Integrity in the Public and Private Domains

This collection of essays addresses key questions on the theoretical and practical dimensions of integrity: What is personal integrity? How do we define integrity in the performance of a public or institutional role and what, if indeed any, is the relationship between private and public integrity? Is integrity of both types always to be desired and if so, is it practically attainable.

The contributions, drawn from a variety of academic and non-academic disciplines, are concerned with the values and practices underpinning the ethical working of societies and their main social institutions. Men and women of varied practical and theoretical experience as teachers, public servants, doctors, psychologists, fund-raisers and scientific researchers engage in rigorous debate in an effort better to understand the specific demands of integrity in their respective professions.

Contributors include: Robert Brown, Anthony Clunies Ross, Margaret Cohen, Paul Flather, Rabbi Hugo Gryn, Alan Hamlin, Donald Hay, Fiona Jenkins, Sir Peter Kemp, Hilary Lawson, Alan Montefiore, Denis Noble, Marie-Hélène Parizeau, Mark Philp, Michael Pinto-Duschinsky, Colin Rayner, Amélie Oksenberg Rorty, René Sève, Anthony Smith and David Vines.

Alan Montefiore is Emeritus Fellow of Balliol College, Oxford and Visiting Professor in the Department of Philosophy. **David Vines** is Fellow in Economics at Balliol College, Oxford, Director of the Global Economic Institutions Research Programme of the Economic and Social Research Council, and Research Fellow at the Centre for Economic Policy Research in London.

Integrity in the Public and Private Domains

Edited by Alan Montefiore and David Vines

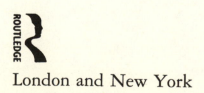

London and New York

First published 1999 by Routledge
11 New Fetter Lane, London EC4P 4EE

Simultaneously published in the USA and Canada
by Routledge
29 West 35th Street, New York, NY 10001

© 1999 selection and editorial matter: Alan Montefiore and David Vines,
individual chapters © their contributors

Typeset in Garamond by BC Typesetting, Bristol
Printed and bound in Great Britain by TJ International, Padstow, Cornwall

Extract of 'Sext' from *Horae Canonicae* © 1995 W.H. Auden
Reprinted by permission of Curtis Brown Ltd.

Extract of 'Sext' from *Horae Canonicae* © 1995 W.H. Auden
Reprinted by permission of Faber and Faber Ltd.

Extract from *Murder in the Cathedral* © 1968 T.S. Eliot
Reprinted by permission of Faber and Faber Ltd.

All rights reserved. No part of this book may be reprinted or
reproduced or utilised in any form or by any electronic,
mechanical, or other means, now known or hereafter
invented, including photocopying and recording, or in any
information storage or retrieval system, without permission in
writing from the publishers.

British Library Cataloguing in Publication Data
A catalogue record for this book is available from the British Library

Library of Congress Cataloguing in Publication Data
Integrity in the public and private domains/[edited by] Alan
   Montefiore and David Vines.
      p.   cm.
   Includes bibliographical references.
      1. Integrity.   2. Professional ethics.   I. Montefiore, Alan.
   II. Vines, David.
   BJ1533.158159   1998
179'.9–dc21   98-9406
                                                      CIP

ISBN 0–415–18031–7

Contents

Contributors

Robert Brown is Deputy Managing Director of Cantrade Investment Management Limited, part of the Union Bank of Switzerland. He has worked in the City for 25 years, spending nearly all this time in the same group, having been a partner of Philips and Drew, the stockbroking firm taken over by Union Bank of Switzerland in 1985. He is a former member of the Stock Exchange Speakers' Panel and regularly writes on investment matters for a wide range of publications. His work includes the Cantrade Calculator, the Cantrade Compendium of Stockmarket Investment for the Private Investor and the Cantrade Compendium of Stockmarket Investment for Charities.

Anthony Clunies Ross was born in Sydney in 1932; was schooled in Sydney, Melbourne, and Cambridge; taught economics at Monash University, the University of Papua New Guinea, and the University of Strathclyde and now lives in Perthshire, Scotland. His publications include *Taxation of Mineral Rent* (jointly with Ross Garnaut, 1983) and *Migrants from Fifty Villages* (1984).

Margaret Cohen is a practising child and adult psychoanalytic psychotherapist, who works both within the National Health Service and privately. She trained at the Tavistock Clinic in London, and has both a BA and an MPhil in Philosophy from University College, London.

Paul Flather has been a journalist with the BBC, *The Times* and the *New Statesman*; a politician serving as Chair of Further and Higher Education on the Inner London Education Authority, a teacher and a university administrator, serving as the founding Chief Executive of the Central European University. He studied at Balliol College, Oxford, gaining a doctorate in modern Indian politics (soon to be published). He is currently a Fellow of Corpus Christi College, and Director of External Relations for Oxford University. He has written extensively on British and Indian issues, particularly education and research.

Rabbi Hugo Gryn, who died in August 1996, was born in Berehovo (Czechoslovakia), now Beregovo (Ukraine). He and all his family were deported to Auschwitz in May 1944, where his grandparents and twin brother were gassed on arrival. After a year in slave labour camps and two death marches, he and his father were liberated by the Americans in May 1945, only for his father to die of typhoid and starvation a mere five days later. After the war he was brought to England together with more than 700 other teenage survivors of the camps, and in 1946 won a scholarship to study Mathematics and Biochemistry at King's College, Cambridge. He subsequently went on to study for the Reform Rabbinate at Hebrew Union College in Cincinnati and became an American citizen in 1956. In 1964 he was appointed Senior Rabbi of the West London Synagogue of British Jews. He held, among many other posts, that of President of the Reform Synagogues of Great Britain; and became well-known to the general public as a broadcaster, especially as a regular panel member of the programme known as the Moral Maze. He was a tireless worker in ecumenical and inter-faith movements of many kinds, and instrumental in founding many of them. He became a British citizen in 1993.

Alan Hamlin is an economist at the University of Southampton whose research interests focus mainly on the links between political theory, ethics and economics. He is the author of *Ethics, Economics and the State* (1986) and editor of *The Good Polity* (1989, with Philip Pettit) and *Market Capitalism and Moral Values* (1995, with Samuel Brittain). He is currently working with Geoffrey Brennan on a book concerned with the design of democratic institutions when individuals are both rational and moral.

Donald Hay has been Fellow and Tutor in Economics at Jesus College, Oxford since 1970. A former General Editor of the *Journal of Industrial Economics*, his research has focused in recent years on the behaviour of firms in oligopolistic industries. His books include *Industrial Economics and Organisation* (1991, with Derek Morris), and *Economics Today: A Christian Critique* (1989).

Fiona Jenkins is currently a post-doctoral Research Fellow in the Department of General Philosophy at Sydney University, working on a Nietzschean approach to art and censorship. She recently completed a D.Phil. at Balliol College, Oxford, on Nietzsche's account of integrity and selfhood.

Sir Peter Kemp is a former senior Civil Servant who was responsible for many of the recent reforms of the British Civil Service. His published works include *Beyond Next Steps – a Civil Service for the 21st Century* (1993) and *A Better Machine: Government for the 21st Century* (1996). Currently he directs a charity which promotes financial education and training in Central and Eastern Europe. He is a member of the Audit Commission.

Hilary Lawson is a philosopher and film-maker. He is the author of *Reflexivity: The Post-modern Predicament* (1986) and editor of *Dismantling Truth: Reality in the Post-modern World* (1989), and is currently completing his next book, *Closure*, an attempt to provide a philosophical 'system' that does not rely on notions of truth or reference. He is also the founder of 'Television and Film Productions' (TVF), which specialises in documentaries and current affairs. TVF has produced many hundreds of hours of programming, for which it has consistently won awards.

Alan Montefiore is an Emeritus Fellow of Balliol College, Oxford, having recently retired after more than 30 years there as a Fellow and Tutor in Philosophy; since then, he has been an Academic Visitor at the Department of Philosophy, Logic and Scientific Method at the London School of Economics, and has recently been made a Visiting Professor at Middlesex University. He is also President of the Wiener Library in London and is a past Chairman of the Froebel Educational Institute. He has published books, either as author or editor or both, on moral philosophy, the university and political commitment, contemporary French philosophy, the political responsibility of intellectuals, and the relationship between causal description and explanation of goal-directed behaviour and that in intentional and normative terms. He is currently working on the relations between personal and cultural identity.

Denis Noble is Professor of Cardiovascular Physiology at the University of Oxford and a Fellow of Balliol College. His research concerns the mechanism of heart rhythm and of the arrhythmias that occur, for example, during a heart attack. He is founder-director of two Biotechnology companies (Oxsoft Ltd. and Physiome Sciences Inc.). He was also a founder of the pressure group Save British Science and serves on several UK government committees on science policy.

Marie-Hélène Parizeau is Professor at the Faculty of Philosophy at Laval University in Québec. Her research interests include bioethics, environmental ethics and moral philosophy. Among her publications are some collective books: *Les fondements de la bioéthique* (1992), *Les mots de la bioéthique* (1993), *Hôpital et éthique* (1995) and *La Biodiversité* (1997).

Mark Philp is Fellow and Tutor in Politics at Oriel College, Oxford. He has published on political theory and the history of political thought, with books on and editions of both Thomas Paine and William Godwin. He is currently working on a book on politics and its corruption.

Michael Pinto-Duschinsky is Senior Research Fellow at Brunel University, a governor of the Westminster Foundation for Democracy and a former Fellow of Merton College and of Pembroke College, Oxford. He has written widely on corruption and on the funding of political parties in Britain, Germany and other countries. He is Vice-Chairman of the International Political Science Association's Research Committee on political finance and political corruption.

Colin Rayner (MS, FRCS, FRCS, Edinburgh) is Surgeon in Charge of the Plastic Surgery and Burns Unit, University Hospital of Birmingham Trust, and prior to this was Senior Lecturer in Surgery at the University of Aberdeen. He won the Pulvertaft Prize for hand surgery in 1975 and a special award for surgery from the Association of Surgeons of Great Britain in 1981. he was the first Chairman of the Ethical Committee of the British Association of Plastic Surgeons and was responsible for drawing up guidelines for ethical practice for that group. He was British Government representative to Russia in 1988 during the Urals Train Disaster. He has published over 40 scientific publications on basic surgical science, plastic surgery and the Piper Alpha Disaster. He has made a number of television programmes including a video on the subject of 'Violent Britain' and numerous other TV and radio broadcasts.

Amélie Oksenberg Rorty is the Director of the Programme in the History of Ideas at Brandeis University. She has published a number of anthologies in the history of philosophy (most recently, *Essays on Aristotle Rhetoric*, 1996, University of California Press) and *Philosophers on Education* (forthcoming, University of Chicago Press). Her essays on moral psychology appeared in her volume *Mind in Action* (1988, Beacon); she is currently preparing *The Political Sources of Morality* (OUP).

René Sève was born in 1954 and studied philosophy at the Ecole Normale Supérieure in Paris. He passed the Agrégation of Philosophy in 1976 and was awarded a PhD in 1982. Since 1981 he has been lecturing in the History of Political Ideas and the Philosophy of Law at the University Panthéon Assas (Paris II) and is editor of the journal *Archives de philosophie du droit*. He has been a guest lecturer in several universities both in Europe and the US, and became Director of Research at the CNRS in 1990. From 1990 to 1993 he was diplomatic adviser to the French Ministry for Industry and Foreign Trade. He has published three books (two of which deal with the philosophy of Leibniz) as well as more than 50 articles on topics ranging from Plato to Rawls.

Anthony Smith (CBE) is President of Magdalen College, Oxford. He was a Producer in BBC TV Current Affairs during the 1960s, and, as a member of the Annan Committee on the Future of Broadcasting, was deeply involved in the national debate which led to the foundation of Channel Four of which he was for four years a Board Director (1981–85). In 1979 he became the Director of the British Film Institute and remained there until he returned to Oxford in 1988. He was for four years a Member of the Arts Council of Great Britain. His books include *The Shadow in the Cave* (1973 and 1976), which dealt with the broadcasting controversy of the 1970s, *Goodbye Guttenburg* (1980), which examined the computerisation of the American press, *The Geopolitics of Information* which dealt with the media imbalances between developed and developing societies, *From Books to Bytes: Information in the post modern era* (BFI Books, 1993) and *The Oxford International History of Television* (OUP, 1995). In 1996 Faber & Faber and OUP (New York) published his 1994 T.S. Eliot lectures under the title *Software for the Self*.

David Vines is Fellow and Tutor in Economics at Balliol College, Oxford, and Adjunct Professor of Economics at the Australian National University. He is also Director of the Economic and Social Research Council's Research Programme on Global Economic Institutions, and a Research Fellow of the Centre for Economic Policy Research in London. From 1985 to 1992 he was Adam Smith Professor of Political Economy at Glasgow University. His research work is on macroeconomic policy, and on international economics, including the process of regional economic integration in Europe and in the Asia-Pacific region. He is a Director of Analysys (a consultancy company which specialises in telecommunications) and of the Scottish Early Music Association. His interest in questions of integrity dates from a six-year period as a member of the Board of Channel 4 Television.

Part I

Introductions

The philosophy, politics and economics of integrity

1 Integrity

A philosopher's introduction

Alan Montefiore

The chapters of this volume are virtually all the re-worked outcome of a small colloquium held in Balliol College, Oxford towards the end of January 1995 under the overall title of Integrity in the Public and Private Domains. Behind that colloquium lay an earlier series of seminars on the same theme, held, also in Balliol, over the first two terms of the academic year 1993/94. These seminars were in fact planned before the recent explosion of public debate and enquiry into the state of integrity (and varying degrees of corruption) in public life that has been taking place not only in Britain but, in one form or another, in many other countries as well. No doubt there has never been a period or a country in which such concerns have been wholly absent. Nevertheless, a widespread collapse of confidence in the integrity of public life presents peculiar dangers for societies that take themselves to be, in one sense or another, democracies; it thus becomes all the more important to think clearly about just what we may mean by integrity in different spheres of life and of how such spheres may or may not be connected.

The initiative for undertaking the present enquiry may be said to have been an academic one, if only in that those responsible for it were themselves academics – and more specifically, tutors within the Oxford Honours School of Philosophy, Politics and Economics. Questions of integrity are, indeed, of crucial concern to anyone working within this general field, whether primarily as a specialist within one of its branches or with interests spreading across all three. (The three chapters in Part One which serve as a joint introduction to this collection are thus by a philosopher, a political theorist and an economist respectively.) Moreover, academics have not only a natural theoretical concern to deepen their understanding of what is at stake when people talk about integrity, and of how the values and principles they thus refer to may or may not be seen at work in their conduct across a whole range of different social contexts; as teachers they are at the same time concerned with the practical contribution that the study of such theoretical matters might make to a proper education, especially (but not, of course, only) one in philosophy and the social sciences. But academics of all sorts are faced with their own practical problems of integrity. They have a prime responsibility for maintaining the integrity of their own profession; and their own personal integrity is at stake in the exercise of that responsibility – however they may understand it. And if one wishes to determine how people actually understand a concept such as that of integrity, one needs to see how they themselves behave and judge each other in the exercise of their own disciplines or in the practice of their own professions; and this is, of course, as true of academics as it is of anybody else.

The best way of coming to a clearer understanding of one's own values and practices is almost always to set them alongside those of others. We were thus fortunate to be able to bring together not only academics belonging to disciplines not usually accustomed to working together, but also people altogether less used to theorising about what they were doing and why, but with long first-hand practical experience as leading players in quite different fields of non-academic life. Our idea was that by sharing their experiences and perplexities as they strove to articulate the demands and conditions of integrity in their own distinct spheres, all concerned might come to not only a better grasp of those demands in their own fields, but also to a greater mutual understanding. The chapters which follow reflect this common concern with what might be called the praxis of integrity, that is with its combined theory and practice in the face of the pressures to be met with in whatever one's own field may be. We also hoped to provide some illustration of the benefits to be derived when academics and those who live and work outside the so-called 'ivory towers' come together – when, as one might say, theory and practice come together – in common debate of matters of common concern. As an appropriately inevitable consequence, chapters of primarily theoretical concern and of considerable theoretical sophistication are here to be found juxtaposed with chapters in which people of extensive working experience in positions of high responsibility in their respective fields reflect very directly upon the values at stake in that experience. We take it that the mutual exchange reflected by such unusual juxtaposition is a necessary condition of any properly focussed moral, political or social theory or philosophy, just as we also take it that the concerns of any such philosophy or theory are bound to overlap very substantially with those of economic theory if it is really to come to grips with the problems of how economies function in societies as they actually are.

It is widely accepted today that the values of economic activity and the market have come to exert an ever increasing influence on all other aspects of life; and this explains why so much of our colloquium was devoted to problems of integrity in financial and economic life and in the market. However, this does not mean that problems of integrity do not present themselves in significantly different ways from one profession to another. There was, of course, no way in which we could aspire to cover the full range of even the most important of these professions within the bounds of one colloquium and one resulting volume. Inevitably, the limits of our actual choice were determined partly by the chance of who in the end was available to participate. In the event, then, we organised the colloquium (at which the participants first met for common discussion of the early drafts of their chapters), around seven distinct sub-themes. These turned around the questions of how integrity might or should be understood in the contexts of:

1   the formation and character of persons as such;
2   the presentation of news and current affairs;
3   scientific research and the academic life;
4   fund-raising;
5   citizenship and social and political structures;
6   finance and the market economy and;
7   the public service.

It is evident that the areas which we might have hoped, but have not in fact been able to, discuss on this occasion are more numerous than those we have been able to cover; the law and the social services in all their diverse aspects are among the more obvious omissions. Still, what we have hoped to produce is not so much a compendium or manual as an exploration of just some of the main possible variations on one broad and central moral theme. General discussion of each of these themes was opened by three participants, reacting in turn to each others' views; these contributions formed the early versions of the chapters, the rewritten versions of which appear here.

It has also to be explained that, as things turned out, not all the participants in the original colloquium were subsequently able to find the time or opportunity to rework their contributions in the light of the discussions following their presentation there; while, in that reworking, others have found themselves led to cut across the (in any case not very determinate) boundaries of the sub-themes as originally conceived. The chapters that now appear have accordingly been somewhat regrouped in order to clarify some of the more immediate ways in which they reflect each other. Most notably, in view of the importance which all those chapters concerned in one way or another with economic life and the market have assumed within the perspective of our project, it has seemed appropriate to place that by David Vines, my co-editor, immediately after the chapter by Mark Philp and my own general introduction as, in effect, a continuation of it, a sort of second introduction to those chapters that belong in one way or another to Part III. But, the point is perhaps worth re-stressing, we have not attempted to put together the chapters of primarily theoretical or more obviously 'academic' concern as opposed to those which remain closer to the concerns and discourse of 'ordinary' working experience; we believe it to be fundamentally important that they should be read in interaction with each other.

Why, though, the especial emphasis in the title of our original colloquium on the distinction between the public and private domains? The fact is that this reflects one of our main motivations in first embarking on this project. One does not have to venture far beyond one's own habitual boundaries to be struck by how different are the assumptions current in different societies as to the connection, or lack of any connection, between the integrity of public and that of private life – or, to put it differently and more generally perhaps, as to the connection between the integrity (or lack of it) of which one and the same individual may be capable when acting in apparently quite distinct spheres or roles. Many may remember the outraged comment (as it was reported) of the then mother-in-law of a then British Government Minister, when his hitherto private relations with a mistress, whose existence the popular press was able to present as spectacularly newsworthy, suddenly became a matter of widespread publicity: 'How can a man who cheats on his wife, be trusted not to cheat in his relations with Parliament and his country?' It is interesting to see how Peter Kemp, in his discussion of integrity in the public service, lays crucial weight on what he sees as the importance of the prior moral quality of those individuals who are recruited to it. From such a perspective, a particular concern with the standards of public morality may very naturally merge into and manifest itself as a more general concern with the standards of individual morality as such. On the other hand, the French, to take a leading, but by no means exceptional, example, notoriously tend to regard the apparently characteristic English view of the relevance of private 'moral' behaviour to fitness for public life with a variable mixture of amusement, incredulity and contempt. It is noteworthy that in his discussion of integrity in the context of the public service in France René Sève lays comparatively greater stress on the nature and significance of the rules, formal and informal, governing the institutional functioning of that service than he does on the personal character of the individuals working within it.

Is this divergence – to the extent that is a real one – simply one aspect of the widely ramifying set of differences that distinguish the two cultures? Or are arguments to be found which show the 'truth' of the matter to lie closer to one side than to the other? Are the standards of public and professional life – whether those of particular professions, of State employment or of the many large-scale 'private' business and financial institutions which together constitute such a dominant part of the national and international contexts in which members of advanced industrialised societies have to lead their lives – best preserved by the elaboration and policing of appropriate sets of rules of institutionally determined behaviour or by the prior moral upbringing of those who are subsequently recruited to the institutions in question? Might the answer to this question depend, in part, on the degree of mobility to be found in different societies between the public and the private spheres and, even more specifically, on the normal sequence of movement from the one sphere to the other and possibly back again? (It may be, for example, that people initially recruited and formed to work in organisations whose institutional integrity depends essentially on the nature and enforcement of the rules governing the performance of whatever might be their roles within the organisation and on the authority of the institution itself, will tend to lack the inner stability of a more personally based sense of integrity when they move 'outside' their parent organisations to take up other – and frequently much better rewarded – forms of employment; and, further, that where return to employment in the original structures is possible, or even assured in advance, the newly acquired flexibility in dealing with the pressures of temptation that those who return may bring back with them, come sooner or later to constitute a threat to the original integrity of those very organisations.) We touch here on the deeper, indeed fundamental, questions of the inner relationship between the individual and society and of where, in the interaction between the two, the sources of moral authority are to be located. Such questions are clearly not to be begged in advance; they are, however, strategic to our whole enquiry.

Clearly, the concepts of the private and the public, and the nature of the distinction between them as they and it vary from one context to another, deserve whole studies in themselves. It would be a serious mistake to take either their stability or clarity for granted. Nevertheless, and although the relation between the morality of the person *qua* individual human being and the morality of the role-holder *qua* public or institutional personage remains one of the major sub-themes of this volume, for many, if not most, of the contributors the main focus of debate has turned out to be that of the nature of integrity itself. Just how this concept is to be understood is already sufficiently obscure for a number of them to have felt the need to start out by making explicit their own understanding of it, before going on to examine the different forms integrity might take in their own particular contexts. It is here, therefore, worth taking an introductory look at some of the most general features of the concept in its relations with those others which, being most closely connected, may also be most easily confused with it.

It is, of course, no longer the fashion to go in for what one might call dictionary philosophy. Nevertheless, there is no way of getting at concepts other than through an examination of the terms whose use is most closely associated with them; and here the *Oxford English Dictionary* (OED) still provides a usefully authoritative starting-point. The root meaning of the term 'integrity' is evidently bound up with a reference to wholeness, and that, unsurprisingly, is where the dictionary starts: '1. The condition of having no part or element wanting; unbroken state; material wholeness, completeness, entirety.' It goes on: '2. Unimpaired or uncorrupted state; original perfect condition; soundness. 3. a. Innocence, sinlessness. b. Soundness of moral principle; the character of uncorrupted virtue, honesty, sincerity.' (None of the dates attached to the passages quoted in illustration of these diverse headings is later than 1678.) By way of cross-comparison and confirmation it is worth noting what the equivalent French dictionary, *Le Grand Robert*, has to say under the heading of 'intégrité': '1. Etat d'une chose qui est dans son entier, complète, intégrale . . . qui est demeurée intacte, inaltérée . . . (Intégrité est plus qualicatif qu'intégralité, réservée généralement à ce qui est mesurable.) 2. Etat d'une personne intègre. Voir Honnêté, incorruptibilité, justice; probité . . .' So far as the terms 'integrity' and 'intégrité' are concerned, the two languages are clearly not very far apart.

In addition to the reference to wholeness, there are two other points to be noted in these dictionary entries. The first is the close connection between the notion of integrity and that of a certain original state of perfection or purity which both entries reflect. Corruption, as the obverse of integrity, is thus thought of as secondary to or as parasitic upon it; it eats away or, like rust, corrodes that which was formerly unblemished or intact; it involves a 'Fall' or a falling away from a (logically, if not necessarily temporally) previous ideal (or 'wholesome') state. Nowadays, of course, when the myth of an original perfection has less general hold than it once had, integrity as a state of perfect integration, of being wholly at one with oneself, may more easily be thought of as a goal at which to aim, even if it is one for which definitive achievement can never be finally assured. This, certainly, would seem to be the view at work in Margaret Cohen's psychoanalytically structured and moving account of the struggles of premature babies to secure and maintain their precarious hold upon life. Overall, however, the choice between forsaken origins, on the one hand, and guiding aspiration, on the other, as governing image would not seem to figure among the immediate concerns of most contributors to the present volume. What difference, if any, it might make to their ways of thinking about integrity; if the choice was pressed upon them, may here be left as an open question.

The other point to be noticed is that, while both the English and French dictionaries are clear in recording the apparently 'natural' passage from, if not indeed the virtual overlap between, the quite general use of the term (to refer to the wholeness or completeness of whatever is 'dans son entier') and its specifically moral use, they are less clear on the question of how far the reference to wholeness is carried over into its common moral understanding. The *OED*'s expressions 'soundness of moral principle' and 'character of uncorrupted virtue' would indeed appear to carry quite general reference to overall moral character; so too in its context would *Le Grand Robert*'s 'état d'une personne intègre'. But then both dictionaries go on to cite, as apparent equivalents, terms which might reasonably be taken to refer rather to distinct virtues or to particular aspects of morality, both of them to 'honesty', the *OED* to 'sincerity' and *Le Grand Robert* to 'justice'. This seeming indecisiveness is perhaps appropriate after all, given that common usage seems to reflect a widespread similar uncertainty in the matter. Indeed, to repeat the point, many of the contributors to this volume feel the need, before going on to tackle the particular problems which confront them, to work out as clearly as they can, for themselves as well as for their readers, the exact sense which they are to attribute to the term.

Broadly speaking, there would seem to be three main tendencies at work in the ways in which different people, and sometimes the same people at different times or in different contexts, understand what is meant by integrity. In the first case, the association with wholeness would seem to dominate. Thus, persons of integrity may be taken to be those whose overall patterns of desire and working principle are fully integrated, as it were, and who are neither at conflict with themselves nor given to wayward departures from their normal patterns of conduct over the course of time. Whether it is better or worse to have to deal with people of integrity in this sense will depend essentially on the particular content of their desires and principles. As Amélie Oksenberg Rorty points out, persons of unbending integrity in their insistence on sticking to principle may in practice be so inflexible in their relations with others as to be a source of great all round unhappiness. In the second case, the association with virtue becomes dominant; and when this goes together with a strong association with the wholeness of integration, then integrity naturally comes to be understood as representing the whole (or, perhaps better, the overall structure) of virtue. (Alan Hamlin, for example, presents the matter in this light.) Or, third, integrity is indeed associated with virtue but, to the extent that the association with wholeness is weakened, it may come to be understood simply as one virtue among others. Among those who tend to this view, however, there appears to be no one steady view as to the particular virtue with which integrity is to be identified. The dictionary goes for sincerity and/or honesty, each of them being incompatible with dissembling; among the contributors to this volume there is also some strong inclination to go for trustworthiness and responsibility. Variations on all these themes are to be found in the chapters that follow.

One might be tempted to explain these variations by putting them down to nothing more than an uncertainty of vocabulary, either the subjective uncertainty of those who find themselves less than sure-footed on the terrain of moral language and/or, perhaps, the 'objective' uncertainty of a given indeterminacy of that language itself. The *OED* after all provides some support for each of these three main tendencies, and further interrogation of it would seem to reinforce the suggestion that such an 'objective' uncertainty is indeed at work. As we have just noted, 'honesty' and 'sincerity' are both given as possible equivalents for 'integrity', at least in certain contexts. But when one looks up the entry under 'sincere', for example, one will find, under a series of different but related headings, repeated occurrences of such expressions as: 'true', 'veracious', 'unadulterated', 'genuine', 'containing no element of dissimulation or deception', 'not feigned or pretended', 'real' and again 'true'; while under 'honest', one finds: 'respectable', 'honourable', 'decent', 'seemly', 'chaste', 'upright', 'sincere', 'fair', 'straightforward', 'free from fraud', 'genuine', 'not seeming other than it is'. Even apart from the fact that 'sincere' appears among the terms given by the dictionary to represent at least one of the senses of 'honest', it is clear that that these two lists of expressions, while not identical, are themselves significantly intertwined. Nevertheless, there are contexts in which some might wish to make explicit what they would take to be an important difference by distinguishing between, for example, sincerity and honesty. One thinks of Kant's famous example of the grocer who is strictly honest not for the sake of any principle of honesty, but simply because he regards it as being good for business in the long term. Such a grocer may certainly be regarded as decent, respectable and free from dissimulation or fraud, and his honesty regarded as real enough, but one can see easily enough why not everyone might be comfortable in regarding it as genuine or sincere. If, against all his calculations and present expectations, the opportunity presented itself to him, by departing from his well-known honesty, of making such a once-and-for-all killing as to enable himself to retire and live comfortably ever after, there would be little reason to rely on his continued honesty. So, although he might up to that point have been quite sincere in his protestations of honesty and in his calculated belief that it was indeed the best policy for him as a businessman to pursue, that would still not have made him a 'genuinely' or 'sincerely' honest man. One might say that although he was *de facto* honest, he was lacking in a certain integrity.

Thus sincerity can not be taken safely as simply equivalent to, or as a sufficient condition of, integrity; the association with wholeness may be weakened, but hardly to the point of complete disappearance. People who change their stance on important issues as often as others may prefer to change their underwear may be perfectly sincere in their affirmation of each new position; but most would probably find it misleading to speak of such an inconstant sincerity as exhibiting integrity. For such persons would be lacking something that is surely essential in anyone on whom one would wish to be able to rely or in whom one could place one's trust, namely, a certain minimum degree of stability or self-integration through time. (Kant might have called it self-synthesis.) Here we come back to the theme of wholeness or completeness in a slightly different form. It is one of the deepest and, in its way, most perplexing aspects of the human condition that, while our immediate awareness is always, and necessarily, awareness of our present situation, that very awareness rests, as on a necessary condition of its own possibility, on the presumption of our own ability, and that of those with whom we share our powers of conceptualisation, to sustain an integrated self-identity across the passage of time past, present and future.[1] Thus, one's sense that a person of integrity is someone on whose given word it is possible to rely, someone on whom one can depend to accept their own share of responsibility in answering for what they may have done, rests on deeper foundations than any mere etymologically punning connection between the terms 'integrity' and 'integration'. Persons of integrity, one might say, are those who are 'all of a piece', who have sufficient stability or weight of character for others to be able to depend on the presumption that if they are their allies today, they will not have changed their opinions and their allegiances tomorrow — not, at any rate, unless they have very serious and well-thought out reasons for doing so, reasons based on certain underlying principles of judgement, principles on which, at that deeper level, their on-going stability of character is founded. In short, one may 'know where one stands' with such persons; once one knows what their real commitments and principles are, they are people who may be trusted.

This reference to principle (or, as some might say, reason) reflects one of the most important aspects of many people's idea of what actually constitutes integrity. (See, for example, Mark Philp's discussion of the concept in Chapter 2.) It receives explicit mention, indeed, under heading **3.b.** of the *OED* entry: 'soundness of moral principle'. It marks the difference between the predict-able reliability of those whom one can 'trust' to behave in a given way on the basis of their known tenacity of habit, lack of imagination or ingrained obstinacy and those whose trustworthiness derives from their sense of moral responsibility, something which both David Vines and Anthony Clunies Ross go almost so far as to identify with integrity itself. Again, there are those whose committed way of life may lead them to spend most of their time behaving in ways which are deliberately designed to make them seem to be 'other than what they are' – for example, professional spies, but who do so on the basis of a principled conviction of the justice of the cause which they thus serve. Though one might hesitate to call such persons dishonest, despite all the lies, subterfuges and dissimulations to which they have regular recourse, one might feel it equally misleading to characterise them as honest; but, whether approving of their behaviour or sharing their convictions or not, one might, in principle, have no problem in acknowledging them to be persons of genuine strength of character and underlying integrity.

Significantly enough, the above points apply not only to individuals, but also to institutions. Be they universities, commercial companies, local coun-cils or governments, their trustworthiness, their integrity, will be seen to depend on their consistency of principle, their reliability in respecting their engagements and their honesty in accepting responsibility for their past actions or commitments. However, institutions can act only by virtue of the actions of given individuals, as they perform their roles within their institutions, whether each on his or her own initiative or in role-governed interaction one with another; and, as with individuals, institutional integrity depends on an adequate degree of consistency or self-integration over time. The present holders of key roles within an institution may be men or women of the utmost personal integrity, but unless the proper mechanisms for the transmission of institutional memory are in place, that is, for the recording of the decisions and undertakings of each succeeding generation of role-holders and for their being passed on for the appropriate attention of succeeding generations, their individual integrity will not be translated into that of the institution that they serve. Of course, it is also true that the personal integrity of those who occupy institutional roles at any given time will be at stake in the ways in which they relate to their roles. It will be at stake in the efforts that they must make to ensure that their institution's memory and sense of responsibility is properly integrated through proper use of their access to the relevant past records. However, in addition to their commitments to their institution as such, they have also to weigh their commitments of loyalty to those who preceded them in the incarnation of that institution, to individuals with whom they may have worked, even perhaps in cases where they may not have agreed with their judgements. This is one of the points at which considerations of personal and institutional, private and public integrity may become most intricately interconnected.

There is a further reason why one should think integrity to have a special connection with principle, and with a soundness of judgement as to how the relevant principle should be interpreted and applied. Once again this is well brought out in the account given by Peter Kemp of how public servants find themselves having constantly to respond to all sorts of claims and counter-claims, often on the basis of manifestly partial information and with little time in which to determine the line to be taken before having to move on to the next issue. In such contexts, and they are but a more extreme typification of life in general, the principles in terms of which a person of integrity may be thought of as operating, will not (because they cannot) be capable of formulation in precisely determinate terms, clearly and invariantly applicable to whatever case may present itself. In the detailed confusion of day-to-day practice, justice as fairness is not to be identified with strictly invariable treatment laid down in advance on the basis of some broad but inflexible classification. The principles of integrity, the principles of a sound moral character, if one may follow on from the *OED* in speaking in this sort of way, are not to be thought of as if, taken somehow together, they might constitute some sort of recipe of how persons of integrity should act over the whole detailed range of circumstances in which they might expect to find themselves. It is better to think of them as principles that enjoin the attitudes to be adopted, along the lines of the famous Kantian injunction always to treat other people never simply as a means but always as ends in themselves, an injunction which, as such, contains no detailed instructions as to exactly how to behave in one set of circumstances or another in order to treat someone as an end in himself or herself, but which leaves that, as Kant might also have said, to be determined in each practical instance by the exercise of a properly formed, though never infallibly guaranteed, judgement.[2]

There is, then, according to both the dictionary and what would seem to be common usage, a tendency, on the one hand, to understand integrity as consisting in a certain wholeness of character, more typically moral character or virtue, and yet, on the other hand, to identify it more particularly with certain specific virtues among others – for example, sincerity or honesty. The explanation for this would seem to be something more interesting than mere indeterminacy of vocabulary, a phenomenon which is, after all, common enough. For even if neither sincerity nor honesty can be taken always as sufficient conditions for integrity, there would seem to be some underlying level at which they figure among its necessary conditions in a way in which, for instance, the virtues of courage or humility would not. Someone who was not fundamentally honest or sincere would have neither the integrity or integrality of 'one who is all of a piece'. Cowardice may, of course, lead only too easily to dishonesty, but it does not of itself constitute a lack of integrity, any more than does arrogance or, if it comes to that, ruthlessness or lack of feeling for others. There is, alas, no reason to suppose that men and women of integrity will always be particularly likeable – nor, indeed, that all those whom one finds most likeable must always turn out to be models of integrity. (Indeed, it is hard to deny that there is some point to Amélie Oksenberg Rorty's suggestion that too much unbendingly principled integrity tends to make life less negotiable and more generally uncomfortable for the common run of humanity. But then it is, of course, only on a broadly utilitarian understanding of morality that one has any right to expect that moral rectitude will not normally lead to discomfort.)

Finally, the question of the nature of the connection between integrity and integrality or wholeness brings us back once again to that opening question of the nature of the relationship, if any, between integrity in the private and public domains. The answer to this question must be in some deep way bound up with whatever conception we may have of what it is to be a human subject. There are, for example, those who think of the human person in essentially individualistic terms, that is in terms of individual autonomy, self-determination and self-responsibility; others hold (or take for granted) the view that individuals are to be thought of and can meaningfully think of themselves only in relation to the society (together with its culture and its language) within which they have been formed and of which, willy nilly, they form a constituent part. To think of them in abstraction from their social embedment is, on this view, a mere abstraction. One might easily suppose that where the first type of view prevailed, it would be natural to think of human wholeness in terms of individual independence and self-reliance, as something to be aimed at independently of whatever the web of social relations in which any given individual might be involved. Conversely, one might expect the second type of view to lead to a vision of the individual as needing to seek the fullness of his or her own self-realisation in the integration (and, so far as possible, harmonisation) within his or her own person of the whole range of differing values and perspectives attaching to all the various social roles in which he or she might find themselves.

The reality, however, is much more complicated than this. In fact it is in what one might, broadly speaking, call the 'Protestant countries', where, one may reasonably assume, the more individualistic view of what it is to be a 'complete' person is generally prevalent, that the assumption of an important connection between integrity in the private or personal and that in the public or social domain is to be found most commonly at work. It is, on the contrary, in countries of a more generally Catholic tradition, where one tends to find a greater emphasis on the integration of the individual into the nation (or nation-state) that little or no inference is normally drawn from the facts of an individual's personal integrity (or lack of it) to his or her integrity as, say, politician or statesman. Why this should be so is no doubt worth a whole study in itself.

My own guess, for what it is worth, would be that this is largely because societies with a more individualistic view of the person tend, maybe as a consequence, to produce a much richer and more vigorous variety of associations intermediate between the individual or the mononuclear family, on the one hand, and the wider political society as such, on the other; while, at the other extreme, strongly integrative or even totalitarian societies tend to a deep theoretical and practical mistrust of such associations as presenting a threat to their own overall unity or 'integrity' (and, one may suppose, centralised control). The greater the diversity of such intermediate associations, the greater the strength that individuals may derive from being members of a certain number of them. For in so far as such associations tend to bring their individual members into different relationships with different fellow-members in each different case, their very diversity both increases the number of different networks from which he or she may derive support, while at the same time emphasising his or her distinctness and at least relative independence from any given one of them. In such smaller and often more nearly face-to-face associations there is inevitably much less of a gap between what may be perceived as the integrity of people's personal or private lives and that of their performance as association members. Thus, to the extent that a political society may be perceived by its members as consisting in a whole set of overlapping sub-sets of variously intermediate associations, it may well be more natural that the demands and possession of integrity be judged in terms of continuity across the whole spectrum; and where, on the contrary, there exist few or, in the extreme case, no such associations intermediate between the individual and the state, equally natural that no such continuity may be presumed to exist.[3]

If for the most part they do not treat of it directly or in explicitly general terms, the chapters that follow provide much material for further reflection on the nature and demands of integrity, on its relationship to an 'integrated' personality (and hence to personal and social identity) and on this central question of the relation, if any, between the personal integrity of individuals *qua* individuals, that of the institutions within which the same individuals may have a role and that of those same individuals as they act in the performance of their institutional roles. This is a subject of crucial concern not only to the original motivations of the project but, indeed, to the mutual relationship of moral and political philosophy, not only in the technical but also in the more broadly informal senses of the terms. If there is one thing which comes through more clearly than anything else in all these papers, it is perhaps the intimacy of the connection between the effort to think one's way through to a greater conceptual clarity about the nature of integrity and that to work out in practical terms what the demands of integrity entail in the manifold complexities of life as it is today. It goes without saying that in these efforts, my fellow-editor, David Vines, and myself, are participants on just the same footing as all the other contributors, except, no doubt, for the fact that we have had the notable advantage of having had all their chapters before us before having to write our own. This being so, it would be inappropriate for me to pretend in this introduction to the provision of any sort of guided tour in advance to the chapters that follow. Nevertheless, there remain three specific points that it would seem right to make here. The first concerns the way in which the two editors have divided their work between them. Although at every stage in the conception and planning of the project we have discussed in detail between us every issue as it arose, we have not attempted actually to write a joint introduction. We decided rather that it should fall to me, as the 'professional' philosopher of the pair of us, to attempt this opening conceptual overview of what we take ourselves to have been about, while David Vines, as the professional economist, has set out to present his own overall reaction to the group of chapters falling more directly into his own immediate domain.

Second, and despite our general resolve not to attempt anything like individual commentaries on the chapters of our fellow-participants, a word should nevertheless be said about the two chapters on the integrity of fund-raising. As Paul Flather points out at the outset of his chapter, the term 'fund-raising' may quite properly be applied to an extraordinarily wide range of activities, most of which have been conducted in one form or another by one group of persons or another for at least as long as anyone can remember, and in fact no doubt a good deal longer than that. It is only relatively recently, however, that fund-raising for socially or politically acceptable purposes has been, in effect, institutionalised, that fund-raising as such has consequently opened up as a career and that those following it have begun to organise themselves into their own professional bodies and to move tentatively towards the formation of their own codes of professional ethics. Paul Flather has himself been, and indeed still is, closely linked in a professional capacity to Oxford University's efforts, through its development work, to raise large sums of money from 'private' donors to replace those which it, along with all other British universities, no longer receives to the extent which it once did from the State; and this lends particular interest to his largely pioneering attempt to formulate at least the outlines of a code of conduct for fund-raisers in Chapter 13. Michael Pinto-Duschinsky, the author of Chapter 14, is widely respected as an expert on the phenomena of political corruption; and he took the (very reasonable) view that the best contribution that he could make would be by the provision, necessarily in considerable detail, of a particular case study. To give sharper point to his study, he took a case that was particularly close to home so far as all the Oxford-based participants in the colloquium were concerned. This was still a very recent case of fund-raising on behalf of Oxford University itself, namely, that of the donation by Doctor Gerd-Rudolf Flick, grandson and heir of the major German industrialist and convicted war criminal, Friedrich Flick, of something over £350,000 over a five-year period for the establishment of a new Chair of European Thought. (At that time Michael was still unaware that his example was even closer to home than he had thought in that the Chair had been allocated to and accepted by Balliol, the College of which both the organisers of the Colloquium were Fellows, in which the whole project had originated and in which the Colloquium was in fact being held.)

Michael Pinto-Duschinsky's chapter thus takes a rather different form from, and is slightly longer than, most of the others that have finally made their way into this volume. Moreover, as things turned out, once his study of the so-called 'Flick case' became known, as it was no doubt inevitable that it should, it became with virtually equal inevitability the focus of a complex, animated and tormented public debate, whose repercussions have perhaps not even now run their full course. In this debate Michael himself became, as again he was bound to, a fully engaged participant. It is in the nature of such controversies that no subsequent account by an actual participant of what he believes it was all about can function as a purely neutral statement of fact. In here publishing the revised version of the paper that he originally presented at the Colloquium, we have to make it clear that it is in no way our purpose to enter that debate as similarly enagaged participants; but equally we have always been quite clear that, given that the original occasion for his study of the issues raised by the Flick donation was provided by the present project, the integrity of the enterprise itself demanded that we publish his revised account of the matter as he sees it and as the important contribution that it is, if not to an impartial appreciation of the balance of rights and wrongs of this particular case, at least to a better awareness of the extraordinary complexity of the issues at stake – not least in the way in which in a given instance questions of integrity that belong properly to the problems of fund-raising itself can run over into questions touching on the integrity of the steps which an institution may find itself led on to take in necessary defence of its fund-raising decisions once taken; and, beyond them, into the sorts of questions that lie at the very heart of our own particular enquiry, that is, questions concerning the demands of integrity, both personal and institutional, on those who find themselves bound to certain lines of behaviour by what they (or others) may see as the commitments of the institutional roles that they occupy.

At the original Colloquium, the third contributor to this section on the integrity of fund-raising, was Rabbi Hugo Gryn. Alas, Hugo died before having had time to put his contribution to the Colloquium into publishable form for this volume. However, both he and I felt ourselves to be very much challenged by the issues raised by the so-called 'Flick case', and we talked about them together on a number of occasions over the year following the Colloquium and as the public debate over the case unfolded. It has been put to me that Hugo's views on such a subject would be especially worth recording and that I should therefore try to put down the main points that he made at the Colloquium and that he elaborated during the course of our subsequent discussions. I have accordingly attempted to do this, as faithfully as possible, in the note that follows immediately upon Chapter 14.

The third point is really a very obvious one. Problems of integrity and of how to integrate the private man or woman with the public person arise in all different walks of life, and the restricted sample of cases that have furnished our basis for discussion and reflection here was constituted not so much in the light of some clearly determined grand strategy as on our sense that these areas at any rate were both important in their own right and hopefully exemplary of others that we have not been able to study in any detail here – and, as I said at the beginning, on the basis of the contingent circumstance of who among our invited participants happened to be avilable at that particular time. There remains much scope for further work.

It remains finally for David Vines and myself to express our grateful thanks to all those who agreed to take part in this enterprise, both those who were able to persist until the end and those who, for one good reason or another, found themselves unable to do so, and especial thanks to those very practically engaged people who, being neither professional academics nor used to theorising about such matters, have nevertheless put themselves to endless trouble in the effort to bring their intuitions to concepts. To Ann Gibson also, for her indispensable secretarial help. To Hugo, who himself once wrote that 'whatever helps us to faithfulness and integrity has been sought',[4] we can now, alas, only give thanks by dedicating this book to his memory.

Notes

1 There would today be a broad consensus among the great majority of those who have pondered such matters on the justice of some version of this apparently dogmatic assertion. The arguments that underpin it have taken a number of different forms. Broadly speaking, however, they stem from the rejection of the generally Cartesian model of (self)-understanding, shared in fact by all the classical British empiricists, according to which each person is in a position to know exactly what he or she is thinking or aware of at each present moment of consciousness, while having no certain access at all to anything external – whether in time or 'in space' – to that immediate awareness. Kant was the first major thinker to point out that such recognitional awareness depends on the ability to conceptualise the contents of consciousness, that concepts are, in effect, rules of classification and that it is of the essence of rules that they are to be understood as having application to a plurality of instances and, as such, as bearing a necessary reference to both the past and the possible future of the conceptualiser or rule-applier. Wittgenstein was, of course, most prominent among those who took the further step of arguing that there is no sense to the notion of applying a rule (or a norm of usage) unless it is in principle possible for whoever is applying it to be confronted with *prima facie* evidence of having failed to do so appropriately; and, as is well known, he went on to argue that that such evidence can only be found in the context of an attempted communication with another member of the same speech community. (There can be no such thing as a logically private language.)

2 It is for reasons such as these that the judiciary, from Left to Right of the political spectrum, object so strongly to the idea that judges, whose very function it is to exercise judgement, should be tied by law to the imposition of fixed sentences for crimes classified according to some predetermined system of classification rather than being allowed to exercise their traditional discretion in the light of the particular circumstances of each case. Kant himself, of course, was led to take the (to my mind unfortunate) step of trying to derive from his Categorical Imperative a set of specific injunctions all of which were supposed somehow to instantiate the one supreme principle of the respect that universal reason owed to itself in all its manifestations of incarnations. He thus exposed himself to the evidently inevitable objection, as it was put to him famously by Benjamin Constant, that, since it was always conceivable that such specific duties might come into conflict with each other, it must be possible for circumstances to arise in which Reason would appear to contradict itself; and to this objection Kant was only able to produce a notoriously unsatisfactory reply. (See his '*On a Presumed Right to Lie from Love of Mankind*', in *Practical Philosophy*, edited by Mary J. Gregor, Cambridge University Press 1997.) He would surely have done better to construe Reason's categorical demand as one to adopt in all circumstances an attitude of respect towards persons, leaving it to everyone's own best judgement to determine the appropriate line of behaviour through which to manifest such respect. In fact, he had already in *Critique of Pure Reason* (translated by Norman Kemp Smith, London: Macmillan, 1978), in the passage immediately preceding that on Schematism, had some striking things to say on the sort of experience through which such judgement might be formed and on the role that might be played in such a formation by guided practice and by example.

   None of this, of course, should be taken as meaning that there are not many circumstances in which a guiding framework of specific rules of conduct may not be useful or even indeed essential. (In order, for instance, to secure a decent degree of equality of treatment of what appear to be similar cases by different judges working within the one overall system.) For those working within such frameworks, integrity may still be thought to demand the exercise of a good interpretive judgement rather than a blindly automatic application of the apparent letter of the law.

3 For the implications for Hungarian civil society, for example, of the largely successful attempt on the part of its then Soviet-style regime to eliminate all intermediate and/or non-Party associations see Elemer Hankiss' interesting and illuminating paper 'The loss of responsibility' in *The Political Responsibility of Intellectuals* edited by Ian MacLean, Alan Montefiore and Peter Winch, Cambridge University Press: Cambridge, 1990, pp. 29–52.

4 In his Introduction, written in his capacity as Chairman of the Prayerbook Committee, to the seventh edition (1977) of the *Forms of Prayer for Jewish Worship* edited by the Assembly of the Reform Rabbis of Great Britain.

2   Citizenship and integrity

Mark Philp

Most adults in most modern states have the status of citizen. This gives them a certain standing in relation to the civil and political institutions of their society, usually involving both rights of political participation and responsibilities towards the public domain and to their fellow citizens. These rights and responsibilities are valued by many because they go some way towards meeting the aspiration that citizens should be self-ruling. Those who refuse to exercise these rights or who deny that responsibilities are entailed by them are seen as apathetic or as opportunists and free-riders, benefitting from the existence of a system but refusing to play their part in it. For those who take this view, it is natural to think that someone who acts in this way lacks, in some fundamental way, the virtue of integrity.

To be a citizen, not merely a subject, was something highly prized by revolutionists at the end of the eighteenth century. It embodied the aspiration that social distinctions could be overcome by each person becoming an equal member of the sovereign legislative body, thereby becoming simultaneously both sovereign and subject. Later political philosophers and politicians sought to realise more fully the aspiration for a politically active citizenry by examining the social, economic and educational prerequisites for effective citizenship. Several post-war European welfare states, not least Britain's, were built with the objective of establishing a degree of social, economic and educational equality sufficient to transform the formally equal standing of citizens into a substantive equality which would equip each to play a role in the democratic institutions of the state. Recent policy developments in Britain have resulted in a shrinking of the universalist and egalitarian component of the welfare state, but they have been accompanied by an expansion in both the rhetoric of citizenship and in the opportunities for forms of 'participation' which draw on an alternative view of citizenship, one in which the independence of the citizen from the state is seen as a prerequisite for effective participation. To this end, the spread of share-ownership, the move to home-ownership in preference to state housing, the emphasis on citizen choice in health and education, and the development of citizens' charters, have all been presented as essential to the development of citizenship in the modern democratic state.

It is not difficult to see the appeal of citizenship. The vision of a virtuous, active citizenry, engaged in deliberation on the proper ends of their association and taking turns at ruling and being ruled, is undoubtedly an attractive one – especially when coupled with the assumption that civic virtue provides the natural completion of the broader moral virtues.[1] Despite our more sceptical age, politicians and political theorists inspired by this view have advocated state involvement in the promotion of these virtues, both through public education and a host of initiatives designed to create and sustain a sense of responsibility to the community, especially among the young. Yet, despite the amount of intellectual activity and political rhetoric devoted to the concept, in most modern democratic societies it remains possible for the man or woman in the street to find his or her status as a citizen of little relevance in everyday life. Citizenship is a status pertaining largely to the political world and in most modern states that world remains foreign to many who have the status. This point does not need to be made in the spirit of John Stuart Mill's anxieties about the working classes having 'too low a standard of political intelligence',[2] but can be made on the grounds that it is entirely possible to live a full and rich life as a private person without one's political standing having any impact on one's basic moral concerns and projects. Indeed, against the ancient ideal of citizenship, which informs many later theories of citizenship and political participation, a distinctive line of argument develops in early modern western political thought which emphasises the virtues and value of the private domain, and sees the public and political world as wholly instrumental to the protection of that domain. One vigorous exponent is Benjamin Constant in 'The Liberty of the Ancients Compared with that of the Moderns':

> The aim of the ancients was the sharing of social power among the citizens of the same fatherland: this is what they called liberty. The aim of the moderns is the enjoyment of security in private pleasures; and they call liberty the guarantees accorded by institutions to these pleasures.[3]

Stated in its most extreme form, this view might be characterised as arguing that the role of the state is to enforce constitutional protections for liberty and security for those within its borders, and that neither the status of citizen, nor any of the egalitarian or participatory claims which are so often evinced in defence of that status, are necessary for that protection. Our responsibilities begin and end with upholding the law – a responsibility we might have to any state we happened to be in, whether or not we had the formal political standing of a citizen.

To take this view is to accept that the role of citizen is one with little moral significance for most people. They can live morally deep lives irrespective of whether they exercise any of the rights that accrue to them as citizens or recognise any responsibilities (beyond mere compliance with the rules which protect their liberty) arising from those rights. Indeed, it is entirely possible to believe that those who live private lives may live more virtuously:

> Storming a breech, conducting an embassy, ruling a nation are glittering deeds. Rebuking, laughing, buying, selling, loving, hating and living together gently and justly with your household – and with yourself – not getting slack nor belying yourself, is something more remarkable, more rare and more difficult. Whatever people say, such secluded lives sustain in that way duties which are at least as hard and as tense as those of other lives.[4]

Modern claims to the calling of citizenship would have been similarly treated by Montaigne. What matters, for him, is the business of one's private life – an active public life cannot be a requirement of integrity, indeed, all too often, it destroys it. We end up taking into our lungs and livers that which we should only take in hand – or bending our reason, when we should only bend our knee.[5] 'Those who realize what they owe to themselves, and the great duties which bind them to themselves, discover that Nature has made that an ample charge and by no means a sinecure.'[6]

This conception of the unrelatedness of our private affairs and our public standing or citizenship suggests, in contrast to the more participatory and classical model with which I began, that there is little positive connection between personal integrity and citizenship. Far from it being a requirement of integrity that one recognises one's civic responsibilities, the undertaking of that role may jeopardise one's integrity.

These contrasting views of the respective claims of integrity and citizenship indicate some of the problems which a discussion of their relationship can generate. I argue here that neither position is wholly tenable. An understanding of the relationship between integrity and citizenship in modern democratic states requires a clearer sense both of the demands of citizenship and of the contexts in which those demands become salient for individuals. In stable regimes the demands of citizenship are less taxing and more easily met than the republican tradition suggests. On the other hand, because they are less taxing, they can also be trumped by other moral considerations. Where the political system is more fragile, the demands of citizenship, and the costs of meeting these demands, are substantially greater, and compliance is significantly less likely to be motivated by moral commitments and considerations of integrity. Yet, not withstanding these sceptical caveats, the arguments advanced here show that modern democratic states will be politically stable only if most of their citizens see compliance with their civic responsibilities as a requirement of personal integrity.

Integrity

A minimum, approximate definition of integrity is the capacity to stick to one's fundamental commitments or principles in the face of other pressures. Intuitively, it refers to a certain way of acting: one where the person not only shows a persistent pattern of conduct but where this pattern is derived from her commitment to a set of values or principles. A person may act well (in the sense of benefitting others or conforming to moral norms), but if she does so unintentionally or mindlessly we would not say that she acted with integrity. The contours of the concept of integrity can be further outlined in three major points.

1   *A judgement of integrity is a judgement about character.* Integrity is attributed to persons, and to their actions only as a way of pointing past the action to the character of the person who acts this way. To say of someone that she has integrity is to make a judgment not just about specific actions but also about the extent to which the act flows from commitments which are central to her sense of herself. As Bernard Williams puts it: 'one who displays integrity acts from those dispositions and motives which are most deeply his, and has the virtues that enable him to do that.[7] To think of integrity as a feature of character is a way of recognising a degree of fixity of disposition – it cannot be opportunistically motivated. Someone who weighs up the pros and cons of an action and decides it is easier or more profitable to stick to his principles does not act with integrity. Equally, people who act well, but out of character are not usually seen as instancing integrity – unless the act is taken to reveal a more fundamental set of commitments than we had previously identified.[8] Similarly, choosing capriciously to act well does not (by definition) involve choosing for the right reasons, nor does it link back to character in the right way.

2   *Integrity concerns actions which flow from choices.* Rote conformity does not instance the appropriate form of agency for integrity. Someone with integrity does the right thing for the right kinds of reason. For example, one conforms not from habit or sheer deference to authority, but because conformity is seen as appropriate and morally responsible. For one's conduct as a citizen to instance integrity it must flow from a principled commitment to the ends one's activity serves.

The element of choice necessary to integrity is complicated by the roles which people perform. Much political activity involves the occupancy of more or less well defined roles within the political system. Part of the way we judge a person's integrity is by asking how far his conduct reflects the commitments he has made in accepting certain roles, and how far he has undertaken those roles with an appropriate degree of reflection upon the responsibilities they entail and the ends they serve. For example, if a man accepts a political office which has serious consequences for the well-being of others but exercises that office in a cavalier or irresponsible manner, his integrity would thereby be impugned. Also, someone who accepts responsibilities which serve ends which he cannot endorse jeopardises his integrity, unless there is some deeper conviction or principle to which he can appeal (as in the case of the person who cannot endorse the ends served by the role she plays, but undertakes it nonetheless in the hope that she may subvert those ends).

Roles combine the right to act in specific areas along with duties to act in certain ways. Choice is thereby limited. This constraint does not reflect on the agent's integrity where the role is one which the agent freely chooses, but where I am forced to undertake a certain responsibility, my exercise of that responsibility reflects on my integrity in a different way than when freely chosen. If the role is freely chosen, my conduct in it must be consistent with my commitment to it; if it is not freely chosen, my integrity is judged not directly with reference to the fulfilling of the role, but with reference to my ability to resist pressures to act in ways or with consequences which I cannot endorse (where this takes into account the consequences of resistance both to myself and to those affected by the role). Citizenship might be seen as one such role. Someone who tries to get out of jury service might not be seen as thereby impugning his integrity, although he would do so if he failed and if he then refused to take the role seriously (on the assumption that the costs to himself of doing so are outweighed by the costs to the accused – and possibly the victim). This suggests that there is a complex relationship between the role of citizen and the issue of choice, and that judgements of integrity may diverge depending on the degree to which the rights and responsibilities are seen as freely chosen.

Issues of integrity also arise from conflicting demands between different roles: for example, the politician who holds public office but who also has responsibilities to his financial backers, his electorate, his political party, his particular ideological faction and so on, where integrity concerns resolving these competing demands appropriately; or the citizen who has competing responsibilities to his family and friends. The competing demands of our various roles may make it difficult to sustain integrity – but they rarely make it impossible. Integrity is not about emerging from a complex set of conflicts unscathed; rather, it is about emerging with one's self-respect and the respect of most others reasonably intact – where they are so because the person has weighed up the different commitments and options and acted in the way that she judges best respects the competing requirements.

3   *Integrity concerns choices which are informed by the person's values or ends.* This claim is complicated partly, as we have seen, by the existence of formal roles. But there is a further complication arising from disputes between those who take integrity to refer to a certain continence of character and those who believe that a judgement of the ends pursued by the individual

are relevant to whether or not we can ascribe integrity to him or her. On the former view, the demands of integrity can be met by the consistency of the agent's commitments and conduct. On the latter view, it cannot be acceptable to ascribe integrity to the Nazi death camp bureaucrat because the ends of his role are so appalling. There is, however, a more nuanced position which deals with some of the concerns of both camps. A direct appeal to the consequences of the act in assessing integrity seems to take us away from the recognition that judgements about integrity are judgements about character. On the other hand, ruling out the consequences of an act or role in the assessment of integrity goes against the recognition that we distinguish rote conformity from integrity, where the latter implies a degree of considered commitment to the principles upon which one acts. Where the consequences of the act are foreseeably vile this must prompt us to ask how far they could have been endorsed by someone acting with a considered commitment to principles. This does not promptly settle the matter against Nazi bureaucrats, terrorists, or professional hit-men. But, if we cannot see how their principles could be endorsed by anyone who has engaged in a minimum degree of serious moral reflection, then we would also resist attributing integrity to their agency. We do not have to agree with the principle a person endorses, but we do have to think that it could reasonably be given priority over other principles, even though we do not share the same sense of its priority. On this view we cannot judge a person's integrity solely on the basis of the internal consistency of her behaviour, or by her conformity to the formal requirements of her roles. Rather, we have an ineliminable element of judgement about whether the commitment from which the act flows can be said to retain its moral character given the presence of clear countervailing moral demands. The man who resists such demands out of a desire to stick to his principles, or who blocks them out psychologically to avoid facing the consequences of his actions, or who acts in the grip of a murderous passion, or who refuses to question his orders – in each case compromises his integrity. On this view, the consequences of the act may lead one to raise questions about the extent to which it flowed from morally serious convictions, but this does not mean that I cannot attribute integrity to someone who acts in accordance with principles I wholeheartedly reject.[9]

The three elements which I have argued are central to the concept of integrity and can be summarised as follows: to say of someone that she is a person of integrity is to make a judgement about a certain consistency of character which is rooted in morally serious commitments to ends and values which are strongly enough felt to enable her to resist pressure to act otherwise. Although this might seem to favour an internal or psychological account of integrity, the characterisation is equally compatible with social worlds which are less individuating in their judgements and where the components of character and sticking to principles are more directly a function of the agent's standing and role in the community. Different cultures operate with different frames for the judgement of integrity. Modern liberal democratic societies tend to operate with more intentional and personal morality-based conceptions of integrity, while in more hierarchical, feudal cultures, judgements about integrity are more concerned with the person's social standing and how far he conducts himself honourably given that standing. Moreover, the fragmentation of moral life ascribed to modern, or post-modern culture, may further exacerbate the tendency to look for integrity at the level of a person's intentions and psychological make-up, as opposed to resting content with the issue of how far the person's behaviour is appropriate to his social and political position or role. In the feudal world, questions of integrity may well have been exhausted by the person's behaviour being consistent with formal role expectations; in the case of modernity, we can see that sticking to one's principles becomes a much more complex act, both to perform and to assess.

To see how far one's citizenship of a modern democratic state might have implications for one's integrity we need to examine more closely the demands which such a role might make.

Citizens' duties

What, then, are the distinctive demands of citizenship? Citizenship is a form of standing in politics which accords the individual the right to be ruled politically – that is, in accordance with some legitimating procedures or principles. It characteristically recognises the right of individuals and/or groups to articulate and present demands within the political institutions of their society and also identifies certain responsibilities as linked to these rights. To deny citizenship to groups and individuals who attempt to articulate demands within a society is to deny them standing in politics and to rule them coercively, not politically.

Within liberal, political thought those who discuss the duties of citizens tend to make two errors. They tend to treat as duties of citizenship things which are owed as more general moral duties; and they often focus on duties (such as the duty to die for the state) which conflict with our sense of the individual's rights and may go against the grain of our moral duties. I argued earlier that issues of integrity can be complicated by the question of how far the role an agent performs is freely chosen. Where the role is not freely chosen the assessment of a person's integrity moves from an analysis of how far she meets the commitments she accepted in undertaking that role to an examination of how far her conduct in the role is consistent with her personal principles and values. Although the issue of the degree to which citizenship is a freely chosen role allows us to raise precisely these questions, there is a long tradition of argument in liberal thought which by-passes these complexities by treating the duties of citizenship as duties which are prescribed by more general moral principles. For example, take the duty to uphold the law of the land. While it is true that each land has a different law to be upheld, it is widely acknowledged that 'when in Rome one should do as Romans do' – and the argument for this can be made in terms of respect for the rule of law, reciprocity (because we are protected by it), or avoidance of harm to others. This means that nothing is added by my being a citizen of a particular country to my general duty to follow the rules which sustain the social and political order of the country in which I currently reside. Some rules and their associated responsibilities might be thought of as coordination solutions – like the rule governing on which side of the road one drives. There needs to be some rule, but the most important feature of the rule is that it is one which everyone knows and with which everyone complies. Clearly, in a choice between radically inegalitarian and radically egalitarian distributions of private property something more is involved than in the question of road etiquette. But the cases are much closer if we recognise that in relatively few instances, at least in liberal democratic states, do our moral principles justify disregarding the current law of the land.[10] In most situations the legal *status quo* is a coordination solution (and one which has additional legitimacy in so far at it is open to change through democratic processes), with which we conform because doing so is sanctioned by general moral principles, such as the duty to avoid harming others, rather than because we happen to be citizens.[11] The result, however, of this grounding of citizenship responsibilities in more general moral principles is that the issue of how far the role is freely entered ceases to be of much significance, and liberal arguments find it difficult to make a morally relevant distinction between the responsibilities of Roman citizens and of those who just happen to be in Rome. The more this type of liberal approach is pressed, the less likely it is that a person's citizenship will have an independent impact upon our assessment of his or her integrity. To resist this approach we need to ask how far specific citizen rights and obligations can be derived from involvement in the political domain: we may have a duty to accept the law of Rome when in Rome, but only Roman citizens will have rights and responsibilities associated with the political process which determines the content of that law, and in assessing the integrity of a citizen we have to weigh the responsibilities that are peculiar to that role.

A second set of difficulties concerning citizenship and its duties arises from the common focus on such questions as: 'is it my duty to fight and die for my state?' Clearly, compulsory military service cannot be treated in the same way as any other law (which is why it is usually applied only to citizens). However, one attractive account of why it might be our duty to fight and die for the state is one in which the primary motivation is not one's citizenship but the justice of the cause or the necessity of acting to defend the people, values or way of life to which one is most deeply committed (which might be a very small sub-set of one's fellow citizens and may include non-citizens).

But that account, again, reduces the question to either a more general or a more particular moral commitment than is generated by one's citizenship.

In contrast to these accounts, the following discussion takes as its starting point the different roles and responsibilities which are associated with the standing which citizenship gives individuals within the political process. I assume that this standing is unique to citizens, albeit different societies may operate with widely differing conceptions of this standing and its responsibilities. In what follows, I focus mainly on the kind of standing which is characteristic of modern democratic societies and I examine how far this standing implies a set of claims upon citizens which cannot be reduced to more general moral principles, and how far, and under what conditions, it can be a requirement of integrity that these be met.

Civic responsibilities can be seen as two-sided: they require that individuals recognise the formal responsibilities which their citizenship entails for their conduct *vis-à-vis* the state and politics; but theories of citizenship also emphasise that, in addition to these formal responsibilities, there is a broader but less well defined requirement that citizens play their part in sustaining a culture of accountability and responsibility to which those who occupy positions of political power and trust are answerable. In the first case, if a citizen makes representation or seeks in some other way to influence the political process and its outcomes, he or she must accept certain constraints on the type of influence that can be brought to bear, and (for the most part) must accept the outcome of the process as legitimate. That is, there are duties to abide by the accepted procedures of the political process whenever one attempts to influence their outcome – which we may term 'procedural duties'. In the second case, the argument is that for the political system to be sustained it must be able to elicit the participation of its citizens, both in the formal institutions of the system, such as elections, and in the broader sense of sustaining a political culture which links the citizen in the street to those who exercise public office. These responsibilities may be termed 'participatory duties'. (Loosely, procedural duties are constraints on conduct which those who act within the political arena must accept; participatory duties concern a level of political and civic activity which is necessary to sustain a common political culture between citizens and their politicians. It is possible to imagine a limit case in which the political system fails because, although procedural norms are not violated by citizens, the absence of participation allows the state to collapse into despotism.)[12]

Procedural duties are essential because a state which distributes formal access to political power and office to all in the absence of a common recognition of the rules and norms of the political process, creates the conditions for extensive corruption – corruption which stems both from individuals seeking to use non-political means to achieve outcomes, and from élites seeking to secure and sustain power by gaining the support and compliance of groups through non-political means – as in patron–client or party machine–type systems. In addition, the political order is jeopardised if those who make representation do not accept the authority of the political institutions to which they appeal. Although there may be an irreducible element of coercion in politics, political authority must be able to secure a fairly wide degree of willing compliance to its commands – not least from those who make representation to it. How demanding these duties are depends very much on their distance from the promptings of self-interest – although that is something which political and social institutions may partly influence. For example, the demand for high levels of (participatory) civic virtue in the classical republican tradition was coupled with the belief that social institutions, not least a religion in the service of the state, would so mould citizens' conceptions of their interests that the disjunction would be slight. In contrast, more modern and parsimonious views of the responsibilities of citizens are often coupled with such a degree of scepticism about people's ability to rise above short-term opportunism that it is difficult to see how even these modest responsibilities can be met.

Participatory responsibilities derive from the view that some degree of civic culture is required to sustain the legitimacy of the political process and the accountability of those who occupy public office and exercise political power. For political action to be publicly legitimated and for leaders to be made accountable to their public we require an active and politically responsible citizenry. An apathetic, uninterested and disaffected public not only places the state at risk through massive rule infraction by citizens (because it diminishes people's sense of their procedural responsibilities), it also creates the conditions under which those exercising political power lose all sense of accountability to their public. Political theorists differ about how much civic culture is required – the less sanguine they are about the potential for positive-sum outcomes for social conflict, or about the trustworthiness of the average politician and the reliability of public officials, the more they want.

Procedural duties involve the acceptance of the norms of the political process and of the rule of law. Participatory responsibilities require activity which sustains the political culture (and its associated norms) and the accountability of those in public office. In each category two basic forms can be identified. Procedural duties concern both:

1   individuals' or groups' vertical relations with holders of public office, where norms of political propriety must be sustained; and
2   individual or group responses to the output of the political system, such as laws and agreements, and their public stand on procedures.

In the former case, it is in the nature of political relations that there be constraints on the kinds of bargaining and influence which legitimately take place between citizens and those in authority. Clearly, on many occasions transgressing those constraints will benefit both parties at cost to a third party or to the public more generally. We might distinguish, roughly, between cases where political norms are being subverted for direct personal gain – as when either public officials or citizens seek to establish profit-maximising, corrupt relations with the other – and cases where group or sectional interests come to trump procedural norms. Such exchanges may be one-off, and symmetrical – such as contractors paying cash to civil servants for the allocation of lucrative contracts; or they may be on-going and asymmetric – the exchange of contracts or goods for political or personal services. As they move to the latter style they become closer to patron–client relations (although these may take various forms, from cases where the holder of public office is the patron, to those in which he or she is the client of some extra-political patronage network). Whether or not citizens act in this way, and whether or not they do so successfully, depends on how deeply ingrained are the norms of political exchange, and on what the opportunity structures, the size of the benefits, and the probabilities of detection are like.

In the second case – 'output-abidingness' – we are primarily concerned with how far groups and communities comply with the spirit of the agreements they negotiate in the political arena, and with whether individuals and groups present themselves in public as endorsing the legitimacy of the political procedures of the state. In such activities, the focus is not on a binary, formally defined, vertical relationship between citizens and public officials so much as on the less formal responsibilities to one's fellow citizens who are subject to the same norms or rules. Keeping to the spirit of one's agreements involves not free-riding on others' compliance – so too does not raising questions about the legitimacy of the process as a tactical move to gain advantage over those who comply without complaint. In neither case is such behaviour necessarily illegal, but nor is it in keeping with the broader character of political negotiation and compromise. Those who deny such citizen responsibilities effectively seek to secure a benefit beyond that which they could legitimate in the political process. I have called these 'horizontal' cases because the benefit is gained by free-riding on other citizens' procedural virtue; whereas the vertical cases are those in which the citizen or group requires the active cooperation of another agent who holds some form of political office and exercises power or controls resources within the political system, to which the citizen seeks preferential access. In the vertical case there is an element of bargaining between individuals who occupy different locations in the political system, which is absent in the pure, horizontal, free-riding case. Derelictions of duty in the two cases may have quite different implications for the stability of political and social orders. Where, for example, the internal structures of employer and employee associations are so weak that they are unreliable performers of public agreements (as in weak corporatist systems), more formal penalties and means of enforcement may be necessary to secure compliance with outcomes. Where, in contrast, the norms requiring conformity with political procedures are weak, the authority of the state can be put at risk, since enforcement can become a trade-able good alongside the other outputs of the political system.

Participatory duties concern, in contrast, (1), responsibilities to be directly involved in the political and also legal institutions of the state – through voting, making representation, interest group activities, joining and acting in political parties, writing letters to newspapers and MPs, demonstrating, performing jury service and so on. In cases where these activities seek to produce a particular outcome from the political system they will also entail certain procedural duties, but such forms of participation also have a broader significance in so far as they help to maintain an active political culture. Classical republicans would have insisted that such participation must be motivated wholly by a concern with the common good but for those who wish to avoid such expressly republican terminology it is possible to recognise that in much participation self-interest is not the only motive. For example, in demonstrating against a policy it is possible to distinguish between the concern to secure a particular outcome and the desire to insist on our right to be heard within the political process; similarly, in voting in an election people may be concerned not only with what would maximally advantage them, but also with some sense of what would be right for the community as a whole. It is through such commitments that we resist the temptation to see the political system solely as a source of personal profit and are able to sustain more general criteria of legitimacy by which to assess the conduct of the political élite. Participation without this more general orientation may become wholly vicious in character, pursuing personal gain without regard for the effects on the political system more broadly, either by exploiting weaknesses in formal procedural constraints, as in various forms of electoral manipulation, lobbying or influence-peddling, or by ignoring procedural constraints completely and using bribery and corruption to attain one's ends.

Theorists of citizenship have also drawn attention to (2) the importance of a civic culture among those subject to political rule – what we might think of as a 'social capital', which exists between citizens outside the directly political arena and which provides a background of shared trust, information, a significant level of political interest and intelligence, and so on. The claim is that without this shared culture the political system will degenerate into factional conflict and strife.

In the case of duties of active participation in politics, the precedent might be derived from classical republican roots – stressing an Aristotelian conception of the citizen taking turns at ruling and being ruled – but it is also captured rather well in more modern accounts of a deliberative rationality or public reason, which is conjured up through participation and which eliminates, to a large extent, the potential conflict between individual interests and the demands of public reason.[13] It is also captured in de Tocqueville's eulogy to the participation found in American townships, which he saw (in Volume 1 of *Democracy in America*) as central to preservation of a spirit of liberty – by which he meant the ability to resist encroachment on liberty by political authorities. For both, civic participation is a central element in ensuring that the state remains true to its function of securing the common good, rather than the good of those who rule it.

The importance of the second type of participation is a major theme in de Tocqueville's second volume to *Democracy in America* and has been seen as his most striking contribution to modern political thought. His concern with the corrosive effects of individualism on the political system and with the willingness of citizens to cede ever greater areas of responsibility to an increasingly centralised and bureaucratic state, is not easily dismissed. But Tocqueville was not entirely *sui generis* in his account. Although he repudiated many of the virtues lauded within classical republican tradition, we can see his insistence on a certain level of public *moeurs* as essentially continuous with that tradition.

This tradition is, however, a divided one in one central respect. In the more Spartan variant, espoused by Rousseau, the sole unit of participation and identification was the general will and one's *patrie*. Secondary associations were seen as inimical to the formation of the general will. In de Tocqueville, and in the liberal pluralist tradition by which he is held in great respect, secondary associations of all sorts are regarded as central to the formation of a public identity and a civic spirit among individuals – hence the litany of community participation reeled off by Robert Putman in his eulogy to the civic spirit of the Northern Italians: 'Neighbourhood associations, choral societies, cooperatives, sports clubs, mass based parties . . .' and so on.[14] Yet interest groups clearly can pose a threat to the norms of the political domain – as Adam Smith recognised when he commented that 'People of the same trade seldom meet together, even for merriment and diversion, but the conversation ends in a conspiracy against the publick . . .'.[15]

The division between those who emphasise the benefits and those who emphasise the costs of association with respect to the state revolves around the issue of how far membership of civil society and its various associations produces a consistent identification with the norms of the political domain, either directly (because of the way that participation enlarges the scope of one's interests), or by default (through the sheer proliferation of interests and the inability of any particular interest to gain ascendancy over all others),[16] and how far such commitments threaten to make the political process hostage to the strongest societal interests. Putnam works with a contrast between corrupt vertical relations and positive forms of horizontal *civitas*, but that distinction is not persuasive: close bilateral vertical relations between individuals and politicians certainly may corrupt politics, but strong horizontal relations (based on class, religious or ethnic identities) may help to create the conditions for such corrupt practices to develop. Putnam is certainly right to emphasise the extent to which horizontal forms of participation are critical for the development of group identities and social capital, but loyalties to a group do not necessarily lead to a more general form of *civitas*. Individuals and groups participate in politics to make the political system more

GENERAL REFERENCE

responsive to their particular needs and interests, but whether the desire that it be so (or more so) is 'procedure abiding' or not depends on which tactic is seen as most likely to succeed, and on whether one's membership of, and loyalty to, a group generates a more general sense of loyalty to the society and to its political system.

This disagreement has taken many forms but in recent years it has shifted its focus from the problems associated with interest groups and associations to those which arise from the presence of different systems of communal value and cultural life coexisting within the bounds of the liberal democratic state. There is a deep concern in liberal circles that the social capital which develops within the communities of multi-cultural societies militates against their accepting the norms and values of liberal political systems. When communities demand collective rights to protect their distinctive cultural values and practices, they are also denying that the citizenship which modern liberal democratic states afford them is adequate (or even very relevant) to their concerns. Similarly, nationalisms within communities can have deeply corrosive effects on the ability of the political order to sustain legitimacy, and state-supported religious tolerance can come to be seen as masking a state-endorsed form of intolerance to certain religious views, as in the Rushdie case. Political theorists are divided on the question of how far the resurgence of ethnic, communal and nationalist movements within modern democratic states can be contained within the liberal democratic tradition and how far this development poses a fundamental challenge to the viability of a conception of politics which rests on a shared respect for rules of procedure and rights of access to those procedures – what Michael Sandel has called 'the procedural republic'.[17] On the one hand, there has been an increasing emphasis on institutionalising respect for 'difference' in all its manifestations and with a 'politics of presence' in contrast to a politics of representation; on the other, many have followed Rawls' attempt to show that the values and conceptions of the good which are sustained by different communities within the liberal state can be reconciled with a common order of political rule through public reason and the development of an overlapping consensus.[18]

These issues are of central importance for an understanding of the relationship between integrity and citizenship in modern societies, not least because recent debates have moved from a perspective which emphasises conflicts of interests (which are, in principle, negotiable and can be organised within a common framework of rules) to a view which emphasises that some of the most basic forms of conflict involve a politics of identity (which is non-negotiable and, as such, resistant to shared political procedures and practices). Moreover, the view that communal, ethnic, and gender-based groups play a constitutive role in the identities of their members, seems inexorably to lead to the view that a person's integrity becomes a function of her acting in line with her deepest sense of self, which flows from her communal membership in a way that is simply not true, for example, for Smith's 'people of the same trade'. If to be black, Muslim, gay or lesbian, or wasp, involves something more than bearing a particular characteristic (something more, for example than being short, red-haired, bald, or allergic to nuts), if it is the constitutive feature of a person's identity, then it will play a fundamental role in framing a person's deepest 'dispositions and motives', and thus in fixing the baseline for assessing integrity. Citizenship, on such a view, seems to become wholly subordinate to questions of identity – in marked contrast to the republican and Jacobin view that the only viable political order is one in which citizenship is constitutive of people's identities.

There are, then, three potential problems which may affect the sustainability of the civic culture which underpins the political order and institutions of a society. Atomism and individualism may so corrode this culture that civil society becomes increasingly prey to state power; interest-group conflicts may be such that groups adhere to or ignore the norms and procedures of the political domain solely according to which best serves the interests of the group; and conflicts between groups which play a constitutive role in their members' identities may assume an unmitigatedly zero-sum character, rendering political norms and procedures completely impotent. Each instance is expressed in an extreme form, but each nonetheless captures a distinct threat to the sustainability of citizenship and its attendant responsibilities within the modern state.

Acting in concert

One way of understanding the impact of interest groups and communal identities is to see them as framing their members' judgements about how they should act when faced with a tension between the norms of the political process and those of their sub-community. Consider, for example, public responses to evidence of political corruption. How we respond depends on how the information is framed and interpreted: for example, whether it is seen as implicating particular individuals in office rather than the political system itself; whether it is taken as indicating widespread non-compliance among citizens, or marginal levels; and whether we think we can trust our fellow citizens to condemn the action rather than follow suit. Most people have limited access to information about what is going on and what the probable outcomes are, and, while they will tend to respond to complex situations by reference to past experience, rules of thumb and existing conventions and norms, they will also need to make some judgement about which is the relevant repertoire of responses in this case. When a black nominee to the Supreme Court is accused of having abused his position of power in the past, the 'facts' of the case are unlikely to be so clear cut that every individual in the community will judge the case in the same light. Although group and communal identities might be thought to solve these framing problems, we cannot treat their presence or absence as a strict structural constraint, nor should we underestimate the complex character of this function.[19] Individuals act, not groups, and we need a better understanding of the factors which affect how individuals will act when faced with conflicts between the demands made by their citizenship and those made by others in their cultural, social or familial context (and the situation may be further complicated if no set of demands is congruent with the individual's conception of his or her interests).

With both procedural and participatory political norms, there is a central element of collective action. Why comply with procedures if you can free ride on the fact that others comply? Why submit to outcomes when recalcitrance can differentially benefit your interests over others? Why perform your civic duties when there are others who will fill one's place and responsibilities? In each case, conforming to the demands of citizenship involves some costs. Sticking to rules, acting with integrity, participating virtuously rather than viciously, are not straightforwardly optimal strategies for self-interest maximisers. That said, where general compliance is widespread, the duties of citizenship are not especially onerous for most citizens. So long as each does his or her share and keeps to the rules, and with disincentives in the form of enforcement agencies (and a general resistance to corrupt practices among one's fellow citizens), most people, much of the time, will find conformity frictionless. This is not to say that no one could ever benefit by free-riding on this broader compliance, but we might follow Hume in characterising the situation as one in which an ingrained resistance develops to such calculation:

> he, it may perhaps be thought, conducts himself with most wisdom, who observes the general rule, and takes advantage of all the exceptions. I must confess that, if a man thinks that this reasoning much requires an answer, it will be a little difficult to find any which will to him appear satisfactory and convincing. If his heart rebel not against such pernicious maxims, if he feel no reluctance to the thoughts of villainy or baseness, he has indeed lost a considerable motive to virtue. . . . But in all ingenuous natures, the antipathy to treachery and roguery is too strong to be counter-balanced by any views of profit or pecuniary advantage. Inward peace of mind, consciousness of integrity, a satisfactory review of our own conduct; these are circumstances very requisite to happiness, and will be cherished and cultivated by every honest man, who feels the importance of them.[20]

For Hume, the free-rider problem is dissipated by the embeddedness of the individual within the social and political order. Our fundamental commitments become rooted in a way of life in such a way that our responsibilities are experienced as an extension of these values and ends. In these circumstances, we have no difficulty in explaining compliance, and integrity unproblematically joins public and private morality. (The only major cloud on such a horizon is the republican view that there is a tendency to slide from virtuous conformity (which is resilient) to habitual conformity (which is not).)

Where there are conflicts between group or communal norms and those of the political system, or where, because of social fragmentation, we cannot count on widespread conformity, the case is altogether different. When the behaviour of others is unreliable, even virtuous motives will not always counsel conforming to rules. Indeed, knowing how others (and which others) will act matters greatly to us. Whether I resist demands for corrupt payments for government services will be influenced by whether I believe others will support me, and by how widespread I believe the practice to be. Such factors greatly affect the level of risk I will run by sticking to my principles and the cost to me of doing so. Where I believe I will not be supported, and where I need the service concerned, I may feel that I cannot afford to resist being implicated in the very practices I find so repugnant.[21]

Widespread doubt about the reliability of compliance has a deeply corrosive effect – and not just for those who are self-interest maximisers and who see the chances of undetected or unpunished non-compliance increasing. Even those who would rather comply may find it impossible to do so – for two different reasons. One concerns a straightforward calculation of cost. Politics is, in part, about the calculated use of one's resources to one's ends. To stand up to a powerful and brutal ruler is irrational, unless one thinks there is some chance of one's action making some difference.[22] Similarly, when it is uncertain whether a collective action will be supported, there has to be some careful judgement about how best to act. Even if one is wholly dedicated to a politics of the common good, one must still have something of Machiavelli's sense that *virtú* is partly the skill of knowing when to act virtuously (where the basic criterion is the likely success of one's action).

The second problem concerns the conflicting ends and values of the individual. Members of modern democratic states for the most part live complex social and personal lives and the status of citizen is only one among many statuses, and not necessarily the one which is most central to their sense of self. Where acting as a good citizen puts in jeopardy other personal, moral and social projects and values, the 'pull' of citizenship is likely to be weak. One may reject compliance not because of its direct cost, but because other values trump those represented by one's citizenship. However, while one feature of this judgement will be the degree of the conflict with these other values, another will be our view as to how those with whom we share these projects and values will act – not least because we take the level of collective action as signalling the extent to which there is a shared reading of the situation and of our responsibilities as members of the group.

Both calculations of cost, and judgements as to how to resolve conflicts in values between one's immediate community and the norms and rules of the political system, will thus depend in large part on how we believe others will act and on whether we think that the 'threshold' for collective (virtuous) action will hold.[23] This 'threshold' concerns the acceptable level of expected compliance by others, which is both a normative judgement about how highly we value collective compliance and a (probabilistic) judgement about the proportion of a group which we would want to see comply (or defect) before we would do so ourselves. If no one else will comply, I would be a sucker (in the technical sense) to do so (because I will pay the costs of others' non-compliance); alternatively, if I do not comply when everyone else does, (and where everyone else also plays a part in the enforcement mechanisms) I cannot realistically expect to profit. The costs and benefits of my action will depend in part on how many others chose to act similarly, so my judgement about the sustainability of this threshold plays a central role in determining how I will act.[24]

However, there will also be individual differences in the way that costs and benefits are calculated and thus differences in individuals' thresholds – i.e., their judgements as to the acceptable level of expected compliance by others. Although levels of horizontal unity, the quality of our information, and the kinds of beliefs we have, all influence which thresholds we confidently expect to be met, more idiosyncratic elements will also play a part in an individual's judgement about what threshold is acceptable.[25] Heroines may be happy to go it alone, so, in the other direction, may 'wide-boys'. In some cases such people will be reckless with respect to costs, although not necessarily with respect to consequences.[26] The student who kills himself publicly in protest at foreign invasion, or someone who acts fearlessly, may nonetheless act with the expectation that the costs they incur will bear fruit in the actions of others in the future. In these and other cases, the person's calculation includes an estimate of the likelihood that their action will subsequently affect the behaviour of others, thereby increasing the probability that they can push collective action over what they believe to be the threshold necessary for success.

Those who are prepared to accept higher risks and lower thresholds can have a major impact on how others will act, since their actions can provide a signal that a more widely shared, higher threshold is viable. In this respect, they function as moral entrepreneurs, setting the moral agenda for others by their example. In fact, the process may involve their action setting off a succession of threshold crossings: a single agent who initiates a collective action may trigger a handful of others to follow suit, and the wider recognition that the action has gathered support (especially if it has not been defeated or blocked by others) will encourage still others to commit themselves to it. This is true both for acts of conformity and for acts of deviance. For example, individual acts of resistance to authoritarian regimes may, if rigorously penalised, prompt few imitators. But one or two examples of successful (or unpenalised) opposition, may prompt others to add their voice; and once there are a few, then many may treat this as a sign that they can oppose without bearing the full costs of their actions. The diverse thresholds for collective action in a population may allow a rapid snowballing effect to follow from a relatively minor incident. In this way, whistle-blowers, dissenters and men and women of especially intense commitment may each help to set the scene for innovative collective action and may make political reform seem a practical possibility, as did the example set by Judge Paolo Borsellino in Italy. Alternatively, virtuous compliance may also unravel in a similar type of spiral. If a university ceases to acknowledge the role of teaching and administration in its criteria for promotion and if it rewards only those whose research productivity is high, we should expect a gradual destruction of institutional virtue. There may be some initial collective resistance, if there is real institutional virtue, but the defection of one or a small number (who will benefit disproportionately by doing so) will signal to others with slightly higher thresholds against defection that the dam has broken, and so on down the line.[27] Similarly, if a trust or honour system of time-keeping and in lieu leave operates in a firm and new management attempts to formalize certain procedures, such as clocking in and sick leave, the sense of fair play on which the old practices (and much else besides) rested may be rapidly eroded leaving a very low level of institutional virtue.[28]

The recognition of thresholds for action and the role of 'entrepreneurs' should not be taken as an argument about the weak-minded masses being swayed by leaders, nor about their susceptibility to conformism. While either is clearly a possible feature of a political system, our concern is with grasping the conditions under which the demands of citizenship become normative for individuals. In recognising that even the most high-minded may have to bide their time where the political system cannot secure widespread compliance, I am suggesting that for the demands of citizenship to exert 'ethical pull' on citizens of a state, those citizens must be able to count on a basic level of reliable conformity, or have a sufficient degree of confidence that their fellow citizens will reliably conform. Where a system cannot cross this basic threshold of effectiveness, its demands on its citizens can have little or no independent normative weight.[29] 'Oughts' imply 'cans', but 'can' is a relative judgement: where the harmful consequences of an individual act of non-compliance are insignificant (given, for example, widespread non-compliance) but the costs of compliance to the individual are high, it is unreasonable to believe that just because it is physically possible for the individual to comply, he or she should do so.

Recognising the importance of threshold judgements and the role of entrepreneurs or leaders also allows us to see how atomism and low levels of identification with political norms might best be seen, not as a basic structural constraint, but as a consequence of people's threshold judgements, which can be influenced in part by leadership and by changes in people's beliefs about what is desirable, what is achievable, and what can be tolerated (the conviction that there is a proletarian revolution waiting to happen around the corner, can make it rational to act, on relatively scanty evidence, as if it is beginning, as Lenin showed in October 1917). These beliefs and values can be influenced by a wide range of factors, but innovative and committed political leadership is certainly one major element. Far from social atomism being irremediable or the politics of identity being non-negotiable and zero-sum, this analysis suggests that much will depend on the vision and the strategies of those who play a central role in defining and interpreting political possibilities and group or community identities. Although, if leadership is essential for collective action in conditions of uncertainty (thereby creating the conditions for citizenship integrity), it is clear that nature of the outcome will be deeply affected by the aims and the integrity of these entrepreneurs and, above all, by the extent of their willingness to achieve a political solution. This does not mean that leaders who emphasise the distinctiveness of their communal identity and the non-negotiable character of their political demands are necessarily acting irresponsibly. On the contrary, groups which have been systematically excluded and oppressed may simply have no better strategy available to them, since settling for the standard citizenship rights and responsibilities of the liberal democratic state may effectively deny the legitimacy of their demands for redress. But, in the final analysis, what has to be found is a political solution – one which secures agreement on a common set of rules and norms by which to resolve conflicts between individuals and groups in the community.[30]

On this account, the depth of personal commitment to certain norms or values is not the best guide as to how most individuals will act in conditions of uncertainty. As Orwell illustrated in *1984*, few of us are so committed to our values that we cannot be brought to betray them through fear.[31] Courage, fidelity and integrity become less exceptional, but more possible, when we can rely on others to lead or to follow suit. Of course, it is also true that our commitments and values are more difficult to sustain when they must be denied by our practice: that involvement in corrupt practices corrodes our judgement; that lip-service and deference to authority debilitates our independence and convictions; and that 'passing' leaves us alienated from ourselves. Sometimes it is possible to develop a counter-culture, or a hidden transcript in which we sustain the possibility of transgression of the existing order. But the more isolated we are the harder it is to do this, and the more long-standing our compliance the more compromised we become.[32]

It is not just that values are not necessarily a good predictor of how people will act. This is a sound, but not exactly startling sociological generalisation. Rather, it is that for people to act in accordance with the norms, rules and values of the political sphere, certain thresholds of political effectiveness have to have been crossed – the procedures and practices of the political domain simply cannot exert ethical pull where basic thresholds of compliance have not been crossed. Politics is not the art and science of noble self-sacrifice. It is at base a deeply practical concern with the resolution of conflict, the negotiation of compromises, and the recognition and pursuit of shared ends, for which a legitimated framework of rules and norms is required. But any such order imposes some costs on individuals and there is a limit to the kinds of costs they can be expected to recognise as acceptable. A great deal hangs, then, on what people will recognise as affordable and thus as politically possible, since that will delimit their sense of their duties in this sphere, and I have suggested that a large role will be played by 'entrepreneurs' and leaders in influencing citizens' understanding of the parameters of political possibility. The account I have given has not, however, done much to distinguish the different types of motive which may lead people to comply with the demands of citizenship and, as such, it leaves open the question of the role of integrity in motivating such compliance.

Motives for compliance

I have suggested that in the absence of general compliance we cannot expect the norms and rules of the political system to have independent normative weight for citizens. This claim needs further examination, not least because it is linked to the complex problem of differentiating 'integrity-motivated' compliance with citizenship norms from other forms of compliance.

We can distinguish, loosely, three different motivations for compliance with political norms: *modus vivendi*,[33] over-determination, and civic virtue. *Modus vivendi* concerns compliance where the motive is the benefit which accrues to individual or group interests – so that conformity to political norms is conditional on those norms offering an interest-maximising strategy for the agent or group. This need not mean narrow self-interest maximising: but it does imply that the interests or values maximised are identified independently of the norms and values which structure the rules of the political domain. Nor does this mean that there is a straightforward calculation for each individual as to whether any particular act of compliance will be interest-maximising. On the contrary, recognising the importance of thresholds helps us see that compliance may be forthcoming, not because the norms of the political system are accepted, nor because conformity with them maximally serves the group's interests, but because non-conformity is not available as a strategy because a certain threshold for collective action would need to be crossed before the norms could be challenged. In *modus vivendi* compliance remains conditional, but the conditional calculation can be a highly complex one, involving judgements about how others will behave.

Modus vivendi compliance is also a feature where the norms and values of the group or the individual carry the weight of motivating compliance. That is, where one's moral and religious values are the sole motivation for political compliance. Such values can be intensely held, just as one's commitment to a group can be an intense form of identification, and in both cases we may acknowledge the integrity with which people act. But their citizenship plays no role in their reasons or complying with its demands, which are accepted or rejected wholly on the basis of their compatibility with the individual's existing moral values or commitments.

Over-determination concerns cases where the interests or values of the individual and the group endorse compliance and where there is also a sufficient degree of commitment to the norms of the political domain for compliance to be motivated independently of the advantage reaped. This case is important because the independently motivated compliance (or virtue) may play a part in shaping and informing the motives for strategic compliance so that there develops an ever closer identification with political norms.[34] But it also raises issues about the possibilities of perverse disjunctions between the two interests – where, for example, conformity to political norms becomes increasingly habitual and unreflective it also becomes less firmly and independently motivated, and thus closer to a *modus vivendi*. The result may be that expectations about the conformity of individual and group interests and political norms become inflated, so that minor disjunctions may come to be treated as throwing into question the validity of the political order.

Civic virtue – or integrity-driven conformity – although also a component in over-determined compliance, is most easily captured in situations where the independent interest in conformity is weak. In such circumstances we can say that we have a case of virtuous conformity only where it is the person's commitment to the rules and principles of the political domain which makes the difference in determining whether she acts in conformity with those principles or not. In assurance situations (where we act only if we are sure others will act), compliance is not virtue- or integrity-motivated if it derives from a calculation that the prudential threshold for supporting the collective action will be crossed (thus rendering our compliance either costless or of cost only to free-riding impulses), nor where it derives from a calculation that it is in our interests to comply. Whether or not citizens comply in the face of possible or actual, partial or total defection must depend on the strength of their commitment to political norms. As we have seen, this does not mean that they must act wholly without concern for how others act, but the acceptable threshold for others' compliance cannot be set entirely by prudential criteria – as when low thresholds for general compliance are generated by the high costs associated with defection and the high probability of detection and punishment. At the same time, people cannot rationally be indifferent to the costs of complying where others do not (they might face, for example, financial ruin or reprisals against their families). So, virtuous citizens are those whose commitment to their citizenship and to political norms takes them beyond an immediate calculation of what is maximally in their interests, and where it is that commitment which motivates them to act in support of those norms. Where some threshold for the compliance of others is set as a condition for one's own compliance, that threshold must be informed by the motive to fulfill, as far as possible, one's responsiblities as a citizen. To say of a citizen that she demonstrates civic virtue is, on this account, to say that it is her commitment to her values and principles *as a citizen* which motivates her compliance – and the cases in which virtue is most sorely tried are those where our principles demand conduct which prudence, self-interest, or our non-political values and commitments, counsel against. This means that when we make a judgement about people's integrity *as citizens*, or their civic virtue, we ask about the commitment from which the act flows, and this requires that we make some assessment both of the motive behind the act and of the extent to which that commitment is embodied in the way that the agent frames her options (in this case, the level at which she sets her threshold). In cases where general compliance is not going to be forthcoming, or where it is extremely improbable that it will be, and where the potential costs of compliance are exorbitant, then we have to say not only that civic virtue has become impossible, but that citizenship has also become impossible, and we are left with the demise of the political order. In such circumstances we might get acts of heroism or instances of great personal courage but the need for this is often an indication that the political order is too weak to be independently effective, which then makes it difficult for us to think of them as instances of civic virtue.

The more general implications of this analysis should be clear. Although we could look at the extensive literature on the types of context in which political participation and procedural compliance are forthcoming and those in which they are not, we must avoid confusing a discussion of the *incidence* of participation with a conceptual analysis which identifies the point at which *citizenship* comes to play an independent role in the motivation of political action and, as such, becomes an independent element within the political system. We have already examined the types of participation and procedural compliance which are required. The issue is whether compliance with these is motivated by our integrity as citizens, or by values and commitments outside of politics. The kinds of commitments which motivate us as citizens include a respect for public reason, a recognition of reciprocal obligations between citizens, an acknowledgement of the legitimacy of the procedural rules governing the formation of law and public policy, and/or a belief that the political domain can defend and promote values and goods which are central to our conception of the good (where it is valued not because this promotes our own good, so much as because it plays a distinctive role in promoting social and moral values which we take to be collective, objective, shared or, even, universal). Such reasons have much weaker motivational force where the political arena is fragile and fractured and where sub-groups, clientalism or atomism systematically undercut political norms. This is why threshold judgements become so important. But, as I have argued, this does not mean that we cannot distinguish analytically the point at which such judgements lose their *modus vivendi* character and take on a properly political character.

The more costly (in terms of virtue) citizenship is, the more fragile is the political order – hence Brecht's 'unhappy is the land that needs heroes'.[35] The more 'frictionless' are the norms of citizenship, the more stable and established will be the political order. But different traditions of political thought have fundamentally different perceptions of what forces render the political order stable and legitimate. Liberals take the political order and the demands of citizenship to be legitimated (and often also as generated) by real or hypothetical agreements between individuals whose interests are conceived of as existentially and normatively prior to that order. In the republican tradition, the interests of citizens are understood as a function of politics.

Threshold judgements about compliance with citizenship norms straddle these two very different accounts. With liberals, thresholds serve to link individuals' motives or preferences with the demands of citizenship; with republicans, the threshold for *citizenship* cannot be understood wholly in terms of a *modus vivendi* based on antecedent interests – there must also be some independent commitment to the values of the political order and a recognition of the normative demands of citizenship. On this account, citizenship plays little or no role in liberalism, since it has ethical significance for us only in so far as it appeals to interests or moral commitments which are normatively prior to politics. For republicans, in contrast, citizenship expresses values which are not reducible to interest-maximising judgements or prior moral values (although there may be some threshold requirement for others' compliance before that commitment can be motivationally effective). On the account I have proposed here, this means that, of the two traditions, only republicanism gives an account in which integrity and citizenship become so intimately linked that the norms and rules of the political domain secure a degree of autonomy from other patterns of commitment and principles of exchange.

Conclusion

Living with integrity means that the individual is able to connect her sense of self and her commitments as a moral agent to her roles and responsibilities in the world. To cease to be able to 'afford' to do this means that one becomes, in greater or lesser areas of one's life, subject to constraints and demands which one can neither resist nor endorse. To that extent one's freedom and autonomy are diminished – as is one's capacity to live a moral life. How far, though, is the standing in politics which citizenship confers an essential precondition for personal integrity?

I began this chapter by contrasting two accounts of citizenship: one which sees a very close connection between citizenship and integrity; the other of which denies the association. I have also noted Aristotle's view that the connection between individual integrity and citizenship is intrinsic – that only through the role of citizen can the moral virtues of the person be developed in their fullest form, because only by taking part in ruling and being ruled, can we develop the attachments and friendships within which we can most fully develop our own unique characters, motives and dispositions, together with the virtues we require to act upon them. De Tocqueville's belief that in the absence of the practices of citizenship egoism would ultimately destroy the moral centre of the agent, offers a similarly powerful account of the interdependence between citizenship and personal integrity. Such accounts press the case hard, but not decisively. The intrinsic view, in the end, claims too much for citizenship in modern democratic politics. The more plausible view is that there is a contingent, albeit strong, connection between the rights and duties of citizenship and the integrity of the individual in the modern democratic state.

In most advanced industrial societies, the denial of citizenship to large numbers of people is often accompanied by the systematic denial of many civil liberties and access to social and economic opportunities. To make their way in society, with such a status and without those civil rights, people are often forced to compromise on issues which are central to their sense of self. Many blacks in South Africa had no option but to pay their toll of self-abnegation to the whites they met and worked for, many women tolerated the intolerable because their societies denied them equal standing to their husbands or fathers, intellectuals in the Eastern Block were often forced to take work which was intended to violate their self-respect and self-esteem, and the threat of expulsion or repatriation leaves illegal immigrants in Britain and America or 'guest-workers' in Germany acutely vulnerable to demeaning forms of exploitation. It is difficult to live consistently in accordance with one's fundamental commitments when one is powerless to protest at the way one is treated by one's political and social institutions and by one's fellow human beings. But this does not mean that citizenship is a necessary condition for personal integrity – if there is an intrinsic connection (and that can still be doubted),[36] it is much more likely to be that a certain basic level of civil rights is centrally important (for most people) to attaining and sustaining integrity.

However, civil rights, such as the right to equal protection before the law, freedom from arbitrary arrest, search, and seizure, and the right to legal representation, are rarely secure unless backed by rights of political representation within the decision-making processes of one's community and society. If the civil rights are crucial to providing a framework of civil liberties, political rights seem important for ensuring that this framework is secured: they are valued because of the part they play in creating and sustaining a domain of free agency for the individual. For the most part we also think certain responsibilities are entailed by them, but, while someone who is cavalier towards these responsibilities is likely to be thought to be free-riding in an integrity compromising way, it does not follow that these duties trump all others. Democratic polities need enough of their people to be good citizens, but it is implausible to think they need all to be so, and that recognition allows us to acknowledge that integrity can equally be instanced by those who openly repudiate their responsibilities as citizens so as more perfectly to realize their deepest commitments. Peace protesters who do not accept that the government has a right to determine defence policy in relation to nuclear weapons, conscientious objectors and refusers who deny that the political system has the right to command them to do certain things (from fighting in a particular war to wearing a crash helmet in violation of their religious practices), and those who are prepared to insist on the illegitimacy of governments which fail to accord standing and its consequent rights to beings which they believe have equal (or at least sufficient) value to warrant it – those in slave societies who stood for the slaves, those who fought for women's rights, and those, perhaps, who fight for the rights of children, or the unborn, or animals, or the eco-system. People who fight such causes in ways which break the rules are bad citizens, but that does not mean they lack integrity. However, all these cases might plausibly be described as ones in which people are bad citizens for (often) virtuous reasons. Much more worrying for those who retain a classical vision of an active and virtuous citizenry, are those whose integrity is realised completely independently from the political sphere – for example, by their dedication to their art or their religion, or to the relief of the suffering of others. In these cases political duties are irrelevant to their achievement of integrity, and in recognising their integrity we break fundamentally with the classical idea that a political life is an essential component for the fully moral life. Moreover, should it come to the point that such alternative lives of integrity become jeopardised by the increasing fragility of the political system, it does not follow that the duties of citizenship 'kick-in' and constrain these other values. They do not do so precisely because that fragility creates the kind of threshold problems we have identified. Faced with those uncertainties integrity may require remaining true to what one holds most dear. To this extent, such commitments may best be understood as contributing to the fragility of the political domain. That is why republicans have traditionally been hostile to sub-political groups and communities and have insisted on the development of a common political culture which dominates all other commitments. But, since we can no longer realistically expect to live in such a state, we are left with the pressing question of just how far value pluralism is compatible with the long-term stability of states and how far modern states should be investing in developing a political culture in which citizens see their political standing and its responsibilities as a constitutive component of their individual identities and as framing their fundamental dispositions, rather than simply as a means for the pursuit of their interests. Although this chapter has not answered this question, it has sought to clarify some of the issues involved in so doing.

My thanks to Diego Gambetta, Alan Montefiore, Alan Patten and, especially, to Jerry Cohen for comments on earlier drafts.

Notes

1 Hence Aristotle's view that although the good citizen is not necessarily a good man, the good man only becomes so by also being a good citizen.
2 John Stuart Mill, 'Considerations on Representative Government', in *On Liberty and Other Essays*, edited by John Gray (Oxford: Oxford University Press, 1991) p. 333.
3 Benjamin Constant, 'The Liberty of the Ancients Compared with that of the Moderns', in *Political Writings*, edited by Biancamaria Fontana (Cambridge: Cambridge University Press, 1998), p. 317.

4 Michel de Montaigne, 'On Repenting', in *The Complete Essays*, edited by M.A. Screech (Harmondsworth: Allen Lane, The Penguin Press, 1991), III.2: p. 912.

5 ibid. 'If I am occasionally pressed into taking some business foreign to me, then it is in hand that I promise to take it, not in lung or liver.' 'On Restraining Your Will', III.10: p. 1135; 'My reason was not made for bending and bowing, my knees were.' 'On the Art of Conversation', III.8: p. 1059.

6 ibid., III.10: p. 1135.

7 Bernard Williams, 'Utilitarianism and Moral Self-indulgence', in *Moral Luck* (Cambridge: Cambridge University Press, 1981), p. 49. With Williams we should resist the idea that it is the desire to stick to one's principles, rather than the sheer commitment to them which matters, since the former leads down the road to what he has called 'moral self-indulgence'. In distinguishing the two cases we implicitly recognise that integrity is fundamentally concerned with character rather than with particular attitudes or desires. See especially pp. 48–51.

8 For example, the case of Max Redlicht in Thomas Kenneally's *Schindler's Ark* (1982) or, more prosaically, that of Rosemary in Bob Dylan's 'Lily, Rosemary and the Jack of Hearts', from the album *Blood on the Tracks*, who 'had done a lot of bad things, even once tried suicide, was looking to do just one good deed before she died.' In both cases it took courage to do what they did, and we may admire that, but this does not mean we are admiring their integrity. Although it may take guts to act with integrity it does not follow that integrity is always exhibited when it takes guts to do something.

9 That an irreducible element of assessment of intent enters ascriptions of integrity means that we run straight into the problem of its observability: i.e., how to distinguish between someone who acts with integrity and someone who simulates such action in order to develop a reputation for integrity. Differences in intention are not readily observable, nonetheless judgements about integrity are also, in part, predictions about the reliability of the relevant behaviour – and while such predictions cannot be fully verified, they can be falsified, and their falsifiability can be made more pertinent through counter-factual reflection. That the behavioural manifestation of integrity can be simulated does not, then, imply that we can never distinguish the simulation from the real thing.

10 These being conscientious refusal – where our beliefs and moral principles will not allow us to perform the act required by the state; and cases where we break a law, although not necessarily the one that we reject, in order to draw attention to a decision, law or governmental action we reject, as in civil disobedience.

11 cf. David Hume, *Enquiries concerning Human Understanding and concerning the Principles of Morals*, 3rd edn., edited by P.H. Nidditch (Oxford: Oxford University Press, 1975), pp. 164–71.

12 As in de Tocqueville's fears for the rise of individualism in the second volume of *Democracy in America* (edited by H. Reeve, revised by Francis Bowen, New York: Vintage Books, 1945. Original French edn. 1840).

13 By theorists such as Jurgen Habermas (*Moral Consciousness and Communicative Action*, Cambridge: Polity Press, 1990), Joshua Cohen ('The economic basis of deliberative democracy', *Social Philosophy and Policy* 1989 6 (2): 25–50)

and, in his recent work, John Rawls (*Political Liberalism*. New York: Columbia University Press, 1993).

14　Robert Putnam, *Making Democracy Work* (Princeton: Princeton University Press, 1993), p. 173.

15　Adam Smith, *The Wealth of Nations*, (Oxford: Oxford University Press, 1976), p.145. In a similar vein Moncur Olson argues, in *The Rise and Decline of Nations*, (New Haven: Yale University Press, 1982), that special interest groups, sub-communities and organisations with limited *civitas* (i.e., limited engagement or commonality of interest with the broader community of citizens) which play a major participatory role in the institutions of the state, can have extremely destructive effects on the political system. See also Joel S. Migdal, 'Strong states, weak states: Power and accommodation', in Myron Weiner and Samuel P. Huntingdon (eds), *Understanding Political Development*, (Boston: Little, Brown, 1987), pp. 391–434.

16　Which, Madison argues, is the virtue of republican (that is, representative) government with a large and diverse citizenry; see *The Federalist Papers*, No. 10, edited by Clinton Rossiter (New York: American Library), pp. 77–84.

17　Michael Sandel, 'The Procedural Republic and the Unencumbered Self', *Political Theory* 1984, 12: pp. 81–96. See also Will Kymlicka, *Multicultural Citizenship: A Liberal Theory of Minority Rights*, (Oxford: Oxford University Press, 1995), and his edited collection *The Rights of Minority Citizens*, (Oxford: Oxford University Press, 1995).

18　See, for example, Iris Marion Young, *Justice and the Politics of Difference*, (Princeton: Princeton University Press, 1990); Anne Phillips, *The Politics of Presence*, (Oxford: Oxford University Press, 1995); and John Rawls, *Political Liberalism*, (Columbia: Columbia University Press, 1993).

19　See, for example, the essays in Toni Morrison (ed.) *Race-ing Justice, En-gendering Power: Essays on Anita Hill, Clarence Thomas and the Construction of Social Reality*, (London: Chatto and Windus, 1993).

20　David Hume, *Enquiries Concerning the Principles of Morals*, edited by Selby-Bigge, IX, ii: p. 283.

21　Being able to afford to fight corruption (and calculations of loss and gain) have to be interpreted in the broadest terms: they do not necessarily concern maxi-mising strategies for individual benefit, but may include a broad range of values, including the desire to act morally where it is possible to do so. How-ever, even impeccably moral motives will often involve a calculation similar in many respects to that made by the opportunist: where it is impossible to both keep to the rules and protect one's family, and where one's principles demand that one does both, some calculation about the best overall strategy sems unavoidable.

22　Of course, there may be cases where principled objection trumps all calculations of cost – there may be some things we believe we should never do. But the class of such acts is relatively small for most people, and the number of cases in which people have the moral will to stick to their commitments is, one sus-pects, a still smaller set.

23　cf. Mark Granovetter, 'Threshold models of collective behaviour', *American Journal of Sociology* 1978, 83: pp. 1402–43.

24 It must be stressed that these calculations concern costs and benefits in the broadest sense – they apply as much to those committed to collective ends as they do to those seeking to maximise self-interest.

25 Granovetter has also pointed out that, because a person's threshold is 'simply that point where the perceived benefits to an individual of doing the thing in question exceed the perceived costs', two people, with different beliefs, preferences and intensity of preferences, may nonetheless end up with the same threshold. Hence the phenomenon of strange partnerships on the barricades. This conclusion is important because it underlines that we cannot assume that just because collective action takes place, there must be a single, widely shared norm prescribing that action – there may be no norm, just a fortuitous conjunction of self-interested calculations, or there may be many norms which serve to different extents to weight judgements of acceptable probability in such a way that collective action becomes possible.

26 Where people are reckless with respect to both we usually refer to them as martyrs or psychotics rather than heroes.

27 There are, of course, other forms of incentives for compliance with norms – not least, coercion and reward. But the ability to exercise coercion effectively depends, in part, on one having persuaded others to support one's action, and that persuasion will rest largely on their sense that one can succeed.

28 See A. Gouldner, *Patterns of Industrial Bureaucracy*, (New York: Free Press, 1954), and the discussion in Gary J. Miller, *Managerial Dilemmas*, (Cambridge: Cambridge University Press, 1992), pp. 207–10.

29 I say 'independent' weight because it might still, on occasion, be able to ensure compliance by appealing to non-political values which inhere in the community, as I discuss below.

30 See Iris Marion Young, 'Together in Difference: Transforming the Logic of group Political Conflict' in Will Kymlicka (ed.), *The Rights of Minority Cultures*, (Oxford: Oxford University Press, 1995), pp. 155–78.

31 See also the case of Max Redlicht's fellow Jews in *Schindler's Ark*, supra, note 9.

32 It is not difficult to understand in this light the need for some cathartic cleansing and empowering ritual by which to liberate oneself from one's past oppression and the shame of one's complicity with it – as in Fanon's call for revolutionary violence. On hidden transcripts see James Scott's *Domination and the Arts of Resistance*, (New Haven, CT: Yale University Press, 1990).

33 Drawing on Rawls' use in *Political Liberalism*, (New York: Columbia University Press, 1993) p. 147.

34 As in Rawls' discussion of overlapping consensus (ibid.).

35 Bertolt Brecht, *Life of Galileo*, (translated by D.I. Vesey, London: Methuen, 1960), p. 108. With thanks to Catherine Audard for the quotation.

36 It seems odd to insist that men and women imprisoned for their beliefs necessarily lose their integrity – especially in the light of so much heroic integrity among such prisoners.

3 Integrity and the economy
Concernedness, trust and responsibility

David Vines

Introduction

This chapter addresses a disquieting gulf.[1] On the one hand there is the economics discipline in which I work, and whose core principles I teach my students. This discipline takes it as axiomatic that individuals are entirely selfish: that they pursue their own 'self-interest unconstrained by morality' (Milgrom and Roberts 1992). On the other hand there is our experience of everyday life, in all of its business, social and political aspects. It is clear to each of us that we nearly all act unselfishly on occasions, and, furthermore, that many aspects of the life that we live are governed by complex moral codes.

The Balliol colloquium on integrity, at which the chapters in this book were discussed, reinforced a sense of this gulf. At the conference, practitioners from a whole range of activities and professions described to each other how their lives and activities were restrained and regulated by intricate considerations of concern, responsibility and integrity, considerations far removed from the pursuit of 'pure selfish self-interest'. In this chapter my aim is therefore to comment on this gulf, as it presented itself at the conference. This chapter has been written in especial response to the chapters in this volume by Donald Hay, Alan Hamlin, Anthony Clunies Ross, Peter Kemp and René Sève, and also to that by Colin Rayner; it is, in part, commentary on these papers, in part it builds upon them.

There are three lengthy, but necessary, preliminaries. These form the subject matter of the next three sections of the chapter. The first is to review why we are here: why is it that economists believe what they do? Then I discuss the difficulties with the economists' argument, even taken on its own ground. And in the last of these sections I review the evidence and the arguments (some very recent indeed) about why people act in concerned and trusting ways.

These three steps form the background to the main argument presented in the following two sections of the chapter. This argument is that an economy can only function successfully if the individuals within it act with consistently exercised concernedness and trust. I want to develop a dynamic metaphor in two-dimensional space, a picture of individuals bound together in a web of relations of what I call a 'horizontal' kind – to the left and to the right of them on a sheet of paper as it were – and of a vertical kind – above them and beneath them on the sheet of paper. 'Horizontal' relations are to do with individuals being concerned about the well-being of others at any one point in time – having the utility of others in one's own utility function at any one point in time. 'Vertical' trust consists in being able to count on commitments made at one point in time being honoured at other points in time; it can also be called promise-keeping. My image of this metaphor is a moving one, of an individual moving forwards – up the sheet of paper as it were – perpetually coming to the points in time at which the promises made in past times have to be honoured, and perpetually fighting temptations to duck and weave, in order both to avoid past promises and to shake off horizontal concernedness to some so as to take up concernedness with others.[2]

This is difficult territory. On the one hand the beauty of economics as a discipline is that we understand very well the extent to which pure selfish self-interest, mobilised through market mechanisms, can work in allocating resources towards desired objectives. On the other hand, we understand very little about the large-scale effects of concernedness and trust, and there is a line of thought (Hayek 1988) which worries that the tendency of human beings to altruism and sympathy actually interferes with the desired workings of the market order. This chapter will therefore raise more questions than it is able to answer.

It is as well to draw attention here to a point which is important in all of what follows. I make continual use of a distinction between what I call 'selfish self-interest' and something else which I merely describe as 'self-interest'. The first form of self-interest is one which exhibits no concern for the well-being of others. The latter form of self-interest is a more general notion. It clearly includes the former. But – or so I will argue – it may also involve 'other-concerned self-interest'. This is because – I will argue – self-interestedness may, in fact, involve, and even require, concern for the well-being of others.

One final preliminary remark might be helpful. I do not actually use the word integrity until more than half of the way through the chapter. But my investigation of concernedness and trust deliberately enables me to build up to a picture of a person whose concernedness and trust is consistently exercised, and who thereby accepts responsibilities which can somehow be relied upon under pressure; such a person I will call a 'person of integrity'. The last parts of the chapter are devoted to an analysis of what can be achieved, in public service, and in the market economy, by such persons of integrity.

The economist's view

Adam Smith's 'boundaries' argument

We can trace the economist's view, and its difficulties, back to Adam Smith. And so I begin, as does Donald Hay in Chapter 16 of this volume, with Smith. Even Smith, who is commonly perceived as the prophet of selfish self-interest, did not believe that a society is, or can be, bound together, if all individuals in it are entirely selfish. Smith instead put forward what we can call a 'boundaries' view.

Sympathy and civil society

Smith's earliest famous book was the *Theory of Moral Sentiments* (1759, see Smith 1976a). This is a book about how societies are held together by the reciprocal interaction of mutual sympathy.

> Nature, when she formed man for society, endowed him with an original desire to please, and an original aversion to offend his brethren . . . [Furthermore] nature has endowed him not only with a desire of being approved of, but with a desire of being what ought to be approved of; or of being what he himself approves of in other men.
>
> (Smith 1976a: 111, 2: 6–7)

The individual is thus subject to two kinds of moral restraint on selfish self-interest – the jurisdiction of both the good opinion of others – what Smith calls the 'man without' – and the good opinion of one's self – the 'man within', that 'great judge and arbiter' of our conduct. Each, by imagining himself in the position of the other, comes to appreciate, and to respond to, both the needs of the other, *and* his own moral perceptions of these needs. Smith discusses at great length the manner in which these sympathies of citizens may be tuned to those of each other, and reinforced, in order to produce desirable outcomes. The chapter by Margaret Cohen in this volume provides a remarkable and sensitive account of the attuning of the sympathies of a carer with the needs of those who are cared for. But in a way Smith goes further than Cohen; he describes how desirable outcomes are brought about by the *reciprocal* interaction and negotiation of mutual sympathies amongst individuals of symmetrical or similar standing (rather than in the asymmetrical relationship of carer and cared for). This is a vision of society in which individuals can and do negotiate their wants and needs into positions of compatibility. Smith does not, of course, think that this is a complete picture of social relations; it is *part* of such a picture.

Self-interest and the market

In contrast to his earlier views, Smith's *Wealth of Nations,* published in 1776, offers a strikingly different partial account of social relations, about the connections between individuals relating to the working of the economy. He carves out the 'economic' as a distinct sphere of human activity, and then argues that within that sphere, individuals are motivated, broadly speaking, by selfish self-interest. 'It is not from the benevolence of the butcher, the brewer or the baker that we expect our dinner, but from their regard to their own self interest. . . .' (Smith 1982: 1, 2: 119)

Smith's ideas were two-fold. First, the voluntary exchange of goods between individuals with different skills is *beneficial.* Broadly speaking, if I specialise in what I am good at, and you specialise in what you are good at and we exchange, then mutual benefit will result. Smith coined a wonderfully expressive term for this specialisation-and-exchange: the 'division of labour'. Examples of this division of labour range from the mundane trade between butcher, brewer and baker to international commerce between nations.[3] In these processes, each, in the pursuit of their own unmitigated selfish self-interest, will produce benefit for others, or general public benefit.

Second, the reliance on a market as an institution will bring about the *most beneficial* amount of exchange. Smith's argument here lays the basis for all modern discussions of the role of the market in economic efficiency, and it is worth spelling it out in a little detail. The argument is in fact very simple. If little of a commodity is produced, then consumers will be prepared to pay a lot for it; the resulting high price will be more than it would cost for additional units to be produced, and that will create incentives for producers of the commodity to expand their output. Conversely, if much of the commodity is produced, then its price will need to be low to induce consumers to buy all that is produced; this low price will be less than it cost to make the last units produced, and that will lead producers to reduce their output. Somewhere between these extremes will be the optimum point – the position where the price which consumers are prepared to pay is just equal to the cost of producing the last units supplied – at which point wants are not under-met or over-met. And our argument shows that the 'market mechanism' will induce producers to expand output if it is below this optimum point and to reduce output if it is above this optimum point. Here is Adam Smith's 'invisible hand' mechanism. Such a vision of the market economy,[4] with its two central ideas (that voluntary exchange leads to benefit and that the organisation of voluntary exchange through a market leads to the maximum of benefit) forms the core of the modern economics of resource allocation.

Smith's claim of 'maximum of benefit' needs to be interpreted carefully, in a way which has only really been understood by economists in the twentieth century (although Smith himself presumably understood the argument). It may be that other third parties lose through voluntary exchange. For example, if the brewer expands his output in response to a high demand for ale, his extra demand for grain may increase the price of grain and thereby harm those who purchase grain for food. One has, therefore, to talk in terms of efficiency, defined as a position in which no one person can be made better off without another person being made worse off. The above argument can then be recast to state that voluntary exchange in a market leads to efficiency. This carefully circumscribed claim no longer asserts that voluntary exchange through a market causes all participants to benefit. Rather it merely says that voluntary exchange produces an outcome in which no further benefit can be had by any one person without at the same time some other person being made worse off.[5]

Smith's invisible-hand perspective was clearly not advanced by someone who believed that people were always selfish; that they were never motivated by the interests of others, or by sympathy. Our brief discussion of *Theory of Moral Sentiments* has made this abundantly clear. Rather, Smith puts forward the hypothesis of selfishness in exactly the same spirit as that in which Alan Hamlin writes in Chapter 17 of this volume – that of 'economising on sympathy'. The bringing of wants and needs into a position of mutual compatibility, in the manner required in *The Theory of Moral Sentiments,* is sympathy-intensive. Smith's radical idea in *Wealth of Nations* is that there are whole swathes of human activity in which sympathy is not necessary.[6] One-hundred-and-fifteen years later Alfred Marshall was to write that '. . . economics is a study of mankind in the ordinary business of life; it examines most closely that part of individual and social action which is most closely connected with the attainment and the use of the material requisites of well-being' (Marshall 1910: 1). Smith's idea was that a part of human life, namely individual and social action in the 'ordinary business of life', could be well regulated – indeed best regulated – by reliance on selfish self-interest rather than on sympathy.[7]

Virtue and the State

But this is not all. At Glasgow University, Smith gave a lecture course with the very exact title of 'Lectures on Justice, Revenue and Arms' the notes from which are now published as the *Lectures on Jurisprudence* (Smith 1978). In these lectures, Smith argued that there are some things which neither the sympathy of individuals, nor the incentives of the market, will provide in sufficient quantity. For Smith, there are three such things. First, the State

> . . . must provide an exact administration of *justice* in order to resolve the clashes of interest which will inevitably arise between individuals, while in addition it must preserve their property – the fruits of gain without whose enjoyment there could be no stimulus to better our condition.
>
> (Skinner 1982: 77)

Second,

> Smith recognised that the State must provide for *defence,* partly as a result of growing technicality and expense, and partly because a modern economy, characterised by the division of labour, would tend to reduce the number of those fitted and available for war. . . . Finally, Smith argued that the state should provide such *public works* as may be necessary to facilitate economic activity.
>
> (ibid.)

> [These are] of such a nature, that the profit could never repay the expense to any individual or small number of individuals, and which it cannot therefore be expected that any individual or small number of individuals should erect or maintain.
>
> (Smith 1982: V, 1: §c.i.)

The examples of such 'public goods' which Smith provided included items like roads, bridges, canals, and harbours (ibid: 78).

Smith discusses rather little the motivation, and the interests, of those who mobilise the state to make such provision. They are deeply important to the argument which follows. Let us label this motivation 'civic virtue', or 'virtue' for short, whilst for the present leaving its content unexplored.[8]

Summary

Thus, we can trace back to Smith a concern with the appropriate boundaries of sympathy, of selfishness, and of what we might call public provision. The 'boundaries claim', which has come down to us from Smith, is as follows:

1   Interactions between individuals in what Smith called 'society' – what we could call the institution of civil society – should be, and are, ones in which sympathy exercises restraint upon the pursuit of individual self-interest.
2   We can, and should, separate out one sphere of human activity, economic activity, and organise it in a market institution in which individuals can and do act entirely selfishly.
3   However, there is a category of things which neither the sympathy of individuals acting within civil society, nor the selfish self-interest of individuals acting within the market, will provide in sufficient quantity. These things should be provided by the institution of the State, mobilised by individuals propelled by the motive of virtue.

The modern economist's boundaries argument

A much more radical boundaries claim was expressed, with characteristic force, by Mrs Thatcher, when she said 'there is no such thing as society, only individuals and their families'. In this she was merely echoing what many economists appear to believe.[9] Sympathy might be important between members of a family, or in clubs and other voluntary associations. Individuals connected in this way might act with concernedness and generosity towards each other (indeed they might even love and cherish each other). But these relations are, for a view of the economy at least, not very important. We are left with a view which may be summed up as *Proposition 1*: Love your family (and perhaps your friends and those whose purposes you share closely). But be selfish in business. And use politics to sort out residual problems.

Then, according to one version of the story, there is rather little of interest for economists to say either about the relations of loving and cherishing within families and clubs and civil associations, or about civic virtue, so by and large they are ignored.[10] This view then boils down yet further to the following stripped-down and simple political philosophy which I may express as *Proposition 2*: there are 'market failures' in the economy, to be sure. It is the role of the state and of politics to correct these market failures. But there is no need for virtue (or for the 'concernedness, trust, and responsibility' in the title of this chapter) for this to be possible.

The third and most radically aggressive version of the economists' argument is that market mechanisms ought to be introduced, with the corollary that the motive of selfish self-interest ought to be relied on, in areas in which this has not hitherto been done. Thus, under the influence of economists' arguments, we have seen (around the world but led by Britain), the privatisation of the public utilities (telephones, gas, water, electricity, railways, etc.). Even more strikingly, we are seeing the introduction of markets into the provision of public services; the most profound example of this has been in the caring professions (in particular health and education) in which motivations of providers have traditionally been thought not to be selfish, but to arise out of a deep concern for the well-being of others. Nevertheless, under the influence of the economists' argument, policy in these areas has been remorselessly focused in the direction of marketisation. Thus, for example, in British medicine, general practitioners have been encouraged to 'shop around' for the best buy for their patients in the process of the onward-referral of these patients to hospitals.

The aggressive version of the economists' argument in this area has *not* only been that one can 'economise on virtue' by the reliance on selfish self-interest harnessed through the market (the Smith claim). Rather, we can express it as *Proposition 3*: without the mobilisation of selfish self-interest through market mechanisms, provision of public utilities and public services cannot be made to work properly. Markets, underpinned by the pursuit of selfish self-interest, are not just a substitute for virtue – the claim goes – but actually necessary instead of it.

In brief, this strong argument may be summarised as follows. The problem of economic organisation within professions such as the caring and educational ones is very serious, because the amount of resources used within them is very large. Furthermore, it will become yet more acute as, with an ageing population, more health services are demanded, and as, with a need for higher levels of skill within a modern economy, the level of education required for effective participation in society rises for all individuals. Furthermore, the problem becomes more acute as the units of production (hospitals and health authorities, schools and education authorities, universities and research communities, etc.) take on larger sizes because of their need for increasingly expensive large-scale technology and for a widening range and scope of activities. The problem is that, in large organisations, to rely on virtuous motivation is to rely on something much too vague and fuzzy. It used to be said that the British National Health Service was the largest employer of labour in Europe except the Soviet army. Such organisations find it hard to weed out inefficiency. More importantly they tend to be 'unprogressive' and experience difficulty in rewarding initiative or promoting technical change.[11] Furthermore, such institutions find it hard to make choices between difficult desirable ends. This problem is compounded by the fact that – with patient demand rationed by unmonitored queuing – there were no clear indications of where need was greatest and where the priorities for the allocation of sympathy were most pressing. The resulting bureaucratic resource allocation battles were legendary.

The 'Thatcher revolution' in Britain – under the influence of the economists' argument – has brought the introduction of markets into the centre of the management of these professions, into the 'heartland' of virtue. The idea has been to create an 'internal' market: to create a purchaser and to separate him or her from the provider, and, as already described, to enable him or her to shop around for the best deal. The aim has been to inject some of Adam Smith's allocative discipline into these activities, encouraging output where it is in short supply, and exerting pressures for closure where there are too many resources employed. In the reformed National Health Service this purchaser is not the patient, but a GP 'fund-holding' doctor acting on the patient's behalf. This new structure in the British Health Service has been called a 'quasi-market', because fund-holding GPs do not own their own practices in quite the way that businesses own theirs, and also because the facilities for hospital provision remain formally owned by the state, even if they are managed by independent hospital 'trusts'. Nevertheless fund-holding general practices are able to keep the money which they save by purchasing cheaply, and hospitals are able to keep the proceeds when they make good 'sales', for improvements to their facilities and for actual financial rewards to staff. In this sense there are 'market relations' within these new structures; indeed the operation of incentives, which is the reason for marketisation, *requires* that they be able to do this.

The next section reviews the problems inherent in Propositions 1, 2 and 3.

Difficulties in the economists' argument

The pervasiveness of 'market failure'

The last 200 years of economic analysis have built up a catalogue of problems in the way of relying on unfettered and purely selfish self-interest, within the institution of the market, to organise economic activity.

If you were to ask most economists about how well Adam Smith's view of the efficiency of the market has survived the last 200 years, you would receive the answer 'only moderately well'.[12] A modern economist would now tell you that an economic system, organised according to the selfish pursuit of self-interest and surrounded only by the institutions of law and defence, would be subject to a very large number of 'market failures'. Almost all economists would tell you that the State can play some role in ensuring that each of the following five market failures is remedied, at least in part.

1   There is a need to ensure an adequate provision of a whole range of goods which would be under-provided by the market. The first category of these is the 'public goods' which Adam Smith described; the list is longer now than justice, defence, and the roads, bridges, canals and harbours of which Smith wrote. A public good is (a) something the consumption of which by one individual does not greatly, or at all, reduce the amount available to be consumed by another; and (b) something for which it is difficult to exclude one individual from consuming, if it has been provided for another person. A good example is street-lighting; which (by contrast with, say, an ice-cream) has both of these features. Any attempt to organise provision of public goods by means of a market economy in a society in which individuals are motivated only by selfish self-interest will lead to too little being produced, since there are clear incentives for any one individual to free-ride on the services provided for another. The second category of goods which will be under-provided by the market is that of 'merit goods': these are goods the properties of which are complex, the benefits from which are difficult to understand, and the desire for which understates their true benefit. They are goods which private individuals would under-consume, if left to their own devices. Examples include the wearing of seatbelts; the taking of preventative health measures, some aspects of education, and public service broadcasting. There is a similar need to deter the consumption of demerit goods such as drugs and pornography. The third category of such goods which will be under-provided by a market is knowledge and information. Once established, any one piece of knowledge should be made widely

available and not restricted, but if all knowledge is free then there will be no economic incentive to produce it. The patent system and trade secrets law exist to provide some protection for the discoverers of knowledge, but subsidies for research and development are also important. The fourth category of goods which will be under-provided by a free market is education and training: individuals, unless they are from wealthy families, cannot invest adequately in their own education because such investments are risky for any one individual (and also cannot be used as collateral); employers will not invest adequately in the education of their employees, because selfishly self-interested employees will not promise to remain loyal when trained and highly marketable.

2   There is a need to control the inflicting of economic damage by one party on another in ways separate from market transactions, for example through the emission of pollution, whose costs fall neither on the producer nor the consumer of a product, but on, so to speak, innocent bystanders. For obvious reasons, these issues have come to be known as 'externality problems' in economists' technical jargon.[13]

3   There is a need to avoid restraints of trade and to regulate monopolies. Restraints of trade cause low output and high prices – and, more generally, low-quality service and restricted choice. The solution may not be as simple as Smith thought – simply to promote competition. There are some kinds of 'natural monopolies' (like water supply and most utilities), and there are some markets in which competition leads naturally to monopoly (like the market for transatlantic aircraft, or that for word-processors).

4   There is a need to provide insurance for members of society against such adverse circumstances as sickness and consequent loss of earning power. Reliance on market-based insurance schemes may be inadequate. One reason for this is that insurance is a merit good in the sense defined above; another reason is that private insurance markets do not function well because (a) those offering insurance seek out the low-risk cases and offer them low premiums, leaving high risk cases uninsurable or with very high premiums, and (b) cost containment can get out of hand, because those insured are able to demand gold-plated service at no cost to themselves.

5   There is a need to regulate the aggregate economy so that overall spending does not become deficient, and mean that large numbers in the economy suffer from loss of employment and earning power, and so that overall spending does not become excessive so that prices rise rapidly, thus frustrating the wishes of many and leading to inevitable subsequent unemployment in over-correction.

The gradual acceptance of the above five arguments, especially in the last half century, has led to a massive increase in the role of the State, compared with the modest role envisaged for it by Adam Smith: instituting a large number of correctives to market forces in order to 'level the playing field'. Such actions are necessary to ensure that the selfish pursuit of self-interest does indeed lead towards efficiency in the way envisaged by Adam Smith's 'invisible hand' mechanism.[14] The erection of a large regulatory super-structure on top of the economy, in order to take these actions, means that part of the realm of economic activity which is left to the unfettered selfish pursuit of self-interest in modern societies has, as a consequence, narrowed immensely compared with that advocated by Adam Smith.

There has also been another development, too, which weakens yet further the Smith 'boundaries' argument. Many economists, although fewer than those who subscribe to the above list of arguments, would also assert that there is a need for the State to redistribute resources to the poorer members of society whose possessions and skills are not valued by a market, even a well-functioning one. However, the basis for this argument that the re-distribution of income is a proper role for the State sits uneasily with a view that, in the economic sphere, life is best organised by means of the selfish pur-suit of self-interest. Why should selfish individuals, whose selfishness is the very engine of a well-functioning economy, move into some other political sphere and display altruism or sympathy, and agree to the State confiscating part of their gains from selfish behaviour in order to improve the lot of those less well-off?[15] Nevertheless, many economists argue both that people ought to do this, and that they actually do.

Problems with using politics to rectify these market failures

Recall Smith's original boundaries argument, and Propositions 1, 2, and 3. It is conceded that there may be 'market failures', but it is argued that there is no need for the relations of concernedness, trust, and responsibility to be introduced into economic life. Instead, it is claimed, it is the role of politics, and of the State, to correct these market failures.

But why should this be possible? Why should individuals who are other-wise entirely selfish be able to come together politically to solve the very many problems of market failure identified above? Does this not give us an incoherent account of politics? There appear to be two difficulties here.

First, why should selfish individuals ever agree on political solutions to important problems? The pioneering work of Arrow in the early 1950s showed that this is a forlorn hope. Here is an example which shows why. Suppose that society is divided into three groups: farmers, fishermen and city dwellers. Suppose that the farmers grow wheat. In the manner discussed above, in a competitive market the price of wheat will settle to that level at which what consumers are prepared to pay for it is exactly equal to the cost of producing the marginal units of output; this price will determine the amount of wheat which is profitable to produce. But suppose now that, if the farmers are not regulated, they use large quantities of a particular kind of fertiliser which kills fish in rivers – say all fish – and ruins the livelihood of fishermen.

This is an example of the kind of pollution 'externality problem' which we discussed above; the 'problem' is that in the buying and selling of wheat, the fishermen are not compensated for the death of their fish. This is the sort of problem to which we ought to be able to imagine a political solution. Suppose that there are three alternatives: the *status quo* (called option A); a tax-payer funded scheme to rejuvenate and manage the river, and to manage and restrict the use of fertiliser, the costs of which fall at least partly on the city-dwellers (called option B); and a simple ban on the use of all fertiliser, which would lead to only partial rejuvenation of the river, but which would cost the city-dwelling taxpayers nothing (called option C). Suppose, as is plausible, that the preferences of the three groups are as follows.[16]

Farmers' preferences:	A is preferred to B is preferred to C
Fishermens' preferences:	B is preferred to C is preferred to A
City-dwellers' preferences:	C is preferred to A is preferred to B

Suppose that the three groups were equally numerous and that there was a vote. Then deadlock would result: although each group has clear preferences, no overall political solution could emerge merely from voting. This is essentially because the preferences of each group are not close enough to each other. If pure selfishness was abandoned one might imagine a solution in which option B was collectively chosen, since the farmers stand to lose the most. But voting amongst entirely selfish individuals could not produce such an outcome.

One is tempted to reply that politics is not just voting and that problems of the above kind could be solved by benevolent political 'leadership'. Continuing in this vein, one might imagine political leaders who not only supported market institutions where markets were efficient, but also adopted policies to rectify market failures and, where there were conflicts of interest as to how to do this, proposed solutions which promoted the greatest good (in some sense).

But we now arrive at the second difficulty. Why on earth should political leadership be like this? Indeed a whole branch of political science has been developed in the USA by James Buchannan and Gordon Tulloch around precisely the argument that political leadership will *not* be like this. Politicians are not exempt from selfishness. Although they are charged with pursuing public duty rather than their own advancement and rewards, inevitably they come – so the argument goes – to pursue what is best for themselves. Furthermore, the public agencies which they would need to use for the furthering of their public duty – the kind of river regeneration agency which would be needed in the above example – are inevitably 'captured' by the parties which they are meant to police (in this example, the farmers). The opposing view, argues Buchannan – that politicians and those who work in public agencies are selfless servants of the public good – is unduly naïve. And it should be clear to us that, if individuals were entirely selfish, such a view certainly *would* be naïve.

We thus conclude that individuals who are motivated only by selfish self-interest could not pursue the kinds of politics required to rectify market failures. This is a pretty big challenge to the economists' view.

Incentivisation and its corrosive effects on altruism

The last problem with the economists' argument is to do with that radical part of it which proposes the introduction of market incentives, whose operation depends on an appeal to selfish motives, into those public provision areas whose detailed operation has traditionally relied on altruism. We reviewed the case of the caring professions above. The economists' argument proposes the introduction of market mechanisms into these areas as a result of the claim that if this is not done, the delivery of these services cannot be managed satisfactorily.[17]

But many are now concerned about the corrosive effects on altruism of such policies. It is quite hard to be precise about how these concerns might be grounded, but they seem to operate at two levels. The first is that market incentives can *distract* practitioners from concernedness for their patients, clients and customers. Thus Colin Rayner, in Chapter 12 of this volume, shows a concern that the doctor–patient relationship should not be compromised by factors that potentially interfere with the practitioner's ability to focus objectively on the patient's requirements, and he argues that this can happen if the doctor is excessively focused on financial or professional advancement.[18]

The second argument appears to be that professional training is important in forming professionals who will be able to resist such distraction, but in a profession in which the rewards come to be greatest for those who pursue their own selfish self-interest, the inculcation of such standards at the training stage will be eroded too. Again Rayner's chapter has interesting things to say on this.

Summary: the nub of the problem

I have reviewed the following argument about the relation between the economy and society in which it is embedded:

1   Individuals are fundamentally selfish.
2   Their pursuit of selfish self-interest in business leads essentially, but with exceptions, to efficient outcomes in business.
3   Even those parts of economic life in which, traditionally, services have been provided by carers whose motivation is concern for others, should be 'marketised'.
4   Politics, regulatory agencies, should be used to sort out the problems caused by market failure.

I have attacked all of steps 2–4. I have argued that market failure is legion. I have argued that a selfish politics cannot solve the problems of market failure. And I have argued that marketisation of areas which traditionally rely on altruism creates problems. So the structure of the economists' argument looks distinctly wobbly. What happens, as a final preliminary, if we also attack step (1), the claim that individuals are fundamentally selfish?

Concernedness and trust

In this overall section I want to discuss evidence, and more particularly the arguments about why people do not always behave selfishly.[19] This will lead me to consider, briefly, what is necessary for sustaining concernedness, trust and consistency.

The relevance of game theory

In this first subsection I want to briefly consider some insights from game theory. The word 'game' has come to be a technical term, meaning a form of interaction between small groups of individuals governed by rules (the 'rules of the game'). In a game, what it is best for me to do depends not only on the rules, but also upon what I believe the other players will do (which is of course itself also constrained by the rules). This dependence, of what it is best for one player to do on what the other player will do, has come to be called 'strategic interaction'. The meanings of these technical terms in quotation marks are, in fact, not far from their everyday meanings: in the game of chess there is clearly something which we would recognise as strategic interaction.

The process of specialisation and exchange in a market, analysed by economists since Adam Smith, is *not* a game. To see this, note that Smith's 'invisible hand' argument, which I presented on pp. 50–3, is set out in the restrictive context of a market in which there are so many buyers and sellers that each can safely afford to ignore the question 'what do I believe that the other buyers and sellers will do?' There is no strategic interaction.

If the process of specialisation and exchange in a market were to become a game, then Smith's 'invisible hand' efficiency argument would completely collapse. For example, if there were only a few sellers, say two, then they might be tempted not to 'follow the signals of the price in the market' in the way in which that argument requires, but instead to ask themselves how they might collude, conspire to restrain trade, and drive up the price. But when trade is restrained and the price of a commodity is high, there are consumers who would willingly pay more for an extra unit of the commodity than such an extra unit would cost to produce – but the collusive restraint of trade prevents this from happening. This is clearly not efficient; the project of demonstrating the efficiency of an economy organised according to purely selfish self-interest is thus clearly undermined.

Economists have, as a tribe, been extraordinarily blinkered since Smith, in that far too much of their analysis has been confined to the analysis of inter-actions between large numbers of buyers and sellers in competitive markets. Precisely because these are interactions in which one can ignore the question 'what do I believe that the other players will do?', these interactions turn out to be a very narrow and small part of economic interactions. Game theory is in the process of liberating economists from their confinement, and in doing so it is in the process of making economics a much more interesting discipline – not just for economists themselves, but for other social scientists, for phil-osophers interested in ethical questions, and, ultimately, for the person on the street.

Altruism: evidence from the prisoner's dilemma game

Consider a 'game' called the 'prisoner's dilemma'. This game has become incredibly well known over the last 15 years amongst economists and social scientists generally. Over this time it has become the most common way of illustrating in detail the 'playing out' of the conflict between selfish self-interest and the common good.

The game is called the prisoner's dilemma because the anecdote most com-monly used to illustrate it concerns two prisoners. Each is in solitary confine-ment for the same crime and each is faced with an offer of a lower sentence in return for evidence incriminating the other, providing that there is no evi-dence incriminating him. The dilemma arises because if neither defects, then the police can convict them both only on the lesser charge; both would be better off if they both stayed silent, but each is at least as well-off if he defects.

The reasoning behind the prisoner's dilemma result is powerful. Each prisoner knows that: (a) if the other has remained silent, then he can lower his sentence by defecting; and (b) if the other has defected, then what he him-self does will make no difference. So whatever the other person does he is at least as well-off by defecting. But the same is true for the other prisoner. So, goes the argument, both defect.

Prisoner's dilemmas are everywhere, but people do not always play the prisoners' dilemma in the way in which this reasoning suggests. And, in a now famous set of computer simulation experiments, the political scientist Robert Axelrod showed why. If a game is repeated over time, then it is much better to play a strategy of cooperate-but-punish-defection. Of such strategies, 'tit-for-tat' is the most famous and one of the best: 'begin by co-operating and do what the other player did last time'. Axelrod explains in his book on the subject, written in the early 1980s:

> What accounts for Tit-for-tat's robust success is its combination of being nice, retaliatory, forgiving and clear. Its niceness prevents it from getting into unnecessary trouble. Its retaliation discourages the other side from

persisting whenever defection is tried. Its forgiveness helps to restore mutual cooperation. And its clarity makes it intelligible to the other player, thereby eliciting long-term cooperation.

(Axelrod 1984)

There is now a wonderful series of real examples which confirm the results of computer experiments: bats who donate some of their spoils from a night of blood-sucking to help other hungry but unsuccessful colleagues; and monkeys who help other monkeys in fights if those others have given similar help in the past. There are also some striking human examples, like the evolution of cooperation between Allied and German soldiers facing each other across the trenches of World War I.

These insights, and this evidence, from game theory help one to understand how and why individuals do not always pursue selfish self-interest in social interactions.

Concernedness

Concernedness amongst individuals can be sustained in at least three rather different ways. The first way of sustaining concernedness is through reciprocity. Concernedness may yield a pay-off if the individual is embedded in a repeated-game structure, in which showing interest in and concern for others is likely to yield the reward of similar behaviour from others in the future. The reciprocity involved in concernedness is 'diffuse', or implicit, in that no explicit promises or commitments are given. It may operate best if individuals are able to signal that they are 'concerned'. Alternatively, concernedness may be motivated by a wish to be esteemed by others. Finally, concernedness may be motivated by a wish for self-esteem − by a wish to be the kind of person who is concerned. The last two motivations we recognise from our discussions of Adam Smith's *Moral Sentiments*; understanding of the first comes from the modern insights about game theory reviewed above.

All of these accounts indicate reasons for which individuals can come to adopt a concern for others, i.e., a lack of selfishness, even if they are in fact self-interested. It may be possible to produce a 'deeper' non-self-interested account of concernedness, but that is not necessary for our purposes. Nevertheless, I return to this question briefly at the conclusion to this chapter.

One might talk of a concerned person as somebody who simply acts, on a number of separate or disparate occasions, out of regard for the interests for others. I will go further than this and talk of concernedness as a disposition, where by that term I mean a habit, a tendency, to act spontaneously in this manner, without extensive, careful or deliberative calculation of the value of the action. Having such a disposition may be a guard against weakness of will: the propensity to choose short-term benefit at the expense of long-term benefit. One could have a disposition for concernedness, whether the underlying motivation for it was any one of the three reasons: reciprocity, esteem or self-esteem. I will use the term 'concernedness' to mean having adopted a disposition for being concerned, independently of for which of these three reasons it was adopted.

One way in which individuals could come to have this disposition of concernedness could be not through their own conscious choice, but because it had been inculcated through upbringing and training. One can tell three rather different stories on parenting. Parents may wish their children to acquire a disposition of non-selfishness because they may believe that it will be in their children's interest to be non-selfish, and that to have this disposition will equip them for this. Or they may want their children to gain esteem by being seen to be the kind of person who is not selfish. Or, finally, they may believe it to be in their own self-interest that their children be concerned, and may, therefore, inculcate an unselfish disposition in their children, since they will have to cohabit with them for a large number of years. All of these stories about upbringing and training point in the same direction.

Trust

One may also sustain trust, or promise-keeping, in two rather different ways. The first way in which promise-keeping might be sustained is if individuals are embedded in an informal repeated-game structure, in which promise-keeping is likely to yield a reward of reciprocity or similar behaviour from others in return in the future. The reciprocity involved in reciprocal promise-keeping is much more explicit than that involved in reciprocal relations of concernedness, in that explicit promises and commitments are given. Since a failure to keep promises is, at least sometimes, an observable dereliction, the failure to keep promises is sometimes subject to much more straightforward enforcement through punishment strategies in a repeated-game set-up. These punishment strategies may operate best if individuals are able to build a reputation for trustworthiness, and/or to signal that they are trustworthy.

One normally thinks of a trustworthy person not as somebody who simply keeps promises on a number of occasions. Instead one thinks of trustworthiness as a disposition – a habit, a tendency to act spontaneously in a promise-keeping manner. Thus trustworthiness is a disposition in the same way in which concernedness is a disposition. Possessing this disposition of trustworthiness will, even within this first repeated-games account of promise-keeping, act as a guard against weakness of will, as a guard against forgetting the long-term consequences of the pursuit of short-term advantage by reneging on a promise.

It is possible to imagine a person who is trustworthy for the reasons just explained as someone who is nevertheless entirely unconcerned with the well-being of others. To act so that 'my word is my bond' may be to act in an entirely unconcerned manner.

By contrast, the second way in which promise-keeping might be sustained is *as a consequence of concernedness*. It is difficult to imagine a concerned person – someone with a disposition to consider the well-being of others in the context of his own actions – who is untrustworthy. But one can certainly think of being trustworthy as possessing a particular kind of concernedness. It involves keeping faith with *explicit* commitments given to others – and only with those. These two, rather different, kinds of trustworthiness have rather different implications, which I will briefly note.

Concernedness, trust, integrity and responsibility

Concernedness and trust must have their limits. I will talk of a person who shows consistently exercised concernedness and trust as someone who, in terms of my physical metaphor introduced at the beginning of the chapter, when travelling 'vertically forwards' through time enters into relationships of concernedness and trust with a stable, or 'consistent' or 'reliable' group. Such a person develops 'commitments'.

There is a connection between these ideas of concernedness and trust, on the one hand, and responsibility, on the other hand. A person who enters into commitments of concernedness and trust in a way which can be relied upon becomes someone who accepts responsibilities for others. Indeed to be 'in a position of trust' is, according to the *Concise Oxford English Dictionary*, to be a person who has the obligation of being in a responsible position. Peter Kemp gives us a very clear account of what this kind of responsibility involves, and the manner in which it has a time dimension.

> People are faced with events as they occur. . . . Faced with the on-rush of events, ministers and civil servants are often confronted with dilemmas. . . . Tensions arise between long-term and short-term policies, between loyalties to personal beliefs and loyalty to the state, between the interests of this set of people and the interests of that other set, between the desirability of taking a decision now and the desirability of thinking it over. . . . Among the stake holders there are many who have to be reconciled . . .
>
> (Chapter 20, this volume)

This is an image of balancing a set of conflicting demands resulting from earlier commitments given. The person whose commitments of concernedness and trust are consistently exercised is a person whose commitments can somehow be relied upon under pressure. We can agree, with Peter Kemp, to call such a person a 'person of integrity'.

A person of integrity does not duck and weave between such commitments; by contrast, a person without integrity enters into commitments which are lightly abandoned. As a consequence, a person of integrity does not enter into commitments capriciously; the notion of wholeness, which is bound up with integrity, conveys a sense that the commitments entered into are carefully considered, and coherent. A person with few commitments cannot be said to have integrity in this sense. Nevertheless integrity cannot be sought in itself; it must be the by-product of commitments. Integrity is revealed (gradually) through pressure. And if the integrity is to be real (rather than 'simulated') these commitments must be difficult ones, the meeting of which has incurred costs.

A person who practices such consistently expressed concernedness and trustworthiness – a person of integrity – will be someone whose commitments can be trusted. The word 'trust' as discussed here has the same meaning as the term 'exogenous trust' introduced by Donald Hay (Chapter 16, this volume). The trust which such a person inspires is stronger than the trust which one has in somebody not to default on a loan. One trusts in somebody not to default on a loan only in as much as one can be confident that it will not be in his long-term interest to do so. One has trust in a person of the kind described here for the same reason that a 'gentleman's word is his bond': one does not need to examine, when the word is given, whether it is likely to be honoured. The absence of such commitments is described in the well-known old English folk-song: 'I leaned my back against an oak/Thinking it was a trusty tree/But first it bent and then it broke/Just as my love proved false to me'. A person of integrity does not have the split in the timber which would cause him or her to break under pressure; he or she can be trusted not to be broken under the unfolding of events.

The limits to concernedness, trust, responsibility and integrity

I began the previous section by noting that concernedness and trust must have limits. These are of two kinds. First, one cannot develop responsibility for everyone. 'Who is my neighbour?' is an old and difficult question. The practice of Adam Smith's 'sympathy' in civil society involves the exercise of concernedness and trust over a relatively small range of persons and issues – the 'opportunities' are small. Virtue in politics, and its exercise in the public service, enables the exercise of concernedness and trust over a wider domain than is normally possible in civil society. But how wide sympathy and virtue should extend is a really difficult question. We feel more concern for the health of our family and our friends than we do for others elsewhere within Britain. Nevertheless for most of us in Britain it is important that there should be a National Health Service which is an expression of our concern for the health of our fellow citizens. We perhaps have less concern for the health of those in Portugal, although we wonder about whether the construction of ever-closer union between the countries in Europe will make our feelings of responsibility towards Portuguese citizens more like those of responsibility towards British citizens. Our sense of responsibility for the health of those in developing countries is less still, but it is not non-existent. Different people will acquire different degrees of such responsibilities as a result of their own different life histories. To judge whether a particular decision is an action of integrity – for example that faced by a junior doctor considering working for the United Nations in Sub-Saharan Africa or in a major London teaching hospital – can turn out to be a very complex matter.

Second, and relatedly, one does not trust such a person to keep such commitments absolutely and irrevocably. When the pressure of events turns out differently from what had been initially imagined, commitments which were originally thought consistent may come to clash, and then one or more of them will have to be abandoned. A person, even a person of integrity, needs to be able to escape from such an unforeseen clash of commitments. That is, there must always exist some kind of 'discretion for non-performance' in a promise. But – and this is the second point – a person of integrity only exercises such discretion when this is a reasonable choice under pressure. Whether such a choice (to renege on a promise) will appear reasonable to an observer will inevitably depend on whether – in some sense – the observer shares the values of the person breaking the promise. This is a second reason why it can be complex to judge whether a particular action is behaviour of integrity.

The value of concernedness and trust

This section discusses the implications for the economy, and for the institution of the 'market', if the individuals in the economy are capable of forming and sustaining consistent relations of concernedness and trust. In the next section I will discuss the implications for institution design.

Politics, public service and virtue

The standard arguments for state intervention in the market have been reviewed earlier in this chapter. But I argued that individuals who are fundamentally selfish could not do the kinds of politics required to rectify these market failures. I would argue that one of the most important aspects of what has been important about the public sector of the economy, at its best, has been the place which it has provided for those with a 'mission' to correct these market failures, to do their work. It has, that is, provided an institutional framework in which virtue can be practised.

In a simplistic view of what underlies the kinds of failures in the market described on pp. 56–61, the actual policies which are needed can be analysed, decided upon (by voting if necessary – which it will be if they involve gain to one party at the expense of another) and then implemented, all in an essentially mechanistic process. Political virtue would be found merely in ensuring the right voting outcomes for policies which remedied the problems listed there.

We have already argued that this misses the fact that fundamentally selfish individuals normally could not agree on such policies by voting on them. But, furthermore, what this also misses is that the analysis is complex, that corrective policy will require advocacy, and that its implementation will require ingenuity. Chapter 20 is exceptionally revealing on this score. From the perspective which Peter Kemp offers we get a picture of the public sector as a place in which concernedness can be consistently exercised by professionals, in pursuit of the goals of correcting market failures, goals for which they feel responsibility.

This exercise of concernedness may be jeopardised by the introduction of market forces. First, because professionals will know more than the public about their particular areas of competence, the correction of market failures will become a merit good; complex policies or actions may be required, which private individuals would under-consume if left to their own devices because the need (or desire) for them is difficult to understand. The professional becomes, and must become, partly discoverer, partly advocate, partly implementer, of better policies. The attempt to separate the purchaser from the provider discussed above may impoverish this process because the purchaser will not know all that the provider has come to learn.

Second, many of the activities in which the state is involved have large system-wide components, for example the education *system* and the *National Health Service*. Disaggregation of provision through the introduction of competition unwittingly destroys these system-wide properties, and with them the possibility for the exercise of concernedness. Thus consider the hypothetical Scottish renal surgeon at Stirling University who has responsibilities in his specialism for the whole of Scotland. If his hospital becomes an NHS Trust whose managers are motivated to expand in profitable directions and contract in non-profitable ones, then he would be prevented from exercising that responsibility. Of course, his concerns could be packaged, marketed and sold, but because his concernedness is a diffuse one there are severe difficulties of contract-specification in the way of that course. In the university world, most academics believe that they have obligations to the wider university system such as external examining and serving on appointing committees in other universities; should they charge a going rate? In the world of science, researchers have, and believe in, an obligation to serve as referees for research council grant applications. They also make their findings publicly available in support of other researchers, in contrast to the world of technology in which research and development (R&D) outcomes are private property. More generally, many academics do many things for the wider political system, such as, for example, writing pieces in the popular press. This is often done not for reasons of personal advantage (by contrast, say, with an economic analyst for a large City firm who will have written into his or her contract of employment a requirement to get on the morning radio in order to increase the exposure of his or her employer). All of these kinds of practice of concernedness are put at risk by the introduction of economic incentives into what has been thought of as the non-economic sector.

Next consider *trust*. There are two aspects of trust connected to the exercise of responsibility that I have been describing. The first is being trusted to tell the truth. Again, the introduction of market incentives can put such trust at risk. To understand this, consider the comparison between the BBC and Sky TV. BBC news is important, and the whole of the BBC's output is important, because we can trust its voice. This is in contrast to, for example, our scepticism about 'news' items in Murdoch papers about how many people have bought Sky dishes,[20] or our concerns as to whether Sky could ever bring us unbiased news about China at a time when Murdoch is engaged in complex negotiations about access to Far Eastern countries. About such news we are likely to say 'well they would say that, wouldn't they', and we have no clear way of knowing whether any given pieces of information are trust-worthy. Will our view of the BBC survive its becoming a competitive global media player? Or consider the relationship between a doctor and his or her patient. Trust between doctor and patient is much harder to sustain when the patient knows that a cash limited fund-holding doctor has a direct personal financial incentive in withholding from him or her a treatment which would be valuable, but very expensive.

My argument thus far about the public sector has been far-reaching, yet limited. I have argued that virtue in politics requires the exercise of respon-sibility and trust by those who work in the public sector; that this is essential if the state is to carry out the necessary task of correcting market failure. I have also argued that we should tread warily in the introduction of economic incentives and marketisation in the public sector. The unintended conse-quences may not be 'more choice, more efficiency', but instead less effective correction of market failure (the reason for which the policies were adopted in the first place). Put bluntly, there is a necessary limit to the extent which markets can be used to solve problems of market failure. But the limitation is that, although I have throughout this chapter acknowledged the need for incentives in the public sector, I have not yet tackled the question of how these incentives can be structured. I return to that question later.

The market economy

When we turn to that central sphere of economic activity organised within the institution of the market, it is also possible to attack the economist's boundaries argument.

None of what we have said *so far* need go against the central part of the boundaries argument as initially expressed by Adam Smith. Indeed it is pos-sible to imagine an interlocutor who would willingly accept the argument up until now, and thereby admit the importance of concernedness and trust *in the public sector* in order to make practically possible the design and implementa-tion of practical policies which rectify market failures.[21] Such a person might nevertheless want to call a halt, to draw the line, at that point.

But why on earth should one agree with this? If concernedness and trust need to be mobilised in the public sector to correct market failures, why should it not be possible for some market failures to be corrected through the exercise of concernedness and trust *in the private sector.* This is the message from Anthony Clunies Ross in Chapter 19 of this volume; his concerns echo those of Will Hutton's best-seller *The State We are In* (1994). Indeed, I take Clunies Ross (and Hutton) to be saying that greater exercise of concernedness and trust is absolutely necessary in the private production sphere, if we are to have an economy as productive as that of the now rising Asia-Pacific countries.

Clunies Ross, following Ronald Dore (1987), compares the community model of the firm with the company law model: in the former, workers make a lifetime commitment to the firm and the firm does the same to its workers. He also discusses the well-known commitments between firms (banks with those to whom they lend credit, large firms with smaller suppliers), commitments which stand in the way of free and open competition. He points out the different nature of competition. He argues briefly, and Hutton argues at length, that the way in which many British firms compete is with the intention of taking their rivals over or of putting them out of business, so as to monopolise the market. By contrast the Japanese-style model of 'managed competition' is designed to improve the way in which, individually and collectively, the firms serve the market. There are other arguments too. The existence of a long-term commitment by managers to their firm – and a sense of concernedness for the fortunes of those in their firm – encourages long-term entrepreneurial solutions to problems: seeking long-term profit opportunity by investing in technology and in product development rather than by seeking short-term profit opportunity in cost-cutting and downsizing. The existence of the long-term commitment by banks to the firms who are their clients encourages this long-term outlook, in contrast to the need to deliver short-term results from investment in a stockmarket-based financial system. The fact that workers stay with their firms means that it is worth investing more in their training, and investing in the kind of plant and machinery in which well-trained, skilled workers thrive. And this spills over from the firm into the wider society: firms who think and operate like this support a social system which expects that all young people are sufficiently well educated as to be turned into trainable, adaptable highly professional workers. And because there are such potential workers available, it is more worthwhile employers investing in modern plant and equipment.

All of this needs arguing in detail of course. For an enjoyable yet anecdotal and unconvincing attempt to argue the case, see Fukayama (1995). For careful comparisons which make the case in detail see Dore (1987). The evidence, both anecdotal and serious, suggests that there is a successful kind of capitalism, possibly a more successful one than our own, in which individuals act in a very different way from the pure pursuit of selfish self-interest which the followers of Adam Smith have asserted is necessary, and all that we need. In such a society, with firms which worked in this way, the kind of concernedness and trust discussed above with reference to the public sector – and which when practised in the public sector I have called virtue – would also be a feature of life in the private sector.[22] On pp. 72–6 I discuss briefly some of the implications for what this rather different kind of private sector would need to look like.

Two anecdotes as examples

I can perhaps best connect with an intuitive understanding of the difference that concernedness and trust would make, both in public service and in the market economy, by means of two anecdotes, both about Mrs Thatcher, and both concerning people at the Balliol integrity seminar.

In the late 1980s, I edited, with a colleague, a book about the effects of increased competition and deregulation in commercial television in this country, in the run-up to the Broadcasting White Paper of 1989 (see Hughes and Vines 1989). In the course of my work for this book, I went to see Anthony Smith, then the head of the British Film Institute, and he made the following memorable remark to me.

> Broadcasting is a particularly interesting place in which to watch Mrs Thatcher at work. She is in favour of deregulated competition. But she is also a political paternalist. In broadcasting we will find that these two principles, competition and paternalism, clash absolutely. The really interesting thing about Mrs Thatcher is that she is baffled by this clash.

More recently, Denis Noble who often works professionally in the Asia-Pacific region, described to me how marvellously Mrs Thatcher went down in Asia.

> They loved her when she came to talk to them about self-interest, ambition, and getting on. But they saw her through the prism of social and cultural restraint as background conditions to the pursuit of self-interest. They did not see that she did not respect these things. And she did not see that they did not see this.

If the reader of this chapter has a sense of both how Mrs Thatcher might not have understood these things, and how this failure to understand could cause difficulties, then he or she will have understood what I am trying to say.

Implications for evaluation of the market

In an economy characterised by concernedness and trust one can no longer rely on Adam Smith's efficiency argument as a justification of the market. This is because efficiency-increasing moves might now be blocked, out of concern for the well-being of those who are damaged by them.[23] Rather the argument for the market must become that it is a delegation and discovery device. Hayek and other Austrian economists base their advocacy of market mechanisms on such arguments, and not on the efficiency arguments derived from Smith.

> In their analysis, the market is an institution which performs the dual function of co-ordinating the . . . division of labour and transmitting throughout society the dispersed information held by private individuals. It achieves this result through the process of competition, whereby rival agents seek their own different objectives. For this mechanism to work, it is not required that agents pursue only their own [selfish] self-interest. What matters is the existence of a sufficiently large number of agents with sufficiently *diverse* objectives to generate genuine competition and rivalry. If this condition is satisfied, the process of exchange will spontaneously generate prices containing the information required to co-ordinate the social division of labour.
>
> (Rowthorn 1996)

Furthermore, one could add, this process allows producers to become more specialised, and to devote more time to finding out how best to do what they are specialised in: the decentralisation of decisions about production in turn leads to inventiveness. This is the market not as an invisible hand, but as a discovery device.

Implications for institution design

The arguments about concernedness and trust developed above can be used to make suggestions about institution design. In this section I am mainly concerned with the public sector, about the creation of an institutional structure in the public sector in which virtue can flourish. But the following remarks are also relevant to responsibility-oriented institutions in the market economy.

Before proceeding, a word of caution is necessary. The suggestions which follow are essentially disconnected insights; we understand very little about system effects of concernedness and trust. And we would do well to remind ourselves initially about Hayek's already quoted worries that the tendency of human beings to altruism and sympathy actually interferes with the proper workings of the market order.

I begin with Alan Hamlin's suggestions in Chapter 17 that one needs institutions which provide an 'outlet' for concernedness, that one should carefully select people for these institutions and reward them appropriately, and then that one should ensure that such institutions are not captured, and that the rewards in them are not 'squandered' in rent-seeking. I now make a number of suggestions building on these insights.

Five principles

Resources for concernedness

Acting with concernedness is not a cost-minimising strategy. This is obvious by construction – I have been rather careful only to call actions 'concerned' if they are ones that markets populated entirely by 'selfish' self-interested individuals would not spontaneously produce. This is a necessary, but, of course, not sufficient, condition for responsibility.

However, we have to distinguish between two types of consistently expressed concernedness. First, there is responsible action within an organisation, of a kind which may be to the organisation's *own* longer term advantage. To sustain this it is necessary to look for institutional support for responsible outcomes. This has been touched on above when discussing 'Japanese capitalism'. I will not go into further detail here, except to remark that much of what follows is relevant to that case too.

Second, there is the kind of concernedness which involves promoting actions and policies which would remedy the list of failings of the market economy discussed on pp. 54–6. This is costly. For that to flourish, it is necessary to create an institutional structure in which there is sufficient 'slack room' for such concerned action. The idea here is that if an *institution* really is a concerned institution, i.e., devoted to the pursuit of concerned policies, then finding some secure source of funding for it is necessary for its concerned activities. An economist would call such funds 'rents' – they are revenue which is secure from being competed away. Put another way, concerned institutions may seem like inefficient operations. They may need some protection from market competition. Where they do, the value of the institutional setting lies in the fact that it provides such protection.

Defence from rent seeking

Second, it is immediately obvious that the resulting institutions – and the rents in them – must be defended from rent-seeking, or more generally from inefficiency. This may arise as a result of either (a) those who are not concerned attempting to capture the 'slack rents' which are designed to be used by those who are concerned, or (b) by a struggle developing between a number of concerned parties within the organisation over the allocation of those slack rents which are supposed to be used to support concernedness, but which are instead merely spent on the struggle. Alan Hamlin is surely right that some of this 'defence' may involve greater competition and marketisation: contracting out, whether of catering or, in the cases of Channel 4 and BBC television, of programme-making.

Screening

Third, a society must screen the right people into the right activities – this is Alan Hamlin's central idea in Chapter 17. There are some activities which require the exercise of responsibility more than others. We should find ways of *screening and sorting* those who – whether by the strengths of their innate disposition or by training – are able and prepared to exercise concern-edness and trust in those organisations. Brennan and Hamlin (1995) point out that it is inefficient for those with these virtues to be located in kinds of productive activities where there is relatively little scope for them to be exercised; and that, similarly, shortages of these virtues where they are needed lead to the under-supply of the benefits described in the previous section. Such screening is clearly also necessary to avoid the type of rent-seeking identified under point (a) in the previous section.

Reward

In addition, ways must be found to *reward* those who are sorted into careers in professions calling for high degrees of responsibility. One important way to ease the problem of incentives in non-market activities discussed earlier may be to pay in a different currency of reward. For academics, for example, systems of peer regard may provide incentives and yet not distort activities in the way in which the introduction of a market can. That is what knighthoods are (or were, or should be) for. After a particularly good meal at Kings in Cambridge a number of years ago a Marxist friend of mine – or Marxist as he then was – said 'Thatcherites just do not realise how cheap dinners are as a way of promoting high quality research.' The form of reward may act as a screening process – large rewards for academics in the form of travel grants, research expenses, book allowances, etc., will be as attractive or more as the equivalent sum of money to those who are committed to the academic process, but will not be for those who are not committed.[24]

Leadership

A theory of such 'concerned' organisations is possible, using ideas of leadership. Consider the position of the leader of an institution that is concernedness-oriented, in the sense that I have discussed this term above. He or she will have a mixture of sticks and carrots to encourage behaviour within the organisation, just as in any organisation. As in any normal circumstances, the exercise of this leadership will rely on a mixture of guilt and shame. But there may be more than this. The leader may be able to manipulate the preferences of his followers, rather than merely change the environment in which they operate. Conspicuous token acts of moral significance made by the leader of the institution may promote a move toward concernedness amongst subordinates.

Tensions

First, if there is not extreme care, then the introduction of markets, or of competition, in pursuit of the second principle above will work against the first principle. If, to take an example, there is ruthless Darwinian pressure in hospitals to cost-minimise, then there will then be no possibility of the required reward to concernedness (if my characterisation of concernedness as costly is correct). No amount of screening to get virtuous doctors will work – the working conditions will not allow them to exercise their concernedness and they will leave. Or to take another example, this is why Channel 4 fought so strenuously not to be privatised in 1989: the correct analysis was that even if commercial television has monopolistic slack in the product market, the discipline of having shareholders would enforce concernedness-destroying cost-minimisation either through takeover-competition in the stockmarket, or through changing the leadership of the organisation. These processes are at present destroying the ability of the ITV network to carry out its public service obligations.[25]

Second, there is a deep contradiction in the current privatisation/ marketisation process. Often that process is presented essentially as a battle *against* rent-seeking of the types described on pp. 72–4. But if that battle is carried out by means of creating ruthless short-run competition in the output market then, as we have argued, concernedness cannot survive. One must find other ways of moving against rent-seeking. The experience of Channel 4 television in its early days is interesting here, in two ways. First, that Channel was securely funded by means of a tax on the advertising revenue of ITV television – in any year the tax on ITV would be based on the previous year's revenue and so the proceeds would be entirely known. Second, it was a lean organisation – a small programme-commissioning staff subcontracted programmes out to independent programme producers, organising in the process a competitive bidding market for work, which encouraged innovation. This process led the BBC by 10 years and effectively re-created the British film industry. The principle that I would attempt to enunciate, drawing on this example, is that there must be 'monopolistic slack' in the markets for outputs of a concernedness-requiring kind, but that one should attempt to introduce competition in the purchase of inputs into the production of those concernedness-intensive outputs.[26]

In brief, although marketisation may well be introduced to improve efficiency, it may have the unintended effect of making the exercise of virtue impossible. This, paradoxically, can result not in more choice, but in less. The television example makes this point clear, but it applies, in different ways, in such different fields as health and education.

Wider social implications

As institutions grow up which select concerned staff in the way described above, and which reward them, the overall expected rewards to those with a moral training in concernedness will expand. Whole procedures will grow up for training agents in concernedness and inculcating the appropriate *moral precepts*. This is the social function of much of schooling and of much religion. It is what 'Victorian values' were about,[27] with their attendant institutions of the Boy Scouts and of Sunday School. The 'morality revival' in British politics, and the result of the 1997 British general election show that the issues are very much alive. In a community in which these precepts are in circulation, devices will emerge with which agents can signal that they are concerned, and the availability of individuals trained in this way will provide the necessary social resources for concernedness. By contrast, for example, if all of the training of young junior doctors is done by lean and hungry consultants who are profit-maximising for their NHS 'Trust' (note the Orwellian use of that word), then these young doctors will quickly imbibe the relevant lesson: that concernedness for patients, and a loyalty to a system-structure in which this might be exercised, is no longer among the moral precepts of doctoring.

The disposition to act in a concerned way is, in effect, a form of 'human capital'. There are things which can be done to encourage its accumulation, just as policies to improve education can assist in the accumulation of knowledge-capital. But, in addition, simply to raise the rewards for concernedness will not only lead to more concerned behaviour, but also to more training of individuals in the dispositions which lead them to perform concerned acts.

It is, of course, also the case that the concernedness-training parts of the economy are also concernedness-intensive. It is likely that the concerned institutions and those who provide training for them will mutually reinforce each in ways which further encourage the accumulation of dispositions for concernedness.

Conclusions

The argument restated

In this chapter, I have reviewed, and attacked at every stage, the following argument about the relation between the economy and society in which it is embedded:

1   individuals are fundamentally selfish;
2   their pursuit of selfish self-interest in business leads essentially, but with exceptions, to efficient outcomes in business;
3   even those parts of economic life in which, traditionally, services have been provided by carers whose motivation is concern for others, should be 'marketised';

4 politics, and associated regulatory agencies, should be used to sort out the problems caused by market failure.

Instead, I have argued that market failures in a free enterprise economy are legion, and that the prospects are bleak for a market-failure-correction type of politics amongst essentially selfish individuals. But, I have argued, because most individuals are not fundamentally selfish, even if they *are* self-interested, prospects for a different kind of market-failure-correction politics, and public service, are *not* bleak (for all that these ideals took a battering during the Thatcher years in Britain). Furthermore, there exists the possibility of market-failure-correction action by individuals, acting within the economy, out of their own self-interest. This is not impossible, I have argued, even if how it would actually operate, and its 'optimality properties', are quite hard to understand. Much work on institution design, for a public service, and for a market economy, is required.

Here is a story from Balliol which contains a small metaphor for my larger argument. It concerns an honest and truthful Oxford tradesman, and Benjamin Jowett the famous cleric and classicist who was Master of the College in the latter part of the nineteenth century. The tradesman – worried about the strain put upon his conscience by the conditions of business competition – decided to seek the advice of the Master of Balliol. The tradesman was a good and upright man, but, as he explained, he had a wife and children to support. Competition was keen, and – it was here that his difficulty arose – his business rivals were unscrupulous. It was impossible to carry on his business successfully unless – to put it plainly – he not only cheated too, but out-cheated his competitors. What was he to do? Jowett listened patiently, and then gave his considered advice: 'Cheat as little as you can'.

There needs, I have argued, to be a supply of doctors and others, like the tradesman in our story, with a desire to act concernedly. There also needs to be a supply of Jowett-figures – selected for office by the kind of screening mechanism that Alan Hamlin describes in Chapter 17, located in the concernedness-intensive sector (if not all at Balliol), and previously produced in it – who will supply the necessary checks and restraints against the pressures not to act with concernedness.

Change any of these three features – remove the background requirements, intensify the pressures or reduce the checks – and two things will follow. First selfish self-interested behaviour will begin to be chosen in preference to consistently concerned and trustworthy behaviour by individuals, and more generally restraints against the pursuit of selfish self-interest, where this conflicts with public interest, will begin to fail. And then, second, if that goes far enough, a kind of Gresham's Law process will begin to set in: each case of acting selfishly will degrade the standards of concernedness and make it that much harder for others to pursue the ideal of consistently exercised concernedness and trust. This is Schumpeter's argument that capitalism not only increases the pressures, but also devours the checks and balances.

The (interim) argument of this chapter is therefore this. It is possible to imagine, and even to take seriously, an ethic for behaviour, *in both public service and the market economy*, which says: 'be as consistently concerned and trustworthy as you can.' A society which had such an ethic would be likely to work well, and the economy within it likely to do so too.[28]

Connections with the 'sources of the self'

I have argued in this chapter entirely from the premise of self-interested individuals, but have been concerned to show the benefits which accrue from such self-interested individuals acting in a non-selfish, other-regarding manner.

Some economists believe that this is – at least in part – a deluded project. I agree with Bob Rowthorn that this is more or less precisely the wrong conclusion to draw.

> attempts to prove that all behaviour is really selfish if only one looks deep enough are, in my opinion, both wrongheaded and harmful. They are wrongheaded because they make the idea of self-interest [what I have been calling selfish self-interest] tautological and therefore deprive us of an important operational concept.[29]

Rather one might attempt to draw the opposite conclusion, that action which consistently exhibits concernedness and trustworthiness shades away from self-interest into self-denying altruism. Some more modern accounts (e.g., those of Macintyre 1981, and Taylor 1989) argue that the self cannot be fully realised other than through a kind of striving for the good, a quest in which the conditions of others have *standing in themselves* as an end for any one individual. For this to have any meaning it must imply that individuals embarked on such a quest perform at least some actions which involve self-denial, at those times when the interests of others conflict with their own interests. An adequate account of peoples' lives – of the beings that we are – must attempt to understand this. Individuals embarked on such a quest, one can argue, engage in acts of self-sacrifice as part of the process of defining, and redefining, what they are and what they are becoming. These acts interact with, and draw out, and enlarge, and reinforce, the capacity of the individuals performing them for concernedness and trustworthiness. I have deliberately not attempted to base my argument on such premises. But if they were accepted, then they would strengthen its foundations.

Political implications

I have been asked: 'is the argument of this chapter a "right-wing" argument or a "left-wing" argument?' I am not sure that I know the answer to this question. To be sure, a 'concern with concernedness' suggests a communitarian, soft, warm-hearted approach. But a recognition of the importance of efficiency, and a respect for the importance of the pursuit of selfish self-interest as the 'mainspring' of economic progress points in the opposite direction. I can only say that I see here a tension between opposites.

We are back to the 'Adam Smith problem'. How can we reconcile the practice of sympathy and the pursuit of selfish self-interest? Smith's enormously ingenious 'boundaries' argument is not really a solution. In this chapter, I myself have certainly not presented a solution either. But if I have merely helped to make the problem, and its implications, more visible, then I will be satisfied.

Notes

1 This chapter has grown out of brief comments presented at the Balliol Colloquium in January, 1995. I am grateful to participants at the meeting for their comments, particularly Anthony Clunies Ross, Alan Hamlin and Donald Hay, for whose papers I acted as discussant. I should also like to thank Phillip Pettit and Bob Rowthorn for helping me to develop the arguments in this paper in more detail. And I owe a special debt to Geoffrey Brennan and Alan Montefiore, who have pushed and goaded me over a period of more than two years into clarifying what it is that I am trying to say. None of these people should be held responsible for the inadequacies of the arguments which follow.

2 It is likely that these two dimensions are not independent, but I do not pursue this line of thought.

3 Few non-economists realise that one of the central purposes of *Wealth of Nations* was to argue for free trade with the American colonies. Smith sympathised with the grievances of the colonists which led to the protests at the Boston Tea Party against the taxation of their tea exports, and he believed that the colonies would not have been lost had better trade policies been adopted, policies which would have benefited *both* colonists *and* mother-country.

4 Opinions amongst scholars actually differ about whether this vision was, in fact, Smith's central insight about the market. On another reading, exchange in a market allows division of labour, which allows producers to become more specialised, and to devote more time to finding out how best to do what they specialise in. In this view, the most important thing about the market is that it allows decentralisation of decisions about production, which leads in turn to inventiveness. This is the market not as an invisible hand, but as a discovery device. I will discuss this view below. Here I simply note that Smith's views on the effects of the division of labour on creativity were mainly negative, namely that it can lead to very-specialised tedium which is mind-numbingly repetitive. These views are hard to square with the 'market-as-discovery-device' strand of thought.

5 This modern 'efficiency claim' is now understood to be subject to very significant qualifications indeed, which are the subject matter of the next section.

6 It was not, however, an unfamiliar idea by the time that Smith used it. See Mandeville's *Fable of the Bees*.

7   This is a characteristically late-eighteenth century form of analysis. To take another example, the founding fathers of the American Constitution wished to devise a structure which economised on virtue; the checks and balances built into the structure were designed to ensure that the resulting political system would function well when not led by persons of virtue. I owe this point to Geoffrey Brennan.

8   It will be one of the chief arguments of this chapter that such virtue requires the practice of integrity in the public service.

9   The Chief Rabbi of Great Britain, Dr Jonathan Sachs, has recently said that, much as he admired Mrs Thatcher for many things, he thought that this was a (morally) dangerous mistake. In what follows I will explore why and how this may be so.

10   Hirschman concludes his thought-provoking essay 'The Passions and the Interests' by remarking on the extent to which the '[a]ttention of both policy and speculative debate came to centre after Smith on his proposition that the general (material) welfare is best served by letting each member of society pursue his own (material) self-interest' (Hirschman 1977: 112, parentheses in the original), rather than on the earlier problem of how the passions and the interests could be reconciled.

The most radical modern extension of this programme is to be found in the work of Nobel-Prize-winning economist Gary Becker, whose project (as I understand it) has been to give an entirely selfish account of the behaviour of members within a family, and so to completely demolish any small, restricted, remaining domain of loving, cherishing, and altruism.

11   Nevertheless, Colin Rayner's chapter has interesting things to say on the extent to which this can be circumvented.

12   The non-economist can find this out, in a very accessible way, by consulting either of two very good, clear and intelligent modern textbooks. The first of these is *Economics* by Begg *et al.* (1987); it is an adaptation by Begg, a Scot who teaches in London, of a text by two eminent Massachussets Institute of Technology (MIT) economists, the first-named of whom is now the Deputy Managing Director of the International Monetary Fund. The second, also called *Economics*, is by Joseph Stiglitz (1997) from Stanford, who, at the time of the initial drafting of this chapter, was Chairman of President Clinton's Council of Economic Advisers, and who is now Chief Economist at the World Bank. Both books are exceptionally clear about the pervasiveness of market failure; indeed the second book takes this pervasiveness as its organising principle.

13   For an extensive discussion, see pp. 58–60.

14   Whether they are sufficient to ensure this is much more difficult to know. There are government failures as well as market failures; the presumption that corrective intervention by government *might* be helpful does not imply that it *will* be helpful.

15   Sometimes economists are genuinely consistent and argue for income redistribution on the entirely selfish grounds that it is really beneficial for the giver (e.g., because it helps to reduce crime). But such an argument can take us only so far. More often the justification given is the utilitarian one of a diminishing marginal utility of income, without the realisation that, for individuals to agree to act in a manner which increases aggregate social utility, it must

involve them in a move away from pure selfishness. Sometimes economists justify re-distribution more tentatively in a Rawlsian manner, appealing to ideas of distributive justice, whilst sometimes too there is appeal to respect for 'the rights of others not to live in poverty'. These last arguments really do suppose the coexistence within the same person of selfishness in the economic world and altruism in the political.

16 I have postulated that the city-dwellers would prefer option C to A because, other things being equal, they like a clean river for recreational purposes, but that they prefer A to B because of the tax burden associated with the latter. Of course, the price of food will be different in the different cases, which would create complications which I have ignored.

17 The yet more radical argument here asserts, in the manner of Buchanan and Tulloch, that there is actually no real altruism and that the 'altruism' of doctors, teachers, etc., is just an elaborate façade for self-interest. Colin Rayner (Chapter 12, this volume) raises, in detail, enormously interesting examples of the kind of places in which the personal, or professional, interest of the doctor could be expected to clash with the patient's interest.

18 Rayner adds an additional complexity here: successful treatment requires the establishment of trust between doctor and patient, and a doctor will only be trusted if he or she is seen to be financially and professionally disinterested.

19 This account is highly selective. Etzioni (1988) surveys some American empirical evidence and Rowthorn (1996) discusses the arguments in a manner complementary to that presented here.

20 There is an occasional column in *Private Eye* called I-BSkyB 'for which readers are invited to submit Sky-plugs masquerading as news in Murdoch papers'. A random example, taken from *Private Eye* no. 906 (September 6, 1996), p. 11 quotes the following report from the *Sun*: 'Church Leaders threw away nearly £2 million by cashing in their BSkyB shares. The Church of England missed out on £1.5 million and the Methodists lost £360,000. They withdrew in November when the Playboy Channel was launched.'

21 A very interesting book (Brennan and Lomasky 1994) can be read in this spirit; its essential argument is as follows. Acts of concernedness and trust have a lower cost in the political sphere than in that of market relations. If I exercise concernedness in my market relations, for, by example, declining to pursue an opportunity in the interests of someone whom it will harm, then there is a direct cost to me. But it costs me nothing to vote for some improving scheme, like universal childcare: I know that the probability of my vote being pivotal (and so of my vote directly causing a cost to me which I would not otherwise have incurred) is essentially zero. I can vote for the scheme – without cost to myself – and give myself the gratification which comes from knowing that I am the kind of (virtuous) person who votes for such schemes. This reading of the Brennan and Lomasky argument can be used to support a claim that concernedness is *easier to achieve in the political sphere*. But it will not support the claim that it should be *kept out of the market sphere*.

22 One can argue that the inculcation of such a sense of obligation in those who work in the private sector, as well as in those who work in the public sector, was the objective of the life's work of John Maynard Keynes, the greatest economist of this century. Keynes is of course mainly remembered for his essentially

narrow and technical argument that a stabilisation policy for the avoidance of recessions, and booms, is a necessary part of public policy, because a free market economy will not avoid such problems of its own accord. But Keynes was interested in a much wider range of problems than this, as the extremely readable biography by Robert Skidelsky (1984, 1992) testifies. In his extraordinary, but not widely-known, essay called 'My Early Beliefs' Keynes writes as follows: 'We used to regard the Christians as the enemy, because they appeared as the representatives of tradition, convention and hocus-pocus. In truth it was the Benthamite calculus, based on an overvaluation of the economic criterion, which was destroying the quality of [our] . . . Ideal', (Keynes 1972: 446–47). Keynes' project was no less than the construction of an institutional framework in the economy in which concernedness and trust were encouraged to flourish, either by means of public policy, or through the agency of private morality, as necessary for the case at hand. The first volume of Skidelsky's biography examines the moral underpinnings of Keynes' project, whilst the second volume makes clear how remarkably all-encompassing that project was.

23 The technical argument is as follows. Consider a game between two players: Row, who chooses between r1 and r2, and Column, who chooses between c1 and c2. The rewards to each player are as follows, where the reward to Row is the first in a pair.

		Column	
		c1	c2
Row	r1	5,5	9,0
	r2	0,9	1,1

In this game, with selfish self-interested players, each player has a dominant strategy (r1, c1) and the resultant equilibrium is efficient – Adam Smith's efficiency result. But now introduce extreme altruism – each individual is motivated to maximise the other player's reward. This transforms the situation into a classic Prisoner's dilemma. Each player has a dominant strategy (r2, c2) and the resultant equilibrium is inefficient. If altruism is less extreme, so that each player is motivated by a weighted average of own and other's reward, then the equilibrium will be efficient for low levels of altruism (i.e. low weights on other's reward) and inefficient for high levels of altruism. The basic idea is simply that of a particular form of externality.

24 I owe this insight to Geoffrey Brennan, who is working on a formal paper on this topic.

25 As Geoffrey Brennan has pointed out to me, what is often at stake here *is* a selection effect: the aim is to replace 'professionals' with 'businessmen'.

26 Of course, some responsibility-requiring outputs are not final goods, and so this principle would get tangled up in the supply chain. But it is surely a start.

27 These are so recently gone. They still pervaded my school in Melbourne (essentially still then a colonial public school) when I attended it in the 1960s.

28 But the ambiguity, laid out in footnote 22, remains, so that one can only say 'is likely to do so'.

29 Rowthorn continues:

> They are harmful because they convert ethics and morality into purely matters of personal taste, thereby inhibiting meaningful dialogue on these topics, and reducing the impact of the social norms which channel human behaviour into beneficial directions. The fact that I do something out of sympathy for someone else, or because I think I ought to, does not in any meaningful sense imply that I am behaving selfishly, even if I feel a sense of satisfaction for having done so.
>
> (Rowthorn 1996: ch. 2, p. 17)

References and further reading

Axelrod, R. (1984) *The Evolution of Cooperation*. New York: Basic Books.

Begg, D. *et al*. (1987) *Economics* (2nd edn). McGraw Hill Book Co.

Brennan, G. and Hamlin, A. (1995) 'Economising on Virtue', *Constitutional Political Economy* 6(1): 35–56.

Brennan, G. and Lomasky, L. (1994) *Democracy and Decision*. Cambridge: Cambridge University Press.

Dore, R. (1987) *British Factory, Japanese Factory: The origins of national diversity in industrial relations*. Berkeley: University of California Press.

Etzioni, A. (1988) *The Moral Dimension: Towards a new economics*. New York: Free Press.

Fukuyama, F. (1995) *Trust: The Social Virtues and the Creation of Prosperity*. New York: The Free Press.

Hayek, F. (1988) *The Fatal Conceit: The errors of socialism*. London: Routledge.

Hughes, G. and Vines, D. (1989) *Deregulation and the Future of Commercial Television*. Aberdeen: Aberdeen University Press.

Hutton, W. (1994) *The State We Are In*. London: Penguin.

Hirschman, A.O. (1977) *The Passions and the Interests*. Princeton: Princeton University Press.

Keynes J.M. (1972) 'My Early Beliefs', in *Essays in Biography,* Vol X of *The Collected Writings of John Maynard Keynes,* edited by D. Moggridge and E. Johnson. London: Macmillan.

Krugman (1995) 'The ties that pay off', review of *Trust* by Francis Fukuyama. *Washington Post*, January 27.

Macintyre, A. (1981) *After Virtue: A study in moral theory*. London: Duckworth.

Marshall, A. (1910) *Principles of Economics*, 6th edn. London: Macmillan.

Milgrom, P. and Roberts, J. (1992) *Economics, Organisation and Management*. Englewood Cliffs, NJ: Prentice Hall.

Rowthorn, R.E. (1996) 'Ethics and Economics', in P. Groenewegen (ed.) *Economics and Ethics*. London: Routledge.

Skidelsky, R. (1984) *John Maynard Keynes. Volume 1: Hopes Betrayed 1883–1920*. London: Macmillan.

Skidelsky, R. (1992) *John Maynard Keynes. Volume 2: The Economist as Saviour 1920–1937*. London: Macmillan.

Skinner, A (1982) 'Introduction' to the Penguin edition of Adam Smith's *Wealth of Nations*. London: Penguin.

Smith, Adam (1976a) *The Theory of Moral Sentiments*. Oxford: Clarendon Press.
Smith, Adam (1976b) *An Inquiry into the Nature and Causes of the Wealth of Nations*. Oxford: Clarendon Press.
Smith, Adam (1978) *Lectures on Jurisprudence*. Oxford: Clarendon Press.
Smith, Adam (1982) *Wealth of Nations*. Harmondsworth: Penguin.
Stiglitz, J. (1997) *Economics* (2nd edn). W.W. Norton and Co.
Taylor, C. (1989) *Sources of the Self*. Cambridge: Cambridge University Press.

Part II

Personal and professional integrity

Section I
Personal integrity

4 A psychoanalytic view of the notion of integrity

Illustrated by the treatment of premature twins in an NHS hospital

Margaret Cohen

My argument in what follows is that the capacity for the exercise of integrity rests fundamentally on the integration of the personality. I will consider how this integration is achieved and against what kinds of odds. This integration is tested continually in life by physically and psychically painful situations which tempt us to fly apart. My belief is that integrity is located at this point in the attempt to withstand this temptation and to remain intact in the face of pain. The attack on integrity can come from outside or from within; so we may be tempted to go against what we know and believe because of the fear of threats or mockery, because holding to what we know is psychically very painful, or the attack may come from a split-off psychotic part of the personality that we are normally well armoured against. I argue that, right at the beginning of life, we work to integrate our different experiences to gain an idea of ourselves and the world we live in. Alongside this work of integration, we usually split-off unwanted, and what are felt to be dangerous, parts of ourselves, for instance hatred of those who care for and love us. So a later task of integration is to recall these split-off parts. It is this process and the way in which it is related to integrity that interests me.

I hope to show in the observations that follow that the baby seeks integration – but that this search needs an answer – something to meet his attempts, something to come up against, something for his searching mouth, eyes to meet his eyes. And this 'something' is what gives meaning and pulls the baby together like a magnet. Normally this would be the mother's arms, nipple, eyes, a mind to think and give meaning and a voice to articulate this. So the baby has an impulse to integration and the mother co-operates with this. This is both a physical and an emotional process. The baby needs to be held and then is held – thus experiencing both the holding and the notion of someone thinking about what he is needing. He also has to sift out what is him and what is not and in good circumstances the mother helps him with this. He needs to know what are constructive, life-avowing impulses and what are destructive. On the Neo-natal Intensive Care Unit (NNICU) we often see mothers making distinctions between these. So one baby pulled out his ventilator and the mother said in confidence that she thought that he had had enough, another baby pulled out her ventilator and breathed and the mother saw this as a great step towards life. Of course, the mothers' judgements may be projections of their own feelings, but not always. As the mother sees her baby in a life-and-death situation she may see a struggle in him and try to support his life-seeking self. Of course, mothers sometimes feel that their babies are rightly giving up, that the task is too much. This integrating function, which is first embodied in the external responses, can then be internalised by the baby to strengthen his own attempts to integrate. So there is the growth of an integrative capacity which can also sort out feelings and thoughts and know them for what they are – that is, know what is good and constructive and what is bad and destructive. So, for example, one might own to racist thoughts (that is, neither deny them or project them into others), but know them for the destructive, anti-life, anti-growth elements that they are. To deny these thoughts or to act them out would mean a loss of integrity, an abandonment of the integrative function either because of the pain or because of the difficulty involved.

There is quite clearly a moral theory implicit in all of this which, as child psychotherapists, we perhaps tend to take for granted, but which it may be important to enunciate. We make a distinction between the good and the bad, between the impulse towards life and growth, and the impulse towards death and destruction and these are seen as closely linked to truth-telling and lying. The truth is thought of as food for the mind, whereas lies are thought to be destructive and closely allied to perverse states of mind. Then there is clearly a moral view about taking responsibility for oneself – owning what is one's own and not splitting it off into other people. When the baby is in a disintegrated state we talk of him having the idea of a good breast and a bad breast. 'Good' here means something like gratifying and is not a moral concept. As the baby heals the split between the 'good' and the 'bad', and has an idea of his mother as a whole person, the space opens for anxiety about her, concern for her, worry about attacks made on her, gratitude for her strength and patience. The stage is set for the internal moral conversation which will continue for the rest of the person's life. Here there is the struggle for integration and the pull back to disintegrated states of mind where a moral viewpoint can be ignored. Here the sifting out between truth, on the one hand, and lying and propaganda, on the other, takes place.

My argument is that we have a life-long task in strengthening this integrative function and then of acting in harmony with it. We are continually tempted to 'go blind' on the things that we see, disintegrating where we had integrated, and I am arguing that integrity is found in the attempt to resist this temptation. Integrity here involves holding to our view, owning the wish to go against it, but not acting on that wish. I am aware that in this description of integrity it is unclear whether integrity resides in the resisting of the wish to go against what one knows or in the attempt to resist it – or, in other words, whether the resistance has to be successful for integrity to be present.

I consider the applicability of this line of argument in the workings of an NNICU which is a particularly fraught workplace. Small premature and sick babies are treated, often with difficult and painful medical procedures. These test the babies' fragile attempts at integration. The mothers have to cope with high levels of uncertainty and with their own maternal needs being frustrated – they are usually unable to pick up their babies, hold them, feed them and so on. The Staff – both doctors and nurses – find themselves inevitably caring about these babies and their parents. They have to work quickly in situations which often have a life-and-death character. The babies are extremely labile and can deteriorate astonishingly quickly – this makes the junior doctors in particular frightened and nervous. Furthermore, ethical questions often arise where a practical decision has to be reached: when do you decide that a baby is in too much pain and should not be kept alive; do you have to wait for a crisis so that the baby can die because of lack of intervention; what do you do when a baby is very damaged, is not really viable and is in pain, but the mother needs a few days to adjust herself to losing her baby and saying good-bye to it? These ethical questions may be familiar to philosophers, but they are hard questions to face in the workplace where the consequences of one's actions are so great. It is tempting to give oneself up to paranoid thinking and to act to cover oneself in the law courts; that is, to protect oneself from blame where this may not be the best course of treatment. It takes integrity to stick with the 'real' questions, particularly where there cannot be any 'good' outcome. My argument is that such a fraught situation inevitably tests everyone's capacity to resist disintegration and that the hope of the staff acting with integrity rests on this resistance. Added to this situation is the atmosphere of the government's health service reforms which, I shall argue, encourage disintegration and thus undermine integrity. I try to illustrate these views with the story of premature twins who were treated in an NNICU.

Before launching into the story of these twins I will delineate my job as a child psychotherapist on the unit. First, I am there as a spokesperson for the babies, to watch them and to try to articulate their experience. Traditionally in medicine it has been thought that babies and even children do not feel pain. I think that it is hard for us to tolerate the thought of babies in pain and so there has been a quite extraordinary denial in the face of clear evidence to the contrary and against the opinion of nurses and mothers. There are risks involved in using analgesia and anaesthetics on small babies, but these are offset medically by the intense stress response caused by *not* using them, which can hinder recovery and may even cause long-term behavioural problems, and ethically by considerations about what kind of experience the baby is going through. Work was done by Anand (1987 and 1992) demonstrating these stress responses and how damaging they can be. Rogers (1992) writes: it is 'commonplace for neo-nates to be rendered immobile or left awake or be given little pain relief during surgery in the belief that this practice minimises the likelihood of anaesthesia-related complications' (p. 55). He concludes:

> We persist in performing 'minor' surgical procedures in infants . . . without giving the same attention to relieving their pain that we give to relieving the pain of adults. . . . It seems that we are better able to tolerate an infant's pain than to deal with our own discomfort and insecurity about the correct dose of pain medication to give the infant.

Xenophon Giannakoulopoulis *et al.* (1994) have published findings about the response of fetuses to invasive procedures showing that the fetus raises a hormonal stress response to invasive procedures (for instance, intra-uterine needling for fetal blood-sampling) and that this response is similar to the hormonal responses mounted by older children and adults to stimuli which they would find painful. They call for further investigation into how these responses might be blunted by anaesthesia or analgesia. But, in the same issue of the *Lancet*, D.A. Clarke (1994) writes in response 'we all believe it worthwhile to avoid the experience of pain, although few of us would insist on morphine or general anaesthesia for simple dental procedure or for routine venepuncture.' He continues:

> What do we know about consciousness of distress in utero – in contrast to the evidence that, as with any living being, there may be physiological responses to certain stimuli? Are there any short term or long term differences after birth between babies who have experienced stress due to intrahepatic vein sampling and babies who have not or who have had needling of their umbilical cord vessels? Is there a greater tendency to depressive illness, for example, or evidence of impaired immune system function?

So these issues about the use of analgesia are hotly debated. I think that it is distressing to accept that babies suffer pain, and maybe there is a lack of integrity, when, in the face of clear scientific evidence of something which it is hard for us to find out about by communication (the babies cannot tell us), doctors deny it and the baby can bear the consequence. So I see the first part of my job as being keeping the babies in mind.

Second, I have a responsibility to support the parents, to listen to their experience, and to help them to make contact with their babies in the face of all this technology. The mothers have often not expected a premature labour and are in a state of shock. They have to bear their disappointment and put up with their anxiety about whether their new and tiny baby will live and whether it will be disabled. A large part of my work is to listen to mothers whose babies have died.

Third, I support the staff both individually, if they ask for it, and in regular Staff Support meetings. I try to help them to keep fresh in their minds an awareness of the impact of the babies on them. The babies, not held or fed or protected by their mothers, often activate the most infantile terrors in those working with them — terrors of being abandoned by one's mother, being delivered over to the persecutor with no protector and so on. Honest junior doctors often admit to suffering from nightmares when they begin working on the unit. Even when they do not have nightmares they are bombarded by images of the babies at night time, and these often interfere with the few hours of sleep which they desperately need for recuperation. My job is to help the doctors not to disintegrate and take refuge in thinking of the babies as non-human little machines who do not feel pain, or by overworking so that they no longer have time to think. Of course, defences develop for reasons, sometimes good reasons. The doctors probably could not do their job without some defences; they need a temporary cessation of imagination. But if this becomes fixed, the doctor will become unable to act with integrity. He may become unable to sympathise with the baby, he may become high-handed and unable to understand the parents and their reactions, he may become bad-tempered with the nurses. Some doctors are able to talk to the babies, tell them what they are doing and even apologise to them afterwards; thus a world of meaning is adhered to and can perhaps begin to be established for the baby — a world in which there is some sense to all this and some hope rather than a world of random pain or, worse still, a torture chamber. Of course, for the doctors and nurses to achieve this they have to be able to bear enormous amounts of psychic pain themselves. They have to tolerate questioning their work, having others question it, caring about the babies and parents, going through the agony of thinking about a particular baby's life and grieving if it dies or lives to be disabled. They have to tolerate not being able to do what is expected of them and knowing that they may cause a death or severe disablement by being slow or clumsy. Finally, if the baby goes home well they have to hand the baby over to its real parents and, often, not have their emotional investment acknowledged. This is a setting which invites people to dismantle their minds, their feelings and their imagination, but an incalculable price has to be paid by everyone if and when this becomes the culture of the unit. So my work at all levels of unit life is essentially about establishing integration and struggling to exercise integrity in the attempt to resist disintegration.

A practical manifestation of this is our weekly unit meeting. It is a multi-disciplinary meeting attended by doctors, nurses, the social worker, the health visitor, the speech therapist, the hospital chaplain, the child psychiatrists and myself, in which we try to think about each baby. We consider: how it is doing medically; how its family is (both emotionally and socially); how they are managing on the unit and how they are supported outside; what is the impact of this baby and family on us and us on them; and how this family coexists with the other families. We also give each other any news we may have of babies who have been in the unit. This is also the setting where we talk about general issues that have arisen in unit life. Sometimes rows have been rumbling around the unit and we have to work hard to get these pulled into the meeting and articulated there. It may be that opinions are split on the management of a baby and need to be articulated before any way of going forward together can be envisaged. One baby was thought to be dying and the doctors wanted her sedated so that she would not pull her ventilator out, first because it would be very hard to reintubate her and second because they thought that if she pulled it out, she would then die in a very horrible way. But a few nurses felt that she was now quite mature, was curious, looking around and wanting contact, and that it was wrong to sedate her so continuously, the quality of life for her in these last few weeks was not only important to her mother, but also to her. It was only when these views got argued out that a compromise began to seem possible, where the other side were no longer seen as cruel or cavalier, but as having an opinion of some importance. In many of these situations there is no ideal answer, it is a matter of trying to work out what is a reasonable way forward where this will involve some bad things. It seems better that these decisions are thought about by people who recognise the cost on both sides and are pained by it.

I will now move from this picture of the unit to thinking about the twins. I first saw the Z twins as they were being wheeled into the NNICU in incubators. There is usually an atmosphere of excitement and urgency around such arrivals. The staff then have to set to work supplying the babies with all the equipment they need to live. I next heard about them at the weekly multi-disciplinary meeting. These were boy twins of 24-week gestation, who each weighed around 600 grammes. Both parents were from Africa, and had only lived in England for a short time. The mother was 24 years old and had previously had a spontaneous abortion at 19 weeks of gestation. On the present occasion she had had to have labour induced because of infection and the twins were given a rather grim prognosis. But Twin I was born in rather good condition although somewhat battered. Twin II was stuck inside his mother and an emergency caesarian section was needed. However, the mother at this point was in a very bad state, hysterical and begging for an injection that would kill her. Eventually the father agreed to the section and Twin II was born four-and-a-half hours after his brother. It was noted that both parents had sickle-cell anaemia trait. It later emerged that the mother had had sickle-cell counselling in pregnancy and was offered the opportunity of a fetal blood test to allow a diagnosis of sickle-cell anaemia, in which case a termination would have been offered. Mother had refused these tests. Both twins were ventilated and it was thought that their lungs were quite good.

I saw the mother on the post-natal ward. She sat slumped in a chair by her bed, saying very little. Eventually she said that she thought she could still feel the babies inside her. She was worried about why her husband was away so long at the telephone. I thought that the loss of her babies from inside her left her feeling confused and frightened. I arranged to meet mother and father in a small room off the unit. I was struck by how much older the mother looked than her 24 years. She spoke very little and I wondered how much English she could understand. I imagined how frightening her labour must have been, so traumatic and in such foreign surroundings. The father greeted me in a very formal way stretching wide his hands and making a speech. He asked me to thank the doctors who were, he knew, doing so much for their babies. This felt like a propitiation of some powerful gods in whose hands he felt himself and his family to be. I was the mediator. He went on to tell me about the labour and the other baby that had died. He seemed to manage his wife and her feelings. In the next few days he asked me what he should do about his wife's unhappiness. He wanted some method of getting rid of it and found it hard to wait and listen. I felt that he was rather bossy and dominating with his wife, but reflected on how helpless he must feel. I asked the parents for permission to observe their twins, telling them that I was particularly interested in twins and they readily agreed.

The twins were born on September 20 and I started observing them at two weeks of age. When I say 'observe' I mean something quite specific and perhaps I should say something about this. It is part of the psychoanalytic training of child psychotherapists that we observe a baby in its family once a week at a fixed time for two years, and record what we have seen in as much detail as possible afterwards. These observations are studied in a weekly seminar group of about five students and a seminar leader. By having to answer questions from seminar members about the details of what we have seen and by recording the observations afterwards we become better at observing, particularly the non-verbal details of, a baby and at remembering (taking in) what occurred. We try to understand something, from what we see, of the emotional life of the baby, its relationship with its mother and other family members. We also observe our own reactions to this experience and try to tease out in what ways we can legitimately use these reactions to help us in understanding what we see. It is in the tradition of this training that I observe babies in the NNICU.

My one modification of the traditional child psychotherapists' method was that I took notes as I watched, because I did not trust myself to record faithfully the little movements of these very premature babies. So on October 5 I went to observe Twin I who had been named Fred. He was under a layer of plastic. He had a ventilator to his mouth, goggles over his eyes because he was under a lamp to counteract jaundice. He was lying on his back on a nappy and was naked. His skin looked very dry and was parchment thin. He had heavy equipment on his left arm and leg. His face was turned towards the ventilator on his right. His right hand was bent over, and went up to touch his left ear which was covered by some padding. His right hand moved around and touched his chin. Both feet flexed. His right hand curled towards his mouth about three inches away from it. His mouth moved rather uncomfortably on the ventilator. He was still and then his mouth opened on the ventilator. His feet were flexing. His right foot was moving against the sheet. He was still and then his mouth juddered against the ventilator. His hand was now two inches from his mouth, and his fingers flexed out a little very gently. His mouth moved on the ventilator, and his hand moved around. His mouth moved, closed and opened rather slackly. He stretched his arms. And his right leg curled up into his open nappy. His right hand touched the ventilator and his mouth, and then closed onto the ventilator near his mouth, and then rested against his open mouth. He explored his mouth and moved away. His hand went back up against his mouth, his thumb went into his mouth and his fingers against his cheek. Then his hand moved one inch away from his mouth with his index finger just touching the ventilator.

This observation continued and I felt rapt and in awe of this little creature. His hand seemed like an adventurer in a new land, plotting the landscape, working hard to make essential links between parts of himself and between himself and the outside world. Here he was, prematurely thrust on the shores of a new kind of world, in air now rather than water, having air pumped into his lungs. He no longer had his brother's intimate company, or the steady beat of the placenta, although he did have the thumping ventilator. He seemed to be working out the relation of the ventilator to his mouth and to be establishing the link of his hand – or more particularly his thumb – to his mouth. Perhaps the link between his mouth and his hand was more familiar, and he was using this as the basis on which to go on to explore the link between his mouth and the ventilator. I thought that Fred was remarkably successful in striving for integration. His hand seemed to move with real intentionality.

I moved on to observe his brother who was still unnamed. His skin too was thin and dry. He was lying on his back on a nappy. He had a hat on which helped to hold the ventilator to his mouth, and he had a tube down his nose. His head was turned to the left. He had a lot of equipment to his left leg which was straight down and his right leg was bent up. His right hand was holding his penis. His right hand moved half an inch away and his index finger was pointing to his penis. His penis moved and he was very still. Then his penis moved very slightly. His left hand fingers, which had to be straight because of the equipment, moved against the bandaging. His penis moved back to touch his right hand – away and up – it was flexing as if it was searching for the hand – backwards and forwards. I found myself amazed. His hand moved slightly away. His penis moved up and down again and again and then touched his index finger and they stayed together. His left leg jerked. He was still. Then his finger and penis moved against each other. His hand bent over and he touched his penis with his bent fingers. His left leg flexed up. He stretched all over – wriggling. Then his hand moved down and his bent fingers were against the length of his penis. His left leg straightened and his right leg bent up. He was still and then wriggling. His nurse came over and turned some equipment down saying that it would be quieter for the poor child.

What can be said about such an observation? I am not sure. But I felt amazed by this little person. I felt convinced that I was not in the presence of random movements, but of a tremendous effort to make connections, to make sense of himself, to explore and perhaps to get some gratification. He did not seem particularly uncomfortable or persecuted. I thought that he was full of curiosity. The nurse was in tune with him, feeling his experience and making him more comfortable. I think that the nurses are more in touch with the babies when they, the babies, are in this curious motivated state and that they are more likely to turn away from them when they are irritable or have given themselves up to mindlessness; or it might be that when the babies are in this latter state, the nurses are in touch with and perhaps unable to cope with the babies' hopelessness. It seems that the couple – nurse and baby – get into a more integrated relationship when the nurse feels able to help the baby.

I went to see Fred again on October 12. He was on his back, his face turned to the right. He was wearing a hat and a nappy, and had a dress lying over him. The ventilator was strapped to his mouth and his left arm was under his dress. He was now being fed by a tube going in through his mouth. He had heavy equipment on his right hand. The nurse came and shielded his eyes. I was hoping that they would open, but they did not. He tried to bring his hand to his mouth, but he could not because of all the equipment. His feet curled up. His right hand stretched out, his arm bending at the elbow. It tried again to come to his mouth and stretched away. He jerked. His right foot beat against the sheet and he rested. He juddered. His mouth, which had been open, opened further and I could see his tongue. His elbow bent and his hand moved away from his mouth. His tongue went in and out. He was sucking his tongue again and again. He stretched out his right foot, which was quite badly scarred from blood-taking.

It seemed to me that Fred was frustrated in his usual activity of getting his right hand or thumb into his mouth and that he beat his foot in protest. Maybe this gesture was to project the hurt or frustration and perhaps we can see here the building blocks from which expression is built. The problem is that a projection of this kind really needs an object that will receive it and I thought of how many times in the day Fred must have felt this kind of frustration and tried to express it without anyone noticing. When I talked to the nurse about this she said that he could not always have the equipment on the other hand. It seemed that Fred lost his way a little after this frustration and then concentrated on his tongue in his mouth. As the observation went on he seemed to be exploring the inside of his mouth with his tongue, and then to be filling the void of his mouth with it. The nurse told me that he was always pulling out his feeding tube. She readjusted it and told me that that morning, while she was doing something for him, he opened his eyes and looked at her. Fred was managing to put up with quite a lot of frustration and to continue his enquiries in the face of it. His concentration seemed to focus on exploring and filling his mouth and then, gradually, on his eyes.

By October 12, Twin II had been named Sam. When I went to see him he was lying on his back, his head turned to the right to the ventilator which was in his mouth. He had a blanket over his legs, and his right leg was bent up. He had a hat and a nappy on. His right hand was against his right cheek, the fingers up towards his eye. His left hand was up against the back of his head. He was sucking on the ventilator, and then his tongue was sucking on the plastic of the ventilator. His mouth was opening and closing. The bleep on the machinery went off. The nurse said that he must like my company because his oxygen requirements had improved. Then he was still. It seemed that his eyes were about to open, but they did not. He was sucking. The fingers of his right hand were under his eye, his hand arched out. The left hand holding the back of his head moved slightly. The nurse said that he liked to hear chatting around him. His right hand arched out again and his left hand moved behind his head. His right hand moved down and he stretched, kicking the blanket off. His right hand fingers went back to pointing to his eye. His eyes opened in slits and closed. His left hand fingers moved behind his head. Both hands moved in a gesture to enclose his head. His eyes opened in little slits, stayed open and then closed. His hands moved to enclose his head again. His right hand moved and he was sucking. Both hands moved, he was sucking and his eyes opened in slits. His hand went to the plastic of the ventilator. His eyes opened wider. His hand was on the ventilator, and his eyes opened, closed and opened. His hand moved away and then back and then away and then further away, then back to the ventilator and rested against it. His tongue went out to the plastic. His eyes opened and his hand moved just away from the ventilator and then right away. His tongue licked around his mouth. His hand came against the ventilator and felt the part furthest from his mouth and then rested against the part that went into his mouth. His tongue licked the inside of the plastic. My time was up, but I was reluctant to leave him.

I felt that what I saw was like a beautifully co-ordinated dance. Sam took the momentous step of opening his eyes to this new world. I was moved by seeing his eyes open, it was a kind of birth, an entry into the world. It seemed that he had to hold on to his head with both hands while he was doing it – a gesture that is familiar to many of us when we have to do something difficult later in life. I wondered if this holding of the head was a very concrete kind of integration where the integrating centre, the head, had to be held together. It seemed then that he was exploring and integrating important zones and activities – his eyes and seeing, his mouth and sucking and then there was the question of what he sucked on. He went away and came back, perhaps checking and perhaps gaining mastery. To watch a baby working in this way is riveting. There was also some acknowledgement by the nurse that this was a human baby who was reassured by human company and throve on hearing friendly voices around him.

By the end of October Sam was in better health than Fred. Neither of them was doing as well as at first. They had both been on ventilators for several weeks and their lungs were in a bad state. The staff felt that the parents did not understand how sick their boys were and that they were rather blasé. They only visited in the evenings.

On November 3 I went to see Fred. I knew that during the previous week he had been on a mask. This is a less invasive form of ventilation, but involves a mask being strapped over the baby's face. Parents usually find this distressing, and feel cut-off from the baby, and I imagine the baby might have similar feelings. I also knew that he had a hernia and that his genitalia were very swollen. I found Fred covered by a light blanket to his neck. His face was to the right and he had the ventilator to his mouth. He had the upper part of his open mouth against the plastic of the ventilator. I could see his tongue lying there inside his open mouth. He was very still. His eyelids moved. A nurse put an antibiotic in through a drip, uncovering his foot to do so. His eyes scrunched up a little as it went in. His tongue went into a V-shape and then flattened out. He was very still. His tongue moved, and then his jaw made rather strong sucking movements almost like chewing. His eyes opened for an instant while he sucked. His eyes opened and closed and then stayed open. But they did not look focused. He blinked as though baffled by it all. They fluttered and closed. I found myself wondering if he was, or would be, blind, an iatrogenic hazard for premature babies ventilated for many weeks. He was very still with his mouth hanging open and his eyes closed. His mouth juddered and his eyelids scrunched a little.

I felt that Fred was giving up his quest for integration and was overwhelmed by a sense of hopelessness and sorrow. Both he and Sam in observations at this time seemed to have lost an exquisite intelligence they had had in the first weeks after birth, a natural will to explore and integrate. The worlds they were inhabiting now – particularly Fred's – seemed to have lost their meaning and he was disintegrating in the face of all his experience.

Fred became sick. He had an infection which was thought might be a fungal infection of the kidneys. His lungs were in a bad way. Sam seemed to improve. The staff worried that the mother did not realise what was going on. She visited very little. An attempt was made to get Fred on to a nasal prong, a less invasive form of ventilation – but he could not manage and had to go back on to the ventilator. He was on a lot of antibiotics for all kinds of infection.

I went to see him on November 10 and he had both arms by his sides. He was very still and his eyes were closed. As she attended him the nurse yanked him with some equipment by mistake. He hardly seemed to notice, he yawned and his right hand curled slightly. The nurse touched him and he yawned again, his eyes opening to a slit. The doctor gave him a heel prick for blood. He opened his eyes, his arms flew out, he screamed and was quickly still again. Probably the medication was making Fred sleepy, but there was a profound sense in which he seemed to have given up, as if the battle was too much. Pain was no longer something to protest against. It was thought that week that he would die. There was a lot of worry about whether the parents understood how grave his condition was. I had not seen mother for some time.

I rang her and encouraged her to come in for a talk. It soon emerged that the mother was not well herself and had been in hospital and that the father was very nervous.

By the end of November the mother was visiting more and seemed more aware of what was happening. I met both parents. The mother talked about how special twins were in her culture, they were the dancers and special songs were sung to them. She had not felt able to sing to them, but I encouraged her to do so. She also talked about the baby she had miscarried and her belief that it had come back as one of the twins. By now Sam was in a headbox, a perspex box covering his head and shoulders, and his mother could quite easily pick him up. One evening she picked him up and sang to him and was delighted that he looked up so intently at her. She was rapturous. With much more difficulty she picked up Fred who was still ventilated. She sang a little to him, but was afraid when he regurgitated some food.

At the beginning of December the registrar was very upset about Fred, telling me that he had a cyst on his brain and that she was not sure that treatment should be continued. I went to observe him. He was quite still, occasionally making little movements. I was taking my notes, but found myself falling asleep. The nurse held his hand saying that he knew when she talked to him and that he was worn out. Referring to the cyst she said what a shame it was, but that it might get better.

As Fred got sicker I found myself giving in to the temptation to disintegrate, to escape, when I observed him. I could feel myself giving up on watching, dreaming off somewhere else or falling asleep, or finding urgent reasons why I could not watch him, or falling into inane platitudes.

By Christmas the unit was in a state of torment about Fred. The consultant felt that it was cruel to go on treating him, that this amounted to torture. Some staff agreed and some did not. He talked to the parents about the almost certain severe brain damage and the mother was devastated. I saw the parents and the father was, once again, very formal, wanting to thank the unit. He said that he was praying to God and that God could do anything. The mother agreed, but said that Fred was in pain, that she pitied him, that he was going through too much. She said how joyful she had been to have twins and that it made up for the lost baby. But this was too much. The father said that she had been suicidal and that he was afraid that she would walk into the road. She was worried about him, saying that he was a good man and should have children.

In the middle of December Sam started to take some feeding bottles; otherwise he was fed through a naso-gastric tube. I had seen him and the nurse enjoying a bottle feed. On December 21 I went to see him. He was lying on his tummy, and needed just a trickle of oxygen. His head was to the left and his right hand was behind his head. His eyes were closed. He was breathing quite heavily. He screwed up his face and sucked on the tubes. He began squirming and wriggling and making uncomfortable noises. His left hand went down and his eyebrows went up. I was worried about the tube which had fallen across his left eye and I moved it. He raised his head and buried it into the sheet, putting up his left hand. I thought that he was looking for something to go into his mouth. He brought his hand to his mouth and nose and cried. He turned his head the other way. He seemed to be searching – his right hand to his mouth and his left hand behind his head. This was a position which earlier in his life had given him comfort and held him together, but now he had had the experience of the teat in his mouth and sucking on it for milk and that seemed to be what he was looking for. He held his right hand to his mouth and seemed more concentrated, less bloated. He was still and then his eyebrows went up and his eyes opened slightly. His hand went away and again he was searching with his head into the sheet. His hand stretched up, feeling the sheet, touching his nose and then his ear. His head turned the other way. His left hand went to his mouth. The nurse asked me if it was alright if she fed him. I said of course, worrying whether she had felt inhibited by my presence. His left hand went away from his mouth and the nurse began to put the feed down the tube. He wriggled. I asked the nurse about bottle feeding. She said that he had about two bottles a day and was disparaging about how much he would take from a bottle. I felt critical because I had seen him enjoying a bottle so much and I also felt that she could have taken him out for a cuddle while she was feeding him. Sam cried and the nurse looked away into space while holding the tube. I felt sad that Sam had nothing for his mouth and asked the nurse if he liked the bottle. She said, rather shamefaced, that he did, but added that it was hard with the oxygen tube. She then asked me if I had recently seen the mother of a baby who had died over a year previously on the unit. I thought that she was telling me to stick to my own job or maybe telling me how it felt to be criticised, or shifting some responsibility to me. Sam settled down with both hands in loose fists on either side of his head. He was still and his mouth was jammed up against the sheet. He seemed uncomfortable. He made a noise and turned his head. The nurse continued to look away. His hand went momentarily to his mouth. He grabbed the tube. The nurse took his hand away and he cried and turned his head the other way. His left hand was exploring and he was making a noise. He choked. The nurse patted his body and he cried. He turned his head back to me, making noises with his mouth against the sheet. I found myself wanting to get away.

I thought that Sam was desperately searching for an object – outside in the real world – to hold him together. Because he had had the experience of feeding from the bottle, this was probably the teat for his mouth, but it might have been arms to hold him or other human eyes to stare into and to have stare back or a voice to talk to him and to begin to make sense of his experience. I had seen him enjoying all of these things with the nurse the previous week. And at this stage it seemed that these were the things that he needed for integration, and that without them he became desperate, flailed around, cried, choked and so on – the things that we commonly describe as 'falling apart'.

I thought that the nurse had likewise not been able to hold herself together. There was something here which she could not, at least at this moment, integrate, and she had blotted out skills and sympathies which I knew that she possessed. She probably knew, at least unconsciously, that she was doing this because she tried to pass on to me some sense of guilt. What precisely she found unbearable I do not know; but it might have been the long haul that this baby had undergone, or the new sense of hope as he was progressing, or the contrast with his very sick brother, or the mother's absence; there may have been things going on in her life which interfered with her capacity to understand and feel for him. Whatever it was, she did not manage to stave off this disintegration, and he lost the opportunity of some human contact which he desperately needed. She did not manage it and I did not help her. I think I allowed myself to enter the world of apportioning blame and I think that she may have been driven further away by feeling my criticism. I think that Fred was my favourite twin – more splitting and a failure of integration, this time on my part – and perhaps I found it hard to see Sam progressing while his brother was dying. This raises the difficulty we commonly have of thinking of one twin except in terms of the other twin.

By the end of December Fred was very ill. I saw that his tummy was very distended and that his genitalia were bloated from his hernia. The nurse looking after him was very gentle and told me that he was very irritable and sensitive to any handling. When the doctor took blood his face screwed up in pain. And when the nurse touched his distended belly very gently he looked as if he was gagging. Even in the middle of all of this his hand went to his mouth as if searching for something.

On December 29 I went to see him again. He had his head to the right. He opened his eyes slightly from time-to-time. His tongue came out, his mouth opened on the ventilator and his tongue was mouthing. His eyes opened slightly. He licked the ventilator strap and the plastic. His eyes opened fleetingly, then stayed open but were rather vacant. I found it hard to watch him and wondered if this was because he was dying. He was screaming as the nurse put something down his drip. She commented that it stung him. She comforted him, rather roughly I thought, and then put some more down. He was screaming again. She asked me if I had seen his right arm – it had become broken or dislocated. She did not know how, she had only just come on duty. She said that it hurt him when it was moved, she demonstrated and he gave his noiseless cry. I asked her what it was like to nurse him, and she said that he was lovely, he had his own personality and that he opened his eyes to see you. She added that, of course, they were not sure that he could see. I asked if his belly was still distended and she said that it was, adding that he was swollen all over. Fred closed his mouth on the plastic.

I thought about how I was about to go on a one-week holiday and wondered if he would be dead by the time I came back. I wondered whether his parents would keep their appointment with me that morning and thought about ringing them. Then I found myself wondering whether I would ever write a book and imagined what the different chapters might be about. I became conscious of all this and realised that my mind was finding it hard to stay with Fred, that it kept on wandering away to escape or maybe to the possibility of another baby (the book). With these reflections I found some strength to come back to Fred. The nurse asked me to move to the other side because she wanted to do Fred's physiotherapy. She seemed rather cross and she asked me sceptically whether I thought that Fred's parents would come to see me. Fred did not seem to object to the physio – this involved his being thumped on the chest to break up the phlegm and dislodge it. The nurse said that she thought that he quite liked it. As she worked, she said that you wonder what you are doing (ethically) and whether it is for the best. I noticed how exhausted she looked and commented that she was looking after two very sick babies and looked very tired. She grinned and said that she was. She had had two days off over Christmas, and had spent most of the time on the M4 so that she could see her parents. Now she was back on and they were short-staffed. She then said that, at the moment, work seemed more like a test of endurance than a part of her life.

It seemed at first that the nurse had dismantled her own sensitivity and judgements and was full of inane comments, and then that she had given herself over to a cruel and meaningless world. She was a nurse whom I knew well and liked. She was generally thoughtful and very sensitive to the babies. I was amazed to see her move Fred's arm so experimentally and to talk about his lovely personality in such a mindless way. As she did the physio, something seemed to come together for her and she suddenly started talking about the morality of what was going on. Perhaps at the moment of feeling she could help him she felt less persecuted and could face this hard question. I think that I could suddenly see her struggling then and could comment to her about how taxed she was. As she felt more looked after, her mood softened both to herself and to Fred. In the face of all this pain and uncertainty it is tempting to forget all kinds of things that you do know, to doubt what you see and to give yourself up to cruelty or mindlessness. It takes hard work to resist this or to retrieve a situation which is slipping downhill. I am arguing that the exercise of integrity is located here. We knew very well the horrible complexity of the situation; all kinds of defences against this kept offering themselves to us and the moral task was to try to resist these so as to treat Fred as well as we could. If we defended ourselves, bad treatment and bad decisions resulted.

While I was away for a week, Fred died. His parents were called in and he was kept alive until they arrived. Both parents held him and wept. Then they disappeared giving the hospital chaplain £30 to arrange a funeral and burial. The chaplain was upset to feel that Fred had been abandoned to him. The parents did not attend the funeral. Gradually we learnt that this was culturally normal for them and that the mother was not supposed to mourn her dead child because it might then come back. However, when the mother reappeared on the unit, she asked me if I had attended the funeral and when I said that I had not been able to do so, she seemed quite annoyed. I wondered if I was meant to do some of the mourning for Fred and perhaps that is part of the function of this chapter. Mothers with one dead twin and one surviving twin are faced with a particularly hard task of integration. It is a very hard task to mourn for one baby while pouring all one's energy into willing the other to survive. In the next few weeks the mother attended the unit daily, feeding Sam, enjoying him and looking very good. Sam throve and it was soon time for him to go home. Eight months later I was sitting on the unit reading through my notes on Fred and Sam in preparation for writing this chapter and I saw some people walking past my table. It was Mr and Mrs Z and Sam coming to visit the unit to celebrate his first birthday. They looked happy and relaxed as the nurses chatted and cooed over Sam. The father was suddenly serious and said that they wanted to thank the staff for saving his life. The Zs looked joyful on that day, but unfortunately Sam has sickle-cell anaemia and it is not known how serious his condition is going to be. He has already had a hospital admission with an attack. This means that his days of excruciating pain are not over and it also means that the doctors cannot reassure themselves that there was a happy ending to this difficult story. They are still left having to answer their own questions about what they have done. It takes integrity for them to face these questions in following up a baby's development into childhood and adolescence, since they can never be sure what the outcome of their work will be.

I have tried to describe an impressive and exquisite fight for integration on the part of the twins. It may be argued that we are fragile creatures and cannot hope for integration – but these most fragile and immature examples of our species are working away to make connections, to explore themselves and their setting. The sight of this work is very moving. It may be that, in the face of such bravery, some would rather not admit that the babies feel pain or that they are having to deal with such a difficult experience, which may prove too much for them. But this involves issues about our own integration and whether we can manage to see what we see and know what we know, or whether we use one of the many mechanisms we have available to split-off, deny or protect ourselves from what is painful to us. I have tried to describe how the staff struggle with, and sometimes succumb to, the pull to disintegrate in the face of pain. We may undermine our own perceptions, look the other way, fall asleep, or, like the mother at one time, just stay away. If we succumb to this temptation we may act with negligence or cruelty and we have, in effect, abandoned the baby. We may also become brutalised so that nothing moves us any more. These are states of mind that we all fall into at times, but there is a question of whether or not we can recover from them. We may find the situation so unbearable that we have to find someone to blame – for instance, the parents, the other staff, the obstetricians, the doctor who resuscitated the baby in the first place, the doctor who did not resuscitate the baby quickly enough, the ambulance staff; the list of candidates goes on indefinitely. It is hard to take responsibility for what is happening and not try to split the blame off somewhere else and again this involves integrity. The other side of this is to idealise the unit, to think of ourselves as a well-intentioned group of devoted people struggling in severe conditions – a kind of World War II mentality, which can make one feel comfortable.

There is one obvious candidate for blame which I have not mentioned, and that is not because I think that they are to blame for all the circumstances, but I do think they are to blame for exacerbating them – and that is the last British Conservative government with their NHS reforms. In the market economy which they have brought into the Health Service, units compete with one another and there is a question of who can deliver the best service most cheaply. Colleagues who were friends and collaborators have become economic rivals. It has been known for one unit to spy on another to see how it is cutting down its costs. Staffing levels are cut to a minimum, which inevitably means that agency staff have to be called in. These are usually less well trained nurses, but perhaps more importantly they are not part of the team. A team has to grow together with people getting to know each other so that there can be trust and cooperation. With a large number of agency staff communication suffers and an even greater strain is put on the permanent staff. But beyond this, a view is fostered that one individual can be slotted into another individual's place without any bad effects; the consequent deterioration in human relationships is ignored. There is, in any case, a constant pressure in a medical context to think in this sort of way; junior doctors are moved on to a new job very quickly and agency staff are used, and this culture has been encouraged by the reforms. This means that there is a continual wearing away of attachment, a pull to trivialise human contact. This situation makes the struggle for integrity more difficult.

Given this fraught, economically competitive situation it is seen as an act of great disloyalty to say anything critical about the unit; a picture of 'everything being fine' has to be maintained. We cannot 'afford' to have our public image tarnished. Any criticism amounts both to suicide and to a murderous attack on the unit. So people mutter about unsafe staffing levels, but these must not be openly voiced. Attempts must be made to hide from parents that the situation is often unsafe. And everyone goes in fear of anything being leaked to the press. Along with this go mutinous wishes that the parents would complain to the press and the whole thing be exposed. The market economy does not facilitate an open discussion of our problems and negative feelings.

Over the last 20 years, complex structures have been developed in the Health Service. Child psychiatrists and child psychotherapists have encouraged an integrated view of the child. This means that the child, not the symptom, gets treated. The child in his family, in his school, in the community gets thought about. This needs a lot of liaison work, but leads to much better practice. The delicate balance of this kind of work has been wrecked by the new way of thinking. Money is so tight that it has become the dominant consideration, and there are no longer the resources to think in this integrated multi-disciplinary way. This is a very plain pull away from integrity in that we no longer think in terms of the health and well-being of our citizens, but of the best delivery of a service (for instance, the ventilation of a baby). Of course, a unit such as the one I work in tries to continue with its tradition, but in the face of enormous opposition. The security of link-workers like speech therapists, health visitors, social workers and child psychiatrists is precarious and most of these people have had their workload increased so that they cannot deliver such a thoughtful service. It is the change in our ways of thinking that seems to be crucial. In such an economically pressed situation it is difficult to find time to think. Exhausted doctors and nurses find it hard to change gear and to attend Staff-Support meetings. But it may be that the injustice, destructiveness and cruelty inherent in the way human beings are being thought about, in our society at the moment is very painful to think about, and so we stop thinking and give up on our integrity.

I want to make it clear that I am not arguing that the NHS is being destroyed purely by lack of funding. There are situations where money is not available and moral choices have to be made about what we can afford and what we cannot; and neo-natal intensive care units may be something we cannot afford, in which case this needs to be said clearly. I am arguing much more that the internal market economy – the atmosphere of economic competition – in institutions designed to provide health care runs counter to the difficult task of thinking people in an integrated way as human beings. To send a mother back to a local hospital from a more specialised hospital after a few weeks may make economic sense even while it does not make emotional sense – the mother has experienced a premature birth and she is being held and helped to get to know her baby in very difficult circumstances, and to send her somewhere else can undermine this restorative work. Ironically, it is probable that looking after people properly and considerately is cheaper in the long run and the cavalier treatment that is becoming commonplace just piles up more and more of the social problems that we are becoming so familiar with.

Postscript

> Turning and turning in the widening gyre
> The falcon cannot hear the falconer;
> Things fall apart; the centre cannot hold;
> Mere anarchy is loosed upon the world,
> (W.B. Yeats, 1919, in *Collected Poems*. Macmillan, 1950, pp. 210–11)

When I began to write this paper, fragments of the first four lines of this poem kept coming into my mind. They seemed to describe so well the states of disintegration that I was thinking about. The image of the falcon and the falconer made me think of the baby needing to hear the mother, to be held in against the desolation of the 'widening gyre'. I thought also of the centre of one's personality – the strength one has been given to take on more and more of oneself, to own it and not to have to split it off into others – and of the mess when this centre cannot hold.

So I looked up the poem to remind myself of the rest, and found it not so comfortable. I could not understand it. I wondered who I could ask to explain it to me. I remembered not liking Yeats' poem to his new-born daughter (W.B. Yeats, *A Prayer for my Daughter*, 1924) with its emphasis on innocence – it seemed a rather attenuated life that he was wishing on her and here again was this valuing of innocence. And then I began to think about integrity and the project to call in unknown parts of oneself and to get to know them. It sounds quite friendly. But I remembered experiences in the analytic setting, on both sides of the encounter, and being very frightened of something emerging – perhaps some rough beast. If we are really committed to integration, we cannot know what will emerge, we have to tolerate the unknown. We cannot ask for any insurance policies, we can only trust to the goodness and strength of our internal objects (by which I mean our internal resources made up from the positive assimilation of good experiences). I worked recently with a pregnant woman who had been told that her baby was going to be very disfigured. She was given the opportunity of an abortion, but eventually decided against. The weeks passed with more tests done and a very bleak forecast. When she was well past the time when she could have an abortion, she arrived at the hospital in a deranged state demanding an abortion. The next few weeks were hell for her. I think she felt so mad because she thought she was carrying a monster around inside her and that that was what she would give birth to. When a human little girl was born, admittedly with many deformities, the mother was overjoyed and put her to the breast. I think that likewise we are afraid of integration because we are afraid that inside somewhere we are not human, but monstrous. Added to this there are the dangers of a false integration; for instance, a sort of law-and-order mentality which holds us together falsely by fear and power rather than by understanding. If someone acted in a behaviourally correct way, but was driven by a harsh super-ego, I do not think that it would be correct to describe him as acting with integrity – he would be acting from, say, fear rather than from a moral view, which he had integrated and felt worth striving for. We have to develop our capacity to hear when we are lying to ourselves, to distinguish the true from the false. This is no easy matter and as with this poem we may find ourselves baffled. But not even to aspire to such a project of integrity leaves the rest of the world at the mercy of all that we have disowned and of our blind selves.

References

Anand, K.J.S. (1987) 'Randomised trial of fentanyl anaesthesia in pre . . . babies undergoing surgery: effects on the stress response' *Lancet* vol 1, pp. 243–47.

Anand, K.J.S. and Hickey, P.R. (1992) 'Halothane-morphine compared with high-dose sufentanil for anaesthesia and pistoperline analgesia' *New England Journal of Medicine* 326, pp. 1–9.

Clarke, D.A. (1994) 'Stress without distress: the intrauterine perspective' *Lancet* 344, pp. 73–74.

Giannakoulopoulis, X., Sepulveda, W., Kourtis, P., Glover, V. and Fisk, N.M. (1994) 'Fetal plasma cortisol and B-endorphin response to intrauterine needling' *Lancet* 344, pp. 73–74.

Rogers, M.C. (1992) 'Do the right thing: pain relief in infants and children' *New England Journal of Medicine* 326, pp. 55–56.

5   Integrity

Political, not psychological

Amélie Oksenberg Rorty

As Milton tells it, Satan addressed the ranks of angels – the Thrones, Dominations, Princedoms, Virtues, Powers – charging them to join him in rebelling against the majesty of God, to claim their liberty and proclaim their equality. And as Milton would have it, only Abdiel, among all the angels, refused to follow Satan – whom we, in our doubly fallen condition, call 'Lucifer', Bearer of Light – in his rebellious charge against God.

> Among the innumerable false, unmov'd
> unshak'n, unseduc'd, unterrifi'd
> His Loyalty, he kept, his Love, his Zeal;
> Nor number, nor example with him wrought
> To swerve from truth, or [to] change his constant mind
> . . . From amidst them forth he pass'd,
> Long way through scorn, which he sustained
> . . . [alone] nor of violence fear'd [he] aught;
> And with retorted scorn his back he turn'd
> On those proud Towr's to swift destruction doom'd

Milton's description of Faithful Abdiel paints one reigning figure of integrity. In obedience to the Power of Divinity, Abdiel mingles awe and fear, justice and piety, loyalty and gratitude. He is alone . . . but safe in the assurance of the justice of divine law.

Political integrity, as we now conceive it, is more difficult to achieve: it is surrounded by uncertainty, and it has travelled inward. A person of integrity acts from her conception of what is right, rather than from impulse or self-interested prudential calculation of advantage. She conjoins honesty and fairness, sincerity and steadfast reliability. Cost what it may, she is stern in the face of personal affections and sentiments. The integrity of a citizen in a totalitarian or unjust state can be extremely searing: it can involve exile or imprisonment as well as isolation and impoverishment. While we admire – and grieve for – the great sacrifices of such integrity, we also envy the clarity of their directions. Unlike most of us, the martyrs of conscience have the luxury of believing that they are wholeheartedly in the right. But the more ordinary, less dramatic cases of political integrity can, even in a relatively just society, also be both clear and costly. Placing conscience before natural desires requires renouncing the benefits of easy access to information, to funds and patronage; it requires being alert to the hidden strings attached to apparently innocent gifts and desirable opportunities.

Integrity is prized as a bulwark against deeply rooted – and highly functional – natural tendencies to self-protection and self-interest. It is valued as an ideal because it is difficult, because it involves effort and struggle. We celebrate rather than praise the integrity of angels who do what is right without further thought, who were never tempted, as even Abdiel must have been, by Lucifer's evocation of equality and freedom. As Plato's story of the ring of Gyges would have it, as the Biblical story of original sin would have it, our natural tendencies are at best amoral: we move to getting whatever we want by whatever means we choose. Unlike the ranks of angels, we are – so the story goes – primarily interested in personal satisfactions, in relatively narrow and short-term benefits. If we were invisible, and unchecked, we would bend the truth, take short-cuts and connive against the near and dear in order to avoid pain and to achieve our heart's desire.

Introduced as a visionary ideal of individual perfection, integrity is thought to preserve society against the impulses of its members. There are, of course, other candidates for transforming our basic animal selves. Theologians like Augustine and Butler focused on varieties of altruistic sentiments. *Caritas*, compassion, pity and love have, at one time or another been introduced as counteractive forces against the basic primitive movements of raw and narrow egoism. These altruistic sentiments have been argued to be as deeply rooted, as natural as self-protection and self-interest. But even if we are naturally endowed with such sentiments, they tend – for good reasons – to be both fragile and narrow in scope, easily eroded in difficult circumstances, only extended to strangers under benign political circumstances, and rarely available for enemies. Strengthening and broadening them requires considerable effort, perhaps even severe training: the work of sustaining altruistic habits is one of the tasks of integrity. But trouble looms even in benign circumstances. Ironically enough, when integrity commands benevolence, when it exhorts us to stand fast against our natural self-protective tendencies, integrity introduces internal conflict.

And the cost of integrity is deeper still. Michael Walzer (1973) argues that the conscientious integrity required by public office can, even in a just state, threaten the personal integrity of conscience or commitment. We are all, in one way or another, public figures with public duties. Our duties as friends or parents, employers or employees, teachers or students can often bring searingly painful conflicts, conflicts that – ironically enough – undermine personal morality. A mayor's duties to her constituents, a doctor's duties to the welfare of her patients, a lawyer's duties to her clients often demand courses of action that may well conflict with their moral principles. To be sure, a lawyer can refuse to defend an alleged child-molester, a physician can refuse to perform elective vanity surgery. But a mayor who – on grounds of conscience – refuses to enforce a law with which she disagrees cannot save her integrity: either she violates the duties of public office or she violates her personal principles; and while she could notionally resign as mayor, she would, in doing so, violate the integrity entrusted by constituents. And so it is, too, for friends and parents, teachers and students. Our many roles carry complex duties and obligations that often conflict with our principled convictions. It is no accident, that the word 'compromise' is a double edged sword, no accident that we are enjoined to compromise, and yet condemned for it.

Recent psychoanalytic theory has attempted to mend the shreds and tears in the fabric of integrity. Margaret Cohen attempts to return us to the Miltonian assurance that integrity and justice coincide, that those who undertake the terrible task of remaining true are, despite (because of?) their suffering, saved, made whole. Her searing, searching story of the Z family (Chapter 4, this volume) has the eloquence of a Dostoyevsky novel. She enables us, at least for a time, to stand fast with them in their struggles. Her version of psychoanalytic theory adds an important dimension to Milton's story; and in doing so, she also enlarges the integrity of the citizen who attempts to combine conscience with the demands of public life. While Dr Cohen acknowledges the inevitability of internal conflict, she attempts to give an account of individual thriving that reconciles the demands of morality with the natural directions of self-protection and self-fulfillment. Her arguments rest on the initial Platonic and Stoic premise that both morality and individual well-being depend on psychological integration, on the consistency and harmony of our beliefs and desires. And while she does not follow Plato or the Stoics in thinking that we naturally strive for what is objectively good and right, she accepts a modification of that view: the natural psychological processes of identification and internalized idealization equip us with a deeply ingrained set of moral ideals that we must, one way or another, integrate with our more self-centred natural equipment. She argues that the personal happiness for which we all strive must incorporate a full acknowledgement of the morality that normal psychological development impels upon us. To mitigate the dreadful burden imposed by overly-idealised morality, constraints are set upon its claims. Morality is not justified in demanding more than we poor, oddly organised, naturally conflicted humans can give. On the one hand, our well-being incorporates the claims of morality; but on the other hand, the claims of morality incorporate the claims of psychological well-being. Integration and integrity are not only mutually compatible; they are mutually dependent. Cohen argues that those who persist in denying the claims of moral integrity eventually end by injuring and diminishing themselves; and those who advance impossible moral ideals eventually end by undermining active morality.

I am suspicious of all this moral and psychological uplift. I want to play Lucifer's advocate, to argue against all this striving after integration and integrity. As Cohen phrases it, integrity depends on effort, the effort of facing – and standing witness to – the painful suffering of life. (Shouldn't integrity also admit that we try to have as much jolly good fun as we can, amidst all this suffering?) The psychoanalytic theories that link integrity with integration seem to me to be dangerously incomplete; their emphasis seems wrongly placed; and by focusing on individual psychology, they may distract our energies from addressing the political conditions that frame and direct our psychology. The work of beneficence begins with structuring the political, economic and social conditions that make compassion possible; and as things stand, that work may – ironically enough – be most effectively done by rogues with questionable motives.

I do not believe that personal integration is – or should be – among our central aims; I suspect there is little connection between integration and integrity; I am convinced that integrity is far from being the most important of our virtues. It does not seem strongly correlated with being set to improve the lot of our fellows. The good work of the world is not always done by those who are good; and those who are humanely intent on doing good are often dangerous bumblers. To be sure, Cohen is not claiming that integration and integrity are *sufficient* for doing good; but many moralists are suspiciously close to saying they are necessary – or at any rate, effective – conditions. I doubt that there is any reliable connection between good intentions and good consequences, though I am sure that a sturdy self-deceptive conviction that there is such a connection is nevertheless a good thing (more about this later).

Psychoanalytic theorists may be right that we strive towards integration; and Margaret Cohen's vivid descriptions of infancy show us how difficult and painful a process this integration can be. But we also have equally powerful, equally canny, and equally beneficial strategies of compartmentalisation, as often driven by fear and by pain as by a sensible division of psychological labor. The striving of babies may not serve as models for us messy adults, who perhaps should not always move towards integration. Neither a model of strict unity nor one of radical division, by itself, can explain the possibility of morally sensitive happiness. Nor can psychoanalysis serve as the model for all fear-filled struggles of discovery. To be sure, honesty is usually a good thing; certainly we should not fear what is not, in the end, really fearful; and facing what we fear – being precise about exactly what we fear – can sometimes mitigate the very suffering we fear. But while we do well to dispel the fears of inner monsters – the fears of ourselves as monsters – flight and self-deception are often wise, even when they deny what is searingly real, even when they divide both mind and heart. If, as Margaret Cohen claims, we should trust 'the goodness and strength of our internal objects . . . the internal resources made up from the positive assimilation of good experiences' then we should also trust the psyche's instinct to flee. People are sometimes destroyed by pain, sometimes destroyed by sharing one another's pain.

To the extent that we can guess about such matters in the lives of others, there doesn't seem to be any strong connection between being a reflectively honest person and having the integrity of what the world considers 'a good person', though those keen on integration will probably be more consistently kind or consistently vicious than those for whom it is not particularly an issue. In Shapespeare's *Othello*, Iago didn't fool himself about his villainy: he smiled and smiled and was a villain. Was he, therefore, less integrated than Othello? If Hamlet helped Denmark to achieve a better form of government, it was not because he struggled with his divided soul, but because he had the good fortune of having the ambitious Fortinbras as his neighbour. If Ophelia's fate be any measure of the matter, Hamlet's struggles with inner and outer truth were far from being a high road to morality. Should he have had a Californian-style heart-to-heart chat with Ophelia? Should he have taken her aside and said: 'Look Ophelia, I keep thinking my father's ghost is telling me that Claudius murdered him to get Mother and the Kingdom. We'd better lay off our Relationship until I get this thing straightened out?' Wouldn't an integrated Ophelia have straightaway run off to create a royal mess by broadcasting the whole story? Sure enough a confused heart spells trouble; but so does a serious-minded struggle for integration. We have divided emotions about what we most want, what we most need. Labyrinthine as we are, we often have as much difficulty acknowledging and integrating our joys and pleasures as our sufferings and pains. Psychological integration, or even psychological honesty in the face of the failure of integration, do not chart the high road to moral integrity. When we are in need, we want the best help we can get, whatever its sources may be. If the very best surgeon is a vain, arrogant, greedy amoralist, and the third best surgeon is a person of manifest integrity, we rightly go for the best surgeon every time. When we are in grief or shame, we don't want to sit with a well-integrated person of integrity; we want to sit quietly with a confused bumbling unreliable person like ourselves, someone who knows us well and (what do you know?) still more-or-less loves us. It would be pretty to think there is a pattern to the matter, a pattern that could help us determine when to look for fix-it, cool competence and when to find a kindred presence, when to look for a shoddy compromiser and when to look for an uncompromising moralist. Sometimes there is such a pattern: after all surgery is one thing, and sitting in mourning is another. But generally, both in need and in giving, we are betwixt and between, without guidance about how to combine the traits that serve our apparently opposed needs. There are no general mottos that can help us live our lives, not even those that convene us towards what we most need. In short, I don't think Cohen's theory is true: it seems unlikely that integrity can be achieved by psychological integration, although we may well be improved by believing it. It is a scandalous terrifying fact about us that we are often genuinely helped by believing what is false. That fact – the human utility of illusion – should never cast doubt on the absolutely important life-sustaining distinction between the true and the useful; nor should it ever weaken our efforts on behalf of both truth and utility, fully aware that they do not always coincide. But that is another dark story for another occasion.

So much for the headlines from darkness. We need definitions and distinctions. First: we need to differentiate three forms of integration: the strictly philosophical, the organisational and the reflective. In the strict Kantian sense, the 'I' – the ego – is implicit in every experience: all of a person's experience is attributable to a single, unified subject. If we can think at all, so the argument goes, we must postulate ourselves as subjects of experience, not only integrated at any given time, but also (in principle) capable of being integrated over a lifetime. According to this upbeat view, the integration of experience – the unity of the ego – is co-ordinate with a systematically coherent world. Absent the ego as the unified systematiser of all possible experience, absent scientific knowledge; absent the possibility of the (same, unified) ego's capacity self-regulation and self-legislation, absent the possibility of morality. But the postulated unity of the ego is not experienced; it carries no particular psychological, and certainly no specific moral consequences.

Cohen is not concerned with this philosophical sense of integration, but with the relation between a person's psychological organization and her moral integrity. Psychological integration can take two forms. A person is *organisationally integrated* when her psychology – her habits, beliefs, desires, emotions, attitudes, what have you – forms a coherent and unconflicted system. She is *reflectively integrated* when she truthfully acknowledges her conflicts, her suffering and (we should add!) her joys, without fleeing from them. Consistency and the absence of ambivalence mark organisational, psychological integration; honesty and sincerity mark reflective integration. Cohen agrees that strict integration of the first sort is acknowledged to be rare; and she also acknowledges that reflective integration does not – as such – necessarily result in integrity and compassion. A person can honestly and truthfully acknowledge her hard-heartedness and do nothing at all about it. She thinks that the mark of integrity is the individual's effort, her struggle to be truthful, and so (then? thus?) her attempt to move from the painful acknowledgment of conflict to their resolution in a well-coordinated harmonious whole.

Cohen introduces a moral component into organisational integration: a person who is strongly psychologically integrated, organizationally and reflectively, is presumptively actively compassionate and beneficent. As she puts it: 'integrity is located at this point in the attempt . . . to remain intact in the face of pain' (p. 88) She wants to convince us that (as she eloquently put it in an earlier draft) 'Our moral lives grow from our investigation of our own honesty . . . and [from] truthfulness with ourselves and then the strength to act in accordance with this'. But it is not clear whether this is a definition or a prediction: if it is a definition, it can't have the powerful normative force Cohen would like it to have. If it is a prediction, then those who become more integrated (and we need some clear criteria for what counts as integration) should be more capable of being present and serviceable to others; and we should expect to find that those who stand fast to serve others are well integrated. I must confess that my experience as a voyeuse and reader suggests that the definition is vacuous and the prediction unconfirmed. Compassion for the near and dear does not always make a person more inclined to be serviceable to the far and not-so-dear . . . and if we can trust the testimony of those intimate with the great human benefactors, devotion to humanity rarely extends to the near and dear. It's true: we are drawn to integrated people of integrity; and because we rely on them, we try to foster their struggles towards compassion, especially when it is directed to us. But when we sense ourselves safe and sound, we are also rightly drawn to interestingly divided rogues and free spirits. And while we hope our near and dear will be worthy and good, we also rightly sometimes wish they had – at least in their dealings with the rest of the world – a little less integrity, perhaps a little less compassion and a little more self-protective, self-deceptive worldly shrewdness.

The criteria for organisational integration are accordion-like: sometimes they are very narrow, and only the unconflicted qualify; sometimes they are broader, and those who are courageously honest qualify; and sometimes they are wide open, and those who expend some effort (sometimes? In which areas of their lives?) trying to pull themselves together qualify. Which is more important to us in the long run: honest integrity to ourselves or to our friends and colleagues? These are, after all, by no means identical; and Shakespeare's Polonius was surely wrong. If Laertes be true to himself, it does not follow as the day follows the night that he will not be false to any man. Nor is it clear just how the connection between integration and integrity is supposed to be achieved. Is it that if we honestly acknowledge pain (and again let's add: joy) – if we don't turn away from them – then we shall become more organisationally integrated, and so persons of greater integrity? Or is it that if we understand what integrity requires of us, we shall endeavor to become more compassionate and by that process become more integrated? These are different stories, and they recommend different therapeutic courses. We are not entitled to be confident that it doesn't matter where we begin. The assurance that integration and integrity in the end coincide is just what is in doubt.

Dr Cohen treats the effort of integration as an important part of its being morally praiseworthy. But we may be as damaged by trying to be what we are not, as we are by trying to flee from what we are. She acknowledges that we cannot know what will emerge from the tasks of integration; unless they are well-guided, they may harden our hearts. Wanting to be integrated in the right way for the right reason, she scorns law-and-order attempts at false integration that are driven by fear and by a harsh, terrorist super-ego (p. 106). Self-terrorizing false integrators are unlikely to have real integrity; and those who are integrated by understanding may not have 'a moral view [that they . . . feel] worth striving for' (p. 106). It would be pretty to think they did; but the voyeuse thinks that those who are integrated by understanding sometimes become dour hermits, while conscience-ridden, self-terrorizing integrators often stand fast in human service.

Let's set aside these niggling theory-construction concerns: after all, even if the criteria for integration are far from clear, we can at least recognise disintegration; and even if we haven't a clue in what goodness really consists, we can at least recognise vicious cruelty and even mild hard-heartedness. Some people seem to be aware – even excruciatingly aware – of 'an inner self', others do not; some are tightly organised, or at least organisable, others are not. Sometimes people who honestly face emotional pain become compassionate; sometimes they become hardened; and sometimes they go mad. It would be nice to think that what happens sometimes, in the best of circumstances, happens for the most part; but we had better not rely on it, even in the best of circumstances. The good can be destroyed by the very things that *are* their goodness; the slimy can be brought to goodness by the very things that *are* their sliminess; and we should not take comfort from the thought that integration, integrity and goodness strengthen us 'as a general rule . . .'. Luck is not something that happens in the corners of our lives; it is all pervasive (cf. Williams 1981a). Yet we would be wholly undone by bearing that truth too vividly in mind.

If a hefty dose of self-deception – denying the extent to which I despair of my fellows – helps me to be decent and kind, if I must choose between compassion and integrity, I hope I would be able to forgo integrity and go full force for self-deception. (Fortunately, magnetised self-deception is one of the few aims we can all confidently expect to be able to realise.) Compassion is often sustained by a little healthy myopia, if not downright blindness, to the ways in which we systematically mistreat each other. That's one of the reasons that children, idiots and young women play such a special role in Dostoyevskian fantasies of morality: our compassion for them can be wholehearted because in our scheme of things, they are, as the phrase goes, 'innocent'.

Compartmentalisation, internal division, self-deception are basic survival strategies. How much of their awareness of human suffering should nurses and doctors bring to wild impish nonsense when they are at home playing with their healthy children? If the answer is – as it might well be – that their connection to their children will be all the more resonant, all the more compassionate if they remember the unbounded and unmeasured pain they see in the clinic, does integrity also require that they remember the echoes of domestic giggly fun when they are at work in the clinic? When we affirm the grief of a woman mourning the death of her husband, by saying 'It will be terrible, the work of mourning is never done; his was a sad and incomplete life', does honest integrity require that we also add: 'Hey, listen, be glad; forget the bad old days; you are much better off freed from your years of servitude to that old tyrant?' If purity of heart is to will one thing, should we be unified and whole at every moment, and so forget one moment in the next? Or should we be wholly, complexly present at every moment, and so be divided, compartmentalised and layered?

Surrounded as we are by pathetically self-seeking amoralists, (including, of course, those within) shouldn't we be glad of their inconsistencies? Of course consistency has great advantages (though they may accrue to the near and dear rather more than to oneself), but so does a Whitmanesque carefree lack of concern for such matters. Whether a person is better off being consistent or being Whitmanesque depends largely on her circumstances, rather than on consistency itself. The success of our struggles to become whole and good depends largely on circumstances, circumstances over which we have no control. It's no good advising us to struggle towards integration if everything in our society – and in ourselves – pulls our many internal personae to *dis*-integration.

Integrity is made possible – or virtually impossible – by social, economic and political structures. Our laws, economy, institutions and public culture express and articulate our ideals and our understanding of what life requires. They form our deepest habits. The increasingly overt and sharp conflicts among the objective interests of different sectors of our society, the presumptive separation of public and private domains block the possibility of integration. Many of us – left, right and centre – believe that this disarray is no accident; it is deeply embedded in our economic arrangements and in our cultural self-presentation and self-understanding. The most powerful and effective moral influence on the possibility of integrity is the economy. Our psychology – as it includes any hopes for integrity – is profoundly influenced by the way that economics drives civic politics. Both, taken together, pervade absolutely every nook and cranny of our lives. We suffer the necessity of fashioning ourselves, forming our abilities and habits in such a way as to make ourselves employable; and worse, we suffer the economy's need to generate the inexhaustible and insatiable desires that define and direct our activities. We have rebaptised greed: it has become the virtue of 'taking the competitive initiative'; we have transformed prudence into short-term monetary cost-benefits analysis; we confuse responsible accountability with ledger income-expenditure accounting. Our role – our place – in the economy shapes our lives; it specifies our virtues, determines our security and pleasures, and results in the kind of recognition we receive. Domestic economy is fixed in a closed pattern that sets the generations at odds: what we give to our children is no longer available for our parents; what we give to our parents diminishes what we have for ourselves. To the extent that any part of the population is hopelessly and structurally excluded from this economically driven civic life, to that extent they have no objective reason to enact its virtues, realistically having no stake in the life those virtues serve and express. Whatever we may say and try to do along the lines of integrity and morality and nobility and goodness and right etc. perforce must – cannot avoid – confronting and complying with the harsh realities of the economic structuring of the 'virtues'. Of course we also continue to admire integrity, to honour fairness, justice, even generosity and kindness. Of course we attempt to promote the ancient virtues, even when we recognise that they are typically exercised at some cost to ourselves. The persona that strives for integration only succeeds in adding yet another voice to the cacophony that is the endeavouring self. Our admiration for the virtues of integrity has become all the more fervent because we recognise that they involve effort and risk . . . and inevitable loss. We wisely try to convince ourselves that virtue is its own reward precisely because we realise that it brings little else.

The point of Dr Cohen's political coda describing the devastation of medical services suggests that the real players in the struggle for human compassion are political, not psychological. Her political coda gets to the heart of the matter: it provides the necessary addition – and correction – to the psychological theory she proposes. We are all – the schools, the universities, the arts, the media – threatened by a political system that is increasingly directed by a market driven economy. Our relations to one another, the minute fabric of our lives, are in grave danger of being directed by short-term narrowly based cost-effective considerations. The readily available integration of a market-defined economic system provides a model for psychological integration – at the cost of the kind of uncompromising moral integrity that refuses cost-benefits analyses.

What should we do? How should we act in the face of these threats? Brecht puts it well: *'Erst kommt das Fressen und dann kommt die Moral'* (first we must eat; and then we can talk about right and wrong). And to make sure that the eats are on the table – that the schools, the social services, the health services – are well financed and structured, we'd do well to lay aside the quest for integration and integrity, and turn to the shrewd hard work of political organisation. We are more likely to be effective in combatting the market-driven turn of what is – to our great shame – scandalously called the 'health-care industry' if we get help from some wheeling, dealing, tough-minded shrewd political organisers, perhaps even from some rogues and thugs whose moral integrity can't bear close scrutiny, and whom we would probably not want as intimate friends or in-laws but whom we desperately need as allies. We need to co-opt a tasteful selection of cold-blooded ruthless people, rich prestigious mass-media moguls like Rupert Murdoch. There is nothing like a little front-office blackmail to preserve what's worth preserving. Certainly moralists agree with the necessity of fairly ruthless political action: but they would add that it must be justified, directed and controlled by moral considerations. But morality is not the only, or even the best control of political thuggery: fear of exposure, sensible calculation or sheer habit will do as well. The insights – the glorious and good work of the world – that now inspire those of us who are bent on integrity were largely the product of wilful, boastful or sniveling egotists, people of low integration and even lower integrity. Having paid homage to morality, we should turn to getting effective powerful thugs (including the thugs within) to work for political reform, appealing to whatever questionable motives we can find. We shouldn't waste time trying to integrate their psychology: doing so might make them less effective. Does this recommendation remain within the frame of integration and compassion, bringing it up a level from the personal to the political? I don't think so. Corrective and corrupt political activity alike are served by pride, by the desire for power, by dreams of great glory. Does integrity differ from corruption in being managed by a crafty, integrated self, striving for its conception of the good? I don't think so: the chaos that we are pleased to call 'the self' is often just along for the ride, desperately grasping whatever crumbs the complex forces – personal and political – throw its way.

As serious educators and citizens, we might reasonably be concerned about the consequences of a general policy of *real psychologie* that has kissed the hope of integration and integrity goodbye. We might well argue that despite our Baroque psychological complexity – indeed because of that complexity – we should promote the ancient 'regulative virtues', developing the habits of honesty, critical reflection and solidarity as best we can. Middle-aged people with good habits can readily, if sadly, shed their illusions; but it is difficult for the middle-aged to acquire good habits when they discover the value of decency. How can we promote decency without its illusions? How can we – in the face of the corrupt habits that we acquire through every turn of economically driven lives – promote the contrary, questioning virtues that striving for integrity was once thought to ensure? Well, we turn to the places that have always moved and enlarged us: to images of exemplary figures (cf. Plutarch's *Lives* and *The Lives of the Saints*), to edifying tales (cf. late Tolstoy), to kindergarten role-playing and to the power of gossip. When mimetic modes and models reveal our many personae, they may – in the best circumstances – provide some counterbalance to the devastations that our contemporary vices paint as luring virtues.

Because Margaret Cohen has so eloquently presented the case for integration and integrity, I have taken the luxury of playing the devil's advocate. Just as Milton's deeply ironic double-play on the name of Satan – his recognising what stands behind our calling the self-proclaimed liberator 'Lucifer', so too, in a far more prosaic voice, integrity requires me to remind the reader that, although integrity is a fine and beautiful thing, it is far from being the only or the best of our projects. Indeed, it is only acceptable when it is constrained in a system of checks and balances, hedged by many apparently contrary moral goods. Complex as we are, our moral and personal projects genuinely and properly pull us in opposite directions. Because a full account of integrity must insist on its limitations, a properly integrated account of integrity must be two-faced. The left hand must take back what the right hand has proffered, and the right hand must again insist on generosity.

Let me end with the right right hand. Having taken Lucifer's role and cast doubt on the connection between integrity and moral goodness, I should, in all banal honesty, also speak on behalf of Abdial, in favor of hope and nobility. With all our reservations, we must nevertheless also join Milton and Margaret Cohen in their estimation of integrity. Most of us are all too clearly aware of our inability to do what we ought to do and our penchant for doing what we ought not to do. We suspect that – as far as the good of the world goes – it makes little difference whether our hearts are pure, whether we are whole-heartedly on the side of Abdial. What is astonishing – what is breath-taking in the midst of our present political darkness – is our persistent desire, our persistent ability to be better than we are, considering the weight of our psychological and political infirmities. Again and again, many among us act beyond our individual and political means, many among us perform actions that we can only call – sensible words are wanting here – noble and beautiful. Those who manage to do such things today cannot count on themselves to do them tomorrow; and as far as the eye can tell, they do not seem to be different from the rest of us fallen spirits. They have little to say about how or why they were able to act as they did: they say 'I saw the fire, I saw the child, of course I had to rush in and get her out.' Or they say: 'I had to keep going; the work was long, it was tedious, it took 20 years of painstak-ing labour, I wrecked the rest of my life over it; I didn't fully understand what I was doing; but of course I had to do it, I had to translate *Remembrance of Things Past* into Hindustani (or join Médicins sans Frontière, or unscramble the genetic code). We do not know how or why some among us side with Abdial, how or why some among us can sometimes surmount our political and economic corruption. Perhaps such people would be revolted if they left undone what manifestly needs to be done; perhaps they just find them-selves in the middle of trouble; perhaps they are possessed by an obsessive admiration; perhaps they are moved by a shudder of fear, perhaps there is no special *reason*, no *because* beyond the large nexus of interlocking causes that *are* the world. If we have theories, they will be general: I rather doubt we can find a theory that can explain or predict the patterns of such individual undertakings; I also doubt that there is one single regimen that could enable those of us who have been systematically malformed by our political economy to do what is right and beautiful. We can be sure of at least one thing: our being able to act well, beyond our means, is not a miracle of clarity or grace sent by an otherwise callous divinity in repentant apology for the harsh-ness of our lives in this, the best of all possible worlds. Yet there it is, the extraordinary human capacity for doing what is simple, what is amazing, what is beautiful and good. Perhaps integrity is nothing more complicated than this: when we are presented with an opportunity to do something that seems helpful or beautiful, we prefer to do that, rather than sit idly by doing nothing, even when things may go badly for us. Nothing may come of it, of course; but other things being equal, we're ready, within the severe limitations of our ability and ignorance, to do a bit of good here and there. Don't count on it when things go badly; but since we are sitting about mul-ling over harsh truths, we must also, in all fairness, celebrate the astonishing, joyous fact that – can we still use these words? – the good, the true and the beautiful sometimes just appear amongst us. The harsh interpretation of moralising integration and integrity is that it is an appeal to a beneficent form of self-deception; the more charitable interpretation is that it reminds us that despite the darkness that is all around us, despite the fact that nothing may come of it, there is room for compassion and goodness; and on the whole – perhaps for no reason at all, and without great hopes for success – we would do well to strive for them and to celebrate them.

References and further reading

Conly, Sarah (1983) 'Utilitarianism and integrity', *The Monist* 66.

Herman, Barbara (1983) 'Integrity and impartiality', *The Monist* 66.

Kekes, John (1983) 'Constancy and Purity', *Mind* 92.

McFall, Lynne (1987) 'Integrity', *Ethics* 98.

Taylor, Gabriele (1971) 'Integrity', *Proceedings of the Aristotelian Society, Supplement* 55.

Walker, Margaret Urban (1989) 'Autonomy or Integrity: A Reply to Slote', *Philosophical Papers* 8.

Walzer, Michael (1973) 'The Problem of Dirty Hands', *Philosophy and Public Affairs*.

Williams, Bernard (1981a) 'Moral Luck', in *Moral Luck*. Cambridge: Cambridge Univeristy Press.

Williams, Bernard (1981b) 'Persons, Character and Morality', in *Moral Luck*. Cambridge: Cambridge University Press.

6 Sense and sensibility

The integrity of vision and response

Fiona Jenkins

The two preceding papers confront us with what, at first sight, seem to be different estimations of the importance of integrity for our moral lives. More fundamentally, their estimations of integrity reflect divergent conceptions of the sphere of action in which moral life is lived. The question they raise is not only that of the importance of integrity in moral life, but the integrity of holding a certain vision of what the moral life demands. Margaret Cohen's rendering of the value of integrity in Chapter 4 suggests that only through it are we open to recognising the moral resonance of experience; her account richly explores the relationship between integrity and the cultivation of powers of judgement, of responsive attitudes, interpretations and sentiments. Amélie Rorty's response in Chapter 5 is, it seems to me, inspired by a profound suspicion of a vision of moral life which makes moral judgement and sentiment central concerns; for on her account, the integrity of our vision of moral life depends upon its being oriented by a concern for practical action, for producing morally desirable states of affairs. The risk of valuing integrity 'too highly' of which Rorty so eloquently reminds us, is in fact the risk of valuing integrity in the wrong way, as though it were sufficient in itself to have 'noble sentiments', or worse, as though it were appropriate to allow noble sentiment to stand in the way of the apparently ignoble actions which our messy moral lives so often demand. Yet the risk of construing moral life so pragmatically is that we lose sight of the importance of what runs counter to pragmatic aims; and that, preoccupied with the worldliness of the world, we forget the need to cultivate a perspective from which to assess, evaluate and interpret our experience. It is of this danger, I believe, that Cohen seeks to warn us. So let me begin by examining how her conception of the prerequisites of moral life informs her account of integrity.

On Margaret Cohen's account, integrity, understood as resting upon the capacity for 'integration', is constitutive of what it is to be fully human. Integration might be said to be presented here as the sign of maturity; it is what the developing human being implicitly aims at in the early stages of infancy as he or she begins to take the measure of world and self, and so too is it the goal of the adult, for whom the task of taking this measure is never complete. The process is very beautifully modelled as one of growing cognisance; this meets, and must overcome, the threat that pain, suffering and the anticipation of death pose for the delicate attempt to apprehend the world as a complex sphere in which a vulnerable life somehow finds its own dignity, its own self, its own sense of both connectedness with and separation from others. The task of the psychotherapist, as Cohen understands it, is to nurture and interpret that process of becoming mature by fostering and displaying two virtues which, her account suggests, require and yet threaten to destroy one another. Honesty and sensibility – a capacity to see truly and a capacity to feel deeply – are ideally brought together in a morally mature response to the world; yet where the experience of feeling deeply is too painful, the eyes of the mind close, cutting off from acknowledgement of the experience provided by sentience. On her account, a delicate sensibility is from the outset fundamental to the capacity to learn about the world, and continues to be so into adulthood; therefore, the impulse to 'shut off', to cease to feel, provisionally blocks and ultimately distorts the learning process because of the fragmentation it produces in what ought ideally to be a rounded and complete view of the world, a view won only by the constant effort to pay attention, to draw the mind back to face what sensibility presents to it. The integrity described here stands, perhaps, for that art of judgement which is based on cultivating and respecting sensibility, all the time attempting to couple its experience, without falsification, to sense – that is, to an honest, coherent interpretation of experience. 'Integration', then, describes the attempt to achieve a view of the world that can be formed only when honesty and sensibility cooperate with one another; it implies that the self is to some significant extent in control of and responsible for what it becomes, that 'effort' is appropriate in striving towards this form of maturity, and that the powers we possess for identification with, and distancing from, different parts or aspects of experience are the proper objects of moral discipline. Here a cognitive and a moral purpose are conjoined with one another. Only by 'integrat[ing] our different experiences [do we] gain an idea of ourselves and the world we live in' (Chapter 4, this volume, p. 88).

What kind of a good is integrity on this account? In brief, with integrity we both display and are enabled to move towards the goal of a moral maturity which has important cognitive as well as dispositional elements. If the end is maturity, integrity might be said to be both a necessary means to that end and constitutive of it. With integrity we both display and take forward the history of our attempt to become mature, for, the thesis suggests, without that history of effort, of striving for 'integration', we would be incapable of – would lack the relevant capacities for – successful performance. Capacities, which are at the outset natural, as illustrated in the example of the babies' struggles to 'integrate' experience, require reinforcement, nurture, assistance, response and guidance if they are to develop properly. Properly directed effort is achievement, hence the apparent ambiguity Cohen notes in her account as to whether integrity resides in the effort to recognise painful experience or in success in so doing. What is being described here is a process; the account of integrity appears within the context of a teleological conception of human life. With integrity we do not become 'better' simply because integrity is a socially desired or useful virtue; rather, with integrity we become better by becoming more responsible for who and what we are, and this in turn by cultivating the capacity for understanding – in a morally rich sense – the world in which we find ourselves. On my reading, it is essential to Cohen's claims about the theory and practice of psychotherapy that its form of knowledge is based not merely on empirical evidence, but on sensibility; direct experience is informed and maintained by an attitude which protects and preserves the capacity for keeping one's eyes open with one's feelings available, precisely because that is what is demanded by the nature of morally relevant experience. Whatever good consequences follow from the possession of integrity must follow from the value, efficacy and significance of this kind of insight and disposition.

Let us suppose for the moment, then, that the value, efficacy and significance of that outlook upon the world is rather limited, and not least because the world which we actually inhabit (the 'real world') is one which cannot in general be relied upon to do other than exploit, deride, take advantage of, betray and manipulate the morally sensitive. Given this, we might imagine that far from being a guide to the world, the form of cultivation encouraged on Cohen's model could in fact be one strategy a society can practice against its members' interests (without there necessarily being any conscious intent to do so, but perhaps merely as a result of the unpunishable vices of naivety and optimism). If this is the 'real world', then to seek 'integration', or to be pre-occupied with one's own integrity, is to withdraw from that world, to pursue a private interest, rather than a public and properly political goal; it is to buy into the moralistic myth that tells us that the path to social justice is for each individual to become 'moral' (whereas in truth by that myth we are individually and collectively disempowered); it is to privilege virtue for its own sake over the ends that virtues ought to serve, and which, since virtues serve only in specific contexts, can never unequivocally be deemed 'good' or 'bad'. On Amélie Rorty's account, it may indeed be considered desirable to produce the circumstances under which it is possible for people to exhibit the virtue of integrity; for integrity is a 'fine and beautiful thing'. And yet it is 'far from being the best of our projects' (Chapter 5, this volume, p. 118). What has to take priority over the pursuit and concern for integrity – which, if we are lucky, produces 'beautiful souls' – are the practical tasks associated with producing desirable states of affairs. Too much 'sensibility', too many scruples, moral squeamishness – are all, on our second account, very dangerous things. Indeed, the rhetorical thrust of this 'paean to Lucifer' is that far from being indicative of strength and honesty, the alleged 'virtues' of integrity are indicative of dispositional and cognitive weakness, and it remains a little unclear why we should even want to create the circumstances under which it becomes possible to display them. Good sense would seem to leave them little place.

It is important to notice how Rorty has shifted the emphasis placed on the terms of analysis of integrity and the context in which it is to be evaluated. Cohen's account of the matter, which I have construed in terms of the cultivation of an orientation towards the world that possesses both cognitive and dispositional depth, is here required to answer to a functional analysis of the social virtue of integrity. I shall take up the question of how it might do so shortly. But let us first consider the exact nature of Rorty's target.

Rorty gives integrity a functional analysis because she believes that our valuations of the virtues naturally are, and rightly ought to be, informed by the consequences and successful results of the projects we undertake. Integrity, she suggests, is assumed to be valuable because it is assumed that its possession by individuals offers beneficial results to the whole society, effects which are supposed to follow from individuals subjugating their selfish, egotistical and amoral motivations for the sake of higher moral concerns. Unclear as we have become in modern times about just what these higher moral concerns demand (for our actions are no longer thought to be informed by 'the assurance of the justice of divine law', by objective moral truths) we have come to value integrity for the sheer effort it represents, for what we assume to be the intrinsic value of the difficult struggle against amoral instincts that threaten to overwhelm us. But, as Rorty wittily shows, this picture and its evaluations beg many questions. It is assumed, for example, that internal conflict (between 'good' and 'bad' impulses) precedes the moral demand that we strengthen the good by resisting the temptation of the bad; and that the 'bad' impulses (those of egotism, violence, anti-sociability etc.) are those that divide and threaten the integration of our nature. But supposing that these 'bad' impulses are – as indeed Cohen believes – entirely natural, an essential part of who we are, then might not our overriding concern to discipline and master them actually introduce internal conflict between what are alleged to be 'moral' and what are alleged to be 'immoral' impulses? Might we not, in relentless pursuit of integrity, generate unnecessary antagonism, increasing inner conflict, and decreasing 'integration' by our resistance to impulses which have – perhaps without good reason – been first labelled 'bad', and subsequently assumed to be the causes of 'disintegration'?

Her question, then, concerns the true source of the rationale of a psychology which divides 'good' and 'bad' impulses along the same lines as those required by the social valuation of integrity; can these really be the same as the 'good' and 'bad' which would contribute to individual psychic harmony or 'integration'? And do we erroneously believe that the achievement of integration is important because we accept a social valuation of integrity which is itself misguided? From these sceptical thoughts two lines of argumentation follow. One line starts by asking whether 'integration', or a disposition to consistency, or self-honesty, or any of the other alleged values which are held to contribute to the good of the self, really do so – and answers that this cannot be resolved independently of the circumstances in which the individual finds herself. Sometimes compartmentalisation, inconsistency or self-deception would serve the good of the self much better. Indeed, what counts as the 'good of the self' cannot be separated from the context of goal-directed activity in which it is considered, hence the gravity of the error involved in retreating from politics to consider independently the psychological conditions of flourishing. The second line of argument challenges the assumption that egotistical or even amoral impulses are rightly labelled 'bad'; for do not such impulses as these have an essential role to play in creating the kind of society in which we wish to live? Rorty contrasts the sheer natural energy of the amoral egotist with what she portrays as the incapacitating effect of a crippling moral discipline that, in the end, risks serving no purpose, not even what it takes to be its own. The moral war, fought against one's own perceived immorality, is comically depicted as losing on all fronts.

We are asked to face – and have what might be called the 'meta-ethical' integrity to face – a set of 'hard truths' which are deeply unsettling to our moral world-view. For on this account, the moral respect for integrity as a 'good in itself' which also has desirable consequences (the reward being reaped in terms of what is thought of as psychological flourishing) inspires a set of erroneous evaluations and interpretations that shape to calamitous effect our conception of the demands of moral life. We falsely assume that the virtues that contribute to the achievement of morally desirable results are identical with those that are involved in the moral war against ourselves, when there is no reason to suppose that the process of acquiring 'virtue' in the latter sense has anything to do with the Machiavellian 'virtu' necessary for the former. We are led, for bad reasons, to resist our natural egoistic impulses to self-interest and self-preservation, thereby increasing our inner conflict and weakening our power to influence events. We come to value moral effort for itself, having long ago lost any clear sense of the value of states of affairs to which effort ought to be directed; for we assume that moral values are more important than any others, and believe them to be realised in actions that we applaud as a pursuit of 'virtue for its own sake', however practically hopeless they may be. We overlook the fact that there are genuine conflicts between equally valid goods and duties, and become grievously dishonest when we forget that in real life it is necessary to adapt constantly to new circumstances, to muddle through, to try any variety of means, even when these seem dubious, in order to obtain valued goals.

Rorty's paean to Lucifer is, in the end, a paean to the kind of meta-ethical integrity that recognises the importance of these difficult truths, and dismisses the all-too tempting myth of the relevance to moral life of heroic integrity. Her account parades its seeming moral perversity in order to trumpet all the more clearly that this is a stubbornly honourable form of political scepticism. We ought not to base any of the more serious expectations we employ in regulating social and political institutions on the unstable and unpredictable quantity of human goodness; and in so far as we rightly attempt, as parents, teachers or leaders, to inculcate a moral character which we hope might at some time lend itself to 'noble and beautiful' action, we do so out of the undeluded recognition that the 'beneficent self-deceptions' of moral conviction are, at best, occasionally useful rudders in waters which only a practical and pragmatic intelligence can properly be trusted to chart.

These are all points well made, and, it seems to me, are proper criticisms of a certain set of distortions that readily attach to our understanding of virtues when, expecting too much of them, we strip them from their legitimate contexts of application and try to make them do the work of redemption. But it is not obvious that the account Rorty gives of the genesis and function of a pre-occupation with 'psychological' integrity is accurate or just with respect to the conceptions animating Cohen's account of the relationship between integration and integrity. The way in which Rorty envisages the person of integrity as rather helplessly debilitated with respect to the achievement of certain goals may not be entirely relevant to the kind of practice that Cohen describes, where the 'goals' appear to be of a different order. This is not merely a question of the differences between the spheres of political and of psychotherapeutic practice, where the very different duties and aims involved will indeed frame the relevant notion of what practical applications of 'integrity' (the integrity which attaches to our everyday ability to carry out a defined role) entail in quite distinct ways. Rather, there seems to be an important divergence – important for meta-ethical reasons to do with our vision of the moral life – between the attention which is paid in the two accounts to different models of action. At the centre of Rorty's concern is a form of consequentialism or what we might call 'action in pursuit of goals', and, crudely put, it entails that the bottom-line for any test of virtue is whether it contributes to getting what we want (where we can make the notion of 'what we want' as morally rich as we like; we may want, for example, to be 'beautiful souls'), but we had better be clear about whether we really want this for the reasons that we think we do and that we fully understand the practical conditions for achieving it. By contrast, at the centre of Cohen's account we find action which, to be sure, does not lack goals (in so far as it is directed to a practice of caring, nurturing and interpreting development, and must judge itself by its criteria of success in achieving results in these fields) but which is thought to result from a capacity for responsiveness. On Cohen's model, appropriate action would seem to be guided by responsiveness rather than, in the first instance, by the positing of goals. Integrity, then, is to be thought of as the expression of a degree of responsiveness which must itself be constantly developed and maintained, and which it involves effort to maintain.

But what, we might reasonably ask, does that 'effort' aim at? Here we need to answer carefully, because it could be made to look as though this is effort directed to the private aim of 'integration', the only apparent alternative being that this effort be directed at practical, public goals in Rorty's sense; in either case a whole set of sceptical questions arise about what integrity 'achieves', which risk distorting its special character. It helps to clarify the first issue to point out that 'integration' is not a state but an activity; as an activity it could be said to move towards the end of maturity, but not because that state is posited as a goal (any more than integration is itself a goal); rather, moral maturity increases as the capacity to experience events both deeply and honestly increases. The meta-ethical significance of this, I take it, is that it suggests the relevance to our understanding of integrity in moral life of an account of the art, sources and resources of evaluative judgement and of moral sensibility. What Cohen highlights in this respect is the co-dependency of cognitive and responsive abilities, the ability to see clearly being linked to the ability to interpret honestly, drawing on an openness to experience which risks becoming blocked through various forms of 'weakness' – cowardice, selfishness or simply fear and exhaustion. Moreover, integrity is construed here as entailing a demand and not merely as a virtue. What it demands is not, in every instance, something that could be recognised within Rorty's framework of goal-directed action; the demand for acknowledgement of one person's situation by another person and the communication of that acknowledgement together entail a pattern of responsiveness to situations of distress even where no 'successful' outcome can be anticipated. Indeed, it is this special aspect of moral life which Cohen's discussion brings so compellingly to the fore. Moral 'effort' is needed in part because we are not always offered the solace of a 'practical' course of action; and it is often the very desire for a practical solution which leads us to deny the reality of what is happening before us, and thus to fail to acknowledge what is available to us to know. Cohen's thesis is that the activity of confronting our passivity is essential to moral development; that it forms a crucial element in our apprehension of moral life which we risk entirely omitting when we 'go blind' on the experience of helplessness.

It is true that a complex set of empirical claims are entailed in specifying the viability of combining qualities in moral development, qualities which, both writers point out, are in tension with one another. We can on no account simply assume an easy relationship between the cultivation of honesty, of sensibility and, equally importantly, of a capacity to pursue courses of action which are very definitely goal-directed. Much of Rorty's argument is engaged in pointing out that the recipe for moral agency is one that requires some trickery in the cooking. Compassion, she notes, is an energetically draining activity which, given our limited resources, exists in competition with the equally draining demands of honesty; the latter, moreover, always threatens to magnify other sources of stress beyond the point that we can bear. Thus, since (goal-directed) compassion is more important in moral life than (moralistically-cherished) honesty, where conflict arises we must maintain compassion at whatever cost to honesty; our recipes must be practical, and being the creatures that we are, 'compassion is often sustained by a little healthy myopia, if not downright blindness, to the ways in which we systematically mistreat each other' (Rorty, Chapter 5 this volume, p. 115).

In order to demonstrate the limitations of this conclusion, I think we must try to answer its concerns at three distinct levels. In the first place we should concede that the recipe for moral education is complex and involves much empirical psychology. But second, we must try to indicate the relationship between what we try to bring the moral agent to be through our recipes for cultivation, and our understanding of the morally relevant features of the world he or she encounters and should be equipped to respond to. Third, we need an account of the importance of 'moral responsiveness' both in informing and directing certain kinds of practical goals and as having significance in itself. We need to say what it is about integrity that transcends pragmatic considerations; and not, I would suggest because it is 'beautiful' but rather because moral life takes its direction at least in part from demands that lie beyond what is ordinarily possible. In conclusion, I shall sketch an outline of such an account.

Cohen would readily concede, I think, that sometimes compassion may need to be sustained by blindness, when a person is not strong enough to cope with what would be seen; but, she suggests, it is better that people should see — see what is around and within them — since only when they do can they make truly sensitive and well-informed decisions. At a very concrete level, the cost of 'blindness' amongst doctors — developed as a self-protective response to intractable problems — is that they become less good at the job of caring. One might explain how honesty enters here into a constructive relationship with practical activity in the following way. There is a need in health care for a 'tragic consciousness', comprising an ability to witness suffering, to accept inevitability, and irreducible conflict, whilst at the same moment maintaining an ability to struggle to do what is best, to make the efforts needed to help and care. One function of 'honesty' here is simply to maintain the space of validity in which two conflicting impulses may both openly operate without eliminating one another, and without the need for the sort of self-deception that would disable one of them: On the one hand, the desire to do what's best (a practical urge which supports itself by reducing the appearance of conflict, removing inconvenient points of view, and so forth); and, on the other hand, the capacity for acceptance, exercised in the recognition that sometimes very little can be altered, but much can be done by 'standing by' a person's suffering, sharing the experience in the awed and grieving mood of tragedy. This attitude can too easily be mistaken for, or even become, defeatism, a ground for despair, but it is surely an essential part of caring that it should involve acknowledgement, validating an activity that may fail to cure but which nonetheless responds to helplessness. Here the 'endeavouring self' is forced to recognise risk and loss as the other dimension of its efforts, or cultivate a blindness that deprives its work of the light of moral apprehension. Within the framework of this conflict, honesty serves compassion in as much as acknowledgement is part of compassion's work.

I think we can take these considerations further in order to approach the special nature of integrity – its non-practical, impossibly demanding character, which leads it to transcend pragmatic evaluation. Let us concede Rorty's point that the virtues conducive to the achievement of certain practical ends may not be identical with those of integrity, and that, since to possess certain virtues is to be one kind of person rather than another, it may be unimaginable that a single individual could embody both sorts of virtue. Let us concede, too, that every practical achievement has social conditions and does not depend upon the individual alone. Can we, nonetheless, imagine a form of moral integrity that may be acknowledged to be more or less ineffective to prevent evil, and, in addition, be considered to be so demanding, that it is more or less impossible to expect that people will demonstrate it; and yet which may, despite this, or perhaps even for these reasons, be urgently and unequivocally called for?

It seems characteristic of the demand of integrity that it calls for us to do what is almost impossible yet utterly morally necessary. *The Drowned and the Saved*, Primo Levi's great work of despairing but resolutely humane judgement, seems to me to be written in the spirit of this paradox. Levi speaks of the fabrications of memory whereby it becomes possible for the perpetrators and also the victims of terrible crimes to learn to live with the past. Such 'lies' are, as he remarks, quite natural; to be able to forget the truth and construct a bearable alternative is a condition of living sanely at all, until the 'stories' that are told become part of the furniture of the mind, its only 'memory', and cannot be attributed to bad faith. Indeed, 'the distinction between good faith and bad faith seems optimistic', for, he writes:

> It presupposes a mental clarity which few have, and which even those few immediately lose when, for whatever reason, past or present reality arouses anxiety or discomfort in them. Under such conditions there are, it is true, those who lie consciously, coldly falsifying reality itself, but more numerous are those who weigh anchor, move off, momentarily or forever, from genuine memories and fabricate for themselves a convenient reality. . . . To keep good and bad faith distinct costs a lot: it requires a decent sincerity or truthfulness with oneself, it demands a continuous intellectual and mental effort.
>
> (Levi 1992: 14–15)

There are many people, he concludes, of whom one cannot expect even the attempt at accurate recollection of past events, for both amongst the perpetrators and the victims of crimes the majority lack the resources and capacities for this effort.

Nonetheless, there remains something that we might fairly call a duty of integrity on both sides. This is linked to the need to account for and to recount past crimes, and it is incurred by the witnesses to, the victims of and the agents of those events. The victim has, Levi believes, a right to be allowed to forget painful memories; yet in doing so she may neglect the important duty of 'standing witness' to the crime and in this way 'standing by' others who suffered from it. The perpetrator, on the other hand, has no right to alleviate his mental pain by forgetting or denying responsibility; the requirement that he should face the truth and acknowledge his deeds as his own is essential to his proper punishment. We find obscene his attempt to excuse himself as the product of his environment, or his actions as the necessity of bowing to orders, though we may offer him our acknowledgment of these pressures.

Integrity, on this account, must put up resistance to the phenomena and forces that ought to be recognised as bad and wrong, even if it is bound to lose in a battle against them. Indeed, Levi's concern is more with the integrity which acknowledges what a human being ought to know, than with the integrity which instigates defiant practical resistance. Even disregarding the question of whether isolated and ordinary individuals might have successfully acted against the Nazi regime, their failure, not only to act, but to see, feel or think condemns them in Levi's eyes. The distinction between good faith and bad faith may be optimistic; nonetheless, it cannot be renounced, for a great deal that is significant in moral life hangs upon maintaining it. The form of effort demanded here is directed at maintaining a truthful, sensitive and responsible moral perspective and, taking its direction from a conception of moral maturity, its judgement transcends social circumstances. Indeed, the historical example strongly indicates that integrity cannot be allowed to be only as good as the society that fosters it, though equally it illustrates a point upon which the two previous papers firmly agree – that we must directly oppose the creation of social circumstances in which it is difficult for integrity to flourish. Thus we may concede that the pressure a totalitarian state can exercise over the individual is truly frightful, that it saps the strength of resistance, and that this is an essential part of what is terrible about it; but at the same time we do not need to accept that during the 12-year term of the Third Reich it had become impossible for the very many people who were directly or indirectly implicated in its crimes, both to see or guess at the sort of atrocities that were being committed and to see that these were truly terrible, unjustifiable crimes. The capacity for taking a good hard look at what is going on, for seeing honestly what is happening to other people, what their sufferings are, how things must be from their point of view, as well as what has happened to oneself, what one has done or not done – all these are essential elements of the kind of integrity Cohen characterises.

Supposing it is right to think that integrity is, at least in certain critical circumstances, amongst the most important moral demands, it is clear that this is not because it comprises the kind of skills that successfully overthrow a ruling political party. Its importance lies, rather, with a form of reflection that 'witnesses' honestly and in a way that implies the practical necessity of adopting certain attitudes. We should be very wary of suggesting that it is sufficient to take up a moral attitude or pass moral judgement as distinct from taking practical action. Nonetheless, the attitude is important in itself, as well as informing a disposition to action. In holding it to be the case that witnesses, as well as agents, of Nazi war crimes ought to have responded with horror and outrage to the evil being perpetrated before their eyes, and to accuse them of a failure of integrity in not having so responded, we do not commit ourselves to belief in some 'divine law' which would clearly differentiate good from evil actions; rather, we suppose that there is a relationship between the internal structure of a person's character and her ability to judge something to be an evil; and in certain extreme circumstances at least, we hold ourselves to be entitled to judge the failure to pass judgement, the failure to witness, the failure of moral maturity.

Reference

Levi, Primo (1992) *The Drowned and the Saved*. London: Abacus.

Section II
Integrity in the presentation of information

7 Integrity in the presentation of news and current affairs

Hilary Lawson

Lost in the web of language, it would be foolish to imagine that we might give a definitive account of integrity. As if with sufficient care and analysis we might tease out its real meaning, and thereby determine how to behave. Yet we are always at risk of this dream, which would enable us to impose our story on others and, incredibly, on reality. Under the guise of 'rationality' or 'analysis' the attempt is frequently made in moral discussion to generate a view, an account, a theory, which will validate our own behaviour, or more precisely our own desired behaviour, and which it is imagined might be used to force others, and (grandiosely) society as a whole, to behave in a similar fashion. The notion that the true meaning of integrity can be uncovered and that rules for behaviour might thus be provided, expresses a desire for power and security: the power to force others to behave as we wish, and the security that we know how they should behave. A desirable and tempting dream perhaps, but a dream nevertheless and one not without its risks. Instead of dreams we have only stories, even when wrapped up as papers and essays. Each story is but one of countless possible narratives distinguished not by an illusory truth or falsity, but by its own particular emotional and theoretical impact. The account of integrity outlined here makes no claim to be other than one such story.

In an attempt to escape the notion that the true meaning of integrity might be uncovered, instead of 'meaning' we shall refer to 'closure'. When we speak of the meaning of a term, there is the impression that the term refers to some distinct identifiable concept. It thus becomes possible to suppose that the term can be analysed, thereby uncovering the real nature of the concept. From the standpoint of this chapter, however, meaning is more elusive. Not only are we unable to discern a single discrete meaning for a term in all its uses, but even in a particular instance meaning is undecidable. So long as we can access a fixed framework of meanings it is possible to propose that we might uncover, or define, the meaning of integrity in some ultimate manner. Such a goal is an illusion. The term 'integrity', like all other terms, is a plaything. It is linked to other terms, but the linkage is loose and available to change. We can do what we will with it, and in the process its very character changes. The term is available for play, and when we play with it, it seemingly becomes something in particular. A particularity which, on closer inspection, itself evaporates. Closure is what we make of the plaything. Unlike meaning, closure is active. Closures are not waiting for us to discover them, but are generated through our own activity. Meaning seemingly points outwards to the world or reality, as if it is a second best, as if what meaning meant was to be found elsewhere. Closure in contrast is nothing other than itself. There is no limit to the number of closures that can be realised from a unit of language, be it a word, a sentence or a book. The plaything is not anything in particular, but a place of potentiality, an opening. Through closure the potential is made concrete, the opening is closed. Closure takes place, therefore, not in the context of reality, but in the context of that which is not closed, which is open.

So having begun, let us begin. At first glance it is not difficult to identify characteristics that we associate with integrity in journalists. Fiction is not peddled as fact; the opinions expressed are their own and have not been bought, or acquired, for the sake of the audience; the material is not presented out of malice or a desire to damage those involved; the individuals quoted or interviewed have not been misrepresented or have themselves been misled or duped. All of these appear to centre around matters of truth. As a consequence we might understandably be tempted to regard truth as the most salient characteristic of integrity in a journalist. What could be simpler? A journalist should tell the truth to others in the obtaining of a story and should present the truth in writing or filming it. If, however, we understand by the term 'truth' some simple notion of objectivity we will be disappointed.

In the familiar terminology of language and reality, the journalist offers a description of reality which may be said to be more or less accurate. The problem with this account is that it makes it look as though journalists could arrive at a true account, as if their descriptions could somehow escape the particularities of time, place and subject, and convey not merely a version of events, but the events as they actually happened. Journalists have traditionally encouraged this view, hiding behind an apparently strict fact/value distinction, with the consequence that they can avoid responsibility for the story by presenting merely the facts of the matter.

As any junior reporter is only too painfully aware, however, the description of an event is not simply a technical exercise in which facts are documented. Even assuming for a moment that the facts are available and waiting to be accessed, which they are not, a journalist must select from a multitude of supposed facts those that are most important or most salient. An account of the Bosnian crisis in terms of the colour of tie worn by the Bosnian Serb spokesman, however true the description, would be unlikely to satisfy either the editor or those seeking integrity. Yet it is difficult to imagine an explanation of how this process of selection could be other than subjective. Are we to suppose that out there in the world there is a hierarchy of facts which in some definite fashion fixes what is important? Such a proposal is surely not credible.

What is important about an event must vary from individual-to-individual, from culture-to-culture, from one historical period to another.

An example may make the case clearer. On the night of the fall of the Berlin Wall should it have been described as the end of the Cold War, the collapse of the Eastern Bloc, the dawn of a new era or the uniting of Germany? On the first night when crowds surrounded the wall none of these events had taken place and yet to have described the event as 'a breakdown in security at the East German border in Berlin' would surely have avoided all that was important in what was taking place. Indeed, one suspects that just such an account may have been given in the Eastern Bloc itself. What the fall of the Berlin Wall 'meant' for a Turkish family living in East Germany was something quite different from what it was for the inheritors of the Zeiss corporation who could see the return of their old factories in the East; and again different for American hawks like Pat Buchanan who saw it as the victory of democracy, and for East German party members for whom it was the end of a life's work. The 'fall of the Berlin Wall' has become the name of the event, although in practice, of course, the wall did not fall, nor was it even broken down until months later. What happened on that night depends on who you are, and it is not possible to access the event independently of all such particularities of culture and individual.

So it is with all description, for descriptions require a selection of facts, and that selection will entail an implicit hierarchy of facts. It is not credible to imagine that this hierarchy is itself a fact in the world. To make a somewhat tedious logical point, such a proposal would involve an infinite regress, since the fact containing the hierarchy would itself require a further fact to determine its importance and so on. But one does not have to rely on such logical tricks to see that there can be no one correct description. In the case of the Berlin Wall how could one begin to formulate what took place without reference to some particular set of concerns. The event as described by a historian, a sociologist or a physicist, would be quite different in character, each calling upon their own set of supposed facts. Nor are the facts mutually agreed, but are themselves closures, ways of seeing the world as a means to understand and intervene in it.

It is tempting to imagine that beneath all these different possible descriptions there is a single event which, stripped of its significance, might be described in some independent manner. As if, taking a God's eye view, one could look down on the Earth and describe what had actually happened, and only then formulate what were the consequences for all of the various parties. No such perspective is, however, possible. There is no Archimedean point or, for that matter, neutral language, which enables such a perspective. However the event is described, the description will embody the assumptions, prejudices, and understanding of the observer. It is not merely that the facts will be placed in a different hierarchy, but that the facts themselves will be different. For the most trivial event an unlimited number of 'facts' can be generated, an unlimited number of closures – although to express it in this manner is in itself misleading. For it gives the impression that behind a description or set of descriptions there is a single event, the sort of event to which the name 'the fall of the Berlin Wall' apparently refers. The notion, however, of a real event beyond the closure is unnecessary and misleading metaphysical baggage. Instead, we should be content with the notion that the journalist offers a text which, if realised, provides a closure or set of closures, which take their place alongside our previous closures and make up our personal space. The closure realised does not refer to something 'other', something out there in the world, but provides a stopping point, a means of holding that which is open, of containing it, of enclosing it for the time being. The enclosure offered by the text is not a version of reality, a second order and hazy version of the real thing, but is a way of seeing, a way that we can be. The phrase 'the fall of the Berlin Wall' is one way of holding a part of recent history, another is 'the end of the Cold War'. There is no 'basic' event that lies behind these closures and which could some-how be accurately described. To paraphrase T.S. Eliot, history is a pattern of intersecting closures (Eliot 1974).

For many who are aggrieved at the coverage of political events, the idea that there is no correct description of an event is not a conclusion that can be easily accepted. They wish to argue that the coverage did not tell the truth. The report interviewed the wrong people. It failed to mention key important facts. The journalist responsible lacked integrity. Often all that is meant by such remarks is that the individuals do not share the closures implied by the coverage, that it was not their perspective. It is for this reason that leading figures in both of the major political parties are of the opinion that the media is biased against them. Such views would be laughable if they were not so widely held.

The notion that a journalist should simply tell the truth, in the sense of providing an accurate account of reality, is not therefore a sustainable position, however straightforward and commonsensical it may at first appear. Instead of looking to objective truth to provide a framework for integrity we will make more headway with the intellectually unfashionable notion of personal or subjective truth. A subjective account of integrity, integrity as truth to oneself, has the advantage that it appeals to the notion of wholeness and singularity with which one assumes the term itself originates. In this sense, to have integrity is to approach singleness of self, to be integral to one-self. To say one thing and do another, or to express a view which one does not hold, is thus a challenge to our integrity. Integrity in this sense is not dependent on objective truth, whether defined in realist terms or in the pragmatists' language of socially agreed statements.

One aspect of being true to oneself is that we should not say one thing and do another, for to do so is to introduce a division in the self. In this context, journalistic integrity requires that the text of a journalist (be it article, report or programme) does not offer closures which are not themselves realised by the author. In this respect journalistic integrity operates on the same basis that we apply to communication in general. Communication on a personal or public level involves a principle of charity. We make the assumption that the closure offered is both possible and realised by the speaker or writer. If, for example, someone says to us 'London is a box', we search for a way of realising closure. We may be unsure – is this an architectural closure perhaps, or a geographical point about the difficultly of getting in and out of a large city? – and as a result leave the text open awaiting further clues to a closure. Only the perversely pedantic would choose to say that the claim was factually incorrect. We assume not only the possibility of closure, but that closure has been realised by the speaker or writer. In the vocabulary of meaning this would be expressed by saying that we assume that an individual holds what is being said or written to be true. One of the differences between closure and meaning is that closures are always true, if they are realised by an individual. In the context of meaning, truth and falsehood are almost accidental characteristics which happen to attach to the sentence. Closure makes this relation less mysterious. In order to have realised a closure we must think it, we must hold the world to be like this. We cannot, therefore, realise a closure which is false, for, having realised the closure, we are holding the world in this manner; for us, therefore, it is true, for it is how the world is. Once we have realised 'London is a box', it is a box. Of course, later we may abandon the closure as false, but if we do so, we will no longer be able to realise it, we will merely be able to utter the words, we will not be able to think them. We know the meaning of the sentence 'London is the capital of France', but we cannot realise it as a closure, we are unable to see the world in this way. Unless perhaps we are attending a speech by a French banker on the dominance of the City.

Integrity, as the principle that individuals should realise the closures offered by their own texts, is in a journalistic context both less stringent than many will desire and more stringent than we can expect. The middle ground we can settle quickly. There are doubtless occasions when journalists (more commonly, one hopes, of the tabloid variety) deliberately concoct stories that they know to be false. In such circumstances they presumably do not realise closure from their own text. We can presumably all agree that this is both a challenge to their integrity and something of which we do not approve. A small caveat we should add to this conclusion is that the text is offered in order that it should be realised. Humour, irony, sarcasm, are modes of expression that do not require the listener or speaker to realise closure, or at least not in any straightforward manner. A journalist who concocts a story headlined 'Second World War Bomber Found on the Moon' may reasonably argue that their integrity has not been undermined by such a fabrication, since readers recognise that it is not intended to be held as true and are merely entertained.

One of the advantages of a subjective account of integrity is that it does not require us to give an account of what it is to misrepresent someone, or to provide a false description, an advantage, since such an account is not possible.

So long as the journalist is able to realise their own text, no misrepresentation has occurred, while if they are not capable of realising the text, it is false. The weakness some will argue with such an account is that it does not guarantee a version of events consistent with current social norms or with what we might describe as the rational liberal consensus. While this is the case, little is gained by the traditional defence of objective truth, and we are still able to counter views we believe to be wrong. Let me take an extreme example.

Let us suppose that a journalist propounds the view that the Holocaust never happened. In the absence of an objective criterion of integrity we are seemingly in the uncomfortable position of not being able to deny the integrity of the journalist on the grounds that the claim is false. We are not, however, in the position of saying that anything goes. If the individual fails to realise their own text, something which we can identify from their behaviour – how they communicate with their friends, whether other statements appear to contradict the present claim and so forth, then its subjective falsity is straightforward with consequent damage to integrity. If, however, the claim is realised by the individual the matter is more complex. It may be that the socially agreed facts are unknown to the individual, or that they are disputed, or that new facts are believed. Once it allows the claim to be realised it is apparent that we are in a position to combat it. If the journalist denies the existence of Auschwitz, and on being taken to the current site still denies its existence, we may be unable to make sense of the claim and dismiss it, not as false but as nonsense. In any case it would fail the principle of charity. We would conclude that the individual had not realised the text either and as a consequence integrity had been undermined. If, however, the individual argued that the present watchtowers and railways lines were built by the victors of the war to humiliate the Germans, further evidence would need to be addressed. Nor is there a limit to such a line of argument. No matter how much evidence is produced, it will always be possible to defend the original claim in support of the initial closure: documents produced are false, or inaccurate, witnesses are themselves involved in a conspiracy, and so forth. Such a defence will, though, require increasingly preposterous claims, and increasing consequential damage to the other closures within the personal space of the individual concerned; but such a response is, in principle, possible.

Can we be content with an account of integrity that would allow such a bizarre and distasteful consequence? Do we not want to be able to say that Auschwitz did exist, that millions were deliberately murdered and that to deny such an event is not a matter of perspective, or selection, but simply false? While it is comforting to imagine that we can outlaw descriptions simply by defining them as false, no purpose is served by such a manoeuvre. The SS guard may account for his own behaviour on the grounds that these individuals were not human. That such a claim has hideous consequences does not thereby mean that it cannot be held to be true, that closure cannot be realised. Furthermore, it is precisely because it is possible to realise such a view that we feel so strongly about its denial. If the SS guard was merely stating something false, we could regard it as an error which could be corrected. We reject it because of the implications it has for personal and social behaviour, not because it is unrealisable or false. We can as a consequence describe the perspective as abhorrent, but we cannot outlaw its realisation, as if we could thereby make it impossible.

A subjective account of integrity may not enable us to rule out views with which we disagree on the grounds that they are false, but we are not, as a result, impotent in the face of such claims. Moreover, the traditional response – the assertion of truth or falsity – is not an effective way of countering those who have realised a different closure. For them it is not false, but true, and the mere assertion of the opposite is more likely to end in violence than in communication. A neo-Nazi unaware of the evidence may be capable of entertaining beliefs which later will be abandoned when faced with socially agreed facts. In this sense the initial belief was in error. It is always possible, however, to deny the agreed facts and to retain the initial view by proposing an alternative closure. For this reason to say that Hitler was in error would be to sanitize his behaviour, as if had he only been told the true situation, he would have abandoned his view. The abandonment of objective truth inherent in a subjective account of integrity may make us feel less assured, but it does not leave us any more exposed to those who choose to adopt closures we find abhorrent.

It is proposed, therefore, that we consider integrity to be concerned with the unity of the self and not with the nature of the closures offered. It is for this reason that the requirement of integrity, as we have described it, may for some be a less stringent condition than they would like. Yet it surely cannot be the case that integrity is only to be attributed to those whose closures we share. Can a Tory supporter not grudgingly accept the integrity of a Michael Foot, or a Labour supporter that of an Enoch Powell?

The real problems with journalistic integrity as the realisation of one's own text is not that it is not stringent enough, but that it is too stringent a condition. Many, perhaps almost all, roles in society require the partial abandonment of this aspect of integrity. Someone selling or advertising a product is not in a position to express all the reservations that they might entertain. A manager working for a large corporation cannot publicly make criticisms of the company. And, in the academic world, for example, are one's real views of colleagues and their work expressed? In each case the requirement to realise one's own text is tempered by beliefs about, for example, how other people should be treated, what doing a good job entails, and notions about what you are trying to achieve.

Certain social roles are directly in conflict with integrity as the realisation of one's own text. The spy provides perhaps the most clear-cut example, since his professional activity requires consistent failure to realise his own text, but the same is true of the barrister or the judge, the doctor or the nurse.

The barrister may believe a client to be guilty, but will propose otherwise in court. The judge may also believe the charged to be guilty, but on account of the law may be constrained from so advising the jury. The doctor and the nurse may know that a patient is in serious danger, but put forward a more optimistic account. A journalist is in a similar predicament. Frequently journalists are required to ensure that their personal views do not impinge on their text. Usually for example a report on the Tory party conference is not expected to vary on account of the views of the reporter, or coverage of the passage of a bill through the House to be dependent on the political persuasion of the individual involved. Some will see in the duplicity of the spy, of the barrister, the doctor and the journalist, reason for saying that these professions inherently lack integrity. Certainly it is more difficult for those in positions of power to realise their own text than for those whose utterances do not have social consequences. The Chancellor of the Exchequer, for example, is not in a position to have integrity on the matter of the future of movements in the exchange rate. It is mistaken however to make the charge that all of these roles lack integrity and that somehow society should be structured such that total integrity was applicable. For it is not only in public life that integrity as a realisation of one's own text is in jeopardy. How many of us on receipt of our Christmas presents provide a text that we do not ourselves wholly realise? In many situations, out of politeness or concern for others, we provide texts which we do not realise.

Integrity is more than the realisation of one's own text, it is the attempt to unify the closures that make up the self. Sometimes the provision of a text which is not realised results in less damage to the integrity of the self than the provision of a text which is realised. It is for this reason that we can make sense of the spy who has integrity. As a result we should modify the requirement that integrity entails the realisation of one's own text, with the addition of the phrase 'where possible in the light of the other closures comprising the individual's personal space'.

So where does this leave the journalist? With regard to the research for an article, report or film, integrity has at the first level the requirement that the journalist should realise whatever is said to the interviewees concerned. At times we may wish to go further and require that the journalist should convey all salient and relevant matters regarding the interview or research. Often, however, the requirement is at odds with the task of a journalist. One of the roles of a journalist is to uncover the misuse of power, and to probe the activities of those given the responsibility of power. Too much integrity on the part of the journalist in acquiring the story will ensure that the wider intent of the journalist is not forthcoming, and thus perhaps a deeper sense of integrity undermined. If a journalist is following a story of corruption in, let us say, the police force, telling police officers all that the journalist was aware of in advance of an interview would be unlikely to result in an illuminating outcome.

The official guidelines on these matters appeal to notions of the public interest. Interviewees should not be misled regarding the use or purpose of an interview unless it is in the public interest. Such guidelines have as little to do with integrity as an appeal to truth, and are in essence no more than a maintenance of the *status quo*, for the public interest is not definable other than in the context of a particular cultural set of values. Journalistic integrity cannot be defined extrinsically to the individual. In Stalin's Russia such guidelines would have stopped a journalist uncovering the death camps, since a court would not have regarded such an uncovering as being in the public interest.

The complexity of integrity stems from its inevitable failure. Total unity of the closures that make up the self is not a possible outcome. We can seek to be consistent, but a thoroughgoing consistency is a mirage. Our closures are frequently in conflict, and the conflict cannot be avoided simply by abandoning some of them. Even the saint must choose, on occasion, between being kind to others and being honest, between acting to ensure a positive outcome and engaging in conflict. The goal of complete integrity is an illusion, for the self contains disparate closures. We can, however, seek to maximise integrity, to reduce conflict between our closures as far as possible, to apply them with as much consistency as possible. What distinguishes the failure to realise one's own text is that the challenge to integrity is obvious and immediate. A journalist with integrity seeks to maximise the unity of the self and a failure to realise one's own text is a threat to such unity. In any instance where journalists are unable to realise their texts, integrity requires that they should be seeking to realise another closure which is held with greater priority. Trying to get a good story, or pursuing their career, are unlikely to be satisfactory alternatives, since the individual is unlikely to be prepared to realise related closures which generalise such a perspective to all journalists, and to all members of society. The requirement that journalists should maximise their unity of self does not, therefore, open the way to blatant abuse in the manner which might at first be imagined. It is tempting to give a list of the circumstances in which the realisation of one's own text could be over-ridden by other closures, but such a desire has nothing to do with integrity and everything to do with our will to impose on others our own views. Journalists cannot be given a set of rules for their integrity, for it is theirs' alone. How journalists acquit themselves in making these difficult decisions is the basis on which the rest of us will choose to determine how much integrity they have. Integrity requires a consistency of behaviour, but the content of the beliefs upheld and the priority given to each cannot be decided in advance.

Similarly with the journalistic text itself, integrity usually requires that closure can be realised by the journalist concerned. There are circumstances in which this could be transgressed without damage to integrity. If, for example, the personal truth of the journalist would expose someone to undue threat, or would break a prior agreement. As elsewhere, there are no rules that can be universally applied. For each individual the character of integrity will depend on the character of the total sum of their personal closures.

There are, of course, many things we desire in journalists besides integrity. A duty of care in the determining of their closure must, for example, come high on the list. But we should be careful not to include such notions within the concept of integrity, for to do so risks weakening the term so that it has no force and becomes, like 'goodness', the name for a somewhat empty characteristic, implying little other than approbation. In recognition of this we should also be aware that integrity is not always to be desired. Individuals who single-mindedly pursue their closures to the exclusion of the closures of others may have great integrity but are often difficult to live with, and sometimes of dubious value to their society. Terrorists may have integrity in the sense that they have not 'sold out' to the dominant democratic culture, but this form of integrity would be one that few of us would seek to encourage. The rationalist would like to believe that such perspectives can be shown to be inconsistent and no doubt thus exhibit a lack of unity of the self. One suspects this to be an illusion based on wishful thinking, as if consistency of belief will automatically yield tolerant, kind individuals.

Some may find this account disturbing. Integrity, as described, has provided no specific constraints on the behaviour of journalists. Dishonesty and deceit are even contemplated as being consistent with integrity in certain circumstances. But we should not look to integrity to police our society in general or the behaviour of journalists in particular. Integrity as 'singleness of self' is itself a closure which enables us to discriminate between individuals in a manner that can be useful. We do not need to use this closure to produce rules of behaviour which are to be applied to all individuals in all circumstances. Indeed the case made here has specifically denied this possibility, since integrity is determined intrinsically and not extrinsically.

If we wish to police the behaviour of journalists, we can draft laws which seek to do so. The laws of libel constitute, of course, one such attempt, and the current guidelines which apply to broadcasting another. Society requires a framework of rules by which individuals and groups are protected from others, but we do not need to defend such rules by an appeal to integrity. If journalists were widely regarded as being too powerful *vis-à-vis* the state, we might wish to contain that power by imposing laws to redress the balance. Such laws might, for example, insist upon disclosure, so that no question could be asked of any individual without their knowing in advance how the answer was to be used. Alternatively, we might conclude that the institutions of society were too powerful and that the power of journalists should be increased. The means of executing such a shift might be a freedom of information act. The balance of power and the way in which we wish individuals to act in society is not, however, a function of integrity, or indeed the consequence of any other supposedly moral characteristic. Furthermore, one suspects that when such notions are appealed to, the purpose is to obscure the authoritarian desire to control others beneath the cloak of moral respectability.

Integrity, as the attempt to make whole one's system of beliefs, is surely part of what it is to be human, and the evasion of conflict in one's closures an undermining of self, and lack of integrity. We should recognise, however, that the pursuit of integrity may not be socially acceptable or desirable, and that integrity in itself is no guide to the character of beliefs held. The advocacy of integrity does not enable us to draw up a set of rules which should determine behaviour. For the content of those rules is going to depend on the individual concerned. Integrity for Marx will not be the same thing as integrity for Nietzsche.

One obvious consequence of this account is that there are as many ways of having integrity as there are individuals. The application of the notion of integrity to the coverage of a story by a journalist will not, therefore, deliver any particular outcome, for it will depend on the framework of closures within which the journalist is operating. Nevertheless, despite the subjectivity of the account of integrity offered here, the constraints on a journalist seeking integrity are substantial. The distortion of events, or more precisely the provision of a text that is not realised by the journalist himself, is only in exceptional circumstances going to be compatible with the pursuit of integrity as 'truth to oneself'. A communist journalist with integrity writing on the night of the fall of the Berlin Wall is unlikely to be able to ignore the events, or to portray them as anything other than a profound setback for the régime. The events may be described as being tragic or reprehensible, they may also be characterised in an utterly different fashion from that of the Western journalist, but these descriptions do not constitute a challenge to integrity. Only those actions or texts which threaten the journalist's own self are at issue.

Finally, on a personal note, it does seem to me that, in the context of current affairs journalism, greater integrity and the more single-minded pursuit of personal beliefs is, in general, to be applauded. It is, however, often the sort of journalism that results in the most criticism and charges of lack of integrity by those who do not concur with the outlook expressed, and is frequently at odds with current Government and BBC guidelines, which seek to impose a notion of balance, which has everything to do with the maintenance of the *status quo*, and little to do with the integrity of the journalist.

Reference

Eliot, T.S. (1974) 'Four Quarters', in *Collected Poems 1909–1962*. London: Faber & Faber.

8   A reply to Hilary Lawson

Anthony Smith

There are many professions where the central task consists in providing descriptions of the world: biologists, historians, psychologists, navigators, economists, financial analysts and astronomers are all trained to provide accounts of situations and events which are intended to be true and are verifiable within a specialist or limited set of criteria. Such professions often work to a self-defined, rather than general, public, but through that public an influence is extended towards a wider world of readers and users. The material provided by these professional groups as it passes through the hands of its various users acquires successive interpretations and re-interpretations; and it is generally accepted that the original description will be influenced by the 'point of view' of the originating observer and has to be judged within that supposed limitation. Nevertheless, the resulting accounts are expected to be re-usable, reliable, accurate, when transposed to different contexts of use. The judgement of the integrity of these and all kinds of reporters begins with the trustworthiness, i.e. the re-employability, of the material that they supply.

One says 'begins with', for there are many virtues (and many vices) built into the practices of reporting. Information cannot be produced or received solipsistically; its production is always, in part, social in character. By its nature reporting takes the knowledge of something out of one context to place it in another, at the very least to remove it from one time-frame to another. And so there are responsibilities to others (audiences, people within the situations described, people who need to keep secrets, competing reporters) attached to the collecting and dissemination of all forms of information. One has to avoid the temptation to apply the label 'integrity' indiscriminately to all of the virtues entailed in what is deemed to be good reporting work: the term 'integrity' must be allowed to enjoy a special, perhaps narrower, sphere of application. Integrity possesses a special relationship with information, since the linking of personal and professional qualities goes with an open-minded knowingness, which opens the individual to temptation, but clarifies the line of duty. Samuel Johnson has Rasselas learn that 'integrity without knowledge is weak and useless, and knowledge without integrity . . . dangerous and dreadful' (Johnson 1976: 129).

The criteria of integrity in journalism – a particularly important example of a describing profession – have always been the object of intense discussion, because the press and, currently, broadcasting have come to construct what one might call our secondary environment, the body of meanings through which we look out upon society itself. The transactions between journalism and society constitute the basis of modern citizenship. Indeed, it is through the collective operations of journalism that our sense of the reality of the world emerges. Though journalism is itself influenced by the ideas inhabiting the world in which it operates, it shoulders (alongside education) the major responsibility for establishing most of what we take to be the 'real' beyond the actual ambit of our own senses. It is through journalism that we come to understand, or feel we understand, the world beyond our families and our workplaces (that is, the world of nations, war, peace and politics) and learn to read the changing values of our own society.

Yet despite the importance of journalism, we find it hard to say in what, exactly, the integrity of journalism consists: there are obvious moral qualities entailed, but there is also a necessary freedom of judgement at work, a taking of risks, the circulation of suppositions and unconfirmable statements, opinions, impressions, provocations. These are, or may be, permissible and necessary. And, paradoxically, all journalism is at some level entertainment, since otherwise it fails to reach its intended recipients. Though the practice of journalism is circumscribed and limited in some countries (e.g., Italy) in a similar manner to the legal and medical professions, it is not really a profession in the commonly accepted sense; no-one can be or should be legally prevented from acting as a journalist and no code of conduct has ever been devised which instructs journalists as to the precise way in which to perform in every circumstance. There is a correct way in which to carry out a conveyance or to perform an appendectomy, but no repeatable or transportable recipe for reporting a war. When the doctor's or the lawyer's work is done, there is little visible evidence of the individual who has carried it out, but journalism revolves (with some exceptions, as in Reuters) around the personalities of reporters. It shares a great deal with showbusiness. It cannot be reduced to procedures, (though it does not entirely lack procedures). So how should we, as non-journalists, tell journalists to behave? How should we instruct them to fulfil our expectations of them?

It is sometimes said that journalism has come to constitute a new, substitute, but inferior, kind of priesthood; where the churches once controlled the symbolic representation of the world, a new class of media people has arrived, without specialist training, which attempts inadequately and arrogantly to lay down shallowly conceived principles,while acting as judge and executioner of the reputations of private persons. The implication of this view is that the inquisitorial weapons of the journalist are flattery and scandal, his moral outlook simplistic, his motivations ultimately self-aggrandising. Certainly journalism seems to concentrate within itself all of the conceptual and moral dilemmas involved in making descriptions of the world, and embodies two conflicts in particular; one which lies between the intellectual liberty of an individual and the responsibility of a communicator towards his or her public and one which is fought out between an employer (publisher or editor), who claims a moral right over the product, and a journalist, who lays claim to the priority of his personal individual right of judgement.

Hilary Lawson deals with the issue of 'integrity' as if the term was not necessarily synchronous with a positive goodness of purpose or approach. I feel that the discussion is not worth our time, unless it entails the attempt to define or describe some of the qualities admired in or necessary to the practice of journalism. I make the assumption that integrity encompasses one part of the bundle of virtues which accompany (or fail to accompany) journalism. The qualities of truthfulness and honesty are surely self-evidently necessary; the question lies in how a journalist succeeds in being true to self, while negotiating the complexities and practicalities of the profession and its institutional context.

Integrity always implies a connecting of personal qualities, a consistency between character and behaviour, or a holding onto virtues through strength of character during trying and testing circumstances. I do not think that we have to be as fearful as Hilary Lawson is of evolving rules of behaviour or of wanting to thrust these upon others. 'The notion that the true meaning of integrity can be uncovered and that rules of behaviour might thus be provided, expresses a desire for power and security. The power to force others to behave as we wish . . .' (Chapter 7, this volume, p. 134). Were Hilary Lawson correct, it would be impossible ever to discuss human behaviour from a moral point of view. The discussion does not lead towards a covert domination of the values of society. The problem, in a sense, gets closer to home than that. To suggest that integrity is an ingredient of good journalistic conduct implies that there is a connection between personal and professional behaviour in a journalist, an inseparability of private and public realms. Hilary Lawson, if I understand him correctly, falls back upon a reductionism of journalism to its procedures.

Of course, every statement, every communication of information, has to be qualified from the vantage point of time and geography. No form of words expressing the truth remains secure or is felt to be accurate beyond a given context. The fall of the Berlin Wall is a good example of a piece of news, the description of which will change as it passes into history and into the consciousness of different ideological communities. There must, of course, be a central physicality of account which could remain consistent though devoid of 'meaning'; it is in the transposition of meaning that interpretations vary and versions multiply. American Hawks and East German Apparatchiks, as he says, will see completely contrary meanings in the dismantling of this piece of masonry. Its history and causes are seen in different ways. Indeed, the history itself alters with the tearing down of the Wall, since it becomes impossible to account for its existence in the first place in the same terms.

As T.S. Eliot says of poetry, the new work changes all the works which precede it (Eliot 1920). The Berlin Wall was a work of politics, the physical emanation of long ideological dispute. 'It is not possible to access the event independently of all such particularities of culture', says Lawson (p. 136). In practice that must be true, but that does not exonerate the journalist who has to provide an account of the event from moral responsibilities. There remains a whole series of obligations, not merely of honesty and attempted truthfulness. The event must have shaken the political or ideological predispositions of all the reporters who saw it happen. A communist reporter would be lacking in integrity if his account carried no hint of regret or of recantation, no ruefulness or indignation. An American Hawk's account would lack integrity if it failed to convey, at some level, the fact of the writer's prior commitment to the Western side of the Cold War. There are occasions when a reporter needs to eliminate predilections in order to be objective, but also occasions when these need to be revealed. Readers can make judgements of the integrity of the reporter accordingly. When we read an account of the Yugoslav wars by a Serb, we should know that fact and should know whether the writer has taken a position previously as a Belgrade or as a Pale Serb, or has attempted to eschew ethnic loyalties. The integrity of the writer can be judged, in part, by the way in which the reader is provided with this secondary level of information.

The question of whom we are dealing with as readers is paramount, not only in in the case of individual reporters but also in that of proprietors. For the reader to be properly and fairly 'placed' in respect of a given text, all sorts of attendant circumstances need to be understood. A respected newspaper is acquired by a wealthy proprietor. In purchasing it he has saved it from being bought by a more successful rival or from being forced to close down. But he is still a businessman with a wide variety of interests. He has enemies and they are bad people. He has the facts about them. He makes his newly acquired editor publish this material, truthfully, but also repeatedly. His commercial rivals are discredited. However, constant recirculation of the story, though a true one, is crucial to the business vendetta – but the repetition is not vital from a journalistic point of view. Does the editor have integrity? Now suppose that the rival and discredited entrepreneurs are friends of the proprietor. And the editor pursues the vendetta on his own initiative, with his boss writing angry letters telling him to desist in these attacks. But our editor insists on continuing the process of revelation. Perhaps he is now to be judged a person of integrity? But if the newspaper loses a lot of advertising revenue as a result of this journalistic enterprise and goes out of business, has the editor been guilty of putting his own egoistic ends before those of his paper or before those of its proprietor? Perhaps there is no easy answer to this dilemma and, in any case, one's judgement must in part depend upon how the story of the affair is told. My point here is that while the behaviour of reporters is something which is perfectly accessible to discussion, it is not reducible to simple rules and measurable criteria.

That does not decrease the (im)moral nature of the actions concerned; rather, it suggests that the integrity of journalism is also a continuous discourse, indeed, a key secondary discourse running alongside all journalism. The trained reader – and all readers are trained to some extent – reads the moral outlook of the journalist, judges his or her moral seriousness, through the text.

People who live in the public eye are – it is widely accepted – available for the public exposure of anything that they do which reveals them to be hypocritical, criminal, pretentious or merely unpleasant. (I myself am not certain that I accept this orthodoxy.) Newspapers, in recent years, have taken to campaigning against particularly famous people who are caught out in some way. What the victims have in common is often their fame and public status more than the heinousness of their misdemeanours. A series of politicians has been overthrown, some of them caught out in particularly disgraceful activities. One of them has been hired by one of the very newspapers which had exposed him and he is now paid handsomely to write a column which itself selects targets and victims from the public realm. Does the decision to give this disgraced individual a job of this nature suggest that the editor concerned is a man of high integrity? If a newspaper proves, or asserts by implication, that a person is unfit to be a Minister, is it not incumbent upon this journal to shun the malefactor? Or is employing him to be considered an act of (highly remunerated) mercy?

A further question which arises here is whether a newspaper is in this sense a person upon whom consistency of behaviour is incumbent. When a newspaper 'exposes' a malefactor, is it not *ipso facto* laying down a moral stricture which must reflect back upon its own subsequent actions as an institution? Or is that merely priggishness? If we look to a newspaper for accurate (with all the qualifications that that term implies) information, do we not require that as an institution – as a juridical person – it has to follow a code of consistency, if only to maintain its own right to continue making moral judgements of others?

Another further issue is that of whether the behaviour which attends integrity entails duties to society and its institutions. At the centre of a society there lie symbols and sensitivities which defy reason or which subsist upon deference. There are flags and anthems, and other symbols of sovereignty including human beings elected as Presidents or Archbishops or simply born as heirs to monarchies. Does a journalist have an obligation to offer reverence or merely normal detachment in dealing with this range of quasi-mystical things and people?

This issue has come to the fore in recent years in connection with Britain's much publicised and much troubled Royal Family. Here is a very unusual group of people who have come into existence, in a sense, in order to provide a special service to a society. Were there no monarchy, these particular people would not even have been born. They have been neither selected nor elected to the job. They have not been chosen from a 'gathered field' of candidates. They have not won their position in a lottery or in the wake of a corporate takeover. They cannot really be considered either rich or poor in the normal sense of those terms. They fulfil a ritual function in a society – so long as the society wills the institution of monarchy to continue. Now, in the twentieth century, a monarchy functions through the media and virtually only with its permission. Without exposure to the people it could not exist. Its role is to fulfil a dignified mystery which links the history of a nation or a polity to its political circumstances in their present. Royals are not celebrities. One might say that a modern monarchy is a collaboration between a specific Family and the media. Is it, therefore, appropriate for the press to treat this group of people in the same way that it might any group of celebrities or would-be celebrities? By stripping them of dignity, as it might (though this, too, raises serious ethical questions) were they football players or film actors or cabinet ministers or bishops captured in inadvertent misdemeanour, the press might be said to be jeopardising the institution of which these individuals are a part.

That kind of decision is properly taken by society as a whole, after open democratic discussion. To put the institution into question by working upon the behaviour of the individual persons concerned, is to decide the issue, as it were, covertly. Would the press consider it its task to destroy any other institution by undermining the morale of the people who uphold it and to do this without declaring its real purpose? The media treatment of the British Royal Family opens up some of the profoundest moral and intellectual issues of journalism at the present time. For it would seem incumbent upon the media to operate here precisely according to different (perhaps 'double') standards. To say that all media should function with an undiscriminating, democratising zeal is to miss the point of what is at stake. There is no simple code upon which to draw, only a complex drawing of lines between what a society requires in order to offer an institution the deference it needs for survival and the freedom a journalist requires to report all that is clearly news and of interest. What cannot, in my view, be asserted is that there exists no dilemma and no area of special concern and no acceptance of the specialness which attends the inner symbols of a society. There can be no society without its containing at its centre something thought to be sacred, for without that a society is but a meaningless agglomeration of individuals, and no society can exist in that condition. A journalist who believes himself to belong to a society will perhaps understand more instinctively than one who does not share that belief how and where to draw the lines concerned. Integrity here can imply only a constant self-scrutiny, a search for one's own motives, rather than the carrying out of strict rules. Current proposals to legislate for the protection of the privacy of prominent individuals can be no substitute for a profession of journalists who base their actions upon a sense of their own integrity. For no law can satisfactorily describe the kinds of situations and list the kinds of people and things who require the intended 'protection'.

The most difficult issues of journalism raise questions of how to behave as much as they do questions of what is truth. The journalist frequently has to decide the nature of mercy, charity, courage or motive. There are times when a journalist should be silent about something he or she has discovered. Perhaps a public figure has committed an error in conduct which would be devastating for family, friends and party, if revealed. If there is no real benefit from the revelation other than the joy of the scoop, then why reveal it?

A journalist functions part of the time as a kind of moral agent of society, and averting the gaze can often be the proper way to behave. It might also be the proper reaction of an editor presented with the information. But, of course, not always. Since the days of Watergate in the late 1970s journalism has arrogated to itself the right or duty of permanent confrontation with the political world. (Certain television interviews are among the current exemplars.) In the mid-nineteenth century there developed in the UK a press ideology by which the rights and duties of statesmen and journalists were divided up: Lord Derby, in a celebrated debate with Delane, Editor of *The Times*, said that 'if the Press aspires to exercise the influence of statesmen, the Press should remember they are not free from the corresponding responsibilities . . .'; to which the reply by Delane was that 'the purposes of the two Powers [sic] are constantly separate, generally independent, sometimes diametrically opposite . . .' (Cook 1915: 277–78). Few today would accept that the Press had so tremendous a role to play. For one thing, the newspaper has been driven more and more towards the condition of entertainment, and in broadcasting the reporting and entertainment roles are even more closely inextricable. Modern liberal thought ascribes very great freedom to the Press – as a social necessity, but less reverence than implied in the Derby–Delane debate of the 1850s. Certainly no-one today believes that journalism is part of the broader process of government, although politicians of the 'television age' usually accept that the media has the role of a licensed saboteur. But does not the social responsibility of the journalist often demand collaboration more than confrontation, and does not close questioning often turn a dangerous corner into sheer harassment? There is, perhaps, an obligation upon journalists to accept that government is today more difficult and more stressful than journalism. And with that obligation might come a realisation that a reporter has no business to make the task of the public figure more difficult, or more nearly impossible, while safeguarding the right and duty of journalistic scepticism. In an age of political terrorism, of nuclear weapons and of instant communication the unintended results of disclosure can be more devastating than a century ago; the need for secrecy is thus often genuine, though it can equally well be merely a familiar cover for political convenience.

The current audience of the media is much greater than that of the middle class newspaper of the Victorian age. The mass audience requires effective, uncondescending explanation, for it exercises political power not only at elections; through the media, all of political life is played out to this new vast audience which requires explanation as well as investigation, a clear account of the normal as well as the lurid disclosure of what has been wrongly withheld. The government of nations and the management of institutions need to be understood as well as confronted, and the tasks of journalism have therefore become much wider at a time when the competitive pressures have reduced journalism ever more towards the condition of entertainment. The integrity of journalism is judged by a broader range of criteria, all of which end up in the reporter's conscience.

Journalists are assisted by many technologies of sound, vision and transmission. But, at the heart of what they aspire to do, there exists a series of modern doubts: objectivity is exploded, balance is derided, language is deconstructed, social structures determine consciousness, circulation wars determine priorities. Professional codes dissolve into relativity. The other reporting professions all know that the world cannot be reconstituted out of 'facts', still less out of scoops. But journalism has long felt confident of its role and of its moral rights within society. However, the self-analogised scientific pretensions of journalism look very shaky in the context of the modern world, which has seen through the heroics of the Watergate era. The scoops all look suspiciously like somebody's handouts. The undaunted reporter shares a social status with the drug-pusher. People feel that journalists have become sources of injustice as much as upholders of people's rights. Journalists seem to want to do things in pursuit of their professional task – in order to gain the material for their accounts of events – which are not permitted to ordinary people. One might feel that, at the end of this century of the media, the journalist of integrity is one who concentrates on rehabilitating the profession, who makes a priority of rebuilding the trust of the reader.

The first question which has to be asked is whether there can be journalism, whether any describing activity can add up to what daily journalism has long aspired (or pretended) to do. Honest men and women may become journalists, but can the procedures and exigencies of the media which carry their work, which employ them, which sell the results, which are directed by great capitalist publishers, which are in themselves great social organisms with their own needs and outlooks, their own positions within an ecology of information firms, ever be a sound basis for creating reliable versions of the world?

Hilary Lawson has taken pains to emphasise the 'close-up' difficulties of journalism; he shows in his Berlin Wall example how interpretations are built into all reporting; or, rather, his example makes us realise that reporting takes place against a background, a repertory of interpretations from which the journalist must select the most apt. Indeed, the facts are incapable of being expressed at all except in a context of meanings and values. If the issue of integrity in journalism simply arose from the difficulties in doing the task honestly, there would be no sense of crisis today. But the problem goes much further than merely encouraging journalists to do their logical best in a task fraught with moral complexities.

Take, for example, the inequality of judgement which exists in most of the world concerning the Holocaust and the atrocities committed under Stalin. Our Press has constantly kept us in mind of the former while underplaying (as we now realise) the latter. We are relatively well informed, 50 years after the event, of what happened under Nazism, but are only just becoming aware of the, probably equal, horrors of Stalinism. To whom do we have recourse? How can we ensure that similar distortions are not visited upon us again? We know that reports of the Holocaust, also, were not fully believed when they started to circulate in the course of World War II. But the facts concerning the nature and existence of the gulags persist in our minds today as if related to half-excused accidents, or as if not fully verified. That can only be the result of a generation or more of faulty journalism. It has great bearing upon the modern world, for today we need to re-determine how to deal with a newly emerged aggressive force in the world: should Islamic fundamentalism be 'contained' or confronted or be appeased by endless concessions? Only history can guide us, but the history we have is, we now know, influenced by wrong reporting, not by a rogue journalist, but by the whole Western project of 'objective' journalism for over half a century.

References

Cook, Sir Edward (1915) *Delane of the Times*. London: Constable.
Eliot, T.S. (1920) 'Tradition and the individual talent', in *The Sacred Wood*. London: Methuen.
Johnson, Samuel (1976) *The History of Rassela, Prince of Abisinnia*. London: Penguin.

9   A reply to Anthony Smith

Hilary Lawson

In Chapter 8 Anthony Smith employs a notion of integrity which relies centrally on a notion of good. While, from the sentiments expressed, Anthony Smith's heart is clearly 'in the right place', it seems to me that the outcome of his proposal may not lead to the utopian outcome he desires. In Chapter 7 I argued against such an approach on the grounds that terms such as 'moral' or 'good' serve merely to endorse a course of action which the particular individual concerned approves. As a result the application of the term 'integrity' to individuals in the journalistic field, or any other, becomes little more than an endorsement, and as a consequence both duplicates other approbatory terms and fails to do any real work. Anthony Smith's chapter itself provides an example of this very outcome.

Anthony Smith is critical of journalism for not giving sufficient coverage to the gulags, and for undermining the 'mystical' role of the monarchy, and implies that if journalists had more integrity these errors would not have occurred. We may, or may not, agree with him in this respect, but these are clearly contentious points of view. Not only may others disagree with his description of the coverage of the gulags and its comparability with the Holocaust, or the risks of undermining the monarchy, but they may hold with equal strength diametrically opposed views. Some might see in a journalist adopting a republican standpoint a principled stand, and conversely a journalist with views sympathetic to the monarchy one who is seeking to curry favour with the establishment. It would appear that by arguing that a journalist with integrity should not undermine the monarchy, Anthony Smith covertly seeks to encourage journalists to his point of view, and to obscure this by the use of moral terminology – namely that such an approach is for the good of society. Moreover, there is always the risk that such encouragement could, in the hands of legislators, become imposition.

To argue that journalists should adopt a particular perspective is inevitably the prerogative of any member of society. To seek to argue that this perspective is required on the grounds of integrity is, however, wishful thinking – as if we could find in the external authority of morality and integrity an endorsement of our particular subjective perspective. Anthony Smith would like to see journalists adopt a more collaborative and less confrontational approach to government. He is, of course, entitled to such a view, although it is, once again, hardly without challenge. Moreover, the personal political perspective that it incorporates is laid bare when one considers that the journalists of Stalin's Russia would be unlikely to gain his support despite their distinctly collaborative attitude to government. Indeed one suspects that their very collaboration would be seen by Anthony Smith as a denial of their integrity.

In giving an account of integrity which does not rely on moral notions I have sought to demonstrate that 'being true to one's text' is not as empty a journalistic discipline as one might first suspect. In fact it turns out to be, if anything, too tough. When applied to the actual practice of journalism it generates starkly different conclusions to those that follow from Anthony Smith's approach. If, for example, we imagine Anthony Smith as a journalist expressing or acting upon the views outlined in his paper on the monarchy, the approach to leading government figures, the gulags and so forth, he might be said to have integrity (so long as we conclude that he is indeed true to his text). However, if another journalist with a wholly different outlook on these matters expressed such views (perhaps because of the editorial slant of the newspaper, the desire for a good story, or the desire for a mention in the honours list) he would not be acting with integrity. The integrity of the journalist does not, therefore, depend on the view expressed, but on the motivation of the journalist in expressing it. In contrast, Anthony Smith's account of integrity makes the view expressed central. It is my contention that to adopt this approach both makes the use of the term 'integrity' redundant and risks the imposition of a single perspective on the press under the guise of morality: a fundamentally anti-liberal and authoritarian outcome.

Section III
Academic, scientific and medical integrity

10 Scientific integrity

Marie-Hélène Parizeau

Introduction

Over the last 15 years an increasing amount of publicity has been given to debates concerning the question of scientific integrity, debates which, going well beyond the self-regulatory framework of the scientific community itself, have centred on cases of major scientific fraud or on clear conflicts of interest. The question of scientific integrity is shown up as if on a negative, thus providing an illustration of one of the conceptual difficulties involved.

There are two different, main angles from which the question of scientific integrity arises. It is seen in the first place as being integral to scientific practice as such. This is, for the most part, the way in which the issue presents itself in what scientists have to say on the question. Alternatively, one may be concerned with the principal ethical features (the virtues, the moral qualities of the scientists themselves) characteristic of scientific integrity. This ethical discussion makes reference to deontology, to etiquette, to the usages and customs which provide the structures within which professional activity may take place and present a model of conduct to those who pursue it.

In what follows, I shall look at the question from both of these angles, first in order to clarify them and then with a view to bringing them closer together. I shall start by looking more closely at the threats which weigh upon the integrity of scientific practice, in particular the phenomenon of scientific fraud. This will make it possible to show, on the one hand, something of the principal lines taken by scientists when they discuss the nature of scientific practice and, on the other hand, the gap that may be seen to exist between the language and practice of science, when one comes to observe that practice as (to an ever-increasing extent) it is carried on by scientists today. I shall then make use of a metaphor borrowed from Alasdair Macintyre to illustrate how the ethical question of scientific integrity carries with it a profound questioning of the identity of scientists as such and of their role in society.

Scientific integrity from the point of view of scientific practices

The reverse side of scientific integrity: scientific fraud

When the question of scientific integrity arises among scientists themselves, it is generally discussed in terms of what may be seen as lapse or abuse. This question frequently gives rise to a sense of unease within the scientific community, which, like any other body of professionals, hardly enjoys having to admit to the public at large that certain of its own members perpetrate frauds or behave as cheats. At the same time, since the end of the 1980s in the U.S.,[1] and more recently in Canada,[2] a number of universities, providing bodies and scientific societies have turned their attention to the question of scientific integrity. They have drawn up a variety of reports and recommendations with the aim of identifying different types of failure of scientific integrity, and have proposed various rules of conduct (often of an administrative type) in an attempt to reduce the numbers of cases of fraud and of conflicts of interest. The areas of scientific research most liable to be affected by such phenomena are those of the engineering sciences (physics, chemistry, the computer sciences, industrial techniques, etc.) and bio-medicine (in particular, the discovery of new medicines and genetic techniques).

If scientific integrity is really threatened, it becomes necessary to measure the extent of scientific fraud. Given the volume of scientific activity and the ever increasing number of researchers who take part in it, we have to ask whether scientific fraud is only marginal or whether it is extensive. The Report of the American National Academy of Sciences (1992) – which will here serve us as a text of basic reference – concludes its study by affirming that, while the number of reported cases is proportionately small, their impact is important since in the eyes of society it undermines the credibility and integrity of the universities and scientific institutions as much as it does that of scientific practice itself.[3] The Report adds that the figures provide only a partial glimpse of a situation, which is in any case hard to quantify.

In giving an account of scientific integrity, it is easier to define its opposite, namely, 'scientific fraud'. Manifestly, scientists find it easier to agree on a technical definition of 'fraud' than they do on a definition of 'scientific integrity'. The discussions that have taken place on the extent and limits of scientific fraud make it possible to identify a hard core of serious cases of 'scientific misconduct'. There is general agreement that such forms of misconduct put at risk the ongoing processes of the practice of science itself. They are defined as follows:

> Misconduct in science is defined as fabrication, falsification, or plagiarism, in proposing, performing, or reporting research. Misconduct in science does not include errors of judgement, errors in the recording,

GENERAL REFERENCE

selection, or analysis of data: differences in opinions involving the interpretation of data; or misconduct unrelated to the research process.

(National Academy of Sciences 1992: 27)

Around this hard core there exist a number of other 'questionable research
practices'. They merit attention, for they serve to undermine the confidence
that scientists, and more generally the public at large, have in the processes
of scientific practice. By way of example we may mention the following:

> Using inappropriate statistical or other methods of measurement to
> enhance the significance of research findings; inadequately supervising
> research subordinates or exploiting them. . . .

(ibid: 28)

Other serious abuses are related to the pursuit of scientific research without
being peculiar to it. Two examples which recur frequently are: sexual harassment and conflicts of interest,[4] in particular as they may arise in relations
between the scientist, the university and the industrial sector.

Scientific fraud may, then, take a variety of different forms of differing
degrees of gravity. Why, all these different Reports ask, is scientific integrity
not respected? Why commit fraud? Two main reasons are generally put forward. The first appeals to the idea of a deviant, even pathological, conduct on
the part of a researcher.[5] This is generally expressed in psychological terms
rather than in the vocabulary of ethics (an intention and a resolve to do harm).

The second reason concerns the numerous pressures to which scientific
research is subjected, now that it is looked on as a form of social enterprise.
Reference is made to such different factors as, for example:

(a) Funding and career pressures of the contemporary research environ-
    ment ('publish or perish');
(b) inadequate institutional oversight;
(c) inappropriate forms of collaborative arrangements between academic
    scientists and commercial firms;
(d) inadequate training in the methods and traditions of science;
(e) the increasing scale and complexity of the research environment
    leading to the erosion of peer review, mentorship and educational
    processes in science;
(f) the possibility that misconduct in science is an expression of a
    broader social pattern of deviation from traditional norms.

(National Academy of Sciences 1992: 30–31)

The multiplication and the extent of these pressures, together with the
phenomena of scientific fraud and of conflicts of interest, weigh increasingly
upon the practice of science to the point where questions may well arise as to
the nature of certain transformations (in, for example, the social organisation

of scientific research, its links with private enterprise, pressures to publish, and so on). Are these merely marginal phenomena or are they, rather, the sign of deep changes in the nature of scientific practice itself?

Accounts of scientific activity: from traditional science to techno-science

In other words, given certain parameters, to enquire into scientific integrity today amounts to raising the question of the very nature of scientific practice. Step-by-step one is led to question its procedures and values *qua* social institution, together with the ethical relationship of the researcher to scientific practice. What, then, can we see?

Empirically, in the first place, the social representation of scientific practice has been progressively modified over the last 30 years. The nineteenth-century image of the solitary scholar, alone with his books and his instruments, has given way to reports in the media of teams of reseachers installed in laboratories technologically equipped to varying degrees of sophistication – computer networks being the common, basic working instrument, whatever the type of research being carried on. Increase in knowledge is achieved thanks, not so much to the discoveries of individual genius, as to the patient and cumulative efforts of several different teams working in different parts of the world upon some hyper-specialised aspect of a given area of knowledge.

In the second place, from the point of view of theory, a number of different philosophers of science have laid stress on the inter-relationship between science and technique and the ever-growing dependence of the former upon the latter, to the extent that the two have become virtually inseparable.[6] The term 'techno-sciences' has been used to describe this phenomenon.[7] The goal of the techno-sciences consists first and foremost in the mastery of operational processes. What counts above all is the ability to make accurate predictions, for it is this which makes it possible to control the phenomena. As the different aspects of knowledge and 'know-hows' become more and more complex and increasingly integrated, so this capacity of control becomes more and more extensive. The tendency of the techno-sciences is to develop the 'technician's imperative', embodying the directive to accomplish everything that it is technically possible to accomplish.

In a parallel development a strong link is established between the techno-sciences and the economy. This link carries with it as a corollary the characteristic ascription of value to such things as the techniques of mass production, efficiency, productivity, standardisation and uniformisation. Thus, an ever-growing relation of dependence is established between Research and Development (R&D) and the market economy. The costs of research continually increase: both the costs of the technology involved and those of the highly specialised training of the researchers themselves. The practical consequences of this are to be seen in a levelling out of the financial commitment of the State to scientific research, a development to be found in the majority of

Western societies. The financing of R&D is progressively taken over by the private sector which, in certain cases (that of engineering, for example), thus becomes the principal investor. These developments lead to changes in the nature of scientific practice as the laws of the market and considerations of profit are introduced among its determining factors. This has an impact upon the directions taken by scientific research, and even upon its methods.

The science of the nineteenth and the early twentieth centuries hardly corresponds any longer to the scientific practice of the last 30 years. Science can no longer be defined as the neutral study of the facts of nature independently of the world of ideas. By the same token, it can equally no longer claim to be neutral with regard to all cultural and social influences. Science, increasingly tied, as it is, by bonds of reciprocity with technique, appears as a form of activity specific to Westernised societies, which possess a growing and effective capacity for social transformation. With the integration of science as a powerful form of social activity within a market economy, it is, then, an appropriate moment to review its underlying values.

Nevertheless, the account which scientists most frequently offer of scientific integrity refers rather to values corresponding to a more traditional conception of science (the state of the relative neutrality of the science of the nineteenth century). I shall try now to bring out the growing extent of the gap between such an account and the ways in which science is carried on in actual practice. In the first part of this chapter I have sought to show how the actual practice of science has come to be modified over the last 30 years by the accelerating interdependence between science and technique within a market economy (the detour by way of scientific fraud helps to throw light on certain symptons of this interdependence). I turn now to the way in which a representation of scientific integrity, understood as a commentary upon the nature of scientific practice, refers back to a nineteenth century vision of science and its values that fails to take adequate account of the changes that have come about in the scientific practice of today.

Once again the Report of the National Academy of Sciences may serve as a typical example. At the very outset the introduction to this document recalls the values underlying the scientific *tradition*:

> Scientific research is grounded in values such as *integrity, honesty, trust, curiosity, and respect for intellectual achievement*. The expression of these values in the diverse styles and approaches of the various scientific disciplines has contributed directly to the discovery of *knowledge* and thus to the achievements of the U.S. scientific research enterprise. Basic to the honour system that binds the community of scientists is *truthfulness*, both as a moral imperative and as a fundamental operational principle in the scientific research process. Ideally, it is the challenge of gaining a measure of truth that motivates scientists to formulate, test, and revise their hypotheses in ways that minimise errors.

Scientific achievement as well as human welfare, which is increasingly affected by the work of scientists, depends on the integrity of the research process. By *integrity of the research process*, the panel means the adherence by scientists and their institutions to *honest and verifiable methods* in proposing, performing, evaluating, and reporting research activities. The research process includes the construction of hypotheses; the collection, analysis, and handling of data; generation of new ideas, findings, and theories through experimentation and analysis; timely communication and publication; refinement of results through replication and extension of the original work; peer review; and the training and supervision of associates and students. The traditions of *scepticism, openness, sharing and disclosure* that are associated with the research process not only provide a means of identifying theoretical or experimental errors that occur inevitably in science, but also imply an obligation to maintain the integrity of the research process.

(National Academy of Sciences 1992: 17–18, my italics)

The state of relative neutrality of scientific practice as so described rests on a certain number of essential values: honesty, confidence, respect for intellectual attainment, curiosity, scepticism, openness of mind, the sharing of knowledge, (which are qualities or virtues that the researcher must possess if he or she is to practice science), and verifiable methods (which are the conditions of validity of scientific knowledge).

On this there are two remarks which may be made. The first is that, if one allows that scientific activity is at the same time a collective enterprise, dimension is here absent from this traditional conception of scientific integrity. In other words, the bonds of interdependence between science and the market economy remain concealed. Private enterprise, whose support in the development of scientific activity is sought to an ever-increasing degree, has as its ultimate aim the profitability of its investments; in certain cases, it will set the goals and the type of research to be pursued. Research for the sake of knowledge as such, the challenge of arriving at a previously unknown truth, the sharing of one's results (one's own knowledge), all of these values are bound up with science and yet may have to take second place to a know-how of expediency, to a functional knowledge placed in the service of other activities, of (patented) property rights over this know-how and of secrecy.

The second remark is the following. If one accepts that scientific activity is very closely tied in with technique, one has, once again, to note that this dimension is missing from the traditional conception of scientific integrity, which (as this inter-relationship grows and other values come to the fore), starts to become blurred. The techno-sciences encourage values which either enter into competition with those traditional to scientific activity or which work to produce transformations of them. Thus, to repeat, technical values are those of utility, of effectiveness, of productivity and of operational autonomy. Technological evolution is ever more rapid, more integrated, more systematic and more controlled. It belongs to the order of means and not to that of ends in themselves. Operational power makes possible an ever more precise mastery of reality. It is particularly in the field of technique that we find a breech opened in the scientist's ethical and social responsibility. It is scarcely possible to go on talking of the pseudo-neutrality of science, given the ways in which reality (society, culture and the relations of human beings to each other) is modelled and manipulated by the operational character of contemporary scientific knowledge and its various forms of know-how.

We may thus take due note of this growing gap between what, on the one hand, is commonly said about the nature of a scientific practice conceived in terms of the model of the nineteenth century and, on the other hand, the way in which it is actually carried on today, when the sciences, their techniques and the economy are becoming ever more closely integrated. We are now in a position to enquire into the ethical question of scientific integrity, that is to say, into how this question presents itself to the scientist in his relation to his work *qua* 'scientist'.

Scientific integrity: the social role and identity of the scientist

Integrity and identity

The ethical notion of integrity relates directly to a person's moral life. Whether it is further qualified or not (physical integrity, intellectual integrity and so on), the notion of integrity makes reference to a form of completeness (a form of totality, or of unity, or of constancy, in one's actions or convictions, for example, as opposed to falling apart or to self-contradiction) and to the fact of being intact (as opposed to the violation of integrity – of physical integrity, for example). The notion of integrity presupposes a form of unity, or let us say, to use another term, an *ideal* of coherence between what is said and what is actually done. Moreover, in the ordinary way of speaking, integrity is readily associated with honesty, with sincerity, with the fact of lying neither about nor to oneself. In the first place, the concept of integrity may be thought of in quasi-spatial terms. Integrity may be attributed to someone either externally, as it were, or internally, as to oneself. What is here at stake is the meaning (the 'making sense'[8]) to be attributed to the actions that may have been performed or to the words that may have been pronounced in relation to others and/or to oneself. The achievement of such a constitution of meaning may involve the making of choices that cause real pain either to others or to oneself in so far as the preservation or the establishment of one's integrity may, for example, commit one to refusing to do certain things in the name of personal or professional values that one takes to be fundamental. In the second place, the concept may be thought of in terms of its relation to time; thus, the way in which events unfold may, in a given context, serve either to reinforce one's integrity or bring it under threat, in which case the question becomes one of its *persistence*.

The contemporary literature on the subject tends to link integrity to the notion of the identity of one and the same person.

> What emerges is a conception of the person as an integrated triad consisting of: (1) a reasonably coherent and *relatively* stable set of highly cherished values and principles; (2) verbal behaviour expressing these values and principles; and (3) conduct embodying one's values and principles and consistent with what one says. These are the elements of integrity. Taken together they constitute the formal structure of one's identity as a person. . . .
>
> Corresponding to its internal and external dimensions, integrity has both internal and external importance. Internally, it provides the structure for a unified whole and unalienated life. Those who through good fortune and personal effort are able to lead reasonably integrated lives generally enjoy a strong sense of personal identity. They know who they are and what they stand for; they will experience the satisfaction and self-respect that comes with living in accord with their deepest and most highly cherished values. An entire life that has been integrated in this way is, in many ways, an enviable achievement. . . .
>
> Viewed from the outside, individual integrity provides the basis for reliance, trust, friendship and love. Social relationships and institutions would be impossible without a certain amount among the individuals who compose them.
>
> (Benjamin 1990: 51–52)

In this analysis, identity and integrity are thus intimately linked and tend each to depend upon the other with the aim (an ideal) of creating that which is peculiar to each human being, that is, his or her own individuality integrated within the horizon of a whole life. These two concepts refer both to that which is internal (one's relationship to oneself), and to that which is external (one's relationship to others and in particular to society at large).

Identity and integrity are thus both closely connected with the social roles which each individual occupies. Our contemporary societies, however, are fragmented, atomised by a whole variety of forces that make it much more difficult for individuals to identify with any one particular social formation (a community). This has, among other things, an impact on the formation of the self.

> Comparatively closed, *homogeneous* societies not characterised by rapid social, scientific and technological change are more conducive to leading integrated lives than the more open, *heterogeneous* and rapidly changing societies of the modern world. The fluidity of many contemporary

social roles and the emphasis placed on social and geographical mobility provide a range of tempting choices not found in the ancient world or in more traditional societies. Nor are we certain in our more cosmopolitan, pluralistic culture as to what values or conception of the good ought to unify or to be at the centre of our life.

(ibid: 71)

What analysis, then, is to be given of what may constitute scientific integrity in the light thrown by these elements on the concept of ethical integrity? In other words, how should one understand the way in which the issue of integrity presents itself to the scientist in his or her relation to scientific practice?

The scientist: a Fallen Hero?

In answering this question, I propose to use the terms of a metaphor that I borrow from Alasdair MacIntyre (cf. 1984). MacIntyre analyses the ethical relation between personal and social identity (taking the latter to be the same thing as the social role). He shows how modernity has brought about a clear split between personal and social identity.

There is thus the sharpest of contrasts between the emotivist self of modernity and the self of the heroic age. The self of the heroic age lacks precisely that characteristic which we have already seen that some modern moral philosophers take to be an essential characteristic of human selfhood: the capacity to detach oneself from any particular stand-point or point of view, to step backwards, as it were, and judge the standpoint or point of view from the outside.

(ibid: 126)

But, explains MacIntyre, in more homogeneous societies, in particular in those of Ancient Greece, personal identity and social identity tend to be indistinguishable from each other, thanks to the exercise of the virtues (courage, prudence, honour, etc.) This exercise of the virtues is a force working for the integration both of the individual and of the society in which he or she lives.

So far as heroic society in particular is concerned, MacIntyre explains its ethical structure by reference to the Homeric poems:

Thus this type of heroic poetry represents a form of society about whose moral structure two central claims are made. The first is that that structure embodies a conceptual scheme which has three central interrelated elements: a conception of what is required by the social role which each individual inhabits: a conception of excellences or virtues as those qualities which enable an individual to do what his or her role requires:

and a conception of the human condition as fragile and vulnerable to destiny and death, such that to be virtuous is not to avoid vulnerability and death, but rather to accord them their due. . . . It is rather that all three elements can find their interrelated places only within a larger unitary framework, deprived of which we could not understand their significance for each other. This framework is the narrative form of epic or saga, a form embodied in the moral life of individuals and in the collective social structure. Heroic social structure *is* enacted epic narrative.

(ibid: 129)

In the metaphor which follows I shall use these three characteristics of heroic society, as described by MacIntyre, in order to show how the scientist may be seen as having once occupied an analogous role as a hero in a heroic society wholly turned towards the goal of scientific and social progress. In the same perspective, I shall go on to show how, as the story develops, the society starts to fragment due to the progressive transformation of the techno-sciences, which offer other values. In this way a crack is revealed at the heart of scientific integrity, leading towards a non-coincidence between the personal identity of the scientist and the identity that is his in virtue of his social role. Today it has become more difficult for the scientist to situate the story which he tells (to himself as to others) of his personal and social identity in continuity with the heroic story which has been handed down to him from the nineteenth century.

MacIntyre explains that the hero is judged by his actions, which themselves are the fruit of the exercise of those virtues belonging to the social role inhabited by the hero. As for scientists, they are judged by their discoveries, by their acquisition of fresh knowledge, by the explanations of natural phenomena that they manage to provide. To that end, the scientist exhibits certain virtues, understood as consisting, on the one hand, in excellence in her activity in the pursuit of science (showing the most rigorous respect for the conditions of validity of scientific knowledge) and, on the other hand, in the exercise of certain individual qualities required of her in virtue of her role as scientist. These latter have been described above in the Report of the National Academy of Sciences (1992): honesty, trustworthiness, respect for intellectual attainment, curiosity, scepticism and openness of mind.

Just like the Homeric hero, for whom glory is the due reward of the courageous warrior and victor, the scientist has to exhibit courage and only the best are rewarded by glory, here represented by the Nobel Prize. Glory is the mark of social recognition. The techno-sciences are here responsible for a certain distortion: glory is no longer so much the aim as money, which has become the most evident mark of social recognition. The courageous Homeric hero relies on friendship and loyalty. For the scientist, this friendship takes the form of a common quest for truth and knowledge. Once again, the techno-sciences provoke a further distortion; scientific research teams become rivals of each other. Secrecy and competition become more characteristic of their modes of functioning, to which the example of the Gallo–Montaigner controversy as to who was the first to discover the HIV virus, may bear witness.[9]

The recognition of heroic figures is linked to their display of the relevant virtues. The stories of these heroic personalities provide sustenance to the story of the individual and help to consolidate his identity. Personalities such as Newton, Claude Bernard, Pasteur, Marie Curie, Watson and Crick – examples of scientific integrity and devotion – belong to the history of science as so many exemplary expressions of what the moral life of a scientist should be like (in terms of individual and social identity). The stories serve as ideals and provide moral content by way of the models of the virtues and of exemplary behaviour that are to be found in them.

The form of a heroic society, explains MacIntyre, must at the same time contain a conception of the human condition, in which the virtuous hero recognises himself to be fragile and vulnerable before fate and death (the third condition). This condition also applies to scientific heroism. At the conclusion of his book *Le hasard et la nécessité* (1970) Jacques Monod provides just such a conception. He proposes an ethic of knowledge to the scientific community and, more broadly, to society at large according to which, in a universe which remains deaf and dumb to all human appeals, the only moral attitude to adopt is one of commitment to the progress of knowledge and of social justice.

In borrowing from MacIntyre this metaphor of the hero, I have tried to show how the personal and social identity of the scientist converge with the notion of scientific integrity in the sense of an integration towards an ideal – that of the scientist–hero, the bearer of social progress and of the enlightenment of true knowledge. Up to the beginning of the 1960s, this integrative force provided the scientist with an assurance of the importance and necessity of his social role, and thus of his social identity. This tended to subsume his personal identity as well through his exercise of the virtues linked to scientific integrity, which, by the same token, provided him with a clear enough goal to aim at: the enrichment of knowledge and the search for truth.

However, both in the analysis of integrity from the standpoint of the ways in which science is actually carried on and in the story-metaphor of the hero, symptoms appear of the profound modifications in the nature of scientific activity brought about by the techno-sciences, leading towards a fragmentation of the social role of the scientist and hence of his social identity. These changes bring about a certain indeterminacy at the heart of scientific integrity. A shift is noticeable: the scientist is less and less the hero, symbol of a progressive and scientific society, but is to be seen more as fulfilling a useful social function (as becoming a cog) in the service of the market economy, which depends, in part, on continuing technological development. This indeterminacy may be experienced by the scientist as a loss of identity, a loss of completeness, even a violation of his personal integrity (a form of betrayal of the ideal represented by scientific integrity).

The gap which thus opens up between the language of scientific integrity and the values that it represents and the actual practice of science, directed by the techno-sciences, introduces tensions, even a dissociation, between integrity and identity so far as the scientist is concerned. Is this dissociation to be put to the account of the over-rapid transition brought about by an instrumental modernity acting as a force for separation rather than integration, as suggested by MacIntyre and others who reflect on the 'crisis of identity' that is shaking our societies?

Are the heroes all dead? No more than others can scientists evade this identity crisis, in other words the necessity of a reformulation of what constitutes scientific integrity. To guide this work, can we not discern the outlines of other forms of integration, less rigid, less all-embracing, more communitarian forms (for example, forms of professional integration), forms doubtless more fragile, but capable of allowing for the expression of a number of different models of identity? Does not the scientific community see opening up before it a polyvalence and increasing complexity of ends and means brought about by the development of the techno-sciences, a development which calls in turn for responsible debate on the goals to be chosen in common for the future of the biosphere and for human beings in general as well as on the guiding principles to be adopted by society at large?

Notes

1 Thus in the medical field, for example, the Faculty of Medicine of Harvard University (1994) published a policy document on scientific integrity, which rapidly came to serve as a model for other universities.

2 For example, in November 1994, the three main Federal providing bodies organised a 'national conference on integrity in research and in scholarly work', which was followed, in 1995, by a statement of policy (Conseil de recherches médicales du Canada *et al.*, 1994).

3 In Québec, for instance, the Deschamps Report's proposals of a series of mechanisms and administrative rules for the governance of research activities in hospitals, constitute an attempt to respond to a loss of confidence on the part of a section of the population in research workers (Deschamps *et al.*, 1995). This report arises out of two 'affairs' (the 'Fabrikant affair' in engineering (1992) and the 'Poisson affair' in medicine (1993)), 'affairs' which raised questions of scientific integrity and which made the headlines.

4 The problem of conflicts of interest is sufficiently serious as to have led a majority of universities to demand of their members that they should make an explicit declaration of their situation, if ever they should find themselves faced with such a conflict. One of the procedures laid down to deal with such contingencies is the setting up of a special Faculty Committee to investigate such cases. The sanctions invoked may vary but may, in certain cases, involve the scientist in question resigning from his or her university post.

In Québec there has been, as yet, little working experience of these procedures – as I discovered when acting as member of an Ethics of Research Committee faced with a situation of conflict of interest presented by a research proposal put forward by a hospital researcher, who, outside his hospital work, also had his own company, the financing of which involved a pharmaceutical company. The ethical implications of this case were very considerable, given that what was at stake was the ownership both of data concerning named persons and of the samples of DNA that had been taken, both of which were to be made over to the pharmaceutical company on the expiry of the contract made with the company belonging to the researcher in question. Neither the hospital administration nor the Ethics Committee had access to this contract.

5 'The Fabrikant affair' provides an illustration, in the eyes of many, of the ways in which the accumulation of pressures and the existence of fraudulent behaviour of varying degrees of gravity in the practice of science (the appropriation of data by someone higher up, the usurpation of one's place in the order of signatures to a publication, insecurity concerning one's salary, the turning of an administrative blind eye to such practices within the institution, etc.) may lead an individual to commit criminal acts. (In 1992 Valery Fabrikant killed four people, members of the Faculty of Engineering and Computer Sciences at Concordia University.) See Arthurs *et al.* (1994).

6 I do not propose to discuss here the importance of this dependence, on the degree of which different authors have different views. Jean Ladrière (1977) is cautious in speaking of 'the extremely close link' that exists between science and technology. With its theoretical models, science provides us with a certain knowledge of reality. By its methods, it makes possible an orderly increase in our body of knowledge as it improves it. The scientific enterprise allows of progress, that is to say, of a certain type of evolution. This knowledge as to how things are, being of an operational type, thereby constitutes a power over the world of things and of human beings. It is technology which gives concrete expression to this power by its transformation of reality. 'In short', says Ladrière, 'one might say that the aim of science is the progress of knowledge, while the aim of technology is the transformation of reality as it is given to us'.

I shall argue that these bonds of interdependence represent a powerful tendency, from which no science, from chemistry to astrophysics, can be considered free – including the mathematical sciences, certain sectors of which are dependent upon computers.

7 This expression is used by Gilbert Hottòis (1984) and has been subsequently taken up by other philosophers, such as Frederick Ferré (1988).

8 Charles Taylor provides a very explicit account of the expression 'making sense':

> Making sense here means articulating what makes these responses appropriate: identifying what makes something a fit object for them and correlatively formulating more fully the nature of the response as well as spelling out what all this presupposes about ourselves and our situation in the world. What is articulated here is the background we assume and draw on in any claim to rightness, part of which we are forced to spell out when we have to defend our responses as the right ones.
>
> (1989: 8–9)

9 This controversy as to who made the discovery first has been complemented by a conflict among major financial interests over the commercialisation of the diagnostic test ELISA and applications for patents and payments for the sale of the diagnostic packs for AIDS (cf Grmek 1989: 116–28).

References and further reading

Arthurs, H.W., Blais, R. and Thompson, J. (1994) (Independent Committee of Inquiry into Academic and Scientific Integrity) *Integrity in Scholarship. A Report to Concerdia University.*

Benjamin, Martin (1990) *Splitting the Dfifference; Compromise and Integrity in Ethics and Politics.* Kansas: University of Kansas Press.

Conseil de recherches médicales du Canada, Conseil de recherches en sciences naturelles et en génie du Canada, Conseil de recherches en sciences humaines du Canada, *L'Intégrité dans la recherche et les travaux d'érudition* (1994).

Deschamps, P. Vinay, P. and Cruess, S. (Comité d'experts sur l'évaluation des mécanismes de contrôle en matière de recherche clinique) (1995) *Rapport sur l'évaluation des mécanismes de contrôle en matière de recherche clinique au Québec présenté au Ministre de la santé et des services sociaux du Québec.*

Faculty of Medicine, Harvard University (1994) *Faculty Policies on Integrity in Science.* Cambridge, MA: Harvard University Press.

Ferré, Frederick (1988) *Philosophy of Technology.* London: The University of Georgia Press, Athens.

Grmek, Mirke (1989) *Histoire du sida.* Paris: Payot.

Hottois, Gilbert (1984) *Le signe et la technique. La philosophie à l'épreuve de la technique.* Paris: Aubier/Montaigne.

Ladrière, Jean (1977) *Les enjeux de la rationalité. Le défi de la science et de la technologie aux cultures.* Paris: Aubier–UNESCO.

MacIntyre, Alasdair (1984) *After Virtue*, 2nd edn. Paris: University of Notre Dame Press.

Monod, Jacques (1970) *Le hasard et la nécessité.* Paris: Le Seuil.

National Academy of Sciences (National Academy of Engineering, Institute of Medicine) (1992) *Responsible Science, Ensuring the Integrity of the Research Process*, Vol. 1. Ottawa: National Academy Press.

National Academy of Sciences (National Academy of Engineering, Institute of Medicine) (1993) *Responsible Science, Ensuring the Integrity of the Research Process*, Vol. 2. Ottawa: National Academy Press.

Taylor, Charles (1989) *Sources of the Self: The Making of the Modern Identity.* Cambridge, MA: Harvard University Press.

Taylor, Charles (1991) *The Ethics of Authenticity.* Cambridge, MA: Harvard University Press.

11 Academic integrity

Denis Noble

Introduction

Throughout this chapter I shall take 'academic integrity' to refer to an academic subject or activity being true to itself and to its responsibilities to society as a whole. This implies that there exist criteria within academic disciplines which must be satisfied and that, in addition to failing these, a lack of integrity could also arise from ceding to inappropriate pressures external to the discipline itself. This interaction is complex, though, for I will also argue that sensitivity to some external pressures on a discipline is also part of what constitutes its integrity. No academic discipline is an island.

Typical internal criteria would include truth (we would certainly wish to say that falsifying data, for example, breaks the rules of academic integrity), acknowledgement of sources, previous work, authorship etc., and whatever concepts of coherence exist within the discipline. An interesting question that arises is whether these criteria differ significantly as between different disciplines (arts and sciences, for example). This will be one of the major issues tackled in this chapter.

Typical external pressures that threaten integrity would include commercial interests (which is why we instinctively mistrust research on cancer funded by tobacco companies), and political pressures, illustrated so dramatically by the implications of the UK Government's recent decision to put the Science Ministry under the ministry responsible for industry. Even those scientists who, like myself, think that a major responsibility of the science base is to be sensitive to the economic and social well-being of a nation, see obvious dangers in making publicly-funded research, which should be independent of particular commercial interests, so obviously subservient to the needs and control of industrialists. It will only be a matter of time before this development produces a major conflict of interest when an industrial member, or even a director, of a research council influences decisions on the funding of research that a company in which he is involved is deeply concerned, either that the research should not be done, or that it should not be done publicly, or that it should be done in a way different to that proposed. Already, there are clear signs that research that is industrially relevant is favoured over that which is not perceived to be so. A condition of some research grants (called 'Realising our Potential Awards' – ROPAs) is precisely that the research team concerned should already be funded by industry. Even though the funding is for 'pure' research, this already sets up a clear bias towards those teams whose research is considered 'relevant' and is therefore a move away from the single criterion of academic excellence.

The issue of integrity in academic work has therefore become an acute one, and not just in the UK. There is, of course, a long history of threats (religious, political and economic) to academic integrity, but some of the pressures today are of very recent origin, arising as they do from scientific research that has generated entirely new ethical problems, and from the immense financial and economic impact of modern research. In the first part of this chapter I shall review some of the ways in which scientists have reacted to such pressures in the past and explain why I think these approaches fail anyway and why they are certainly inappropriate to the modern situation. In the second part, I shall briefly extend some of the argument to work in other areas of academic life.

This definition of academic integrity implies that, in addition to the requirements for personal integrity in general, individuals who practise or profess an academic subject are also constrained by the integrity of their subject. It might be questioned whether there are, or at least whether there need to be, such constraints, defined as they are by non-personal criteria. It will be part of the purpose of this paper to argue that such subject-constraints must exist and that it is through these that individuals acquire additional duties and responsibilities to society as a whole. For society can and does hold whole disciplines to account for their effects on society. To a large extent, therefore, academic integrity is a question of the human, moral integrity of people with special aptitudes working in special fields. And one of the reasons why society as a whole can hold those individuals responsible as a group is that there is always a potential threat to society in the production of such specialist knowledge. Knowledge generally is subversive and there is no guarantee that society will successfully adapt to its discovery, particularly when it is generated on the immense scale that we see today. Whether, as academics, we like the analogy or not, there is now an academic industry with risks and benefits that others in a democratic society have a right to judge. These judgements, as they evolve in political debate, must also enter into the determinants of academic integrity. To give a very specific example relevant to my own discipline, it is inconceivable that those working in fields which use animal experimentation could regard the issues involved, both for the integrity of the discipline and of the individuals concerned, in the same way today as their predecessors would have done a century ago. No-one now, for example, would repeat the Rev Stephen Hales' experiment in 1733 to determine the blood pressure of a horse by inserting tubes into the arteries of an unanaesthetised animal. Academic integrity, then, evolves. This evolution is an interaction with society as a whole that is two-way, with immense implications, as I hope will become clear towards the end of this chapter.

The problems of science

The 'totally neutral' view

A solution to these problems that found favour with earlier generations of scientists was to defend what they saw as the intrinsic neutrality of science. The argument here is that since science is, ideally at least, an entirely objective process, the results of research are also entirely objective. It is the researcher's job to follow this 'neutral' study of nature wherever it may lead and not, *qua* researcher, to worry about the wider implications. The most severe form of this approach was espoused by Karl Pearson in *The Grammar of Science* (1892). Pearson was a highly influential Professor of Mathematics and, later, of Eugenics at University College London. He influenced British science in its formative years between 1890 and 1930 (he retired from his Chair in 1933). His philosophy of science is summed up by the statement (in the preface to the 2nd edition of his book, Pearson 1937) that 'all science is description and not explanation' (p. 5). In the book itself he wrote 'The scientific man has above all things to strive at self-elimination in his judgements' (p. 11). On this view, the experimenter should even leave his theories outside the laboratory, with his overcoat as it were, so that the pure detection of objectively hard facts should not be influenced by theory. Pearson's view essentially reduced science in this 'pure' form to collecting observed correlations between sets of facts: 'The classification of facts, the recognition of their sequence and relative significance is the function of science' (p. 11).

It is implicit in this view that almost any venture into theoretical interpretation already contains the seeds of compromise of integrity, and that objectivity automatically guarantees neutrality.

The problems with this view of scientific integrity are well known. First, and most fundamentally, it is impossible to achieve. There cannot be an activity of the human mind that is independent of any form of theory. We must already hold particular beliefs about the world, ourselves, and how we come to know anything about either, in order to experiment at all in the systematic way that we call science. Paradoxically, Pearson himself recognised this when he wrote 'All great scientists have, in a certain sense, been great artists; the man with no imagination may collect facts, but he cannot make great discoveries' (ibid: 31). (Yet, in the same paragraph he also wrote that 'the imagination must not replace the reason in the deduction of relation and law from classified facts' (p. 31).) Moreover, and most importantly, these ideas must also be ones that could conceivably be challenged by argument or by further research. Science, like philosophy, can make no plausible claims to incorrigible ideas.

Second, even if it were possible to achieve such independence in practice, the 'science' that would result would be a particularly arid activity. It is hard, for example, to see how the theory of evolution could have emerged from such activity although, interestingly, Karl Pearson refers frequently to Darwin's work to illustrate *The Grammar of Science*, helped enormously by Darwin's own description of his research activity: 'I worked on true Baconian principles, and, without any theory, collected facts on a wholesale scale . . .' (Darwin 1887: vol 1: 83). Yet the creationists were surely, on Pearson's view of science, quite right to point out that Darwin's facts did not, and could not, prove the theory of evolution. Indeed they didn't. What did happen is that the same facts could not be seen in the same way once the theory was formulated. For those who were convinced, there was something deeply satisfying about the theory in relation to those facts (features like explanatory economy, for example – but recall that, for Pearson, science is not about explanation!); and for the intellectually adventurous there was the excitement of such a fundamental change in world-view.

As an aside, but a very relevant one from the viewpoint of assessing personal academic integrity, it is fascinating to see how Darwin struggled with justifying his leap of imagination and how, in a Pearsonian manner, he tried to keep his fact-collecting immune from its influence by not even writing his theory down even after he had hit upon it: 'Here, then, I had at last got a theory by which to work; but I was so anxious to avoid prejudice, that I determined not for some time to write even the briefest sketch of it.' He says it was 'four years after the inspiration [that] I first allowed myself the satisfaction of writing a very brief abstract of my theory' (Darwin 1887, vol 1: 83) (and even then he did so only in pencil, just in case he wanted to change!). Of course, there were many other possible reasons for Darwin's caution, not least the social, religious and political consequences of such a momentous theory. But can one imagine a scientist today waiting 4 years before even venturing into a preliminary sketch of a theory with such insight? An Archimedeian 'Eureka' is much more likely (see, for example, James Watson's account (1968) in *The Double Helix* of the frenzy associated with the discovery of the structure of DNA) – followed, of course, by an immediate application for a research grant!

The 'relatively neutral' view

Even though this extreme view of the nature of science would attract few overt followers, today it remains influential as a cultural background. I have encountered scientists, reacting to argument with philosophers about the nature of their work, resorting to the claim that they are 'only seeking truth'! – implying of course that there is only one form of truth. And it has been one of the standard defences of scientists and engineers that they, as discoverers, are not responsible for the uses to which society may put their discoveries. Moreover, the philosophical cousin of the totally neutral view has a very major influence indeed. This is the view that, while we must admit to the ideas that make experimentation possible, these are the only ideas that should influence what we do. Science must remain neutral in all other respects. It should not be influenced by the rest of the philosophical and political culture in which we live, nor should science pronounce on such matters.

This view must be taken much more seriously, of course. The experience of biology (e.g. the Lysenko disaster) and psychiatry ('psychiatric' prisons) in the former Soviet Union are severe enough warnings of the dangers that this approach seeks to forestall. And lest anyone thinks it is only totalitarian regimes that pose such threats, I shall deal later with threats that arise from capitalist society.

The first problem with this view is the very one that the totally neutral view attempted to avoid. This is the question of where does one draw the line between ideas that are relevant to systematic experimentation (which would presumably include, at least, ideas on existence, matter, time, dimensionality, regularity, coherence, etc.) without which we could not practice science at all, and ideas (such as political views on racial equality, religious views on the nature of life, etc.) which we should presumably ignore. (In fact, the relatively neutral view is the one that Pearson himself would have recognised. He regarded space and time, for example, not as 'realities of the phenomenal world, but the modes under which we perceive things apart'.)

Even a few years ago, a plausible answer to this problem was to say that while there might be a few boundary problems posed by questions such as 'Can we really measure human intelligence?' (cf. Gould 1981), there is no serious difficulty in drawing the distinctions in a general way. The argument would have been that we should not let a few difficult cases determine the central foundation on which integrity in science must be built.

The problem is that we are not dealing just with a few difficult cases. There are too many such problems in science today. I also recommend Gould (1981) as an antidote for anyone who still imagines that objectivity confers neutrality. Some of the nineteenth-century craniologists were highly objective in their measurements of cranial and brain dimensions in different peoples and races, but we would today regard them as far from neutral, not only in their interpretations of the data, but also (and this is the point I am making) in the criteria they used for conducting the research in the first place. As Gould puts it 'They have gotten nowhere, not because there are no answers, but because the answers are so difficult to get *and because the a priori convictions are so clear and controlling*' (ibid: 112, my italics).

The ethical impact of modern research

What has thrown this approach into disarray is the fact that modern science raises very deep ethical dilemmas that have forced scientists to enter into public debate on the issues. More importantly, having done so, they cannot fail to be influenced, even as scientists, by the outcome. To follow are a few examples.

- If experiments on the human foetus were ruled unethical after a certain age there would probably be no funding for them even if the researcher himself was convinced of their value. All research foundations now require proposals to be subject to ethical judgement and they must certainly be within the law.
- The possibility of direct alteration of the human genetic line (as distinct from the indirect 'natural' alteration that occurs through choice of partners, differential fertility rates, genetically-linked diseases and their treatment, etc.) cannot conceivably be regarded by society as an entirely 'neutral' experiment. Society must have a view on it which the researcher cannot ignore 'with integrity'.
- Commercial interest in, for example, research on HIV can – indeed must – conflict with the interests of society, as can both with the interests of competing researchers; witness the bitter public controversy between the American and French teams working to identify the virus. Here, virtually all the relevant factors were involved: reputations were at stake (pretty certainly the award of a Nobel prize would have occurred – one was given for the discovery of the Hepatitus B virus), the commercial interests were immense, and academic integrity (had the American team, led by Gallo stolen the French virus?) was one of the central issues that brought it all out into public view.

It is not a new situation for scientists to find themselves pressed to justify the freedom of academic inquiry. And this is the essential issue of integrity raised here. Beyond the question of what is ethically right, there is the obvious conflict between the internal criteria like academic freedom, and external criteria that would restrict that freedom. Earlier examples included the dilemma faced by those who worked on the nuclear bomb project, resolved by some scientists by the founding of the Pugwash conferences on the public responsibility of scientists. (The foundation responsible for the Pugwash conferences was recently awarded a Nobel peace prize jointly with one of the founders, the former nuclear scientist Joseph Rotblat.) Issues of public ethics are involved, but so also is that of academic integrity. It was certainly a matter of integrity to Rotblat that he should draw attention to the issues in such a dramatic and persistent way.

The economic impact of science

A second source of problems is already evident in these examples. The economic impact of science and, in turn, its cost to society are too great for it to be possible, even if it were desirable, to return to the nineteenth-century values of the self-financed 'gentleman researcher' working in his own basement: this is exactly how G.H. Lewes, common law husband of George Eliot, did his physiological work; the most recent example, but surely the last, is that of Peter Mitchell (see Slater 1994), who won a Nobel prize for work done on mitochondrial function in his own laboratory in Cornwall. Most science of any value is now impossible without substantial public or private foundation funding, and the protection of intellectual property has become a central feature of university research administration. To measure the change over 50 years simply consider the fact that the discovery of the therapeutic value of penicillin, if made today and exploited via the formation of a company, would be worth much more than the whole of the funding of research at Oxford University where the therapy was first demonstrated. The equivalent in Cambridge would be monoclonal antibodies. Even governments as antipathetic to public funding as recent ones in the UK recognise, some of them reluctantly, the economic impact and the value of such investment. Government funding of the science base in the UK is around £2 billion, and this is small compared to the USA, Germany and France (all at nearly twice this level on a per capita basis).

These pressures are sometimes portrayed as adversely affecting the balance between pure and applied research. The point seems obvious (applied research is, by definition, more applicable(?)), but it is nonetheless, mistaken. In one of the most extensive studies of this question (Comroe and Dripps 1977) it was shown that around 40 per cent of research publications necessary for certain practical applications in medicine to occur were from researchers who could not possibly have seen these particular applications of their research at the time that it was done. The most dramatic example from this study is that of how the nineteenth-century physicist Tyndall's analysis of why the sky is blue led to a practical test for lung function (not for nothing do we refer to 'blue skies' research!) Tyndall showed that the blueness of the sky is attributable to light scattering by particles in the upper atmosphere. This led to a test of lung function since the lungs absorb particles so that the last parts of the air expelled on breathing out should be clear of particles and so show no light scattering. Applicability, then, lies in the eye of the beholder and is only fully clear with the great benefit of hindsight. Pharmaceutical companies (amongst the greatest investors in research in the UK and world-wide) understand this point very well. They themselves fund a great deal of curiosity-driven research even in their own laboratories. In fact, the economic value of basic research is literally incalculable since it changes the market in which these values must be calculated. The former British Prime Minister, Margaret Thatcher, in a speech to the Royal Society in 1988, correctly remarked that the value of Michael Faraday's nineteenth-century work (leading, amongst other things, to the discovery of electric light) must today be greater than the capitalisation of the whole of the London Stock Exchange. Lasers (initially dismissed as not having any practical importance) form a more recent example; super-computing looks likely (though who knows for sure?) to be another; and every industrialised nation looks for the clue to super-conductivity with its promise of vast energy gains in an energy-hungry planet. These are yet more reasons why placing academic research increasingly under the control of industrialists, as is now happening in the UK, is unwise. Not only will this lead to conflicts of interest (already pointed out in the introduction to this chapter), but it will not necessarily achieve the desired aim of making research more relevant in the long term. Future relevance is almost impossible to guess.

Bio-technology also features strongly in this economic race. Here the economic issues, which inevitably challenge academic integrity (see below), are closely bound to ethical issues. Should we, for example, allow patents on pieces of the human genome? If not, why do we allow them on animal genetic material? The reason, of course, is that no bio-technology company would make the required investment without a patent, and if human material is excluded, so also would be many medical benefits. The development costs of a new drug are typically measured in hundreds of millions of pounds.

It is very important here to emphasise that I am not arguing that there is more intrinsic integrity in the pursuit of pure research. I am, rather, arguing that to force research to be more applied is to challenge academic integrity, for it leads, amongst other things, to funding agencies compromising their standards in favour of particular forms of research. There is, of course, nothing inherent in applied research that in itself compromises academic integrity. And, as I have already emphasised, it is a mistake anyway to think that more applications will necessarily come from research that is classified today as 'applied'.

A personal example

My own field of research fully illustrates these issues and their historical development. In 1952, when Alan Hodgkin and Andrew Huxley made their discovery of the ionic mechanism of the nerve impulse (for which they received a Nobel prize), practical application seemed remote: it seemed that the work was of purely intellectual interest.

Forty years later, in the hands of researchers on the heart, these ideas have become the basis of a super-computer reconstruction of the mechanism of a heart attack: the most dramatic killer of otherwise healthy people often at the peak of their careers. What price would one put on a solution to this particular, and widespread, scourge of modern society? In economic terms it is vastly more important than AIDS. Drugs and other therapies needed for cardiovascular disease represent a $30 billion industry in the USA alone.

In such a field, it is impossible for academics to occupy an ivory tower even if they want to, for at some stage it is essential to commercialise the products if they are to be of value to society. The distinction between the worlds of academe and industry then become very blurred indeed with all the issues this raises on freedom of publication, personal financial interests of the researchers themselves (which almost certainly played a role in the HIV virus scandal) and, since universities themselves want to benefit from such commercialisation, one even sees the term 'institutional greed' enter the vocabulary of the finance houses! (For an amusing parody of all this, see *Nature*, 1994, 4 October issue.)

Conclusion

The pressures on academic integrity in science are so great that they have changed the relationship between universities and industry and transformed the way in which scientists themselves would defend the values of their subject. It is easier, though, to describe what has happened than to arrive at new definitions of what academic integrity involves in this environment.

The problems of the humanities and social sciences

Arts and *science?*

Some would argue (doubtless Karl Pearson himself would have argued – certainly many popularisers of science do so today) that the sciences and humanities are so fundamentally different in nature that little, if any, discussion of integrity in the natural sciences could be relevant to the humanities and social sciences. In one form or another, such a view – emphasising the fundamental differences between science and the humanities – has dominated thinking in the Anglo-Saxon world during the twentieth century, though it never has done so, or at least never to the same degree, outside this intellectual empire. The very word 'science' still carries its old connotation in continental Europe, for example. An interesting reminder that the separation is fairly recent even in the Anglo-Saxon world is the persistence in The Royal Society Club (dating as it does from the seventeenth century, before the separation of the disciplines) of the toast 'Arts and Science', used at all its dinners. East-Asian cultures in this respect resemble more closely the continental European tradition than the modern Anglo-Saxon one. The relevant Chinese character carries the connotation 'knowledge' or 'study' in general.

The first part of my argument here will be to challenge what I shall call the Anglo-Saxon view. I shall do this by considering the various criteria often used in arguments for separation.

Science discovers, the arts create

This view is, of course, the basis of the claim that science generates 'hard' facts about the world, whereas the humanities express judgement about 'softer' features. The hard facts are objectively determined, the softer features are subjectively assessed. The trouble with this view is that we are all so familiar with it – and think that we understand it – and most of those who hold it even consider it to be so obviously true as to require merely stating. Yet it is patently false! With regard to science, it depends on separating science from technology, from mathematics, and even from its own theoretical foundations. My argument here bears close resemblance to some of the points made in Chapter 10 of this volume. Clearly, technology creates. It can only be said to 'discover' in the sense that it discovers what is possible, the boundaries of which are indeed a matter for science to investigate. But then, so too does music (could we plausibly hold that the relevant sense in which there are boundaries to this creativity are independent of the science of hearing?); so too does poetry (consider some of the highly technical achievements of Troubadour poetry – for example Arnaut Daniel's *Sestina* – or Chinese poetry – at least equally demanding technically – and ask whether these could be independent of the technical limits that might be revealed by a scientific study of human language and communication).

In an earlier age, one might have taken the view that science could, even should, be divorced from technology. In an age of super-computers and highly concrete modelling of scientific theories, that is increasingly implausible. Some of the most important theoretical work in modern science depends on this particular technology. Some fields of science and mathematics, such as non-linear theory, complexity theory and the study of what is technically called 'chaos', would not exist were this technology not to have been developed. These are forms of science that have literally been made possible by advanced technology.

In this context, and given what I have written about Pearson and Darwin earlier in this chapter, it is intriguing to note that some of the most advanced work on the theory of evolution (such as the investigation of self-organising systems, the dynamics of populations, and questions concerning the speed and range of natural selection, including the extinction of species) must necessarily be done using computers. The practitioners of this art of investigating the principles of emergence and how life may have evolved, are the direct intellectual descendants of Darwin, yet they could not possibly do what they are doing were they to take Darwin's view of the relation between theory and observation. They must not only write their theories down, they must do so directly in the form of computer programs in order to make any 'experiments' at all. They literally create possible worlds in order better to understand the world as it is (cf. Coveney and Highfield 1995; Gleick 1987; Waldrop 1992).

With regard to the humanities, the Anglo-Saxon view is guilty of distorting whole disciplines and cutting them off from much of their proper domains. I will give one example of this from my own experience, over the last 30 years, as a scientist who has been privileged to interact extensively with philosophers. Much of what I had to read to make myself competent to take part in these interdisciplinary debates (for example, Strawson's *Individuals* 1959, Ryle's *The Concept of Mind* 1949, Hampshire's *Thought and Action* 1959) was clearly written within a tradition that not only accepted a clear separation between matters of science (the empirical) and those of philosophy (the conceptual) but almost seemed to revel in not needing to enter the domain of science. Indeed, one of the earliest debates I was involved in (concerning Charles Taylor's *The Explanation of Behaviour* 1964) required, but then raised doubts about, a clear distinction between the empirical and the conceptual. (The philosophically-minded reader will readily understand why I then found Quine so exciting). Today, one has only to read recent volumes in this area (such as Daniel Dennett's *Consciousness Explained* 1991 or Derek Parfit's *Reasons and Persons* 1984) to see that such a separation would now be infinitely harder to draw. So much so that when six of us (three philosophers, three scientists) wrote up the results of our discussions on Intentionality (cf. Montefiore and Noble 1989), we found the boundary of the arguments continually crossing any notional 'divide' between the scientists and the philosophers.

Science is falsifiable

Here we are surely on safer ground(?) With Karl Popper's falsifiability criterion (Popper 1959) we can even clearly distinguish science from pseudo-science. Of course, this was a major milestone in the philosophy of science and is therefore fundamental to any concept of scientific integrity. Some have even used the claimed absence of a falsifiability criterion to challenge the integrity of whole fields of science.

Nevertheless, there are worrying rough edges. First, even some theories that would clearly rank as scientific have had a hard time earning their falsifiability credentials even after they had become widely accepted. The most notable example here is the theory of evolution. Second, the criterion is itself a version of the strict separation between the empirical (which can be used to falsify) and the conceptual (which cannot be used to falsify). But one has only to raise the last question to see that there is a gaping hole in the thesis. Large areas of theoretical work have internal criteria (like coherence, compatibility, creativity) that certainly occupy a higher priority than strict falsifiability at the time the work is done, and which often lead to theories being abandoned before they are ever put to empirical test. How, then, does this activity differ from many areas of the humanities? Doesn't a historian, for example, use similar methods: create an interpretation, investigate it for coherence and compatibility, even ending up checking it against known facts? I am not, here, championing the idea that history should be reinterpreted as a science. I am merely noting that there is enough similarity for there to be similar issues relating to questions of academic integrity. There are even areas of science that have history-like characteristics. A good account of this view, as applied to evolution, can be found in Stephen Jay Gould's wonderful book *Wonderful Life* (1989).

It is also important to note that lack of falsifiability cannot, in itself, be a challenge to academic integrity. Someone whose work is not intended to be falsifiable, and who may not even make a claim to falsifiability, does not thereby lack integrity. Even someone who falsely claimed falsifiability does not necessarily lack integrity: he may simply be wrong! If being wrong were a criterion for lack of integrity, then academic integrity would be an impossible ideal.

Science as progress

A powerful feature of scientific research is the way in which each piece of research stands on the foundations established by its predecessors. There is an accumulation, both of empirical discovery, and of theory that virtually guarantees a definition of progress in science. In my own field, for example, I can trace this heritage back at least to William Harvey, through to the discovery of animal electricity, to electrochemistry, and more recently to the work of Alan Hodgkin and Andrew Huxley on the nerve impulse. It is a fundamental aspect of scientific integrity to acknowledge and document these connections in scientific papers in a very explicit manner. In the humanities, at the least, there are different traditions in the way in which these debts are acknowledged. Philosophers, for example, divide into those who write with extensive acknowledgement of the history of their discipline and those who appear almost deliberately to ignore it. And surely it is deliberate? One cannot, for example, imagine Wittgenstein's work having the impact it has had, if it had been written in a totally different way, full of specific references. The writing technique was itself part of the essence of the work. Yet no-one surely would accuse him of a lack of integrity in employing such a technique. This difference is important, particularly in a discussion of academic integrity, but we should be careful not to overplay it. For equally surely, no-one would imagine that someone like Wittgenstein was unaware of his predecessors, even if he reveals a contempt for their efforts and errors (be careful, though: so do angry young scientists!). Indeed, the acknowledgement, and therefore the evidence of integrity, is built into the work in an implicit way that simply does not require extensive overt statement. To put the point in a Wittgensteinian way, we know by what the work shows what it is not necessary for the work itself to say.

There is, of course, a criterion for academic integrity here that the sciences and humanities clearly share: plagiarism always involves a lack of integrity.

Conclusion

This section could readily be continued with other examples from the standard criteria used to define the way in which the sciences and the humanities differ. But what I have written on these three central examples will suffice to illustrate the thesis that I wish to propose. This is that there is more to bring the sciences and the humanities together in their attempts to define academic integrity than there is to separate them. As I made clear in the first part of this chapter, it has taken a major public debate on the costs and ethics of science to bring about an acknowledgement of this state of affairs, but that is an incidental historical fact, not a necessary feature of academic life.

I want to finish this chapter on an urgent note. I see this breakdown of the division between the sciences and the humanities as crucially important to a major challenge the academic world faces, and one which will test academic integrity very seriously indeed. The challenge arises from the obvious fact that knowledge, particularly on the scale on which we now possess it, is deeply subversive. This is obvious in a historical context, but it is also obvious as a fact of contemporary life. The structures of society – social, political, religious – are creaking heavily with our inability to absorb what we know into ethical and social systems that are capable of being widely accepted. The problem is urgent because we cannot avoid some of the ethical questions referred to in the first part of this chapter. One possible outcome is, of course, a retreat into fundamentalism of various forms, which would certainly challenge academic integrity severely. The alternative – and I would rank this as a matter of academic integrity – is to acknowledge that there is an obligation on the part of the creators of this stockpile of knowledge to work out how to disarm its ability to destroy us.

References

Comroe, J. and Dripps (1977) *The Retrospectroscope*. Menlo Park, CA: Von Gehr Press.

Coveney, P. and Highfield, R. (1995) *Frontiers of Complexity. The search for order in a chaotic world*. London: Faber & Faber.

Darwin, F. (1887) *The Life and Letters of Charles Darwin including an autobiographical chapter*, 3 vols. London: Murray.

Dennett, D.C. (1991) *Consciousness Explained*. Harmondsowrth: Penguin Books.

Gleick, J. (1987) *Chaos. Making a new science*. London: Heinemann.

Gould, S.J. (1981) *The Mismeasure of Man*. New York and London: W.W. Norton.

Gould, S.J. (1989) *Wonderful Life*. Harmondsworth: Penguin Books.

Hampshire, S. (1959) *Thought and Action*. London: Chatto & Windus.

Montefiore, A.C.R.G. and Noble, D. (eds) (1989) *Goals, No-Goals and Own-Goals*. London: Unwin Hyman.

Parfit, D. (1984) *Reasons and Persons*. Oxford: Clarendon Press.

Pearson, K. (1892) *The Grammar of Science*. London and New York: J.M. Dent; Everyman (1937).

Popper, K. (1959) *The Logic of Scientific Discovery*. London: Hutchinson.

Ryle, G. (1949) *The Concept of Mind*. London: Hutchinson.

Slater, E.C. (1994) *Peter Dennis Mitchell, Biographical Memoirs of Fellows of The Royal Society*, 40: 281–305.

Strawson, P.F. (1959) *Individuals*. London: Methuen.

Taylor, C. (1964) *The Explanation of Behaviour*. London: Routledge & Kegan Paul.

Waldrop, M.M. (1992) *Complexity. The emerging science at the edge of order and chaos*. Simon & Schuster; Penguin Books (1994).

Watson, J.D. (1968) *The Double Helix. A Personal Account of the Discovery of the Structure of DNA*. London:Weidenfeld and Nicolson.

12 Integrity in surgical life
What happens if it is missing?

Colin Rayner

Integrity in the doctor–patient relationship

Professor Calne, the noted medical writer and pioneer of liver transplantation in the UK, once made an observation that, in peace time, surgeons are the only people who constantly live in a situation akin to the state of war. The use of the hand to inflict injury with a patient's consent has immediate effect. There is nothing abstract about it. There is no distance between action and effect. Cutting with a knife touches and threatens the very substance of life itself.

Integrity and individual responsibility under the pressures of consensus decision-making

To bring a patient to the operating table normally requires the final decision concerning treatment to be made by the surgeon himself. This means that, ultimately, the responsibility rests with one individual – the surgeon – to make a correct decision. This is then followed by the operation itself which is initiated by that individual making the first incision.

When making a clinical decision on a complex situation leading to operation, a large amount of information may have to be considered. In addition, resources will need to be organised to support the patient pre- and post-operatively. Furthermore, other concurrent conditions may have to be managed by different specialists, and conflicting issues and interests may have to be reconciled. In such circumstances, that is in a situation of collective decision-making, responsibility is shared. There may be a general tendency to compromise. Worse, responsibility may be deferred, or, worse still, avoided.

However, surgery cannot function on that basis. Ultimately it is under the control of one individual: it requires the decision of an individual to act on the patient's behalf. But for this act not to be compromised the surgeon must be able to withstand the pressures imposed on him by his complex situation. We may describe this by saying that the effectiveness of the surgeon's action in these circumstances is dependent on the surgeon's integrity. We may also say that the surgeon's ability to act with integrity in such circumstances is an attribute of his personality.

Integrity and the pre-requisite of disinterestedness

The essence of the Hippocratic Oath is 'first do no harm'. The fundamental prerequisite for the proper initiation of medical care is that the doctor should aim to act in the patient's best interest. This concept is expressed in the British General Medical Council's guidelines on professional conduct. An operation is an exercise in surgical technique. A technically correct result will be achieved when it is applied to redress an appropriate patho-logical or anatomical condition. However, a technical success is not neces-sarily the same as a satisfactory outcome. 'The operation was a success, but the patient died.' A less facetious example – a male patient with a nose deformed due to trauma may ask for surgical correction. Anatomical norm-ality could be restored, but not necessarily the pre-injury appearance. If the injury had occurred in an assault, the patient may be seeking restoration of the pre-injury state in order to be relieved of feelings of anger or humiliation. Failure to achieve that, despite a technically correct result, could reinforce the adverse psychological state with disastrous consequences. The surgeon looks for indicators, based on his experience, that may weight his judgement in this situation. Such patients have been known to resort to self-harm or other forms of violence. It is not sufficient to present the patient with the above scenario and then simply act as the patient's agent, absolved of respon-sibility. In this case 'acting in the patient's best interest' may be to decline to act at all! Parallels exist in all other specialities.

How, without arrogance, can one decide what is in another individual's best interest? How does one avoid the pitfall of making a decision based on an inadequate understanding of the patient's best interest? First, a conscien-tious effort must be made to obtain a good appreciation of the patient's his-tory and motivation. This may include such factors as emotional or material support or isolation, intelligence and religious attitudes. Second, the clinician must be detached from personal rewards – be they material, emotional or intellectual – whilst trying to weigh-up the other individual's condition. These matters cannot be pursued inexhaustively and therefore there is always the possibility of error. Failure to recognise this, and over-confidence, can lead to a paternalistic approach to medical care. This may be avoided by not making decisions for people who are of sufficient maturity and sufficiently informed to make their own. Where the surgeon's view conflicts with a patient's decision, time should be taken for reflection and possibly a second opinion sought. Paternalism seems to imply taking responsibility on another's behalf when that person wishes to delegate his own responsibility through diffidence or some kindred inhibition. Whilst it could be used to the patient's benefit when exercised with humanity and integrity, in reality it should be recognised that that situation arises from an inability of the patient to reconcile his wishes with his ability to act. This situation has to be managed by the two parties, based on communication and the clinician's willingness to take some *risk* (on his own account) to reassure the patient. Again, the clinician's integrity must be the 'broker' in this situation. Old-fashioned paternalism (strong versus weak) really has no role in modern practice. The basis for the establishment of the doctor–patient relationship should be such that it is not compromised by factors that potentially interfere with the practitioner's ability to focus objectively on the patient's requirements. An example of the application of this principle leads to the traditional view that doctors should not treat their own families. Compromising circumstances can arise if the doctor is so focused on financial or scientific advancement that the patients are primarily considered in the light of those requirements rather than their own needs.

The profession exists in a competitive environment that demands that the clinician demonstrate ability in science. When trying to reconcile biological measurements with the effects of applying craft techniques to a constantly varying subject such as the human body, the product of research cannot be expressed in rigid mathematical or scientific terms. The ethics governing what it is acceptable to do to a human being impose severe restrictions on experimentation. If an operation 'works well' in the hands of its originator, but the same results cannot be achieved by his peers, then he may have unique skills or else the procedure is based on a false premise and the results are not really as reported. Possibly the preliminary laboratory work did not translate into the same effect in human anatomy or pathology. Medical history is full of examples of clinical blind alleys that were either mistaken pathways or sinister ways to advancement and success. Of course, there are all shades of grey and the risks of being overtly discredited as dishonest are low unless the effects are lethal. Whilst these problems are doubtless always in existence, it is nevertheless greatly to the credit of the profession's *corporate* integrity that the vast majority of patients are dealt with honestly.

The antithesis of a proper doctor–patient relationship is the use of patients by a doctor to further his own interests. As doctors suffer from human frailty themselves there is always a tension between pursuit of the interest of the patient and that of the doctor. If one pictures these pursuits as weights at the opposite ends of a balance, then the factor that tips the scales in one direction or the other is integrity or a lack of it (or even the relative *strength* of integrity).

Integrity and trust

The decision on treatment *on the patient's behalf* is normally made in consultation *with the patient*. This introduces an additional complexity into the meaning of what it is for a surgeon to act with integrity. There is a need to establish *trust* between doctor and patient. Whilst professional introductions can give some immediacy to this, the process nevertheless needs an element of time to develop. In order to evaluate an individual's needs his situation has to be understood and this may need confidential information to be given. It is privileged information and, like 'insider' information in business, should not be used inappropriately. This information gives the recipient opportunities for personal advantage, for example, sexual favours, bequests, gifts etc. Clinicians can justifiably enjoy the respect and friendship of their patients – effectively this is obtained as a privilege controlled by integrity which does not allow them to cross the boundary and abuse trust.

This point is connected with the previous one. A surgeon will only be trusted if he is seen to be disinterested.

Some observations on the development of integrity

Irina Ratushinskaya, the dissident Russian poet, in her book entitled *In the Beginning* (1990) describes her upbringing surrounded by institutionalised falsehood. In this work, she tells how she learned to be truthful. Two other quotations give some insight into this process of learning. Thomas à Beckett was originally a playboy with powerful connections. Eventually his life led him to a moral crossroads:

> Now is my way clear, now is the meaning plain;
> Temptation shall not come in this kind again.
> The last temptation is the greatest treason:
> To do the right deed for the wrong reason.
> (Eliot 1968: 47)

Finally an anonymous, strangely inverted quotation emphasises that some qualities of character are acquired by conscious effort. 'Innocence is something acquired, an act of the will.'

If temptation did not exist, integrity as a moral virtue would have no meaning. Integrity is, therefore, essentially about making choices. The term 'moral maze' is often used to describe difficult and complex clinical situations. A surgeon serves extensive training (formal education) and apprenticeship (experience modified by circumstance) over a long period of time. In addition to one's innate personal attitude or motivation, professional development lays an additional obligation to act properly on a patient's behalf. It takes time and willingness to learn to understand the complexities involved. A surgeon must, therefore, confront these issues and systematise his response. This can never be wholly mechanistic but should become progressively more disciplined. Along the way temptation will always be a factor – not in every situation, but often enough to require a moral effort to do the right thing. Integrity governs that effort.

A composite medical scenario: integrity in the NHS hierarchy

I now examine pressures on, and the exercise of, integrity within the British NHS system, starting at the level of the Consultant, then going 'upwards', through the management structure and disciplinary processes, to the General Medical Council.

'Moral hazard' pressures on the integrity of the NHS Consultant

If we picture the Consultant in his or her interview room at the time he or she is assessing a patient, towards the end of the interview there will come a time when a choice has to be made. In many instances there are different treatments that can be offered to the patient. Under normal circumstances, one hopes that the basis of this choice would be strictly ethical. That is to say, the doctor will aim to do what is optimal for the patient. However, it is not unreasonable that where a wide range of possibilities exists, the surgeon should select that treatment which he felt most able to execute with good success. In other words he would, to use a sporting metaphor, 'play to his own strength'.

If, however, integrity is not quite so powerful, the Consultant may simply select a treatment which is most favourable to himself. The patient may not feel disadvantaged by this. He or she will not possess all of the information at the Consultant's disposal, and will not know of the other quality outcomes that could be achieved.

There are powerful reasons why a practitioner might choose to act in that way. The Consultant may consider that there are wider issues in the nature of his practice other than simply treating particular patients well, e.g., it may seem important to establish a wider base to his practice for it to flourish effectively and the service to become known. On occasion this leads to the indiscriminate acceptance for treatment of all patients referred. This can be irrespective of whether or not the referral was appropriate and whether or not there are the resources actually to deliver the care promised. In this way the practitioner can begin to create a need. As need becomes apparent more cases are referred. Following indiscriminate acceptance of treatment, it may then become apparent that it is not possible to deliver this within a reasonable length of time. The patient may seek other sources for treatment or indeed be pushed towards the private sector. A variant of this is for the Consultant to suggest that the treatment required is not available on the NHS sector and the patient should seek to get the treatment done in the private sector, under the care of the Consultant himself, on a fee-for-service basis. The unscrupulous Consultant can thus use the pathways of referral in his own interest. Furthermore, the direction or control of patients in these situations can be reinforced by the professional or personal 'aura' of the practitioner, which can be extremely powerful.[1]

There are, however, many occasions when these same pathways of referral can be followed without serious ethical compromise. There will always be treatments which are too new or experimental or expensive to be available on the NHS, and there will be times when waiting lists and queues make the treatment under the NHS – even an identical treatment – inferior for the patient. Referral of the patient by the Consultant into the private sector, even referral to the Consultant himself, will then be in the patient's own interest.

It can thus be seen that there may be the possibility for creating need and that the Consultant can turn this possibility to personal advantage. But such unscrupulous behaviour will be difficult to detect, since only the practitioner will know whether he is acting in his own interest or in the patient's interest. It therefore rests on the integrity of the practitioner not to abuse these pathways.

Professional integrity also requires practitioners to state the needs of patients – real needs, not manufactured ones – and to try to ensure that resources are made available for them. Fighting for these 'stated needs' becomes part of the professional responsibility of the consultant (see below).

Pressures on doctors' integrity created by management priorities within the NHS

Often management priorities involve numerical targets. Qualitative objectives are often identified, but in reality these are largely nominal; and often the pursuit of the objective is at the expense of the quality of outcome following a course of medical or surgical treatment. As an example, consider 'Waiting List Initiatives'. Where waiting lists have become excessively long and are a political embarrassment, money may be provided to buy extra work in order to reduce their length. Patients on waiting lists will have a wide range of priorities, but their treatment is purchased indiscriminately simply to meet time deadlines. They will also have been accepted and counselled by a specialist, often with individualised treatment plans according to their needs and the specialist's skills. However, the patients may then be transferred elsewhere to a clinician who in this instance need *only* be motivated by financial consideration. On such occasions the clinician may carry out a treatment plan that he would not have 'owned' had he been taking primary responsibility for the patient. In effect he is acting as an agent for a third party (i.e. to meet a managerial directive) and the patient's interests become more peripheral.

The second management priority is 'to control the medical environment'. This is usually in response to policy guidelines. Administration will identify need within the guidelines and will then plan development. However, any needs of which they are advised – the 'stated need' discussed above – may meet with resistance or denial if they do not relate to the given guidelines.

Another management priority is to project the image that within set parameters 'all is well'. The advice goes out: 'Look for good news stories!'.

All three priorities can create practical problems for clinicians. It may be difficult for them to obtain formal recognition that a problem exists. This can lead to frustration and to them looking to other spheres of influence to obtain a response. That then leads to management resentment and political instructions may be given to managers to counteract this unwanted situation. Covert warnings may be issued to try to suppress the problem.

Does the management structure create a dilemma?

The higher management structure has public and political accountability. In a huge organisation managing vast sums of money this level of management (usually non-clinical in background) cannot be close enough to the point of action – the clinical realities – to be involved with organisational decision-making at that level. When major strategic decisions are translated into detailed action at 'shop floor' level many inconsistencies emerge and these can profoundly affect clinical outcomes.

Problems are compounded by the fact that, in the UK, management has undergone radical change in the last few years. 'Trusts' can no doubt bring decision-making closer to the point of delivery of medical care.[2] But within the present transitional period a major dilemma has emerged. Senior management makes major decisions and defers detailed management to 'directorates'. But these directorates are not empowered to act without counter-signature of the senior management above them. Furthermore, the directorates are also subject to professional resistance 'from below'. They are perceived to operate by means of an autocratic system; although such autocratic systems may be found in different cultural circumstances, they are not appropriate to the medical world. Thus, senior management will not act, but middle management cannot act. In such an immobilised system, reports of clinical difficulty are not easily acceptable. Therefore to bring about change is doubly difficult.

Finally, there are conflicts created by the fact that, whereas managers and administrators are 'easy' to sack and therefore vulnerable, clinicians with complex contracts, security of tenure and considerable freedom to act independently are not easy to dismiss. This creates difficult attitudes to the risks of openness and change.

If clinical realities demand that major decisions be taken by higher management, how do those managers trust the advice given? Is there not a history of 'empire building' by Consultants? Does the Consultant hold renegade but plausible views? A system which can respond rapidly must always contain some element of risk for the decision-maker. A system that evaluates situations based on listening to advice and testing the premises of that advice (does it really take two hours to transfer a patient from Ward A to Operating Theatre B?) would help. If the system allows agreement in principle that there is a problem and it has certain dimensions, then a plan of correction can be set up. Orderly though such a system could be, the reality is that there are still major human factors influencing the way it is presented and responded to. Higher management must be able to believe in the motivation and honesty of the clinician – his or her integrity – and the clinician needs to believe that the administration is willing to respond in an *unfettered* way, or at least that it will admit to limitations. One would wish to see that the organisation had the equivalent of moral integrity.

The NHS 'policing' system

For a system to be one which seeks to ensure the integrity of those working within it, it is not sufficient that it merely allows all individuals within it to be self-regulating and self-policing. There must also be mechanisms for improvement of clinical practice, and for the punishment of failures of intgrity.

The introduction of compulsory *clinical audit* is an effective way of inducing constructive self-criticism and peer review into clinical practice. It is not primarily concerned with wrongdoing or fault. Instead it provides external support for the raising of clinical standards.

Where wrongdoing occurs, the methods of handling it are very variable. Some establishments have an *'untoward incidents procedure'*. This is aimed at defusing potentially damaging situations and taking remedial action. A circumstance is reported to senior management who may appoint medical auditors. The role of such auditors is totally different from those who conduct clinical audits. The auditors can conduct a secret investigation and prepare a confidential report. On the basis of this, action against the relevant parties may be undertaken. Or the Health Authority may decide not to act if it perceives that such action would be against its own interests. Or other steps may be taken to redress damage.

The code of the General Medical Council (GMC) lays an obligation on all medical practitioners to report 'wrongdoing' by colleagues. The GMC is morally effective when dealing with practitioners who wish to act within the guidelines. It is relatively easy to pressurise a 'good' person to comply with its code. The less scrupulous assess the limits of the code and then find ways to comply technically but avoid the spirit of them. An examples of this is surgeons who work in cosmetic clinics that advertise to the public, who gain by the promotion whilst avoiding the censure of advertising themselves. Furthermore, when a doctor reports a colleague to the GMC, it has to be in the form of a sworn affidavit. There is no anonymity allowed. There is therefore a potential risk of reprisal – for example, if the complainee has criminal backers. The GMC, however, has no powers of investigation so the complainant must act as accuser and investigator.

The GMC was asked to raise this issue of principle with its Council, i.e., it was asked about how a reporter might be protected. The request was never acknowledged.

Ambition, trouble and the failure of integrity

A surgeon may develop a long waiting list. There are insufficient facilities to treat patients. The Health Authority may be pressurised to finance treatment and/or invest in dubious technology. The patients are not offered effective alternative treatment. They may even have been incorrectly offered treatment in the first place. Pressure mounts to divert them into the private sector.

This has three types of costs. Financial costs spiral as extra financial commitments are required. There are physical costs: patients suffer. And there are moral costs: effort must be expended to convince patients of the truth about advice previously given (where that appears contradictory) so as to avoid damaging confidence in the medical profession.

There may be no accountability for such behaviour. There will be none on the part of the surgeon, if his practice is unchallenged. There will be none on the part of the Health Authority, if it chooses not to expose an embarrassing affair. And there will be none on the part of the GMC, as it is not obliged to expose weakness in its own disciplinary system. But behind all this is the risk of ultimate exposure where there has been complicity due to silence, despite knowledge of the circumstances.

Patients too have obligations. Many instances exist where patients deliberately withhold information from attendants in order to obtain their desired procedure. Once committed, the surgeon may not easily change his commitment. Since the advent of the 'Patient's Charter' the most streetwise patients exert the most effective pressure in their own interests.

Conclusions

A definition of integrity is difficult. If we cannot define the quality of integrity we can at least recognise it by its peripheral attributes, something like identifying a black hole by the activity around it. Integrity is a personal quality; someone of integrity respects the rights of others, even (in extreme cases) to his or her own detriment or risk. Integrity does not seem to me to be an isolated characteristic. Rather it is a moral control mechanism that steers the individual to behave with truth, humanity, fairness or responsibility when dealing with issues that impact on other people. In surgery it is about acting in the patient's interest without necessarily obtaining self-gratification.

The exercise of integrity is voluntary, but may need support. It is necessary sometimes to identify matters which need to be brought to account. But if accountability is optional, who will ensure that this happens? It requires integrity and the support of an intrinsically upright administration, to bridge this gap.

Notes

1 Such aura can be harnessed to good purpose in medical practice rather than to bad, as, for example, in using the 'placebo effect'.
2 This still leaves room, or creates scope, for parochial factors such as inter-personal rivalries and 'old boy networks'.

References

Eliot, T.S. (1968) *Murder in the Cathedral*. London: Faber & Faber.
Ratuskinskaya, Irina (1990) *In the Beginning*. Translated by Alyona Kojevnikov. London: Hodder & Stoughton.

Section IV
Integrity in fund-raising

13 Should Mother Teresa accept money from the Mafia?

A note on ethical dilemmas raised by fund-raising and giving

Paul Flather

[Paul Flather is Director of External Relations at Oxford and involved in supporting the University's fund-raising work. However, the ideas in this chapter represent the authors own personal views, and in no way reflect University policy.]

Introduction

Money, it is claimed, is the root of all evil. But economists would only be the first in a line of objectors to point out that money, as such, only serves as the means for transaction and exchange. Moral assertions of good and bad must pertain to how money is obtained and how it is used. Such questions have been given urgency world-wide by the increasing phenomenon of fund-raising by public and private institutions. Non-Governmental Organisations (NGOs), charities, campaigning bodies and pressure groups, even freedom fighters and terrorist organisations, all are now driven to seek external funding from individual donors, corporations, communities, foundations and trusts. Does this kind of fund-raising cause any moral dilemmas? After all, it could be argued that as long as the fund-raiser sets out to spend it on recognisable and acceptable public goals which will, in some universally agreeable way, benefit the common or public good, even for a small group or specific community, the fund-raiser can, in some legitimate sense, ignore any questions posed by the ways in which the funds were earned or acquired. This might be deemed the 'hang it all, what matters is the good we're now doing' approach. Why should Mother Teresa not accept gifts from any dictator in the world, not to mention the Mafia, if she is going to spend the funds on rescuing orphans and the dying from the slums of Calcutta.[1] Indeed Mother Teresa may herself not wish to judge others. In ethical terms, the argument would be that the 'rightness' of the ends supersedes the 'goodness' or 'badness' of the motive of the donor. Fortunately, perhaps, for us, and unfortunately, perhaps, for the fund-raiser, this just will not do.

Fund-raising involves a relationship, from donor (through the act of giving) via the fund-raiser (who organises the transaction) through to the recipient bodies and individuals. Ethical dilemmas may arise at both ends of this relationship, as well as during the process; they may also arise in relation to the overall, cultural, context in which such acts take place. However, it must be noted right from the outset that fund-raisers are *naturally* inclined to accept funds that they are offered. This is, after all, the assumption on which they undertake their professional work of raising funds. But certain ethical considerations do intervene and fund-raisers recognise this, even if they can be both reluctant, and unsure about how to react to them.[2] The rest of this chapter seeks to explain why, and it does so for the following sets of reasons:

- first, the means by which the donated funds were originally obtained may provoke moral considerations about whether or not these particular funds should be accepted;
- second, the donor may require a certain implicit or explicit return or benefit for the donation which may prove unacceptable;
- third, the donor may seek to interfere or intervene unacceptably in the way the donated funds are to be spent;
- fourth, certain morally unacceptable levels of pressure may have been placed on the potential donor by the fund-raiser or receiving institution in the solicitation of the gift;
- fifth, the purposes for which the donated funds are to be spent may fail to meet certain public, and private, levels of individual or collective good; and
- finally, the donated funds themselves may have a morally corrupting influence on the aims and style of the receiving institution.

It is assumed for the purposes of this chapter that a donation should be accepted *unless* certain rules or provisos, as described below, are breached. The issues posed in this paper are couched largely in what would be termed normative (or first order) questions; meta-ethical (or second order) questions are largely ignored.

I

The first set of problems, and in some ways the easiest set of dilemmas to identify, though not the easiest to respond to in terms of developing an acceptable moral code map for fund-raising, is to do with the origins of the donated funds. As mentioned above, there is a school of opinion that says as long as the funding is to be used freely by the receiving institution 'to do good', it does not matter where it comes from.[3] Thus Mother Teresa setting up an orphanage in Calcutta with external funding would clearly seem to fit the bill. But intuitively, in some very clear sense, it would seem morally wrong to accept donations that were earned from, say, pimping, the sale of child pornography videos or drug-smuggling. Similarly, funds earned through racist exploitation, for example money made by the sale of diamonds dug by black slaves, or fortunes made by confiscating property of, say, non-communists or Jews. Equally, funds earned from arms-dealing, even where legal, may fall foul of a general moral code, and certainly that of pacifists. These are among the more obvious areas of ethical concern, but the list could continue indefinitely. An attempt to develop some clear framework for identifying the unacceptable limits – and by implication the acceptable types – of giving is clearly needed. But matching rules is not simple. For example, ruling out funds that are earned by 'corrupt' means might seem sensible, but would be too all embracing, given the variations of definitions and meanings.[4] A simple approach would be for **Rule One**, therefore, to state that all funds earned illegally should be rejected automatically, thereby immediately excluding drug-related or pimping earnings.

It can be argued that the definition of what is legal/illegal also gives rise to dilemmas – both in terms of the scope for interpretation of the law, as well as in terms of questions of civil disobedience against 'bad' or 'wrong' laws; equally in non-moral régimes (dictatorships, racist or chauvinistic societies) the law itself may sanction or support what we would take to be non-moral positions. **Rule Two**, therefore, would state that funds earned through the exploitation or destruction (morally or physically) of others, should also be rejected. This should exclude, for example, funds earned through even the apparently 'legal' destruction of others, for example under totalitarian, non-benevolent dictatorships, communist, nazi or other similar régimes. **Rule Three** might add restrictions on accepting funds from corporations or individuals involved in the destruction of the environment.

Even these apparently 'simple' rules throw up very significant difficulties. First, where and how to draw the line. For the purposes of this chapter, the answer will have to remain, in no small degree, a subjective assessment. Within a broadly acceptable liberal democratic framework, where morality is defined in terms of a set of prescriptions for promoting collective good in which the interests of all are treated equally, it is affirmed that there ought to emerge a broad measure of agreement on the positive and ethically negative, on 'goodness' and on 'fairness', even if assessments may, in the final analysis, still involve degrees of personal preference or intuition.[5] Of course, it has to be conceded that, as such, personal interpretation could easily allow a funding receiver to 'escape' a moral dilemma: an arms dealer may also produce hospital equipment, and the donation may be claimed to have come from the profits of producing the latter, rather than the former. But, for the purposes of this chapter, it is not proposed to wrestle further with such difficulties: the context of the moral dilemma has been established, along with a working hypothesis.

A second difficulty is just how does a potential fund-raiser discover the origins of the donated funds? There ought to be an onus on the receiving institution to investigate the background of the donor, whatever that involves. Equally, there must, and will, be practical and financial limits on the extent of such an investigation. Clearly, the blind man outside Waterloo station cannot be expected to check the *Who's Who bona fides* of everyone dropping a coin in his tin as they pass — just in case the money is tainted. Therefore, **Rule Four** might be that a receiving body should take 'reasonable steps' to discover the origins of funding contributions, commensurate with the size of the donation. Here the receiver does have some luck: it is a fact that the larger the sum involved, the easier it is, in practice, to have a rough and ready idea of its origins. Thus, the origins of a donation from the likes of the Rockefeller Foundation, the Kellogg Foundation, the Wellcome Trust or, indeed, the Open Society Foundation of George Soros, are fairly simple to identify, at least in general terms.[6] It is the source of the smaller sums which is more difficult to ascertain; yet the implications of moral uncertainty over the receipt of a donation must surely apply equally to a small sum as to a large sum. Clearly, given the costs of research, it would seem reasonable to incorporate into the rule-of-thumb, some element of correlation between the size of the donation and the amount of effort put in to divine its origins. Most significant fund-raising organisations, including the University of Oxford, now incorporate research units which are able to draw on the full range of public sources to build up profiles of potential major donors. Such background work is clearly geared to enable the fund-raiser to identify potential donors, to prepare a case carefully, leading, eventually, to a successful 'ask'. But such research should also reveal helpful information on the background of the donor and the funds to be donated, allowing ethical considerations, if necessary, to be taken into account.[7] It is those donors who do not, in any sense, feature in the public domain, who inevitably raise potential difficulties with regard to background investigation. Also difficult are private and unlisted company and family accounts, not open to public scrutiny. Ultimately, some information must also be accepted in good faith. This does tend to have some force behind it, as the risk of exposure and discovery by the investigative teams of the Sunday newspapers can easily outweigh any benefits expected in the giving.

A further difficulty arises if money, accepted in good faith, is subsequently discovered to have been obtained illegally, by fraud or by other unacceptable means. Thus, a good historical example might be the Tate Gallery, built with profits earned through the exploitation of plantation slave labour. While the Victorian establishment was happy to have the Tate built as a national gallery, the dilemma now is what, if anything, should be done, in changed times, and given the emergence of a multi-racial Britain. Clearly, no-one could rationally advocate pulling down the Tate. But if the same set of circumstances were to arise today, let us say on an offer to build a major new art gallery with profits made from Apartheid, clearly the nation would hesitate, and might well wish to refuse such a gift were it offered. Perhaps, in the case of the Tate, some definite acknowledgement of its less savoury antecedents should appear somewhere in the gallery. An interesting variant of this dilemma arose for an institution which had named a room after one of its benefactors, Sir Jack Lyons. When Lyons was convicted for fraud, a meeting was called to discuss whether the room should be renamed. In this case it was never suggested that the actual money given was fraudulently obtained but just that *he* was a crook.

II

Giving away money to benefit others makes one feel good. Well, that, at any rate, is the theory of donation: in the words of St Francis of Assisi, 'it is in the act of giving that one receives'. This, however, raises the second set of main difficulties outlined in the introduction: in modern parlance, there is no such thing as a free lunch. As the eighteenth-century satirist, Bernard Mandeville, put it, selfless benevolence is a contradiction in terms, 'sheer hypocrisy' (Mandeville 1998: x). Donation to charity, he argued, was either to develop – selfishly – a reputation for generosity, or a mechanism to assuage guilt. Perhaps this is going too far, but it is clear to all experienced fundraisers that the donor who does not want anything at all in return is indeed rare.

What do they want ? At the most basic level, it may indeed be simply to assuage guilt, or salve their conscience. In certain cases, in the reverse of the parable of the widow's mite, it might not even amount to generosity, which to be invoked must surely involve some sense of hardship foregone, in economic jargon, an opportunity cost. George Soros, the American–Hungarian philanthropist, who has given several hundred million dollars to support projects in East-Central Europe, has talked of the fact that his donations do not amount to charity because even donating such large and significant sums do not in fact tax him, as they do not in any way reduce his personal well-being. For someone on an average salary, (a humble Oxford don?) it may be the equivalent of donating £250 to a charity of our choice – not a noticeable hardship – the price of owning half a dozen new monographs as opposed to borrowing them from a library.

Two other forms of relatively harmless but nevertheless apparent 'benefit' to donors might be first, the notion of seeking recognition in posterity, and second a personal affinity to an institution and its goals. Thus, some donors may be seeking their own expression of *virtual* immortality, by endowing a perpetual scholarship scheme, or funding a building that will live on for centuries. Both are essentially charitable acts but with a personal motivation involved. Donors commonly also wish to support institutions that will somehow deliver the goals they share, or at least believe they share. Thus, I believe that everyone is entitled to a certain minimum standard of living regardless of race, gender, age and where they live, and I can 'enact' this belief indirectly by donating to Oxfam. This might be deemed 'selfish', but hardly in any serious, negative sense. Indeed, this notion of common affinity may well be the primary identifiable motive among groups of donors: the reason why so many Oxford *alumni* supported the University's Campaign for Oxford was, surely, at least partly because they shared the goals of the institution (as well as to say thank you!).[8] But the perceived private and public benefits to a donor may be even simpler: I sometimes feel that Mr Bill Coolidge, a great benefactor for Balliol College students to visit the US, who seemed to seek so little reward, nonetheless enjoyed the company of bright, young brains, and managed to achieve his goal of promoting better British awareness of the United States, as well as companionship with young people through virtue of his scholarship scheme. So far, though, no significant ethical problems have been unearthed.

Difficulties begin to emerge when the motivation involves seeking 'acceptability', perhaps access to higher, or certainly new and different, layers of political, economic or social influence,[9] or for corporations, the buying of an improved image by association. Thus, the *nouveau riche* can use charity to gain access to the Establishment; the immigrant can 'buy' the comradeship and gratitude of the host community, even proving that he or she is at least as good as 'them' (probably better). A major beefburger chain might support simplistic 'green' projects like Keep Britain Tidy, even though the sale of billions of burgers may be indirectly contributing to the wholesale destruction of the rainforests. A major telecommunications company can support arts and disabled groups to counteract its poor image for making excess profits or over-paying its top directors.[10] Thus it happens that a new museum dedicated to the history and traditions of native inhabitants, harshly treated following an invasion, has been established. The founder, a businessman, had set up the museum as part of a series of philanthropic activities, in the process ensuring his own personal access to the country's ruling elite, its 'great and good'. Effectively, therefore, a highly worthy, desirable and charitable act, was also a sound investment for him. A leading financier, a man dogged by controversy, hosted a dinner for 200 specially invited great and good, from all political parties, to celebrate a life of successful commercial and philanthropic activities. Mr Said has said that his gift of £20 million to Oxford for management studies was in part his way of expressing his gratitude to Britain, a country he admires and one that gave him a home. John Paul Getty is another whose gifts appear with the gratitude of a native American more at home in Britain. All these forms of indirect 'purchasing' of cultural acceptability would thus seem to share a very common rationale behind the worthy charitable donation: the return or 'pay-back' might come in the form of informal meetings with other well-known figures linked to a particular charitable cause; there might be photographs taken with these well known figures for publicity purposes; or the naming of a particular scholarship scheme, room or project after the donor. Thus, a picture of a financier in the company annual report with, say, a Vice-Chancellor of a world-famous university, following a donation, could be a relatively cost effective price to pay for the Company to gain the goodwill of other great and good, keep shareholders happy and gain credibility within the community.

By and large though, **Rule Five** would say that donations should be accepted if the gift is freely offered, and the receiver freely accepts any *quid pro quo* as a fair price to pay, and, if the donated funds can still be spent in the way that he or she wishes. The moral judgement from the man on the Clapham omnibus, Adam Smith's 'impartial spectator', may already have become hard enough. But if, for example, a donor subsequently demanded a seat on the relevant institutional governing body, or began to imply that a vice-chancellor personally endorsed his company's product, or, let us say, that the product had been tested successfully in the university laboratory, then clearly an unfair or immoral pay-off is being exacted.

All this looks just a little more sordid when political fund-raising is involved, and the issue of pay-off is brought into much sharper focus. If one tries to gauge the benefits that, for example, companies might seek to gain by donating to the Conservative Party (tax breaks, economic de-regulation, liberal labour laws) and equally the benefits for trade unions in backing the Labour Party (support for union members, improved welfare and health arrangements, distributive justice arrangements), then the pay-offs move into the realms of individual, corporate or interest group gain (possibly at the expense of others) – in other words egoism. Given the likelihood of direct or indirect pay-backs being involved in purely political fund-raising, it must be the case that the tests of free agency involved in **Rule Five** – both in the giving and the receiving – should be applied all the more stringently here.[11]

In order to explore further some of the underlying factors which may be at work, follow a hypothetical example: in return for endowing a new Chair in cosmic philosophy to be named after him, a particular donor seeks, and obtains, a visit by a vice-chancellor to his astrology gift factory where photographs are taken to be used for publicity purposes, in the annual report, to impress shareholders, with a feature on the new Chair. Here, acceptability is being merged into advertising – and the institution may even be largely ignorant of the real agenda. Pursuing the example, the vice-chancellor may then be invited to a relative's wedding, and, eventually, in comes a request for a university place for a niece. The first feature to note, and **Rule Six**, therefore, is to *expect* a *quid pro quo* in the act of donation and, as so many institutions now do, anticipate this by developing policies of reciprocation that involve various explicit means of saying 'thank you', which have been vetted in advance by the institution as agreeable and acceptable. If the donation is simply motivated by a wish to do good or by conscience or guilt, and no more so, the rule is still not infringed. Usually, though, there is much more to it, and it may well be that it is only in the medium to long term that the real pay-off emerges. A reciprocation framework is therefore best laid out clearly to avoid future misunderstanding on both sides. Thus, a major university could offer an honorary degree to donors, or perhaps more appropriately, invent a new form of degree-related recognition, arrange dinners, lectures, provide naming opportunities, plaques, inscriptions, scrolls, garden parties and the like. The ethical test for any institution really arises when its own operating principles are, in some unacceptable way, challenged in return for a donation. Thus, a political party may be asked to drop a campaign pledge, a hospital to arrange speedy and special treatment, the university to admit a candidate of lesser ability.

This latter was, allegedly, the story behind the headline-grabbing case of a Hong Kong millionaire and Wadham College donor in 1985, when it was alleged that, in return for a donation of some £500,000 towards a student block, a relative of the donor had apparently secured a place in the college. Whatever happened, it is clear that the matter might have been better dealt with by stating, at the outset, the mission of the college involved that all students had to win admission on merit and that whatever extra was donated – even if not explicitly as an inducement, was to be considered an entirely separate matter, along the already agreed lines of college reciprocation policy. However, the college could mount a sound, neo-utilitarian, defence: the student block would not have been built without the donation; many highly meritorious students would then not have been admitted each year. Once the block had been built, adding one more student to the roll did not disadvantage any other student or member of the institution. Thus the price of this alleged special admission was therefore small; in any case, admission judgement is an inexact science, and the potential of the applicant may have been deemed high.

III

Sometimes, the ethical dilemma may arise in the reverse way – namely the receiving institution has placed undue pressure on the donor. One extreme example would be in the case of the Mafia, which might raise funding from a protection racket, the kind 'you really have no choice about joining'! Here the unethical aspect of fund-raising is pretty clear-cut. Equally, the case of a liberation movement which has turned to armed struggle – the IRA comes to mind – which raised some funds from some Catholic supporters in a way that implied those who did not contribute were unsympathetic and liable to community hostility, ostracism, and even reprisals. Clearly, if the donor donates, the overriding urge would be for the receiving institution to take the money and spend – whatever the alleged dilemma. But **Rule Seven** would state that a receiving institution should not exert undue pressure on a donor by whatever means, and that the donor must be a free agent in the process of giving; otherwise the act cannot, as such, be deemed charitable. But what if the donor agent really does have freedom to give, but is either deliberately misled (and the rights and wrongs of the motivations are not the issue here) by propaganda. Thus the IRA's fund-raising campaigns in the US in recent years are clearly deemed suspect by the British Government in that 'the Troubles' were presented as a war of liberation against an oppressive colonial power rather than on troops acting to keep the peace. Thus, it appears that British water companies encourage you to support what is ostensibly a 'Third World' development project, WaterAid, which, while no doubt being entirely worthy, actually involves the placing of their own equipment in the project. False propaganda may come in a much more mild form: 'If you give £10 today, you may save a child's life'. Well, that statement may be true but probably only in a few cases. Dramatic licence has been used to emphasise the emotional appeal. Again, say the charity only ever intended to spend a small sum of funds raised in this way on that particular programme and channelled the rest elsewhere, or indeed if on the basis of that appeal, too much − several million perhaps − is raised and the money is channelled into other worthy but less appealing campaigns, other issues of concern are surely raised. **Rule Eight** would therefore state that fund-raisers must take all reasonable steps to provide full and fair information on what funds are to be spent on; **Rule Nine** that as far as possible the funds should be spent on what they were intended for − and, if this is not possible, the donor must be informed, even consulted. In practice, of course, donors learn to trust the spending and operational policies of those organisations who appear to work according to such rules in any case, for example, Oxfam or Amnesty International.

A donor may also be subject to singular community or peer-group pressure. Fund-raising activities within certain ethnic or religious communities or groups comes to mind. For example, within certain communities individuals are clearly motivated by well-established and laudable commitments to support the well-being of their community as well as society as a whole, to support those sometimes less fortunate than oneself out of prudence and precaution (it might be you who needs help on another occasion) to put something back into the society which gave them their chance. But is there not a degree of identifiable coercion at work, for example, at a community event, when, say, a receptacle is passed around and guests are expected, under the attentive gaze of others present, to put in an item of jewellery as it passes, a process I have personally witnessed. Ethnically related appeals are actually a well-known feature within general fund-raising strategies − thus Greeks are approached to fund ancient or Hellenic studies, or Indians to fund scholarships for poor students from the sub-continent, and so on − though in a still young profession, perhaps the ethical dimension of such appeals is not fully appreciated.[12] Thus, newly settled Sikh communities in Canada, partly homesick, but partly under community pressure, have provided funding and support for armed struggle for the creation of an independent Punjab state in India − Khalistan. Equally, there can be unfair professional peer-group pressure to donate. At certain professional gatherings, guests are 'embarrassed' into matching gifts by fellow professional colleagues: this is certainly a feature of some Hollywood fund-raising events in support of AIDS research. But, while there clearly is peer-group pressure at work, it can be pointed out that, strictly, a donor can still refuse to give − and perhaps the donor has really made the decision to give by choosing to attend such an event in the first place.

IV

It may seem trite in the context of the rest of this discussion, but it should be noted, for the sake of completeness if nothing else, that if the donated funds are themselves to be spent on morally corrupting ends, then a fresh set of ethical problems will, by definition, clearly arise. Clearly, funds that are (mis)spent, for example, on furthering the career or prospects of family members of the receiving agent, would seem to breach standards of private integrity – though once again note should be taken of cultural variety, as in certain societies the onus, the sense of private duty, is so strongly geared to the promotion of the interests of the family – most of all on the father promoting the son – that this heavily outweighs the sense of impropriety or nepotism that might be felt in the Westernised world. **Rule Ten** would say that, in any moral assessment, an element of cultural assessment is essential.

Where charities are involved, there is some degree of legal protection to ensure that donated funds are spent on the purposes for which they are donated, as stated in Rule Nine. But, **Rule Eleven** states that donated funds should be spent on collective good and not on ends that might count as the promotion of self-interest. I once sent, albeit very reluctantly, some funds to a persistent letter writer from Bangladesh, who was, it seemed to me, spending unnecessary money on sending registered letters with repeated pleas for funds to alleviate poverty in his village. On receipt of my relatively small money transfer I received a further letter saying the money had done much to relieve the poverty of the said individual, and could I send out a further instalment! Needless to say, the correspondence ended at once.

That case was pretty clear-cut, though once again a hypothetical example can help to illustrate more of the potential complexities involved: imagine, therefore, using funds donated to an educational institution for scholarships for overseas students, to pay for the repair of a college building, or carpets for a faculty dining room. Surely this would traduce the motivations of the donor. Of course, it might be argued that the building might otherwise fall down, threatening the very students who might stand to benefit from the scholarships. It would seem harder to justify the carpets – though as fund-raisers know only too well, it is often these kinds of items which probably most need new, non-recurrent, fund-raising support.

Rule Twelve would also be breached if an agency decided, again for whatever motives, to allocate only part, perhaps a very small part, of the funding towards the advertised programme. There would certainly appear to be ethical problems if significant sums are spent on the fund-raisers themselves and their work environment. If, say, 20 per cent of funds raised went on administration and further fund-raising preparation, this might be deemed by some as misuse of funds raised. Thus, Oxfam was criticised for allegedly refurbishing its offices after a particularly successful Africa emergency appeal had netted more than £20 million some years back, exceeding expectations by more than one-third. Oxfam would counter, as would other charities, that the morale and salaries of its staff (including its fund-raisers) are in themselves part of the equation for a successful operation and, therefore, such spending was justified. But full information should be put before donors. The argument could also be made that if so much is raised, the excess cannot legitimately or easily be spent on the original programmes concerned: the money would simply be frittered away, wasted or become corrupting, a powerful and valid point. All fund-raisers know that considerable funding must be invested at the start in order to mount a successful campaign. Thus the University of Oxford was prepared to spend £12 million in order to achieve its Campaign target of some £200 million, eventually raising some £340 million. **Rule Thirteen** then, would require fund-raisers to state the full facts about their fund-raising objectives; and **Rule Fourteen** that they take all reasonable steps to spend the funds raised on these stated objectives, and to reveal to donors the proportion of funds spent on operational overheads such as administration, travel, training, salaries and so forth.[13]

V

Finally, surprisingly perhaps, as indicated by the Oxfam example above, the case of charities having more money than they can usefully and properly spend, is not so unusual.[14] This can lead to a morally corrupting influence, as I discovered on a very recent trip to Nepal, where I visited a well-established environmental protection charity, working in the Annarpurna foothills. This charity is, deservedly, flush with money from Western overseas aid programmes, and in a little danger, according to some of its grassroots workers, of being 'morally undermined' by having 'too much money'. Specifically, workers are being well paid and losing their zeal, not to say their links, with those with whom they are supposed to work. Also, the charity's well established philosophy of avoiding 'handouts' in favour of providing sparse and limited pump-priming funds to promote self-help projects – much harder work in terms of assessment and monitoring – may itself be undermined by having too much money to give out. It may also be argued more generally that certain organisations are so confident of their continuing fund-raising abilities that they become slack and wasteful in their spending policies. Certainly, Mr Soros feels this as a constant 'threat' with his own philanthropic activities, especially within established institutions, because they become confident that, in the end, he will be on hand to 'bail' them out whatever they do, always assuming that it was done for the right motivations, namely to help the re-emergence of civil society in East and Central Europe. By-and-large, I do not think this to be a significant worry, but the point is well founded. Any small organisation that hits the fund-raising jackpot is liable to what might be termed motivational decay; equally those extremely badly off, I suppose, may be tempted to cut financial and moral corners. But the more useful response to any surplus – the unexpected or unplanned luxury of having a surfeit of funds, is that there is still not quite enough to cover the entire 'Wish List', and the fund-raisers must simply continue their good work. **Rule Fourteen** would say that fund-raisers have a duty to raise that level of funds required for justifiable projects, and to continually review their targets in the light of their success (as well as failure).

To try to conclude, six distinct series of ethical dilemmas between donor and receiver involved in the process of fund-raising have been outlined above. Essentially, it has been assumed that the receiving agents will want to accept donated funds – an essentially positive act of charity – but that a host of caveats – essentially negative factors linked to ulterior motive or undue pressure, may well be involved in the process. It is therefore suggested that the following 14 rules, should be applied to test the charitable act involved.

- **Rule One:** any funds earned illegally should be rejected automatically.
- **Rule Two:** any funds earned through the exploitation or destruction, morally or physically, of others should be rejected.
- **Rule Three:** any funds earned through the partial or wholesale direct or indirect destruction of the environment should be rejected.
- **Rule Four:** a receiving body should take 'reasonable steps' to discover the origins of funding contributions, commensurate with the size of the donation.
- **Rule Five:** a donation should be accepted only if the gift is freely offered, and the receiver freely accepts any *quid pro quo* as a fair price to pay, and if the donated funds can still be spent in the way that he or she wishes.
- **Rule Six:** a receiver should anticipate a *quid pro quo* in the act of donation and develop internally agreed and acceptable, clear and explicit policies of 'reciprocation' in advance, to say 'thank you'.
- **Rule Seven:** a receiving institution should not exert undue pressure by whatever means on a donor, who must be a free agent in the process of giving.
- **Rule Eight:** fund-raisers must take all reasonable steps to provide full and fair information on what received funds are to be spent on.
- **Rule Nine:** donated funds should be spent on the intended proposal as far as possible; if this is not possible, donors should be informed, and, where any significant sums are involved, consulted on the changed objective.
- **Rule Ten:** 'cultural' factors should be taken into account in making ethical decisions about giving and receiving funds.
- **Rule Eleven:** donated funds should be spent on promoting collective or individual good, and not for private or self-interested gain.
- **Rule Twelve:** fund-raisers should provide full information in advance about their fund-raising objectives and the purposes for which donated funds are to be used.
- **Rule Thirteen:** fund-raisers should reveal to donors the proportion of funds donated to be spent on operational and administrative overheads.

- **Rule Fourteen:** fund-raisers should aim to raise the appropriate level of funds required for their stated objectives, and continually to review their targets in the light of success (as well as failure).

These rules will prompt certain moral uncertainties which should require varying degrees of moral analysis *before* the act of giving should be completed. Even then, it should be remembered that further ethical dilemmas can arise retrospectively as a result of subsequent discovery or development. Finally, it must be admitted that while these rules may serve usefully to stimulate discussion of some of the ethical dilemmas that can be involved in the process of fund-raising, this chapter has not set out to produce a practical ethical code for professionals. Further work would be needed before the suggested rules can be applied fully in practice.

Notes

1 This particular issue is very much implicit in Christopher Hitchins' book, *The Missionary Position* (1985), in which he condemns Mother Teresa for providing her 'saintly' stamp of approval to a range of tyrants from Albania's Enver Hoxha to Papa Doc Duvalier of Haiti, who visited her to support her work.

2 There is an increasing sense of awareness of such dilemmas among the professional fund-raising community. Thus, for example, the University of Oxford set up an Ethics Committee to discuss any such issues during the fund-raising work undertaken under the auspices of its highly successful Campaign for Oxford (1988–94). The Committee has met on a number of occasions, most recently to review the background of the donation by Dr Gert-Rudolph Flick for the new Chair of European Thought at the University. This donation (worth *c.* £360,000 over five years) was subsequently returned to Dr Flick by the University at his personal request following public discussion of his family's Nazi links. The Chair is now supported by a new benefactor, who wishes to remain anonymous, who came forward after being irked at the public hounding of Dr Flick.

3 It is assumed that 'good' is something characterised very loosely in a neo-utilitarian sense of improving the general happiness of all (as Sidgwick argued), is something that should be done (as Kant would have it), but in a 'fair' and 'just' way (as Rawls argues). Thus, Mother Teresa impelled to set up an orphanage in Calcutta is deemed to fit the bill.

4 It is true that the *Oxford English Dictionary* definition of corruption: 'moral deterioration . . . the widespread use of corrupt practices, especially bribery or fraud; irregular alteration (of text, language etc.) from its original state . . . decomposition of a corpse or other organic matter', would seem pretty convincing. But if money earned through 'corrupt' means was, in some morally ordained way, banned, there would be endless scope for interpretation both of what was, or was not, corruption, and what corruption entails in different cultural and national contexts, leaving fund-raisers forever engulfed in ethical knots.

5 An interesting variation on this theme was illustrated by Cambridge University's decision to accept funding for a new Chair by the BAT conglomerate, which has major interests in tobacco. As smoking is seen as directly linked to the destruction of lives – it can be said to contribute to the 'physical destruction of others' (but directly and indirectly through passive smoking and the knock-on effect on dependants of a death by lung cancer) and hence open to objection. Equally it could be considered a personal choice issue. After a public debate, the dons at Cambridge voted 2–1 in favour of returning the BAT Chair. While no dons have yet resigned, the cancer research charities have threatened to switch their funding to other research centres. See 'War declared on tobacco sponsorship' in the *Observer*, 21 July 1996, p. 3. Interestingly, no major complaints appear to have been aired about the fact that a leading American University (Duke) was, by and large, founded on money donated by the Duke family, which made its fortune through tobacco sales.

6 Thus, for example, it may be clear that monies donated by the Hypothetical Foundation are largely earned from the profits of selling magnets the world over. But it may be that the profits are the result of exploitatively low wages paid to Bolivian miners. This would be deemed unacceptable by the receiving institution, if only it were able to ascertain all the facts and trace the resulting products back through a chain of economic links to the Bolivian miners. The case of the major donation by the international businessman Wafic Said to help fund the new Said Business School at Oxford University may be a case in point. It is alleged that he is an arms dealer. This Mr Said emphatically denies. It is true he played a role in the Al Yammah arms deal, which led to a major Saudi Arabian purchase of British arms. But he is very clear that he played no role in the negotiations and received no fee. He merely brought together the British and Saudi Arabian sides, suggesting the British offer was superior to the French. A university, even Oxford, clearly does not have the equivalent of an Insight team to guarantee this, though the University's Ethics Committee when it looked at the issue was absolutely clear his was a *bona fide* gift. See reports in the *Sunday Times* ('A gift for getting on in high society', p. 3), *Sunday Independent* ('Out of the shadows', p. 15) and *Observer* ('Who'd give £20 million to make Roy Jenkins happy?', p. 7) of July 21st 1996.

7 But no system, and no amount of research, is foolproof.

8 For a good outline of the philosophy and guiding principles behind the Campaign, see Drucker (1995), originally given as the Frank Geden Foster lecture.

9 In other words, the gaining of entry, and acceptance within the Establishment and élite circles, is OK, perhaps with the hope of an honour.

10 Note must also be taken of the fact that charitable contributions are, in any case, tax-deductible.

11 Perhaps in the case of donations to political parties, this very unevenness, involving 'pay-offs' and 'pay-backs', strengthens the case for a system of state-funding of legitimate political parties. But whether such a system would eliminate political bribery and corruption is far from clear.

12 An interesting case arose when a Chair in Middle Eastern Studies was endowed and accepted by a leading British University with the proviso that the post could not be held by an Arab. The outrage that this created led to the Jewish Community, on its own initiative, raising sufficient funding to allow

a new Chair to be established *without* restrictions on who might fill it. [This case is not the same as that referred to by Michael Pinto-Duschinsky (Chapter 14, p. 238). Eds.]

13   This in itself may serve as a useful external sanction on keeping such spending within reasonable levels, as donors would surely be averse to supporting organisations whose proportionate spending on its own administration was unduly large. An acceptable working average seems to be 8–12 per cent. One small, private, charity that I know, uses such data as a qualifying yardstick: any charity spending more than 20 per cent on overheads is excluded.

14   This is not to say that too much is being given to certain charities or to charities in general.

References

Drucker, Henry (1995) 'Why people give', *Royal Society of Arts*, Jan–Feb: 42–52.
Hitchins, Christopher (1985) *The Missionary Position*. Oxford: Blackwell Publishers.
Mandeville, Bernard (1998) *The Fable of the Bees*. New York: Hacket.

14 Fund-raising and the Holocaust

The case of Dr Gert-Rudolf Flick's contribution to Oxford University

Michael Pinto-Duschinsky

Paul Flather's arguments are so convincing that it is easy to assume that he is doing no more in his chapter than stating the obvious (Chapter 13, this volume). His view that institutions such as universities should conduct their fund-raising campaigns according to certain moral standards and that it is useful for fund-raisers to give careful consideration to what those standards ought to be seems to be no more than common sense. Yet, his insights are far from being platitudes. In fact, they are highly controversial. This emerges clearly from an examination of a real life controversy in which he and I were both participants – the debate about whether Oxford University was justified in accepting an endowment from Dr Gert-Rudolf Flick and about whether it was also justified in naming an Oxford professor the 'Flick Professor'. This controversy started shortly after he had completed the original draft of his chapter. During the debate, a number of commentators came close to the view that Mother Teresa should accept money from the Mafia.

The history of Oxford's 'Flick Affair' illustrates how different moral discussions become when they move from theoretical to actual situations. Questions of principle intertwine with those of factual detail, especially when the perceived interests of powerful institutions are involved. This justifies the relatively detailed examination in this chapter of the public arguments raised during the controversy.

In 1992 Dr Gert-Rudolf Flick was appointed to Oxford University's Court of Benefactors in recognition of his contributions to an initiative called the Europaeum. This was a network of universities in Western Europe created mainly by proponents of closer political integration in Europe.[1] Dr Flick's gift to the University of some £350,000 was used to create a five-year position whose holder would be titled the 'Flick Professor of European Thought'. Initially, the Oxford authorities proposed to allocate the post to St Anne's College. Dr Flick reportedly objected on the ground that he felt it was a relatively new institution and was less distinguished internationally than some other colleges. In accord with his desire that his endowment (and hence the Flick name) should be associated with an old and famous college, Balliol College (founded between 1263 and 1268) was asked, and after considerable discussion agreed, to accept the appointee as one of its Fellows. Balliol's qualms about accepting the professorship stemmed from a sense of solidarity with St Anne's. The new professor took up his post in the Trinity (Summer) Term of 1995.

One year later, on 12 April 1996, Dr Flick wrote to the Vice-Chancellor requesting that his name be removed from the Chair and that the endowment money be returned to him. His decision resulted from an intense controversy about the Nazi provenance of his inheritance and his failure (along with the rest of the Flick family) to provide compensation for the Flick Concern's former slave labourers. The debate, largely private but partly in the national press, revolved around two different clusters of issues: the legacy of the Nazi era, and the problems of universities faced with financial pressures and with the need to attract funds from wealthy individuals and from business sources.

First, this chapter will summarise the facts about the origins of the Flick fortune. Second, it will review the history of the controversy about the donation. Third, questions about the memory of the Holocaust, compensation for victims and reconciliation will be analysed. Fourth, the chapter will discuss the light the 'Flick Affair' throws on the broader questions about integrity in fund-raising raised in Paul Flather's chapter.

The Flick family and its fortune

The family's industrial empire was created by Dr Gert-Rudolf Flick's grandfather, Friedrich Flick. Flick was a self-made entrepreneur who achieved success mainly after World War I and, in particular, during the Nazi period (cf. United Nations War Crimes Commission 1949: 6 and *Der Spiegel* 1984: 26ff.). In the 1930s, Flick was one of the most active and most ruthless of German entrepreneurs in using Nazi laws (and the accompanying threats of expropriation, imprisonment and physical ill-treatment) to acquire at knockdown prices enterprises owned by Jews. His 'aryanisations' were later characterised by one prosecutor at Nuremberg as 'a form of industrial piracy' (Chernow 1993: 464). They included the purchase of mines formerly owned in Germany and Bohemia by the Petschek family, Luebeck's largest firm, known as the Luebeck Blast Furnace Company (ibid: 463), as well as iron resources in Lorraine (cf. Hilberg 1961: 76ff.; Ferencz 1979: 156; and Duchene 1994: 60). An article in the *Frankfurter Zeitung* of 21 June 1936 listed four earlier Flick 'aryanisations' (cited in Simpson 1993: 62). According to the official record of the Nuremberg Military Tribunal, by World War II, the

> Flick Concern constituted the largest privately owned and controlled enterprise in Germany for the production of iron, steel products, and armaments.
>
> (US Government Printing Office 1954: 26)

Flick was arrested by the Allies on 13 June 1945 and became the principal defendant in 1947 in the first of three Nuremberg trials of industrialists (the others being the IG Farben and Krupp cases).[2] The case was brought by the American authorities under Brigadier-General Telford Taylor. In December 1947, Flick was sentenced to seven years for war crimes. He was convicted on three counts: for taking part in groups or organisations connected,

- Count I: with 'enslavement and deportation to slave labour' of concentration camp inmates, civilians and prisoners of war;
- Count II: with 'plunder of public and private property, spoliation, and other offences against property' and;
- Count IV: with 'murders, brutalities, cruelties, tortures, atrocities and other inhuman acts committed principally by the SS.[3]

The US prosecutors produced detailed evidence that Flick 'enjoyed the special blessing of the highest [Nazi] Party and government officials in his pursuit of property owned by Jews' (United Nations War Crimes Commission 1949, VI: 102).

Flick was a member of and funded the Nazi party. He was a leading member of the 'Circle of Friends' of Himmler (Himmlerkreis). Among other events organised by the Circle, Himmler presided over Flick's pre-war guided tour of Dachau. In December 1943, the SS fuehrer received Flick and the Himmlerkreis at his eastern headquarters. Flick's chief business assistant until 1939, Otto Steinbrinck, who was convicted in the same Nuremberg trial, had the position of brigadier general in the SS (ibid: 409).

Robert Wistrich (1982: 76) sums up Flick as a 'supporter of the Nazi movement and one of the most prominent employers of slave labour in the Third Reich.' He states that '[d]uring World War II Flick's enterprises bought and used 48,000 slave labourers, 80 per cent of whom died.'[4] One surviving forced labourer, Trude Levi, has recounted in a recent autobiography how 206 women in her camp at Hessisch Lichtenau, who had become too exhausted to work, were returned to Auschwitz, from whence they never emerged (Levi 1995: 17). A survivor testimony, held at Yad Vashem in Jerusalem, records the conditions at Dynamit Nobel's munitions factory at Ludwigsdorf. David Glicksmann recorded that 10 Jews out of 800 employed there died each day from malnutrition ('generally there were only cooked leaves of red cabbage and spinach'), from being forced to handle an explosive powder that led to severe lung disease in 50 per cent of them, from long marches, from toxic injections, from being subjected to successive hot and cold showers and, finally, from being left to freeze to death in a room designated as a 'death chamber'.[5]

The distinctive feature of Flick's trial was his defiance and lack of remorse. 'Nothing will convince us that we are war criminals,' he stated in his closing comments (United Nations War Crimes Commission 1949, VI: 1187). He explained away everything. Of his visit with Himmler to the Dachau concentration camp he testified that:

> People worked in large airy rooms. They did carpentry work. . . . In the canteen one could buy practically everything except alcohol . . . the kitchen was like a kitchen in a large hotel with all installations . . .
>
> (ibid: 409)

He explained away his recorded anti-semitic statements as 'howling with the wolves.' He explained away his activities as an employer of slave labour during the War on the grounds that he had acted under compulsion (Simpson 1993: 270–71). When the prosecution produced documentary evidence bearing his signature that disproved the claim, he explained this away too:

> I initialled every document that came to my desk without regard to whether I had read it or not. . . I couldn't possibly accept the responsibility for every letter and for every little incident.
>
> (US Government Printing Office 1954: 808)[6]

And he explained away his special payments to the Circle of Friends of Himmler. He claimed they were solely for cultural projects supporting the SS leader's interests in the origins of the Aryan race. For example, the Circle arranged visits to midnight ceremonies at the grave of King Henry in the Quedlinburg Cathedral; it subsidised the 'anthropological' exhibits at the Ahnenerbe Institute in Berlin, excavations on the Lueneberger Heide and even a large expedition to Tibet (US Government Printing Office 1954, VI: 409).

Evidence produced in the course of several of the cases tried by the US prosecutors revealed a far more sombre story. The Circle acted as the meeting place between hard-core Nazi industrialists and SS generals and colonels. Its members included SS Lieut. Gen. Oswald Pohl, later condemned at Nuremberg and hanged for his role as the SS official in charge of the concentration camps and concentration-camp labour, and SS Brig. Gen. Otto Ohlendorf, later condemned at Nuremberg and hanged for killing 90,000 Jews in the Soviet Union in 1941–2 as commander of Group D of the *Einsatzgruppen* (mobile killing squads).[7]

The Circle's regular meetings provided useful informal opportunities to conduct a trade in slaves between industrialists who wished to lay their hands on stocks of labourers, and the top SS officers who controlled the concentration camp system. Some of the Circle's formal lectures consisted of topical briefings on the progress of the Holocaust. Ohlendorf (just back from the eastern front) reported on his 'anti-partisan campaign' in the Soviet Union. Flick was on the distribution list of a secret report dated 19 November 1941 describing the elimination of all the Jews of Kiev, Krivoy Rog and other towns in which 'those who did not escape were liquidated' (Ferencz 1979: 157). Reinhard Heydrich (Himmler's chief lieutenant) lectured to the Circle on the work of his SS security police; SS Col. Hermann Behrends, of the SS Racial and Settlement Office (another member of the Circle of Friends), talked on the resettlement of racial Germans in the territories captured by the Wehrmacht (Nuremberg Prosecutor, I.G. Forben Case, in US Government Printing Office 1954, VIII: 860). There were further briefings on groups considered as enemies of the Reich – Jews, homosexuals and Freemasons.

As far as the Circle's financial contributions to the Ahnenerbe Institute were concerned, they were partly used to fund medical experiments on prisoners organised by a further member, SS Col. Wolfram Sievers. It was from Ahnenerbe that Sievers instructed Eichmann to transfer 109 Jews from Auschwitz to Natzweiler so that they could have their anatomical measurements taken while still alive and be questioned about their ages and backgrounds; they were then killed and chemically preserved to make a 'scientific' collection of Jewish skeletons.[8] Funding from the Circle of Friends – of whom Flick was one of the most generous and most prominent donors[9] – also subsidised Sievers' macabre and cruel experiments conducted mostly at Dachau on responses of live prisoners to high altitudes, freezing, malaria, mustard gas, sea water and spotted fever.

After his conviction, Flick was permitted to continue to manage his business interests while in Landsberg Prison. He was released in August 1950. By this time the Cold War against the Soviet Union was leading to increasingly conciliatory policies by the victorious Allies towards the industrial giants of the Hitler era. According to Tom Bower,

> By mid-1949, the Americans were very anxious that German industry should expand to help the West resist communism . . . One key to German recovery and cooperation, Abs [himself a convicted war criminal and banker to the Hitler regime] told [US High Commissioner] McCloy, was the release of the industrialists in Landsberg.
>
> (Bower 1995: 404–5)

The fate of Flick's mines and factories in the years following Germany's defeat was to become a topic of the Oxford debate in 1995–96 (see Appendix 2; Keegan 1996). As described below, one argument used by those who sought to defend acceptance of Dr G.R. Flick's donation to Oxford University was that the assets he inherited in 1972 from his grandfather derived from Friedrich Flick's postwar fortune and that this was a new fortune distinct from, and therefore free from, the taint of his wartime activities. The fact that Flick's wartime business interests were so varied and extensive makes it difficult to reach uncontroversial conclusions about the precise connections between his pre- and post-1945 holdings (assuming that the question is morally relevant, which is itself open to disagreement). As Flick said during his trial, he had no fewer than 75 different plants in Germany under his supervision during World War II (US Government Printing Office 1954: 834). There are several clear points which lead to the conclusion that, at the very least, Flick's business activities during the Hitler period formed a significant basis of his postwar industrial conglomerate.

1   The Communist takeover of Central Europe and of the Soviet zone of occupation in what became East Germany led to the loss of Flick's holdings situated in these territories. They comprised a regularly quoted 75–80 percent of his wartime empire. Nevertheless, this means that Flick retained the rest. A 1955 study of Flick's postwar holdings published in the West German news magazine *Der Spiegel* makes this clear. 'Certainly, Flick retained in 1945 barely 20 percent of his mammoth holdings from the wreckage of the collapse. All the same, this remainder still represented a value of 500–700 million marks'.[10]

2   The restitution law passed in May 1948 by the British authorities in Hamburg obliged Flick to reach agreements with the Hahns and the Warburgs, whose pre-war interests in the Luebeck Blast Furnace Company had been taken over by Flick in 1938. Nevertheless this did not result in Flick's losing the company (Chernow 1993: 472).

3   Decartelisation decrees were enforced in the early 1950s by the Allied Control Council. Their aim was to break up some of the business trusts and to restrict the monopolistic practices of Hitler's Reich. Decartelisation did not entail expropriation. When existing owners were obliged to sell factories, they kept the proceeds, which they were then free to reinvest. Flick was not permitted to remain the owner of both coal mines and steel plants in West Germany. It nevertheless proved easy for him to cope with this rule. In some cases, Friedrich Flick transferred ownership to his two surviving sons; in other cases, he sold holdings in West Germany and used the handsome proceeds to buy into similar enterprises in France and Belgium, and to purchase other companies in Germany (Fishman 1986: 69).

4   Despite the ravages of war, occupation, and imprisonment, Flick appears to have remained at all times a very rich man. According to a contemporary report in the *New York Times* (1956), he netted 180 million marks (US$51 million) from the sale of his majority interest in just one of his companies, the Harpen Mining Company of Essen in 1953. In 1953 values, $51 million was a huge sum. Espelage has recorded that, when Flick emerged from prison in 1950, other holdings remaining in his possession included the Maximilian Works in Bavaria, the Luebeck Blast Furnace Company, and further interests in the Ruhr.[11]

Building on this extensive base, Flick made a series of (frequently secret) acquisitions. He became the major shareholder in a number of large and growing corporations such as Daimler-Benz. When he died in 1972, the Flick fortune was 'an empire embracing holdings in some

300 companies, including a 40 per cent stake in Daimler-Benz' (*The Times*, 4 September 1972). He had reputedly become the richest man in West Germany and the fifth richest in the world (Ferencz 1979: 170).

Three factors seem to have been important in Flick's business success from the late 1940s. First, and probably most important, was the wealth he retained from the Nazi era. Second, was the inflow of funds from the United States for industrial expansion under the programme of Marshall Aid. Third was the assistance of associates such as Dr Hermann Abs. As a leading director of the Deutsche Bank during the War, his post-war position in the Bank Deutsche Länder gave him an important role in the distribution of Marshall Aid funds in West Germany. Abs assisted Flick in his purchase of Daimler-Benz and Flick, in turn, ensured that Abs became Chairman of its Board of Directors.[12]

5   Several of Flick's former colleagues from the Nazi business establishment had prominent positions in his companies. They included several former board members and executives of I.G. Farben, such as Dr Hermann Abs.[13]

From the early 1960s, the Conference on Jewish Material Claims against Germany conducted a series of fruitless negotiations over a decade with Flick's representatives to secure limited compensation for the former slave labourers of the Dynamit Nobel company. Flick had been a wartime director of the company and became the major shareholder in 1959. The talks have been fully described by Ferencz, who had served as a prosecuting lawyer in Nuremberg. Flick's mixture of promises, delays, evasions and a final refusal to give a penny to his former victims is in keeping with descriptions of his character and record by a number of historians and writers. They include Paul Johnson (1987: 515), Ferencz (1979), *Der Spiegel*, *Das Handelsblatt* (cited in Espelage 1984) and Ron Chernow (1993: 659).

In 1967, several years into the talks, Flick (who had meanwhile agreed to the principle of compensation) refused to pay the US$1.25 million then under discussion on the ground that Dynamit Nobel was short of cash. At the time, his personal fortune was some $500 million and he had given to his 16-year-old granddaughter, Dagmar, a gift of more than the total amount being requested for the thousands of Jewish claimants who had survived in companies controlled by Flick (Ferencz 1979: 164). When the former US High Commissioner in West Germany, John McCloy, who had been responsible for Flick's early release from prison, wrote to him in 1969 with an appeal on behalf of his former slave labourers, Flick did not even reply. Instead, his legal representative Eberhard von Brauchitsch wrote that 'Dr Flick is of the opinion that under no aspect, nor under a moral aspect either, would it be indicated or justifiable for Dynamit Nobel AG or the Flick Group to fulfil the demands of the Claims Conference' (letter of 7 January 1970, cited in Ferencz 1979: 168).

During the 1960s, Flick had fallen out with one of his two surviving sons, Otto-Ernst. When he died in 1972, his main heirs were his other son (Friedrich-Karl) and Otto-Ernst's two sons – Friedrich's grandchildren – Gert-Rudolf (who was to become the donor to Oxford University), and Friedrich-Christian (*The Times*, 22 July and 4 September 1972).

The most highly publicised episode in the history of the Flick Concern (i.e., the main holding company) in the ensuing period was a corruption scandal that became known as the 'Flick Affair'. (This earlier West German scandal is quite separate from the 'Flick Affair' involving Oxford, which is the subject of this chapter.)[14] There is no evidence to suggest Gert-Rudolf's involvement in this earlier 'Flick Affair'. Its relevance to this chapter is that it led, in 1985, to the sale of the Flick Concern to the Deutsche Bank. It was only after they sold Dynamit Nobel that any compensation was forthcoming in 1986 and not from them but from the Deutsche Bank, albeit on an insultingly inadequate scale.[15] The researches undertaken into the Flick family have so far failed to reveal any evidence that any member (including Dr G.R. Flick) has ever provided compensation to the firm's wartime victims. The single exception was a payment of DM3,000 to one ex-slave as a reward for his appearance as a witness at Nuremberg.[16]

The DM5 million offered as compensation, when compared with the DM5 *billion* paid by Deutsche Bank for the Flick Concern, means that the compensation was one-tenth of one per cent of the total sale value of the Flick Concern. According to *The Times*, the motive for the belated compensation gesture could be understood as follows:

> An explanation less concerned with humanitarianism is that a new controversy about the lack of compensation threatened to damage the forthcoming flotation of shares in the group, especially among American investors . . . Herr Heinz Galinski, the chairman of the West Berlin Jewish community organisation, who had long campaigned for Flick to pay compensation, said that the sum was not enough. So long as it was solely owned by the Flick family, the firm always refused to pay. It had post-war West German law on its side, but not, in the view of many Germans, post-war West German morality.
>
> (9 January 1986)

The renewed controversy over the compensation issue had arisen after a remark by a Bundestag member, made in response to Jewish claims on behalf of the former slave labourers. The Christian Social Union MP declared that these demands had 'neither a legal nor moral basis', and that they fostered the impression 'that the Jews quickly speak out when money jingles somewhere in German tills.' He denied that the Germans had become insensitive to Jewish sufferings in the war, 'but the Jews should not embarrass us with these demands' (ibid. see also Janssen 1986).

From the lump sum of DM5 million, the administrative and banking costs had to be subtracted. Dynamit Nobel's surviving former slaves received some DM2,000 each. The settlement provided nothing for the families of those who had died or for those who had laboured for other Flick firms. Considering that there had been some 48,000 Flick slave labourers, the compensation would have amounted to a mere DM100 had it been averaged out.

Four historical conclusions emerge. First, Friedrich Flick's criminality is beyond reasonable question; second, it was from Friedrich Flick that his grandson – the donor to Oxford University – inherited his fortune; third, no evidence has emerged so far that any of the Flick family provided compensation to the slave labourers employed by Friedrich Flick's plants during World War II. Fourth, the compensation provided in 1986 came from the Deutsche Bank, not from the Flicks, and in any case was derisory.

The debate in 1995–96 about Dr Gert-Rudolf Flick's donation to Oxford University

The debate about Oxford University's Flick Professorship of European Thought had its origin in the conference on Integrity in the Public and Private Domains, held at Balliol College on 27–29 January 1995 and organised by the editors of this volume. Paul Flather, the late Rabbi Hugo Gryn (himself a survivor of Auschwitz and other Nazi camps) and I, were invited to give presentations during a session on 'Integrity in fund-raising in different domains.'[17] It was a matter of chance that Balliol acted as the host of a meeting at which questions about one of its Fellowships were to be raised. It was not until the meeting itself that I discovered that Balliol had provided the college affiliation for the new Flick professorship.

In the week before the meeting, the conference organisers, other panel members and a limited circle of friends were consulted or received copies of the draft notes which I had prepared for circulation on the historical background to the Flick donation. At the suggestion of one friend, who had served for many years on some of Oxford University's senior committees, it was informally agreed that those attending the conference should, for the time being, be asked to keep private the concerns that were to be raised in the notes. By avoiding early publicity, Oxford's authorities would have a chance not only to consider the matter calmly and to take action, but they could behave in a manner which protected the reputation of the University's fund-raising campaign.[18]

It was clear that this voluntary silence could not last indefinitely. The notes prepared for the seminar were based on publicly available materials. The family connection between the donor and Friedrich Flick would inevitably become a subject of comment at some stage. Moreover, the organisers were firm in their decision that a chapter based on the presentation about the donation would be included in the book of the conference proceedings which they intended to publish.

In the end, there was no leak throughout the months when the issues raised by the donation were under internal scrutiny. However, signals from the administration implied a desire to delay and then to bury the matter. Shortly after the Balliol meeting of January 1995, Rabbi Gryn expressed the wish that my chapter should set in motion for the university 'an extraordinary process of looking at themselves' as far as the Flick donation was concerned. Over the following months, there were few signs that Rabbi Gryn's hopes were being fulfilled.

Shortly after the Balliol seminar, it was unofficially reported that the Flick donation had been referred to a little-known University body called the Ethics Committee. Created in 1989 to review potentially controversial donations to the Campaign for Oxford, it had previously hardly ever met. The university authorities refused to divulge its membership and declined requests by some of those present at the Balliol seminar for access to the Committee or even to the Vice-Chancellor.

In June 1995, just before the Long Vacation and five months after the matter had been raised, the Ethics Committee held another of its widely spaced meetings and still failed to reach any conclusions about the Flick donation. The University authorities gave instructions that no information was to be conveyed to those who had been involved in the Balliol seminar beyond the fact that the issue remained under review. It was becoming evident that the Committee intended to recommend no change in its previous decision to accept the contribution and that it did not even wish to suggest a change in the title of the professorship. This was confirmed in the autumn. When it became clear that the University had decided to take no action about the endowment, I put the matter into the public domain, having given prior notice to the University and to Balliol and after consulting with a number of colleagues.[19]

On 18 November 1995, *The Times* published my feature article about the Flick donation. The university released a previously prepared press statement on the afternoon of 17 November in response to an approach from an educational correspondent of *The Times*. The Vice-Chancellor and the Master of Balliol responded to the article in a letter to *The Times* published on 23 November.

In the ensuing weeks there was little further public discussion. It was nearly two months before the *Jewish Chronicle* published a letter by Trude Levi, a former Flick slave labourer (26 January 1996). She described the poverty-stricken condition of some of her fellow survivors who were living in Hungary and the failure of the Flick family to address the compensation issue.

It was not until early March that a combination of several uncoordinated initiatives led to a sudden explosion of press coverage. First of all, a vital, isolated behind-the-scenes role was played by one of Oxford's best known dons, a political scientist who had seen Trude Levi's *Jewish Chronicle* letter and who had been alarmed by the silence of his colleagues. Unknown to me, he now approached Dr Flick through a go-between in an effort to persuade him to consider compensation for the poorest of his grandfather's former slaves. In addition, he briefed several journalists.

Second, the peg for a fresh press report about the controversy was the University's decision to change the name of the controversial position from the 'Flick professorship' to the 'Gert-Rudolf Flick professorship'. This move was intended to make clear that it was not the war criminal, but his grandson after whom the post was named. The option of adding 'Gert-Rudolf' to the title of the professorship, which had been considered and rejected in 1995, was accepted by the University after protests to the Vice-Chancellor from Greville Janner, who had complained about the University's previous failure to consult with official Jewish bodies about the endowment. Janner, a Labour MP and chairman of the Holocaust Educational Trust, was also a former president of the main representative body of Anglo-Jewry, the Board of Deputies of British Jews.[20]

Third, a report in the *Daily Telegraph* of 4 March 1996 about this renaming sparked immediate interest. On 7 March, the newspaper published a letter from a former Balliol student, the prominent moral philosopher David Selbourne.[21] For some time, he had been conducting a correspondence with the Master of Balliol. Selbourne had become convinced that Balliol's explanations ignored the serious moral implications of the donation. In particular, two arguments disturbed him: first, the Master's implication that because three leading Jews – Lord Weidenfeld, the former Master of Balliol (Professor Baruch Blumberg) and Sir Isaiah Berlin – had been involved in establishing the new professorship, other Jews had weak grounds for objection. Second, as Selbourne wrote in the *Daily Telegraph* about his correspondence with the Master, some of the detailed factual points that had been raised in defence of the endowment showed a 'poverty of argument' as well as blindness to the serious moral dimensions of the matter: for instance, the endowment was excused on the ground that there were two separate fortunes, Friedrich Flick's wartime wealth and his post-war fortune, built anew (it was argued) 'on the basis of bank loans'. Selbourne's letter to the *Daily Telegraph* attacked the 'moral disgrace' and shame which he thought had been brought upon Balliol by the 'Flick connection'.

The College's case was put the next day in a feature by the *Daily Telegraph*'s defence correspondent, John Keegan, himself a Balliol member and benefactor. Keegan had received a rushed briefing from the College ('Nazi gold didn't fund this gift', *Daily Telegraph*, 8 March 1996). Further letters and features followed by the day in the national broadsheets. On 11 March Lord Weidenfeld wrote to the *Telegraph*. He stated Sir Ronald Grierson and he had been responsible for introducing Dr Flick as a donor to the University. As a Jew whose family had suffered in the Holocaust, Weidenfeld justified the professorship on the basis of liberal values and the need for reconciliation with Germany. The same day, Balliol's governing body had a long discussion about the affair and issued a statement that seemed to give full backing to Lord Weidenfeld's judgements.

In fact, the justification of the donation offered by Balliol was not unconditional. Senior members of Balliol had become concerned about the fact that the press coverage had concentrated on the college, whereas the endowment given by Dr Flick had been given to the university. The Ethics Committee, too, was a University body whose proceedings were not revealed to Balliol and not even to the Master, who was the Vice-Chancellor-elect; Balliol was effectively being challenged to back the findings of an investigation in which it had played no part, findings that were beginning to appear flawed.[22] On 13 March, the *Telegraph* carried two parallel letters, from the Vice-Chancellor and from the Master of Balliol. The letters appeared to reflect pressure from Balliol on the Vice-Chancellor. The Vice-Chancellor stressed that it was the university – not Balliol – which bore the central responsibility for the matter. The Master of Balliol, while expressing support for the professorship 'for as long as the university is associated with it', stressed that Balliol's role had been limited to giving 'house-room' to the Flick Professor.

On 20 March Dr Flick entered the same correspondence column. He wrote to the *Telegraph* 'reiterating' his total abhorrence of what took place in Germany during the Third Reich and his 'profound personal shame for the involvement of my grandfather in these dreadful events.' Did this mean, asked the *Jewish Chronicle* of 22 March 1996 that he was prepared to compensate his grandfather's former slaves? Answering the *Jewish Chronicle* that this was 'absolutely possible', he also expressed reservations: first, he owned only 10 per cent of the family fortune; second, compensation could leave him 'destitute'; third, '[h]ow can you compensate for human tragedy with money?'

There had already been two abortive, private efforts to open discussions about compensation for the former Flick slave labourers during 1995, while the concerns about the Flick professorship remained unpublicised. One of these had been made by Rabbi Hugo Gryn. A third attempt had been reported in the *Telegraph* of 4 March. Despite the failure of earlier efforts to negotiate with Dr Flick about the compensation issue, the president of the International Council of Christians and Jews, Sir Sigmund Sternberg issued a press statement and made a further approach to Dr Flick, through a prominent German statesman associated with Balliol. In a separate initiative, a former Flick slave labourer wrote directly to Dr Flick to request that he establish a trust fund on behalf of the poorest ex-slave labourers, some of them living in Hungary.

At this stage, Balliol's governing body had given its support to the Flick professorship and editiorial coverage had been largely favourable to the University's position. However, there could be no assurance that the matter was over. The inaugural lecture of the Gert-Rudolf Flick Professor was due to take place in early May. Such a lecture is normally the occasion for a dinner and reception in honour of the donor. The Flick camp apparently feared –

almost certainly without foundation – that there might be an organised student demonstration and further unfavourable publicity.

Dr Flick gave no further response concerning the compensation issue. Instead, on 15 April, the university published an exchange of letters between Dr Flick and the Vice-Chancellor of Balliol. Dr Flick asked for his name to be removed from the professorship and for the return of his endowment.[23] The Vice-Chancellor complied. There was a further burst of press coverage, but the withdrawal of the donation effectively ended the matter as far as Oxford was concerned.

Before proceeding to discuss the broader issues raised by the controversy, it will be useful to summarise and assess the main arguments put forward on each side. Arguments in favour of the endowment are given first and rejoinders are then presented in italics. A number of the points made in favour of the donation are taken from the University's press statement of 17 November 1995 and the statement from Balliol issued in 1996 to its Old Members. These documents are reproduced in the appendices. The review of arguments and counter-arguments suggests two main conclusions: first, that it is difficult to combine the roles of institutional defender and of neutral guardian of moral standards; second, that financial interests may have some significant effects upon academic judgements.

1 Defence of the University's fund-raising procedures

My article in *The Times*, which opened the public debate, criticised these procedures, reporting that the University's 'Ethics Committee' had not even met at the time the Flick donation was originally made. In its press release of 17 November 1996 and in the Chancellor's letter to the *Daily Telegraph* of 20 April 1996, the University gave three defences: first, that the University had not known of the background of the Flick family until the Balliol seminar of January 1995; second, as soon as doubts had been raised, the Ethics Committee had conducted a thorough review; third, the distinction of the members of this Committee gave a solid imprimatur to its findings.

First, the experience and personal honour of the members of the Ethics Committee is not in doubt, But (except for the student member) the roles that they occupied made it difficult for them to be seen as neutral. The membership of the committee was effectively secret until revealed by Oxford's Chancellor, Lord Jenkins, in a letter to the Telegraph *of 20 April 1996. The Ethics Committee was chaired by the Vice-Chancellor; its secretary was also secretary to the fund-raising campaign. The other members were Sir Patrick Neill (then in his final year as Warden of All Souls), the Reverend Ernest Nicholson (Provost of Oriel), Mrs Ruth Deech (Principal of St Anne's), and Hopi Sen (President of the Oxford University Student Union). The senior members were all College heads. Three were distinguished lawyers.*

Nevertheless, in terms of their positions they arguably lacked a sufficient distance from the matter they were asked to review. The Vice-Chancellor had a strong interest in protecting the University's development campaign. The other senior members were active in university administration – one was a former Vice-Chancellor, another a candidate for the Vice-Chancellorship, the third a pro-Vice-Chancellor.[24]

Moreover, some members of the committee occupied positions that involved their continuing to raise funds with the assistance of some of those whose earlier actions regarding the Flick endowment were relevant to the investigations of the Ethics Committee.

Second, the claim that the Ethics Committee set to work as soon as the Nazi background of the Flick family came to the University's attention is without foundation. Dr Henry Drucker, who headed the Campaign for Oxford at the time of the Flick donation, acknowledged in the Jewish Chronicle *of 22 March 1996 that he had known of the background before the Balliol seminar and had taken the decision not to submit the matter to the Ethics Committee. When the University's press statement claimed in November 1995 that no information had been before the University about the matter in the early 1990s, it apparently made this claim without having consulted Dr Drucker. That the Nazi connection of the Flicks was known at an early date to a small, senior circle within the University administration has been authoritatively confirmed to me.*

2 Views of prominent members of the Anglo-Jewish Community

Proponents of the donation stressed the active role that had been played by 'senior' or 'prominent' British Jews in soliciting the endowment and in serving on the committee which appointed the first Flick Professor. The two men responsible for arranging the donation – Lord Weidenfeld and Sir Ronald Grierson – were both Jewish, as were two of the board of electors to the chair, Professor Barry Blumberg (then Master of Balliol and a former winner of the Nobel prize for medicine) and Sir Isaiah Berlin.

In addition, the Ethics Committee stated that it had consulted senior members of the Jewish community during its enquiries. In particular, leading Jewish historians had been approached. Of all these Jewish figures, the participation of Sir Isaiah Berlin carried the greatest weight, as indicated by Lord Weidenfeld, in his autobiography published in 1994.

The involvement of Lord Weidenfeld and Sir Ronald Grierson helps to provide an explanation of the University's failure to accept the endowment without scrutiny. The assumption that such leading personalities were representative of British Jewry is understandable. But it does not justify the use of the 'Jewish defence'. This argument caused offence to some Jews. They found it objectionable on the ground that it appeared to imply that Jews who were prominent in British public life were entitled to present themselves or to be regarded as representatives of the Jewish community, irrespective of their actual communal roles. It implied, further, that there was a monolithic Jewish view of the matter.[25]

Certainly there was a time when rich, socially prominent Jews were regularly chosen to head Anglo-Jewish institutions. In the 1990s matters are different. The elected leaders of such institutions as the Board of Deputies of British Jews are rarely public celebrities. Conversely, famous Jews are frequently marginal or untypical in Jewish affairs. Yet, with one possible exception, the 'protracted . . . substantial . . . thorough and professional' enquiry conducted in 1995 by the Ethics Committee apparently failed to approach any of the main representative or religious bodies of British Jews.[26] Among the bodies not consulted were the Board of Deputies of British Jews, the Holocaust Survivors' Centre, the Wiener Library, the United Synagogue, the Reform synagogues, the old-established Spanish and Portuguese Congregation, the Oxford Jewish Congregation, or the Oxford Centre for Hebrew and Jewish Studies. The identity of the historians who were consulted and who approved the donation has never been revealed. It is known that authorities who were not consulted included Sir Martin Gilbert.

As far as the Jews principally involved in the endowment and in the appointment of the Flick Professor are concerned, two subsequently made public and private statements distancing themselves from the Flick connection. Baruch Blumberg[27] and Sir Isaiah Berlin both made clear that they had been unaware of the wartime role of Friedrich Flick at the time they had participated in the appointment process. They made it known that they would have acted differently had they been aware.

The main burden of arguing in favour of the donation fell to Lord Weidenfeld. Of relevance to this chapter is the fact that his views on Jewish relations with Germany and Austria were not necessarily the same as those of many British Jews. This was shown by Jewish responses when the Flick controversy became public.[28] Contrary to the university's claims, Jewish opinion was largely critical of the donation. The poor Flick record concerning the compensation of former slave labourers was the fundamental concern. Public critics included the Board of Deputies of British Jews,[29] the Jewish Chronicle,[30] and leading members of the Holocaust Survivors' Centre,[31] the Association of Jewish Refugees,[32] the Wiener Library,[33] the Anglo-Jewish Association and the Conference on Jewish Material Claims against Germany,[34] the Holocaust Educational Trust,[35] Oxford University Jewish Society, and the Jewish community of Frankfurt.[36]

Moreover, the justification that prominent Jews supported the Flick donation can be turned on its head. There was unease in at least some German quarters about naming institutions and professorships after wealthy servants of the Nazi regime. While the controversy over the Flick professorship was in progress in Britain, a group of non-Jewish secondary school students in Germany was mounting a protest at a school funded by the Flick Foundation of Duesseldorf. The school should be named after Anne Frank, they argued, not after Friedrich Flick. As in Oxford, the school authorities rejected this on the ground that renaming would lead to the withdrawal of financial support by the foundation.[37]

The publicity generated about Dr Flick's gift to Oxford's Europaeum programme produced the information from a top German University that it had considered and rejected a proposal to honour Hermann Abs on the ground of Abs' war record. As mentioned earlier, Abs was a banker and close colleague of Flick. In contrast to Abs's rejection by German academics, his name featured on the list of donors to the Campaign for Oxford.

3   The decision in January 1996 to change the title of the chair from the
'Flick Professorship' to the 'Gert-Rudolf Flick Professorship' was sufficient to
remove any connection with the war criminal, Friedrich Flick

It was never the intention to name the chair after a war criminal. As the Vice-Chancellor and the Master of Balliol pointed out in a letter to *The Times*, the chair 'was named [the Flick professorship] after its donor, Dr Gert-Rudolf Flick'.[38] To protest against naming a professorship in honour of Dr G.R. Flick on the ground of his grandfather's record amounted to 'guilt by descent'.[39]

The change of name did not deal with the objection that Dr G.R. Flick, while ben-
efiting from his grandfather's inheritance, had failed to provide compensation for his
grandfather's slave labourers. It was viewed by some (such as the Old Balliol MP,
Toby Jessel) as a cosmetic measure.[40] *Others feared that, as long as the Flick name*
continued to be included, the professorship would in any case continue to be associated
with the best known – and most notorious – member of the family, Friedrich Flick. In
practice, the first names of the donor would tend to be omitted and the chair would con-
tinue to be called the 'Flick chair'. Indeed, it was in this way that the Oxford Gaz-
ette *and the Trinity Term lecture list referred to it even after the official name change.*

The fact that Dr G.R. Flick was not only Friedrich's grandson but also his heir
arguably made it implausible to claim that the title of the endowment had no connec-
tion with Friedrich. As one Times reader pointed out, it would have been possible for
Dr Flick to provide an endowment without making stipulations about the title of the
chair.[41] *The insistence that the Flick name feature in the title meant, in the view of*
some critics, that Oxford was effectively being asked to provide a mark of public
approval and (as one former Oxford Head of House put it) to 'wash the family's name'.

4   Rejection of the notion of 'guilt by descent'

This is a central argument of the Master of Balliol's note to Old Members of the College, reproduced in Appendix 3. It is alluded to in the university's press statement of 17 November 1995 (Appendix 2) in which the reference to Dr G.R. Flick's date of birth implies that it is absurd to hold him responsible for events that occurred when he was just a baby. Lord Shawcross set forward the same view in a letter to *The Times*.[42]

Critics of the donation generally made clear (publicly and privately) that the case
against the Flick endowment was not based on any notion of revenge or of guilt by
descent. This was stated in the author's original article in The Times *of 18 November*
1995 (see Appendix 1), in leaders in the Jewish Chronicle *(22 March 1996) and*
in the Holocaust Survivors' News *(March 1996), in David Selbourne's opening*
letter to the Daily Telegraph *(7 March 1996) and elsewhere. The major worries*
of the critics were: (a) the record of the Flick family and of the donor relating to

compensation of World War II slave labourers; and (b) the fact that the donation was tied to the inclusion of the Flick name in the title of the professorship.

5 The need for reconciliation: the War was a long time ago

These propositions formed the basis of Lord Weidenfeld's letter to the *Daily Telegraph* (11 March 1996) and of statements by the Vice-Chancellor and the Master of Balliol. Given their importance, they will be discussed at greater length in the next section of this chapter.

6 The money given to the university by Dr Flick was derived from a post-war fortune that was a new and distinct one, untainted by Friedrich Flick's wartime activities

That Dr G.R. Flick's wealth derived from his grandfather's inheritance was not in question. Rather, the university authorities based their defence on the view that there were two Friedrich Flick fortunes. This position was alluded to, though not explained, in the university's opening press statement of 17 November 1996 (see Appendix 2). Subsequently, the Master of Balliol elaborated in correspondence with an old member of the College: 'My understanding is that a new fortune was made after the War, originally on the basis of bank loans.' Later, the university's position altered. It was admitted that Friedrich Flick's post-war fortune was not completely separate from his wartime one. The amended argument was that his later fortune was largely but not totally distinct. As John Keegan put it, in the rebuttal of David Selbourne's protest that has already been mentioned:

> Friedrich Flick . . . was rightly condemned as a war criminal and deserved to lose his money, which he did. Just enough remained, however, to give him a new start. It was from that postwar fortune, the Ethics Committee decided, that the endowment came. Hence the decision not to repudiate it.[43]

In some quarters, the argument was given an extra twist. The factories which Flick retained in 1945 were in the Western zones of occupation. These particular factories had not used slave labour. Such labour was employed in factories in the Russian zone of occupation or further to the East, which fell into Russian hands. It was from the 'pure' factories that Flick's 'just enough' derived from the war to act as the basis for his post-war fortune.[44]

This pleading is implausible both for factual and for moral reasons. (a) As described in the opening section of this chapter, the factories which Flick retained after the War were substantial. The scale of the sale of the Harpen Mining company alone – DM180 million – demonstrates this. (b) As far as bank loans are concerned, they normally require collateral which, of course, Flick was able to provide. (c) It is not correct to suggest that the plants which employed slave labourers all fell into territory behind the post-war Iron Curtain. To give just one example, Hessisch Lichtenau was situated in West Germany, near Kassel. (d) Moving to the moral plane, the university's position is based on the dubious assumption that it is possible to divide someone's fortune into watertight compartments. Assuming that Flick's slave plants had all fallen into Russian hands and that his post-war fortune had been based on relatively 'pure' plants, would this have absolved Flick from all responsibility to his former victims? (e) Likewise, even if Flick had made a completely new fortune after the War, he would arguably have still had the duty to use his new wealth to pay off his old moral debts. Certainly, as far as charitable contributions are concerned, there are strong grounds for the view that the claims of slave labourers should have had precedence to those of universities.

Apart from the propositions themselves, proponents and critics of the Flick donation were divided by the forms of reasoning they employed. It was precisely the willingness of the university authorities to present highly detailed defences that struck the philosopher David Selbourne as unacceptable. To base the debate about the justification of accepting Dr G.R. Flick's gift on the extent of Friedrich Flick's bank loans at particular periods of the 1940s and 1950s, or on the precise size of the 'just enough' of Flick's wartime fortune which survived the Nazi defeat, or on the location of particular factories, showed a failure to face up to the enormity of the Holocaust. The resort to technical detail constituted a deliberate attempt to evade the central moral questions involved in an acceptance of the donation.

Selbourne's point was reminiscent of the letters in which the former US High Commissioner in Germany, John McCloy, appealed for compensation for Flick's ex-slaves. Writing in 1969 to Hermann Abs, McCloy said:

> *I find the legal position of the firm {Dynamit Nobel} to be unbearably legalistic and really irrelevant to the main moral issue. It is not a matter of 'claims' and 'time of filing'. It is a fact that the firm did employ Jewish slave labor.*

To Friedrich Flick himself, McCloy wrote:

> *I deeply feel that a legalistic approach to this matter entirely misses the point . . . Most of the Jewish concentration camp inmates who managed to survive the horrors of the camps . . . are old women broken in health and living in straightened circumstances.*

> *(Ferencz 1979: 166–67)*

7   Dr G.R. Flick's statements of abhorrence of Nazism and of Friedrich Flick's wartime record

From the time that Dr G.R. Flick's endowment was mooted, his supporters stressed his personal character and opposition to Nazism. The University's initial press statement of 17 November 1995 said that 'Dr Flick's abhorrence of a dark period in the family history has been made very clear.' When critics pointed out that this form of words omitted to mention whether Dr Flick abhorred his grandfather's activities, Dr Flick wrote to the *Telegraph* to reiterate that he did (20 March 1996).

Dr Flick's personal character is incidental to the main issues of compensation to victims and of the name of the chair. The significance of Dr Flick's expression of regret must be judged by his actions on the central issue of compensation. As mentioned earlier, Dr Flick expressed reservations to the Jewish Chronicle *(22 March 1996) about compensation, though he did not rule it out. Informal approaches about the compensation issue proved unproductive (at least until the time this chapter has been written). A later justification for his refusal to heed the pleas for compensation was annoyance about his treatment in the British press and by opponents of his endowment. Yet the issue of compensation had been raised with the Flick family or with intermediaries – without effect – at least since the early 1960s.*

Apart from compensation, the history of Dr Flick's statements about his grandfather remains unclear. While this chapter has been in preparation neither the university authorities nor some of Dr Flick's closest supporters, from whom information was requested, have produced any earlier statements by Dr Flick in which he publicly condemned his grandfather. On the other hand, his close links with his grandfather are described in one (admittedly hostile) East German publication. After his grandfather's death and after his inheritance, Dr Flick is cited as saying that Friedrich had been a 'wonderful person' (Ohlsen 1985: 414–15).

Dr Flick's views are also the subject of a more recent interview reported in the Telegraph *(5 April 1997):*

{Dr G.R. Flick} *himself argues that there is no reason to feel guilty over an inheritance that grew out of seed money the Allies had allowed Friedrich Flick to keep, because his grandfather was so clever he would have made a second fortune whether or not the seed money was available to him. 'I know he would have made it anyway.'*

8 Pragmatic considerations: refusal of Dr Flick's gift would endanger the University's future fund-raising efforts; fortunes derived from slave labour a normal feature of Oxford's history

In the early stages of the debate pragmatic arguments were stressed in private. They later were presented forthrightly by the university's defenders, though they were usually not stated by university officials. Again, Keegan's article in the *Telegraph* written in response to David Selbourne's letter of protest laid the basis for a defence that was then elaborated by others. His article opened with the quotation from Balzac that 'Behind every great fortune, there is a great crime' (28 March 1996). He pointed out that some of Britain's richest families, including that of the Liberal premier, William Ewart Gladstone, owed their wealth to the slave trade.

In a similar vein, the religious affairs correspondent of the *Independent* cited the editor of the *Oxford Magazine* as saying that 'almost all the colleges were themselves founded as acts of reparation by powerful men with a great deal on their consciences' (Brown 1996). Simon Jenkins, a former editor of *The Times,* argued that the founder of Balliol had been no angel. Mocking Dr Flick's critics, he suggested that they could hardly urge the name of Flick to be removed from the Professorship of European Thought without also demanding the removal of 'Balliol' from the title of the college. He added that '[i]f historians are to crawl over the family trees of every donor, universities will wither.'[45]

The general argument that universities should accept donations regardless of their origin will be considered in the final section. Three points apply to this particular debate. First, the university's defence was based on contradictory arguments. Initially, the Vice-Chancellor and the Master of Balliol wrote to The Times *(23 November 1995) arguing that a code of conduct regarding fund-raising was unnecessary since it was unreasonable to suggest that Oxford could ever accept money derived from slave labour. The justification of the Flick endowment then changed. From the time of David Selbourne's letter to the* Telegraph *of 7 March 1996, press articles based on official Oxford sources argued that, far from being unknown, gifts derived from slave labour and other dubious sources were a norm.*

Second, when supporters of the donation cited other instances of endowments with immoral origins, they implied that the Holocaust was a run-of-the-mill event. The former editor of The Times *argued that it was inconsistent to object to naming a chair after Flick without objecting to the naming of the famous journalistic prizes after Joseph Pulitzer. Pulitzer, he explained, had been 'the most scandalous muckraker in newspaper history.' The implication is that on the scale of immorality muckraking journalism and genocide should be undifferentiated. This line of argument proved intolerable to the author of* Blind Eye to Murder, Tom Bower. *He stressed that it was easy to slip from defence of the Flick endowment to belittling the enormity of the Holocaust (*Guardian, *13 March 1996).*

Third, apart from the moral issues involved, there were – as I had written to a senior University representative early in 1995 – practical grounds for refusing to accept the donation. The loss of money in the short term would prove worthwhile if it avoided bringing Oxford's development programme into disrepute. If Oxford were seen to accept the profits of the Nazi Holocaust, this could deter future donations from other sources. One counter-argument was that Oxford had received a half dozen other contributions which could be seen as similarly tainted by Nazi associations. This provided, in my view, all the more reason to tighten fund-raising standards.

9 Balliol was unjustifiably attacked in the press for accepting Dr Flick's cash whereas it had only given 'room-space' to the new professor

Senior members of the College felt strongly that press headlines had all too often mentioned Balliol rather than the University in their reports. The reputation of the College had been unjustifiably sullied.

This was a largely justified feeling. It was the University, not Balliol, which had received the Flick endowment. Moreover, the College authorities had made genuine efforts to meet with those worried by the donation and to address their questions.

Nevertheless, Balliol had brought itself into the firing line by loyally refusing to dissociate itself from the University's conclusions. The Master of Balliol, who had been designated as the next Vice-Chancellor, took pains in the early stages of the controversy to give public support to the incumbent Vice-Chancellor and lent his name to their joint letter to The Times *of 23 November 1995.*

In conclusion, despite the public justifications that have been listed, there is little doubt that even the most forthright defenders of the endowment realised that they were on weak ground and that Oxford's arrangement for screening potential donors had been shown to be inadequate. To my knowledge, from the time of my article in *The Times* until the Vice-Chancellor's announcement five months later that Dr Flick had asked for his money back, no ordinary member of the Oxford faculty wrote to the press in defence of the endowment. The uncomfortable task was left to senior University and College officials. A famous former College head summed up the affair of the Flick professorship as follows:

> The name is an embarrassment, as everyone here, by now, knows . . . I am quite sure that if the electors, or Members of Council or Fellows of Balliol (including the then Master, who was a very loyal and identified Jew) had had any idea of whom Flick had been, the thing would not have gone through.

The Holocaust after a half-century: notes on the meaning of reconciliation

The controversy sparked public interest partly because it involved one of the most celebrated colleges at Britain's most famous university. It also raised moral and historical questions of much wider importance. Lord Weidenfeld's main public contribution to the debate was an appeal for the deepening of the reconciliation between Germans and Jews, and especially the State of Israel. This had started with the historic handshake between David Ben Gurion and Konrad Adenauer:

> Many Jewish leaders, and especially the political class in Israel, share the perception that although the past must not be forgotten, the innocent descendants of former foes must not be rejected.
>
> (*Daily Telegraph* 11 March 1996)

The statement to Old Members of Balliol (Appendix 3) presents similar sentiments. Yet issues of guilt, responsibility, compensation, remembrance and reconciliation arising from the Holocaust are complex and frequently confused. Some of these questions will be discussed in this section.

The idea of 'reconciliation' has a variety of connotations. It will be argued that some, but by no means all, are desirable.

Some of the most noble, heartening acts of reconciliation have been performed by individual Germans, often from the younger generations. An elderly Oxford Holocaust survivor reports that a teacher in her former home village in Germany regularly works with groups of his students to tend Jewish graves that would otherwise fall into disrepair. The legal expenses of a current compensation claim brought before the German courts are reportedly being paid – anonymously – by the son of a Nazi as a practical act of atonement. A German political scientist at an Austrian university takes his students each year to visit Auschwitz. A German student at Oxford, the grand-daughter of another German Oxonian executed for his part in the attempted assassination of Hitler, is so active in a Jewish student society at the University that she becomes its chairperson. A woman who has quietly attended a number of meetings in London about Holocaust-related subjects finally makes a hesitant approach to one of the Jewish organisers: she has a terrible admission to make. Her father served in the SS at Auschwitz. She does not know what she can possibly do. The Jew assures her that she cannot be to blame for her father's actions; she will be treated with friendship, not hatred; he proposes they should continue to meet together to explore their feelings.

Such acts have at least three essential ingredients. First, they express genuine feelings of regret. There cannot be a reconciliation without some form of sincere acknowledgement to the victims of the wrong that has been done. Frequently, this will involve an apology. Nothing is more distressing to those who have been harmed than the attempt to evade such an acknowledgement. Friedrich Flick's prolonged and brazen effort to deny moral as well as legal culpability was a notorious example of such denial.

However, mere verbal apology is not sufficient. There are occasions when a formal apology is self-serving – an insincere gesture made for the record and to evade more substantial actions and expressions.

Second, reconciliation often requires recompense, particularly where victims have suffered material loss. Money frequently has a symbolic as well as a practical value. A thief who has become wealthy from the proceeds of crime cannot expect to be reconciled with his victims while he retains his booty. Where a criminal has squandered his takings and is in no position to provide realistic compensation, some form of community service may reasonably be expected instead.

Third, the offence must be such as to be capable of reconciliation, if not of forgiveness for the acts which were perpetrated. Some offences may be too serious for this.

Where crimes have been too heinous to permit reconciliation with the perpetrators themselves, two questions arise: first, the blameworthiness of bystanders whose sins were those of omission; second, the question of whether reconciliation becomes possible with the passage of time or of generations.

An answer to both questions lies in the clear distinction between guilt and responsibility. It would be an unacceptable morality that believed that guilt could be collective or could pass down through generations. The perpetrators alone can be held guilty. By contrast, responsibility is not subject to the same limits. Where the material proceeds of crime are concerned, the obligation to compensate victims does not end when the criminal passes his gains to his family or friends. An heir is not entitled to enjoy his inheritance before he has met any outstanding debts. Moreover, the inheritance of debts applies at the social as well as the individual level. A new government is obliged to take responsibility for the debts incurred by its predecessors; a new generation of electors inherits long-standing obligations to make social security payments to older generations, and so on.

Proceeding from this outline of genuine reconciliation, it will be necessary to note several unsatisfactory, though common, uses of the term.

1 Reconciliation as victory

A core meaning of 'reconciliation' is the grudging acceptance by the vanquished of the finality of their defeat and the loss of will to expect their rights or to preserve their culture. When it comes from the victors, the call for 'reconciliation', forgiveness or to 'draw a line under the past' is tantamount to a demand that victims should abandon their claims and their hopes.

2 Reconciliation by denial

It is no coincidence that campaigns for reconciliation have sometimes stressed that both sides have been guilty; there has been suffering all round. An example of this approach was Helmut Kohl's controversial invitation to President Reagan to visit the cemetery at Bitburg, where the graves of SS officers lay side by side with others. The implication was that all of the war dead were innocent victims.

Another example is the campaign to rebuild Dresden, heavily bombed in 1945 by the Allies, and the partnership between Coventry and Dresden. There may be a moral comparison between the bombings of Coventry and of Dresden (though even this is unclear). But this parallel all too easily leads campaigners to ignore Nazi deeds far more serious than the bombing of Coventry, such as the deeds committed in Auschwitz. Despite the sincere values represented by the campaign for reconciliation between Coventry and Dresden, its premise of equal guilt not only produces distortion of history, but tends also to minimise the atrocities that constituted the Holocaust. On the fiftieth anniversary of the bombing of Dresden, a senior British delegation (including a representative of the Royal family) attended a remembrance ceremony in Dresden. The architectural memorial consisted of equal columns each marked with a name. 'Dresden' was side by side with 'Auschwitz' – a statement that the two represented equal horrors.

It is because of the potential for minimising Nazi guilt, that Christian groups are not alone in their focus on the bombing of Dresden. It is an equally popular theme for the far right.

3 *Reconciliation for others*

The more remote the struggle, the easier it is to recommend reconciliation between warring parties. The policy of reconciliation can all too easily reflect lack of understanding or sympathy. This applies to some of the appeals for forgiveness made by those who were unaffected by the Holocaust or only marginally involved in it.

The shooting of schoolchildren in Spring 1996 in Dunblane was so closely felt in Britain that there were few demands for reconciliation. The Archbishop of Canterbury took a tough line. It was not for him or anyone else to dispense forgiveness to the killer, Thomas Hamilton. 'Sometimes after a tragedy like Dunblane the word 'forgiveness' trips too lightly from people's lips . . . others cannot do the forgiving on behalf of the one who has been wronged.'[46]

4 *Reconciliation by forgetting*

A technique that is sometimes an aspect of 'reconciliation as victory' is the attempt to forget or to divert historical attention from a controversial past. Usually, this does not involve outright denial but consists of techniques of distraction. During the controversy over Kurt Waldheim's record of Nazi service, the Austrian foreign ministry stepped up its efforts to publicise the country's musical history. If Austria was seen as the land of Mozart and Strauss, its poor record in the World War II would be 'put into context'. The promotion of European studies and European thought (the subject, incidentally, of the Flick Professorship) sometimes appears to have had similar, diversionary motives.

The Flick debate provided dramatic evidence of the extent of ignorance about major aspects of the Holocaust among senior members of the University. It is probable that some dons involved in the endowment had some idea of the background of the Flick family and chose to say nothing. However, it is clear that a number of well-known Fellows acted in good faith and without any knowledge.

My examination of the contributions to the debate over the Flick Professorship indicates that the divide was not between those who favoured and who opposed a process of post-war reconciliation. Rather, it was between those who asked for few conditions and those who felt that reconciliation needed to have a more solid basis.

Underlying the worries of the critics was a feeling that the temptations of money had led the University to minimise the justifiable demands of Holocaust victims; that the appeal to 'reconciliation' had been a convenient slogan. The University had no answer to the point that compensation to the Flick family's slave labourers had priority over a University endowment; thus, this was almost invariably ignored in University and Balliol statements. The University refused to provide evidence of any past expressions by Dr Flick of abhorrence of his grandfather's actions, taking refuge in the policy of secrecy of investigations by the Ethics Committee. There was also no explanation of why the University was prepared to accept the stipulation of the donor that the professorship bear the name of Flick.

Integrity in fund-raising: comments on Paul Flather's chapter

The 'Flick affair' highlights the relevance of Paul Flather's chapter, which was drafted before the 'affair' started. Since the present author is in agreement with it, the following paragraphs will underline some of its points and will stress its originality.

The subject of the financing of election campaigns, political parties and lobbies has rightly been the subject of a large academic literature as well as of frequent press comment in many countries. By contrast, Flather's analysis of fund-raising in the university domain and in similar fields is a lonely, pioneering effort. Yet, the topic is of great importance for a number of reasons.

First of all, there is the sheer scale of university fund-raising, which in Britain greatly exceeds that of the political parties. Wafic Said's gift to Oxford University in 1996 of £20 million exceeds by far the largest reported or rumoured payment to any party at any time in history.[47] Similarly the £3 million donated to Oxford University in the 1930s by Lord Nuffield for clinical medicine overshadowed the considerable political contributions recorded in his papers. The several dozen professional fund-raisers employed by Oxford University and its colleges form a larger corps than the fund-raisers of the national organisations of the British parties combined.

Second, there is the question of the influence derived from endowments to universities. Unlike payments to parties and election campaigns, gifts to universities do not directly influence the struggle for political office. However, they arguably may have a far-reaching effect on the development of élite opinion and, thereby, of public opinion as a whole. In his contribution to the well-known debate about the nature of political power, Stephen Lukes (a former Fellow of Balliol) suggests realistically that influence over the assumptions underlying politics is crucial. The fact that certain issues and views become prominent, whereas others appear beyond the realm of reasonable debate, owes much to the way in which opinion-forming institutions operate.

Given the importance of educational fund-raising, the next question is how the fund-raising process affects the integrity of the modern university. In this area, as in so many others, the problem of integrity arises from the existence of conflicting pressures. In Benjamin Disraeli's words, uttered in the House of Commons in 1873, '[A] University should be a place of light, of liberty, and of learning.' It could be argued that fund-raising from private sources promotes these objects and thereby contributes to the integrity of universities.

A present-day university cannot be a place of advanced learning without incurring huge costs. Libraries, laboratories and the time needed by scholars for research and for teaching require funding on a scale that neither government grants nor teaching fees are able to provide. Consequently, fund-raising from rich individuals and corporations is required in order to permit the university to fulfil its primary mission.

Private fund-raising arguably helps the university to become a place of liberty. By relying less on public funding and more on donations from a whole series of sources, university programmes are themselves likely to become more varied and innovative. According to this view, it is no bad thing if donors make conditions for their gifts. This process will make universities more aware of the real world, less stuffy, and less dependent upon the tyranny of funding agencies of central government.

While these are weighty considerations, there are significant contrary arguments. These will be discussed under Disraeli's headings.

1 The university as a place of light

In accord with Disraeli, Flather's paper indicates that universities have a moral role which makes it as inappropriate for them as for Mother Teresa to accept money from the Mafia. This argument, though accepted by the present author, remains disputed.

The Flick donation was wholly exceptional in that it involved a consideration of Nazi war crimes. The debate which it occasioned led to a heightened awareness of the broader moral issues raised by the fund-raising efforts of British universities. Qualms about a £1.5 million gift from the tobacco giant BAT to create a chair in international affairs at Cambridge University led in July 1996 to a ballot of dons. In the same month, the shadow of the Flick debate fell over a £20 million donation to create a business school at Oxford.

The way in which these donations were handled indicated that University leaders felt under greater threat of criticism about their sources of funds. It showed also that they were determined to resist the pressures and to accept the controversial contributions. One fund-raiser acknowledged frankly that the standards to which universities need to conform when it comes to accepting donations are lower than those of political parties. And as a letter to *The Times* (George Racz, 24 July 1996) put it:

It is offensive, and it will deter from further offers those whose munificence has kept our most prestigious institutions alive, if before a donation is accepted the donor has to prove that the moneys did not come from arms deals, or from the killing of endangered species, or the sale of seal-skins or elephant tusks. The potential use of money is far more important than its origin.

2 *The university as a place of liberty*

The increased pressure of fund-raising – a result, in part, of government funding restrictions – has affected the structure of power within universities. It has contributed to the process of increased managerial control and to the reduction of freedom for individual academics. Fund-raising has generally become a task of teams answerable to university administrators, and other senior managers.

As they have become more closely involved in meetings with millionaires and captains of industry, the lifestyles and values of university leaders have often altered. They have tended to lose a sense of identity with the scholarly community.

A sub-text of recent debates has been the challenge they have presented to senior university administrators. They have tended to regard fund-raising as a function that should not be subject to the consciences and whims of 'the congregation of dons'.[48]

3 *The university as a place of learning*

Accepting that learning requires money, some of which needs to be raised from private sources, it is still necessary to guard against the distorting and possibly damaging effects of fund-raising on academic standards.

The search for private funds may all too easily become an end in itself and the money that is collected may have limited benefits. There are several reasons for this. Private funds may be offered for purposes that are marginal to a university's central needs. Sometimes established university positions of central importance remain unfilled because of a shortage of funds; meanwhile, new posts in exotic or marginal subjects may be created simply because they are of special interest to a donor.

The time and concentration required for collecting funds may lead to a neglect by university managers of financial efficiency. This was the topic of a heated discussion in 1989 in the *Economist*. The distinguished journalist, Godfrey Hodgson argued that Oxford University would do better to concentrate on improving the yield on its investments and on tapping the large endowments of the richest colleges than on launching a fund-raising campaign. The Vice-Chancellor gave a detailed rebuttal.[49] Irrespective of the details of this exchange, there have certainly been cases where the priority given to fund-raising has allowed wastage and inefficiency to go unchecked.

Also, the advent of active fund-raising by British universities (itself a consequence of government-imposed stringencies) has arguably made possible further reductions of public funding and has contributed to a policy of over-expanded but under-financed institutions of higher education.

Apart from these pragmatic considerations, fund-raising may distort the direction of university teaching and research. Defenders of controversial endowments tend to be too sanguine when they declare that the source of money will have no influence on curricula or on academic output. Denis Noble discusses the problems that can arise in the scientific field in his chapter in this book. In universities that train future politicians, civil servants, writers and intellectuals, influence over the curriculum and over research is especially important in subjects such as politics and modern history. For those seeking to manipulate the curriculum in these subjects, it is usually unnecessary to interfere with appointments. It is enough to determine the subjects for which appointments are made.

To give a foreign example, one leading university agreed some years ago to use money collected from Arab sources to appoint a professor of Arabic and Middle Eastern studies. Not surprisingly, this professor interpreted the Arab-Israeli conflict from an Arab perspective. Thereupon, Jewish sources raised money for an Israeli professor. He gave courses on similar topics. Students came to feel that their marks depended on providing the appropriate interpretation of the origins of the Six Day War to each professor. This variety may have provided an interesting educational experience. Nevertheless, it illustrated how the courses offered depended on fund-raising, and not solely on academic criteria.

As suggested earlier, the heavy inflow of funding from foreign sources has, in my opinion, had a considerable effect on the teaching of modern history at some British universities. Among other consequences, it seems to have contributed to a relative neglect of the Holocaust, which has sometimes been segregated from the mainline study of modern Europe.

To summarise the argument so far, fund-raising may either enhance or damage the integrity of universities. A strength of Flather's paper is that, unlike most university administrators, he recognises that fund-raising may lead to serious problems and that there needs, therefore, to be a conscious effort to anticipate them. In my article about the Flick professorship in *The Times*, I argued for a code of conduct about fund-raising:

> At present the University has no code governing its fund-raising practices, and there is no bar, for instance, against accepting money based on the proceeds of slavery or other grossly immoral practices. Moreover, the Ethics Committee is secret, and as a 'self-standing' body is not required to report to the Congregation of Oxford dons. Clearer safeguards and more accountable procedures are needed, if only to protect the interests of donors who have nothing to fear from scrutiny and to safeguard the

reputation of the fund-raising that has become essential under present conditions for all universities.

The public response from the Vice-Chancellor and the Master of Balliol in the same newspaper was that a suggested code was 'frankly preposterous' (23 November 1995). There are nevertheless strong indications that, in private, Oxford University's procedures for vetting potential donors have been considerably tightened as a result of the Flick controversy. As a member of the Ethics Committee later told me, the Flick donation 'has raised our consciousness of the ethics of every single gift.'

The broader debate about the legitimate boundaries of fund-raising by universities has not ended.[50] The discussions initiated by the seminar at Balliol in January 1995 have established that the issues of fund-raising in universities are of moral and intellectual importance.

Appendix 1

Extracts from the author's article in **The Times** *of 18 November 1995*

When the Fellows of Balliol College, Oxford agreed to accept the newly endowed Flick Professorship in European Thought, they were not informed that the chair bore the name of a major war criminal sentenced at Nuremberg. . . . The Oxford University fund-raisers accepted the case that the Second World War is a long time ago . . .

It is possible to take another view. The issues raised by the donation certainly do not involve an implication of 'guilt by descent' against the member of the Flick family who endowed the chair in his family's name. Yet, several questions arise from this matter:

First, though it is possible to have endless metaphysical discussions about whether the money contributed to the University is the same as that obtained during the War by the use of slave labour, the links are uncomfortably strong . . .

Second. . . . There is a strong case that any charitable donations from Friedrich Flick's heirs should be directed to the firm's former slave labourers and their families.

Third, . . . is it fitting to append the name of Flick to a professorship at Oxford University, especially a chair devoted to European thought? . . .

There is the question of the corporate responsibility of German enterprises. A study by the former Nuremberg prosecutor, Benjamin Ferencz, has documented their generally miserly record of compensation to their wartime victims. Though the 1940s may seem a long time ago, the slave labourers – especially those surviving in Eastern Europe and in the former Soviet Union – are often living in penury having never recovered from their terrible experiences. Is it not the primary task of the corporations that ran the slave camps to compensate the slaves rather than to sponsor symphony orchestras and universities?

Finally, is the cause of reconciliation best served by naming a professorship after a war criminal? Rather than honour, directly or indirectly, an industrialist who served the Nazis, it would be more fitting to commemorate a German such as Adam von Trott zu Solz, a Balliol graduate executed for his part in the resistance to Hitler, or to establish a chair in the name of the victims of the Holocaust.

Appendix 2

University of Oxford

Press statement

At the end of January this year the attention of the University authorities was drawn to the involvement of the German industrialist Friedrich Flick with the Nazi regime, and to the view that because of that involvement the University ought not to have accepted the substantial benefaction made to the University in 1991 by Friedrich Flick's grandson, Dr Gert-Rudolph Flick (b. 1943), for the establishment of a Professorship of European Thought. No information about this matter had been before the University at the time when the gift was accepted . . .

When early in 1995 the concerns about the Flick family were reported, the University authorities, as Dr Flick himself readily accepted, had no choice but to refer the matter to [the Ethical Committee established in 1989]. The committee . . . pursued inquiries both in this country and in Germany, and it consulted in particular senior members of the Jewish community. It endeavoured, as in fairness to all parties it was bound to do, to investigate the matter carefully and dispassionately.

The committee found no grounds for associating the name of Dr Gert-Rudolph Flick with the appalling events in Germany in the 1930's and during the war, or for supposing that Dr Flick, or the various recipients of his very considerable personal generosity, could be regarded as beneficiaries of those events. Indeed, Dr Flick's abhorrence of a dark period in the family history has been made very clear. . .

If these matters had come to the University's attention at the relevant time, the University would have investigated them before the gift was accepted. Having investigated them subsequently, it wishes only to reiterate its gratitude for Dr Flick's far-sighted benefaction.

17 November 1995

Appendix 3

Statement prepared for distribution to old members of Balliol
College, 1996

During March 1996, there was considerable controversy in the Press about a gift made to Oxford University by Dr Gert-Rudolf Flick. Hostility was expressed because the donor's grandfather, Friedrich Flick, had used slave labour in his factories during the Second World War and the survivors were not subsequently compensated adequately.

Much of the press comment stated that Balliol had received an endowment from Dr Flick. This is not true. The College received no money from this source. Dr Flick's gift was made to the University about three years ago, not to the College. University Professors are allocated colleges which give them house-room at college expense. Balliol accepted the allocation of this Professorship; but the College does not benefit materially from this benefaction.

Nonetheless, the Fellows have certainly felt that the association of the Chair with the College has meant that they should consider the source and implications of the endowment, even though the duty of investigation did not fall upon Balliol. The University's Ethics Committee has undertaken a protracted and substantial enquiry. To the best of Balliol's belief, this work was carried out in a thorough and professional manner, and the College understands that a number of prominent British Jews were also consulted. The Committee concluded that the money was not tainted.

Furthermore, on March 20, 1996, Dr Flick reiterated in a letter to the *Daily Telegraph* his 'total abhorrence of what took place in Germany during the Third Reich' and expressed again [51] his 'profound personal shame for the involvement of (his) grandfather in these dreadful events'. The College notes that the *Jewish Chronicle* reported (March 15, 1996) that the chief executive of the Board of Deputies has said that the Board does not object to the University accepting this money, which 'comes from a source which can be regarded as acceptable'.[52] Moreover, the College understands that Dr Flick has given benefactions elsewhere that have not caused controversy, especially one to Hammersmith Hospital in support of one of its principal researchers, a devout Jew.

Balliol does not accept that Dr Flick bears guilt by descent, nor that anyone can do so. The College is glad to note that this view is explicitly endorsed by Lord Shawcross (*The Times*, March 14) The College has always deeply held anti-authoritarian and anti-racist principles; it also has a tradition of reconciliation and tolerance. It has never accepted the demonisation of the enemy, let alone the demonisation of a whole people. The College Chapel has a memorial to all those Balliol men who died in both wars, whether they fought for the Allies or for Germany. It has publicly celebrated the bravery of its old member Adam von Trott in his resistance to Hitler and one of the main function rooms in its new building will be named after him.[53]

In late April, Dr Flick found the press attention on this matter too personally distressing and withdrew his benefaction from the University. Old members will understand from the above that the College did not solicit this decision from him.

Acknowledgements

It is always hard – and especially in this instance – to act as a participant observer. I owe a special debt of gratitude to the editors and to Paul Flather, who throughout the debate over the Flick donation remained faithful to Balliol and to the University and, at the same time, extended the hand of friendship to me. It was due to them that sympathetic and constructive exchanges of views continued at all times. I wish to acknowledge help and advice from Shelley Pinto-Duschinsky. All of the above have read and given valuable comments on successive drafts of this chapter.

I am grateful to the following (as well as to others remaining unnamed) for information and assistance: the late Sir Isaiah Berlin, Baruch Blumberg, Vernon Bogdanor, Tom Bower, Ruth Deech, Henry Drucker, Jackie Ettinger, Benjamin Ferencz, Jennie Frazer, Sir Martin Gilbert, the late Rabbi Hugo Gryn, Lord Holme, Ronnie Hooberman, Helen Jacobus, Anthony Julius, Saul Kagan, Rudy Kennedy, David Klass, Anthony Lerman, Franz Levi, Trude Levi, Raphael Loewe, Colin Lucas, Sir Claus Moser, Neville Nagler, Clemens Nathan, Rev. Ernest Nicholson, Rev. John Nightingale, Lord Perth, Adam Roberts, the late Stephen Roth, Hans-Peter Schwarz, David Selbourne, Adam Shapiro, Sir Richard Southwood, Sir Sigmund Sternberg, Alice Teichova, Ned Temko, Trisha Ward, Lord Weidenfeld and Regine Wosnitza.

This chapter contains an account of a contemporary matter. Because of this, some of the sources cannot be named. In all cases, those sources have been discussed with the editors. Late drafts were also read by a senior Oxford official and by a former official, acquainted between them with the University's fundraising and with Balliol's position. They confirmed the factual accuracy of the chapter but did not comment on the interpretations and characterisations it contains. Despite these checks, responsibility for the text and for any errors it may contain are my own.

Notes

1 For a description of the political objectives of the Europaeum, see Flather 1995.
2 The Flick case was one of twelve brought under what came to be known as the Nuremberg Subsequent Proceedings. These cases, conducted by United States authorities, followed the International Military Tribunal, which tried the leaders of the Nazi regime.

3 'The Flick Case' (Military Tribunal IV, Case 5, *The United States of America – against – Friedrich Flick {and others}*. See also *History of the United Nations War Commission*, London: HMSO 1948: 340). Flick was also charged with crimes against humanity involving 'persecutions on racial, religious and political grounds' (Count III). These accusations related to Flick's involvement in expropriations of Jewish property as part of the Nazi aryanisation programme. However, the Court ruled that it did not have jurisdiction to consider the charges under this count since they related to the period before the invasion of Austria (US Government Printing Office 1954, VI: iv).

4 Inevitably, judgements about Flick's war record vary. The judges at Nuremberg accepted some of the pleadings of his team of defence lawyers. See the summary of the Flick case in United Nations War Crimes Commission (1949: IX). Authors such as Simpson attribute the Court's failure to pass a stiffer sentence than seven years' imprisonment to political pressures within the United States against prosecutions of industrialists. 'Washington hobbled the prosecutions with budgetary restrictions, and some U.S. agencies in Berlin tacitly refused cooperation, particularly during trials of German industrialists' (Simpson 1993: 270). This interpretation is supported by *Der Spiegel*, 29 October 1984: 30. Even so, the evidence produced at Nuremberg was sufficient, by any reasonable standards, to establish Flick's status as a leading war criminal.

5 Translation from the Yiddish by David Dimson and Franz Levi, London: 1996. According to Glicksmann, Jews formed 800 out of a workforce of 2,500. Franz Levi has also kindly supplied the translation of a further eyewitness report concerning the same factory completed in 1948 for the historical commission at Lamtsberg, Lech, by a nurse, Giza Klein. This second report tells a similar story.

6 Flick was particularly evasive about his companies' use of slave labour, estimated by the prosecution to have consisted of some 40,000 workers at any one time (ibid: 55). 'When it started,' claimed Flick, 'I assumed that the workers came of their own accord . . . In my home in Toelz a Ukrainian was employed and she told us and assured us again and again that . . . she liked it very much in Germany . . . As time went on . . . I gained the feeling and the moral conviction that not all of them . . . had come voluntarily to Germany. But that was my own surmise. I had no knowledge to this effect' (ibid: 806–7). Asked whether he had ever spoken to one of the foreign workers, Flick said 'I do not know. I cannot remember. I do not think it is very likely, but it is not impossible . . . I must decisively refuse to accept responsibility for internal matters within a plant management which did not touch me at all . . .' (ibid: 828).

7 See, for example, the list of those attending the meeting of 12 December 1943, reproduced in US Government Printing Office (1954, VI: 274).

8 Letter from Sievers to Eichmann, Medical Case (US Government Printing Office 1954, I: 751–52).The number of Jews murdered for the sake of this 'skeleton collection' is stated at one point as 112 and at another as 109.

9 See the list of donors sent by Baron von Schroeder to Himmler, 21 September 1943 (in USG PO 1954: Vol VI: 270).

10 'Flick-Konzern: Wo stecken die Millionen?' *Der Spiegel*, 3 August 1955, p. 18 ff. See also Karl Bosl, *et al.* (1973, vol 1, col 700) and *Der Spiegel*, 29 October 1984, p. 30; 'Herr Friedrich Flick: Millionaire industrialist' (obituary). *The*

Times, 22 July, 1972; and Niall Ferguson, 'Shame for Oxford, not Dr Flick' (*Daily Telegraph*, 17 April 1996).

11 See Espelage (1984: 30) and, for a contemporary notice about the sale of Harpener Bergbau, *Der Spiegel*, 6 May, 1953: 3.

12 Bower (1996), and entry on Abs in National Council of the National Front of Democratic Germany (n.d.) For a description of Flick's further influential contacts in the early years of the German Federal Republic, including Robert Pferdemenges, see *Der Spiegel*, 29 October 1984: 30–31.

13 National Council of the National Front of Democratic Germany, *Brown Book* (pp. 49–50) and Ferencz (1979: 161). Quoting from the magazine *Stern*, Bower gives an indication of an authoritarian, and arguably Neo-Nazi, atmosphere within Mercedes-Benz after World War II. In the aftermath of the kidnapping by the Red Brigades in 1977 of Hans-Martin Schleyer, president of the Federation of German Employers, it transpired that Schleyer had not only been recruited in 1951 as personnel director of Daimler-Benz, but that he had joined the SS in 1935, had become director in 1938 of the Nazi party training school at Innsbruck University. After the War, Daimler-Benz – according to *Stern* – only recruited from amongst those who, during the Nazi period, were the 'high and mighty in the economy'. Schleyer ordained that when it came to young recruits, only right-wing graduates be chosen. Though Flick became the major shareholder, his role in such alleged postwar practices is unclear (Bower 1996: 463–64).

14 In 1976 and 1978, the Flick Concern sold DM1.9 billion worth of its Daimler-Benz stock. Under German law, the sale would give rise to a heavy tax liability unless the government decided the sale was in the German national interest. This favourable tax decision was duly taken.

In 1981, the matter became the subject of intense press comment. It was revealed that the Flick Concern had made a series of massive political donations to all the main parties. Between 1969 and 1980, they amounted to over DM26 million. (See Ulrich von Alemann, 'Bureaucratic and Political Corruption Controls: Reassessing the German Record', Arnold J. Heidenheimer *et al.* (1989: 865). The contribution figure is derived from *Bericht des 1. Untersuchung-sausschusses zur Flick-Affaere*, Bonn: Bundestages-Drucksache 10/5079 von 21.2.86.)

In particular, it was suggested that the Flick Concern had obtained its tax concessions in return for political donations. The affair led to the resignation of Dr Rainer Barzel, the president (i.e. speaker) of the Bundestag, and of the two implicated economics ministers, Dr Otto Graf Lambsdorff and Dr Hans Friderichs.

The Flick scandal led to a parliamentary investigation, to a presidential commission on party funding, to a new parties law and, finally, to a trial. In 1987, a senior Flick official received a two-year suspended sentence. The two former economics ministers were fined on minor charges. They were found not guilty on the main corruption charges, though the judge announced that 'the chamber continues to maintain considerable suspicion' that some of the allegations had been justified:

The judge described the so-called Flick case . . . as 'extraordinary' since . . . almost all the 80 witnesses had suffered a 'conspicuous loss of memory.' (Keesing's Contemporary Archives 1987, p. 35015. The official report of the case is Landgericht Bonn, *Urteil in der Strafsache gegen Eberhard von Brauchitsch, Han Friderichs, Otto Graf Lambsdorff von 16.2.1987*, 27 F 7/83.)

In the wake of adverse publicity caused by the Flick Affair the main (family) shareholders decided to sell the Flick Concern to the Deutsche Bank for DM5 billion.

(The Flick Affair has been the subject of a great amount of report and comment by German scholars of political corruption and party finance. See, for example, Landfried (1994: especially chapter 5: 'Parteienfinanzierung und Korruption' – Party financing and corruption). An English language account of the scandal is given in Erhard Blankenburg *et al*. 'Political Scandals and Corruption Issues in West Germany' (in Heidenkeimer *et al*. 1989). For the ramifications of the Flick Affair in Spain, see Pilar del Castillo, 'Financing of Spanish Political Parties' in Alexander 1989. See also *Der Spiegel*, 29 October 1984.)

15 Trude Levi, a former Flick slave labourer, has kindly shown me copies of her correspondence with an official German body, the Compensation Treuhand. A letter from the Compensation Treuhand dated 1 February 1989 stated to her: 'I am sorry it has taken so long for payments to be made. If the Flick Group of Companies would not have been bought up by the Deutsche Bank, in all likehood not even this small amount of DM5 million would have been paid . . . I share your anger concerning the level of the compensation and the long period which the descendents of the slave holders have allowed to pass by.'

Criticism of the Flick record on compensation spurred a debate in the European Parliament on 16 January 1986. Resolutions calling for 'compensation for persons formerly employed as slave labour in German industry' were tabled by the Socialist Group and the Rainbow Group and were passed by the Parliament. A German Socialist MEP, Mrs Wieczorek-Zeul, declared that it was 'a disgrace' that 'there has been no genuine compensation for the forced and slave labourers put to work in Germany's industry':

> This long-repressed problem has come into the public eye again with the sale of the Flick concern. Flick is a particularly scandalous case, since although in the 1960s a compensation payment was agreed upon with the Jewish Claims Conference, the concern simply refused to pay. It was only the public debate on the occasion of the sale to the Deutsche Bank which brought about the change. However, we agree with Heinz Galinski, the President of the Jewish Community in Berlin, that the sum involved is a pittance. The discussion surrounding Flick revealed how abysmally Germany has failed to come to terms with its past. (*Debates of the European Parliament*, No 2-334/181.)

16 Payments by Friedrich Flick or by members of the Flick family to former slave labourers: considerable care has been taken to check whether any such payments were ever made. I am grateful for help on the matter from Benjamin Ferencz, Saul Kagan (of the Conference on Jewish Material Claims against Germany), Lord Weidenfeld, and the Oxford University authorities. For information on Flick's exceptional payment of DM3000, I am grateful to Rudy Kennedy, who supplied a copy of a letter giving the relevant information from the German lawyer who had represented the former slave labourer.

17 Hugo Gryn and I met for the first time just before our joint session at the Balliol conference on Sunday morning, 29 January 1995. He had to rush back to London to attend that afternoon's fiftieth anniversary ceremony of the liberation of Auschwitz, where he would meet the Russian general who had liberated the camp. Our rushed discussions in the margins of the conference revealed that we had much in common and had been in neighbouring ghettos in May 1944, just before he was deported from Beregszasz to Auschwitz. There started an all-too-brief friendship which was cut short by his death. Though his private attempt to negotiate compensation for the former Flick slave labourers failed, he was much valued by a wide spectrum of those involved in Oxford's 'Flick Affair'.

18 At the time of the Balliol seminar of January 1995, one argument which cropped up a number of times was that Dr G.R. Flick's acceptance as a member of the Athenaeum, a prestigious London club, showed that his credentials had already been sufficiently examined. Moreover, those who had supported his election included prominent Jews, some of whom had also been involved in the creation and appointment of the 'Flick professor'. (See also Knight Bruce (1996: 13).)

19 One purpose of giving this notice was to ensure that Dr G.R. Flick could be informed and would not be taken by surprise by an article in the press.

20 There had been another representation from a distinguished Old Member of Balliol that the Flick name be dropped altogether and that the professorship be renamed after a major European thinker such as Copernicus. In *The Times* of 18 November 1995, the present author argued that the professorship should be renamed either after Adam von Trott zu Solz, an Old Member of Balliol executed for his role in the plot against Hitler, or after a victim of the Holocaust. The unofficial reaction to these suggestions of a former Oxford college head, who was close to some of the central figures in the affair, to these suggestions was that the donor would ask for his money back if the University refused to accept the Flick name in the title.

21 In the 1990s, David Selbourne has occupied a distinctive and prominent place in British intellectual life. Living in Urbino, Italy following a highly publicised departure from Ruskin College, Oxford, he has produced a series of works setting out the moral and political philosophy which had earlier occasioned the wrath of some left-wing Ruskin students. His work has been characterised by his personal independence, by his rejection of socialism and of laissez-faire alike, by his stress on 'civic values, civic purposes and civic problems' above self-interest, and by his open acknowledgement of his debt to several traditions, including the Jewish ethics expressed in the writings of his grandfather, Rabbi Moshe Avigdor Amiel, 'one of the greatest of modern rabbinical thinkers'. In 1994, Selbourne's book titled *The Principle of Duty* was serialised in *The Times* – something exceptional for a volume of political theory.

In a preface to a revised edition of *The Principle of Duty* (Selbourne 1997: xiii) he remarked on his freedom from 'the dead hand of 'academia' ' and of the need to play the 'academic game'. The confrontation between Selbourne and the Master of Balliol may be taken to personify that confrontation between different concepts of integrity, which is the theme of this volume. To the Master, integrity may have appeared to entail loyalty to his institution; to Selbourne, it meant the pursuit of civic duty.

22 Though the Master of Balliol had not been a member of the Ethics Committee in the academic year 1994–95, when the Flick donation was initially under discussion, he joined the Committee in 1995–96 in his capacity as Vice-Chancellor-elect. It was only from the academic year 1995–96 that the University's annual Calendar included the names of the Ethics Committee's members.

23 The account by Fiammetta Rocco (1997) suggests that Dr Flick's action was influenced by a depressive illness, aggravated in 1995 by divorce proceedings. Referring to Dr Flick's record on compensation, Professor Vernon Bogdanor, of Brasenose College, Oxford remarked to The *Sunday Telegraph* 'If he's ill, it's a psychosomatic consequence of guilt' (12 May 1996).

24 According to a later report, there was fear in some senior University circles that Wafic Said's projected gift of £20 million to establish a business school could be placed in danger if the university failed to stand by Dr Flick.

25 The Master of Balliol later acknowledged the absence of a single Anglo-Jewish view. 'Looking back on it, I think . . . that British Jewry was divided over it. I think we found ourselves for a while in the midst of a debate that we didn't quite understand. A debate between one generation of British Jewry – which is very integrated – and who believed in moving forward. And there's another part of British Jewry who say we must never forget, we must never give in' (*Daily Telegraph*, 5 April 1997). The Flick Affair certainly reflected and raised issues of identity among some British Jews. However, the division lines were, in my view, more complex and different. Some Jews who were most forthright in criticising the Flick contribution took this action precisely because they felt sufficiently 'integrated' to feel able to express themselves. The premise that 'integration' requires forgetting the Holocaust struck some readers as inappropriate.

26 A former director of the Institute of Jewish Affairs, the late Dr Stephen Roth, was approached for factual advice by a member of the Ethics Committee. Since Dr Roth was asked to make his enquiries discreetly, he consulted with his successor, Dr Anthony Lerman, without informing him of the reason for his query. Dr Lerman's investigations into the text of the notes I had presented at the Balliol seminar reportedly confirmed their accuracy. Unfortunately, Dr Roth died suddenly in the summer of 1996.

27 See, for example, *Jewish Chronicle*, 15 March 1996.

28 Jenni Frazer (1996) recalled that Lord Weidenfeld had 'provoked considerable controversy with his support of Dr Kurt Waldheim, the former secretary-general of the United Nations, amid the controversy over Waldheim's role during the war.' The two strongest criticisms of Lord Weidenfeld in the national press came from Tom Bower (*Guardian*, 13 March 1996) and Melanie Phillips ('College cash that leaves a Nazi taste'. *Observer*, 17 March 1996) 'There are Jews,' wrote Phillips, 'who, for whatever psychological reasons, want to draw the kind of line under the past that helps obliterate it.' Lord Weidenfeld justified his support for Waldheim in The *Observer*, 24 March 1996. He wrote 'Waldheim and I were fellow students at the Vienna Konsular Akademie in 1937–38. During the five months between the Anschluss and my departure from Austria, he was one of the few Christian colleagues who was demonstratively friendly towards the few Jewish students . . .' Weidenfeld added that 'for those of us who work, battle and beg for charitable causes, the intemperate outbursts of armchair moralists can leave a bitter taste.'

29 The Board of Deputies – Anglo-Jewry's parliament – had not been consulted by Oxford. It was thus left to its director-general, Neville Nagler, to make comments on its behalf. His initial caution, reported in The *Jewish Chronicle* of 15 March 1996 misled the University into thinking that, having changed the name of the professorship from Flick to Gert-Rudolf Flick, it had the Board's support. In fact, Mr Nagler's position (clarified in the same weekly on 19 April 1996) was that the acceptability of Dr Flick as a donor to Oxford was linked to his willingness to make some sort of reparation. As he wrote in an (unpublished) letter of 9 April 1997 to The *Daily Telegraph*:

'The position which I expressed on behalf of the Board was that we did not object to the use of the funds in question for the proposed chair. But more suitable philanthropic uses might be found for the Flick fortune, for example by making some sort of reparation to the surviving slave labourers so cruelly abused by Friedrich Flick during the Nazi era or to their descendants. Such a gesture might prove a more tangible indicator of his grandson's humanitarianism.'

30 Editorial, 22 March 1996 and Ned Temko quoted in *The Times*, 12 March 1996.
31 *Jewish Chronicle*, 8 March 1996 and *Holocaust Survivors' News*, March 1996.
32 *Jewish Chronicle*, 8 March 1996 and Association of Jewish Refugees, 'What's in a name? Reflections on the Flick donation to Oxford.' *AJR Information*, May 1996. The same issue of AJR Information announced a talk by George Clare following the annual general meeting of 9 June 1996 entitled 'Adolf's Grand-children, Balliol and We'.
33 David Cesarani quoted in *The Guardian*, 12 March 1996 and in The *Times Higher Education Supplement*, 15 March 1996.
34 Clemens Nathan, a director of the Conference on Jewish Material Claims against Germany and vice-president of the Anglo-Jewish Association, quoted in The *Jewish Chronicle*, 15 March 1996.
35 Greville Janner, quoted in the *Guardian*, 12 March 1996.
36 *Jewish Chronicle*, 15 March 1996.
37 Regine Wosnitza, *Jewish Chronicle*, 5 April 1996.
38 23 November 1997.
39 Letter to an Old Member of Balliol.
40 *Daily Telegraph*, 12 March 1996.
41 Letter from Ziona S. Strelitz, *The Times*, 16 March 1996.
42 *The Times*, 14 March 1996. Defenders of the University's position were repeat-edly to cite this letter of support from the former Nuremberg prosecutor. Though this letter to *The Times* had attacked 'guilt by descent', Shawcross had also been a leading advocate in the House of Lords against the War Crimes Bill, which permitted the prosecution in Britain of alleged war criminals themselves.
43 Keegan (1996). As the controversy was attracting attention in the press, a further line of defence was investigated by one of the College's Fellows. He read through the 1,200-page summary of Friedrich Flick's trial at Nuremberg, held at All Souls' Codrington Library, to see whether a more favourable account of his record could be presented. He decided that, though a number of pleas of

extenuation had been put forward on his behalf, it would not help the College's image to justify itself on this basis.

44 Further variations on the theme are reported by Rocco (Daily Telegraph, 5 April 1997): 'The Flick family and their friends split hairs even more finely. The explanation given by one of [Dr G.R. Flick's] closest friends is that Friedrich Flick had already made a lot of money before he joined the Nazis . . .' (*Daily Telegraph* Magazine, 5 April 1997, pp. 26).

45 'Sins of the founder revisited,' *The Times*, 16 March 1996. For a variation of the pragmatic argument for accepting the Flick donation, see Gregor (1997). Gregor argues (a) that 'Flick was not unique among German industrialists' (p. 56), (b) that 'at the root of much of the controversy' was the 'myth' and the 'misrepresentation' that 'Flick was unique' (pp. 56 and 58), and (c) that, because Friedrich Flick was only one of many guilty German industrialists and because of the 'unanswerable' question of 'where do we draw the line?', Oxford University should have accepted the Flick donation (p. 57). In fact, there is little evidence for the second of these propositions; the case for criticising the Flick donation in no way rested on the idea that the Flick Concern had been alone in its involvement in exploiting slave labour during the Nazi period. (See Appendix 1; my letter to the editor, *Patterns of Prejudice* 1998, 32(4), pp. 103–7.)

46 Gledhill (1996). The Dunblane massacre occurred when a gunman entered a school and killed a large number of children and a teacher.

47 The only parallel is Sir James Goldsmith's outlay – reportedly, also of some £20 million – to found and to finance his own party, the Referendum Party, in the British general election of 1997.

48 Such is the argument of despair of an editorial in the *Times Higher Education Supplement*, 19 April 1996. Those who had raised doubts about Dr Flick's endowment had been responsible for Oxford's losing £350,000, the journal suggested. 'Beggars who want the luxury of picking and choosing – and those who expect to expose donors to public mauling – must find other ways to live.' In fact, Oxford almost immediately recouped its losses when a new donor contacted the University with an offer to replace Dr Flick's money.

49 'Oxford University: poverty ringed with riches,' 8 July 1989; letter from Sir Patrick Neill, 29 July, 1989 and response, 5 August 1989.

50 See, for example, Kingston (1996) and a feature on the controversy at Cambridge University over the sponsorship of a professorship by a cigarette manufacturer (Popham 1996).

51 With reference to this, see Section 3, no. 7 above. As described, requests for information from the University authorities produced no evidence of any earlier statements by Dr Flick in which he publicly condemned his grandfather.

52 The quotation as given from the *Jewish Chronicle* is again in my view misleading. The Balliol statement omits to report that the *Jewish Chronicle* of 19 April reported the chief executive of the Board of Deputies of British Jews as saying Dr Flick 'ought to have made some gesture towards the survivors of his ancestor's activities.' He said there was a case for Dr G.R. Flick using his money 'to help survivors'. For a more detailed discussion of the opinions of the Board's chief executive, see footnote 29.

53 There is reason to regard this as a response to the conclusion of my article in *The Times* (reproduced in Appendix 1). The commemoration of Trott that I

had suggested in the article was, however, that the professorship in European Thought should be endowed in his name, not in the name of Flick. The Balliol statement does not address this particular suggestion.

My proposal to rename the professorship after Trott is itself a refutation of any idea that criticism of the Flick donation implied 'the demonisation of a whole people.' For a fuller response to the 'demonisation' argument, see section 3 subsection 4 above.

References

Alemann, Von, Ulrich (1989) 'Bureaucratic and Political Corruption Controls: Reassessing the German Record', in Arnold J. Heidenheimer *et al.* p. 865.

Alexander, H.E. (ed.) (1989) *Comparative Political Finance in the 1980s*. Cambridge: Cambridge University Press.

Anon. (1984) 'Flick: Zahlmeister der Republik'. *Der Speigel*, 29 October.

Bosl *et al.* (eds) (1973) *Biographisches Woerterbuch zur Deutschen Geschichte*. Munich: Franke Verlag.

Bower, Tom (1995) *Blind Eye to Murder: Britain, America and the Purging of Nazi Germany – A Pledge Betrayed*. London: Little Brown.

Bower, Tom (1996) 'Shame behind the name'. *Guardian*, 13 March.

Brown, Andrew (1996) 'The high price of a chair at Oxford'. *Independent*, 9 March.

Chernow, Ron (1993) *The Warburgs: A Family Saga*. London: Pimlico.

Duchêne, François (1994) *Jean Monnet: The first statesman of interdependence*. New York: W.W. Norton.

Ferencz, Benjamin B. (1979) *Less Than Slaves*. Cambridge, MA: Harvard University Press.

Ferguson, Niall (1996) 'Shame for Oxford not Dr Flick'. *Daily Telegraph*, 17 April.

Fishman, Jack (1986) *Long Knives and Short Memories: The Spandau Prison Story*. London: Souvenir Press; Gregor Espelage, *Sprengsstoff und Kunstoff*.

Flather, P. (1995) *The Times*, 8 December.

Frazer, Jenni (1996) 'Agenda'. *Jewish Chronicle*, 15 March.

Gledhill, Ruth (1996) '"Our role is not to forgive", says Carey'. *The Times*, 23 March.

Gregor, Neil (1997) 'Big business, barbarism and benefaction: The Flick affair'. *Patterns of Prejudice* 31(2): 51–58.

Heidenheimer, Arnold J., Johnston, Michael and LeVine, Victor T. (1989) *Political Corruption: A Handbook*. New Brunswick: Transcription Books.

Hilberg, Raul (1961) *The Destruction of the European Jews*. London: W.H. Allen.

Janssen, Karl-Heinz (1986) 'Sklavenarbeit: Flicks boeses Erbe: 22 Jahre zu spaet: Die Deutsche Bank begleit eine fuenf-millionen Schuld'. *Die Zeit*, 17 January.

Johnson, Paul (1987) *A History of the Jews*. New York: Harper and Row.

Keegan, John (1996) 'Nazi gold didn't fund this gift'. *Daily Telegraph*, 8 March.

Kingston, Peter (1996) 'Temptation of filthy lucre'. *Guardian*, 23 March.

Knight, Bruce Ross (1996) 'Those Flicks in full'. *Sunday Telegraph* magazine, 28 January.

Landfried, Christine (1994) *Parteifinanzen und politische macht* (Party Finances and Political Power). Baden-Baden: Nomos Verlagsgesellschaft.

Levi, Trude (1995) *A Cat Called Adolf*. London: Vallentine Mitchell, The Library of Holocaust Testimonies.

National Council of the National Front of Democratic Germany (n.d.) *Brown Book: War and Nazi Criminals in West Germany*. East Berlin: Verlag Zeit in Bild.

New York Times, The (1956) 'Zur Geschichte der Dynamit AG Ausgege' (Explosives and Synthetic Material: Extract on the history of Dynamit AG). 12 April, p. 5.

Ohlsen, Manfred (1985) *Milliarden fuer den Geier: oder Der Fall des Friedrich Flick*. East Berlin: Verlag der Nation.

Popham, Peter (1996) 'Lucky Strike or poisoned chalice'. *Independent*, 20 May.

Rocco, Fiametta (1997) 'The sins of the grandfather'. *Daily Telegraph* magazine, 5 April.

Selbourne, David (1997) *The Principle of Duty*. London: Little Brown.

Simpson, Christopher (1993) *The Splendid Blond Beast: Money, law and genocide in the twentieth century*. New York: Grove Press.

Spiegel, Der (1984) 'Flick: Zahlmeister der Republik' 24 October, pp. 26ff.

Times, The (1996) Letter from George Racz. 24 July.

United Nations War Crimes Commission (UNWCC) (1949) *Law Reports of Trials of War Criminals*. London: HMSO.

US Government Printing Office (USGPO) (1954) *Trials of War Criminals before the Neruenberg Military Tribunals under Control Law No. 10 (1946–49)*. Washington DC: US Government Printing Office.

Wistrich, Robert (1982) *Who's Who in Nazi Germany*. London: Weidenfeld and Nicolson.

15 Fund-raising, guilt and responsibility

Rabbi Hugo Gryn
As reported by Alan Montefiore

At the Colloquium from which the chapters in this volume originate, the third participant in this section on the integrity of fund-raising, was Rabbi Hugo Gryn. Hugo Gryn's participation at this point was peculiarly appropriate; not only did he have a wide (if non-professional) experience of fund-raising, but he was himself a survivor of Auschwitz, having been born and first brought up in just the same part of Europe from which, as it happens, part of Michael Pinto-Duschinsky's own family also originates. To the immense sorrow of his countless friends, Hugo died before having had time to write up his (largely extempore) contribution to the Colloquium into publishable form for this volume. Although he and I did indeed discuss the issues involved many times together, issues with which Hugo was deeply and characteristically concerned, it would be quite wrong for me now to try to write up that contribution for him and to present it as if it were his. I may, however, just outline the points that he already made at the Colloquium and that I know from our subsequent discussions he would have wished to have recorded here.

In the first place, he would certainly have stressed not only his rejection (along with virtually all other participants in the debate) of all ideas of hereditary guilt, but also the importance of never completely closing one's mind or one's heart to the possibility of sincere repentance on the part of the criminal for even the most terrible of crimes. (Which is not, he would have added, the same thing as to say that such crimes may ever be forgiven. While he wanted, I think, to reflect further on what it could mean to 'forgive' the criminal while continuing to hold that his crime had been unforgivable, he was clear enough that the distinction was of great importance.)

Second, however, while the idea of hereditary guilt is one thing and wholly unacceptable, that of hereditary responsibility, although immensely complicated, is another and altogether different thing. Indeed, Hugo thought it so complicated and yet so important that he would, he said, have been more than happy to participate in any subsequent study of this idea in its own right; and we even embarked on some preliminary discussion of the form which such a study might take.

Third, he thought that there was something seriously wrong – something that showed a lack of proper integrity, indeed – with any gesture that one should know might naturally be taken to indicate that it was not necessarily unacceptable for someone to have been involved in major criminal activity or to have profited directly from it, and yet to have made no subsequent effort to make effective compensation. In certain circumstances, to accept money known to have been derived from such a source might well be construed as such a gesture. Hence, to know all this to be so and to accept such money notwithstanding might well be judged to involve a lack of proper integrity. (Hugo did note, however, that delicate and essentially contestable matters of judgement might be involved in seeking to set the importance of the cause for which one was raising money against the magnitude of the crimes from which the proposed contribution ultimately derived, and the consequent undesirability of seeming, in any way, to condone them.)

Fourth, he thought that the nature of the circumstances in which such questions might present themselves would depend crucially on whether one could be satisfied that any repentance for (or repudiation of) the original crime was genuine, and that any relevant responsibility had been properly acknowledged and, so far as possible, fulfilled. Here too he recognised that honest judges might well disagree in their assessments of such matters.

Fifth and sixth, he was, (a), nevertheless clear that a 'merely' verbal affirmation of repentance or apology, or acknowledgement of responsibility, could not easily be taken as sufficient were it not accompanied by some appropriate act or acts; and, (b), that in assessing them, nobody should underestimate the importance of the symbolic, in addition to that of the more obviously practical, significance of acts of compensation and contrition.

Seventh, however, he was well aware that in stressing the importance of the symbolic, he was touching on what could often turn out to be not only the most important, but also the most difficult point. For actions can have very different symbolic values for different persons, differences that those most closely concerned may find almost impossible to appreciate or even understand. Similarly, he could see how those who had had no direct or even indirect involvement with a catastrophe such as the Holocaust would find it very hard to appreciate the ongoing impact that it would have on succeeding generations, the children and grandchildren of those who had been caught up in it; and this could only too easily give rise to a certain impatience with the continuing symbolic sensitivities that they might display, especially when they seemed to interfere with the pursuit of important contemporary projects. Moreover, Hugo said to me in one of our very last discussions, he could well see how very much more difficult it must be to repudiate or to apologise for what someone else very close to one had done than to apologise for anything that one might have done oneself. However, how exactly one should bring all these considerations to bear on Michael Pinto-Duschinsky's account of the many different aspects of the Flick affair, or indeed on the proposals of Paul Flather's chapter, is something that we have now all to work out for ourselves; for Hugo was never able to see the finally written up versions of either of these chapters. His death leaves an immense and deeply felt gap and we can but salute in sadness, affection and respect the passing of a man of exceptional human wisdom, warmth and integrity.

Part III

Integrity, the economy and the public service

Section I
Integrity and the economy

16 Do markets need a moral framework?

Donald Hay

A moral framework for the functioning of markets?

The issue I wish to explore in this chapter was stated succinctly by Hirsch (1977) in his significant, but neglected treatise, *The Social Limits to Growth* (see especially Chapter 10). His starting point was the relationship between Adam Smith's economic analysis in the *Wealth of Nations*, and his social analysis in *The Theory of Moral Sentiments*. He quoted with approval a summary provided by Coats:

> Men could safely be trusted to pursue their own self-interest without undue harm to the community not only because of the restrictions imposed by the law, but also because they were subject to built-in restraint derived from morals, religion, custom and education.
>
> (Coats 1971: 9)

Hirsch interpreted this to mean that without standards of truth-telling, mutual trust, and obligation to fulfil promises, the market system will tend to fail. Fewer goods and services will be produced because potential transactors are not able to trust each other sufficiently to trade with each other. According to Hirsch, such standards were previously sustained by moral sanctions outside the market system, and he is clearly referring to the sanctions provided by Judaeo-Christian religion and ethics – what he calls 'the depleting moral legacy'.

Three possible solutions to this problem were discussed by Hirsch. The first is that proposed by the Hayek–Friedman school of liberal economists. Market behaviour is to be controlled by the provision of statutory rules with incentives for compliance. However, as Hirsch observed, law can only imperfectly substitute a sense of social obligation. Arrow illustrated the limitations of liberal thought with an extreme example. If the market extends to the judicial and administrative system, so that judges and regulators are willing to be bought by the highest bidders, then any attempt to regulate market behaviour by statutory rules is bound to fail. Arrow remarked: 'The definition of property rights based on the price system depends precisely on the lack of universality of private property and the price system' (1975: 24).

The second solution, mentioned by Hirsch only to be dismissed, is a revival of religious sanctions. Griffiths (1984) is more sanguine about this solution. Indeed, he argues that a Judaeo-Christian moral code is essential for the functioning of a market economy. In this he rejects the neo-liberal position that markets are morally neutral, being no more than mechanisms by which different value systems can be expressed in terms of the types of goods and services being produced in the economy. On the contrary, markets cannot function effectively without a clear basis for individual rights (including rights of property), and notions of obligation to others (which restrains self-seeking behaviour in markets). Griffiths' contention is that Judaeo-Christian thought, with its conception of human beings in the image of God, and with its emphasis on obligations to one's neighbour, especially the weak and disadvantaged, provides precisely the moral ingredients required. Hirsch presumably would not disagree with this diagnosis, but would doubt whether a revival of Judaeo-Christian ethics is an option in current circumstances. More surprisingly, a Christian ethicist, John Atherton (1992), has counselled in a recent book against importing 'Christian values' into an essentially secular social organisation like the market, and has proposed that our focus of attention should be the values that the market itself develops, something akin to a natural law ethic.

The third solution, proposed by Hirsch himself, is to foster a new social ethic.

> Individuals' motives can remain self-interested, provided their actions within the relevant sphere are conditioned by a social interest. The purpose is served if individuals act *as if* they put the social interest first, even if they do not, and merely follow convention or the social ethic that influences individual behaviour. The key shift needed is, therefore, in that social ethic.
>
> (Hirsch 1977: 178–79)

But how is this social ethic to be generated? Hirsch suggested that 'the functional need for a change in social ethic can be expected over time to promote it' (ibid: 179). But he was unable to identify any particularly satisfactory mechanism to bring this about, though he believed that collective action would be needed, since no individual would have an incentive to change his or her behaviour alone.

The common feature of these three options is that they propose bringing an 'external' moral or legal framework to bear on the problem identified by Hirsch. The problem is that the scope of self-interested behaviour, which the freedom of the market system permits, includes actions such as deception and failure to fulfil promises, which could, if they became widespread, deter people from trading. Note that this problem is quite narrowly defined: we are not addressing here the general evaluation of the morality of markets, e.g. the value of market freedom, or the justice of market outcomes. But it is a problem which has attracted considerable attention in a number of cases, such as Maxwell Communications, the Blue Arrow affair at County Nat. West, and the Guinness share support operation during the bid for Distillers. More generally, it is known that the Bank of England has been concerned to promote ethical behaviour in financial markets in the aftermath of the financial deregulation of the 1980s: no longer it seems is 'a gentleman's word his bond', and there is considerable lack of clarity about what gentlemen are allowed, or not allowed, to do.

Given this interest, it seems worthwhile to give the problem a more detailed analysis. Our objective is to try to delineate more accurately the circumstances in which individualistic behaviour is likely to prove destructive of the market mechanism. This will be the focus of discussion in the next section. A subsequent section will return to the need for external moral and legal frameworks to enable markets to function effectively.

Market incentives for good market behaviour

We rely, in this section, on the analysis developed by Dasgupta (1988), which focuses on the concept of trust in markets. He notes first that standard economic theory presumes that people are trustworthy in transactions, without explaining why, and so presumably appealing to social obligations or institutional sanctions. In exploring trust, Dasgupta keeps within the framework of rational economic behaviour, and does not appeal to any external moral code which generates a sense of obligation on the economic actor to fulfil a promised action. Hence, if there is no punishment or loss involved in a failure to fulfil contracts, then there is no incentive to fulfil a contract, and no transactions will take place. Any punishment threat must be credible, in the sense that the 'enforcement agency' must itself be trustworthy, where the nature of the agency varies from society in general (social ostracism) to the aggrieved individual or individuals. Given the scope for punishment implied in a contract, you rationally trust another person to do something, not just because he says he will, but because you believe it is in his interests to do so. So, when entering into an agreement with someone else, you need to look at the transaction from their point of view at the point in time when they have to fulfil their part of the contract. That is, you form expectations about the actions of the others, and those expectations then affect your willingness to enter into an agreement or contract. (Note here that I am excluding the possibility that one is able to control or monitor the actions of the other party directly, within the terms of the contract.)

Economic analysis has identified two areas where trust is important in market transactions. The first is where one person's choice of action depends on the actions of others which the first person cannot directly control or monitor. The second is where a person's actions depend on information held by others, and those persons cannot necessarily be relied upon to tell the truth. We will look at examples in these two areas, to illustrate the general points under discussion.

In the first case we may examine two firms entering into a joint venture where each has to contribute its expertise in some fashion which is not directly measurable. The success of the joint venture depends not only on the contributions of the firms, but also on market uncertainties, which are also difficult to measure accurately (e.g., the size of the potential market for the product produced by the joint venture). Given the uncertainty and non-measurability, it is simply not possible to write a contract to cover all contingencies. Each firm then has the option of putting in a low- or a high-level of expertise with commensurate costs to itself in terms of effort and commitment of resources. What emerges is a typical 'Prisoner's Dilemma' problem. The best outcome (in terms of joint profits) is for both firms to put in a high level of commitment. However, for each individual firm the best outcome is when the firm gives a low level of commitment; when its partner gives a high level, the firm is able to free-ride on the commitment of its partner, and to take its share of the (lower) profits with very little cost to itself. For this reason, neither firm will be willing to put in a high-level of commitment, and the outcome will be low commitment and low profits for both firms. This may be sufficient to deter the firms from entering the agreement in the first place; lack of trust means that a market transaction which is privately and socially beneficial will not take place.

However, the analysis is not quite so bleak if the transaction is one of a continuing series rather than a one-off event. In this case, the prospect of foregoing profitable future joint ventures may be sufficient punishment to deter the firm from a low commitment to the current venture. One firm can then 'trust' its partner to behave positively, because it is *rational* for the partner to do so. That will not work, of course, if the partner could behave badly in one venture, collect the profits from so doing, and promptly put itself up for sale to a new management. However, that is perhaps a rather implausible scenario.

This analysis can be extended to a wide range of market transactions where the parties are required to perform. The incentive to behave positively is the threat of losing out on future transactions. Obviously, this threat of punishment is strongest where the parties to the transactions remain the same over time: but it can also be strong where reputations for performing contracts will spread widely in the business community.

The second area of potential market failure is lack of trust in the truthfulness of the person on the other side of the transaction. Dasgupta (1988) has given a subtle and detailed analysis of this case. His example is an extension of Akerlof's famous analysis of the 'market for lemons', where a 'lemon' is American slang for a used car of low quality (Akerlof 1970). A potential customer is considering whether to enter a particular used car showroom. He does not know whether the salesman is honest (will sell a good car) or dishonest (will pass off a lemon as a good car), but he does know the proportions of honest and dishonest sellers in the whole population of salesmen. In a simple model, the customer acts on the basis of his expected net benefit from entering the salesroom. Suppose initially that this is negative: the customer does not enter the salesroom and a potential transaction is foregone.

There are two routes out of this apparent impasse. The first appeals, once again, to repeated transactions and the building of reputations.[1] The dishonest salesman compares the returns from selling a stream of good cars over time with the one-off gain from selling a lemon, after which (to take an extreme case) he stands revealed as dishonest and no-one will deal with him again. If the long-term returns exceed those of the one-off gain, then the dishonest salesman will act *as if* he were honest. Knowing this, the customer will not hesitate to enter the salesroom: he will expect to be sold a good car regardless of the nature of the salesman. (Once again, there is a problem if the dishonest salesman has decided that the time has come to retire: he passes off his entire stock of lemons before his dishonesty becomes common knowledge, and decamps to the Caribbean to eat the lotus.)

The second route focusses on the actions that honest salesmen may take to signal their honesty to potential customers. An example is an advertising campaign which would only be worthwhile for an honest salesman who planned to stay in business, and could recoup the outlay from a stream of sales over time, but would not be worthwhile for a fly-by-night dishonest salesman who was going for a short-term gain. Unfortunately, it is also easy to construct examples where what is worthwhile for the honest salesman is also worthwhile for the dishonest salesman (in the sense that he is prepared to spend the same amount to avoid being revealed as dishonest).

Alternatively, and perhaps more plausibly in this particular case, it may be worthwhile for the honest salesman to offer a guarantee to replace any car that turns out not to be up-to-standard – an offer which the dishonest salesman would not be willing to make. Unfortunately again, this simple solution encounters a different problem, which is the dishonest customer who drives the car to destruction for six months and then claims under the guarantee.

Although these examples are somewhat artificial, they do suggest that rational behaviour can be 'good' behaviour in markets despite the apparent temptations to short-term gain from failure to fulfil obligations or from deception. The incentives for good behaviour are strongest where firms are involved in an ongoing series of transactions, so that bad behaviour can be punished, and where information about bad behaviour can be quickly spread among market participants. Anecdotal evidence suggests that this situation characterised the London financial markets before the financial liberalisation of the 1980s. It was, indeed, an exclusive club to which general entry was denied: but within the club a strict code of conduct could be enforced by the simple expedient of expelling any person or institution that was perceived to break the rules. Since financial liberalisation such strict sanctions are no longer in place, and there is a general perception that 'standards' have slipped.

Similarly, the existence of long-term vertical relationships between firms may reflect a recognition that repeated transactions over time are the best way to ensure that suppliers and buyers perform their obligations.

Another example is the growing economic power of major retailers in the UK. The broad mass of customers are unable to distinguish good quality products, so they rely on the retailers to do it for them. The incentive for the retailer is the knowledge that a failure to supply high quality goods could quickly damage their reputation with consumers. The incentive for those supplying the major retailers is that only by supplying goods of high quality will they be accepted by the retailers, and that without access to the major retailers they would be excluded from mass markets.

The irony of these arrangements is that they almost certainly constitute barriers to the free-market competition so enthusiastically expounded by neo-liberal economists. Indeed there may be a trade-off here: more long term relationships between firms in organised markets may be the means to ensure that contracts are fulfilled and that dishonest traders are excluded. But there may be offsetting losses of economic efficiency as more efficient, but untried, suppliers are unable to get access to markets.

Is an external moral framework necessary?

The analysis of the previous section has shown that Hirsch's thesis on the need for a social ethic to sustain the functioning of markets in a market economy is overstated. Even within the rather restricted purview of economic analysis, with its emphasis on rational economic behaviour, we have been able to identify circumstances in which there will be incentives for good behaviour. With a broader model of human behaviour (Frank 1988), it may be possible to extend the circumstances in which we may expect good behaviour to occur in markets, without recourse to any external moral code.

However, it seems implausible, empirically at least, to believe that markets can always generate their own patterns of good behaviour. The examples of consumers being duped by fraudulent schemes or products, the incidence of white-collar crime, and the continuing roles of consumer watchdogs in the media suggest otherwise. One response would be to appeal to legal or regulatory frameworks to fill the gap. However, there is good reason to believe that these are not likely to be sufficient.

Statutory frameworks for regulating market behaviour clearly have an important role, witness the size of the legal and accountancy professions that deal with business. However the costs are high. Many business deals, especially those involving real estate and development involve armies of lawyers on both sides of the transaction. Audit fees for major companies are high, and there have been some spectacular failures to identify corruption and fraud, witness the BCCI and Maxwell cases. It seems quite likely that pro-fessional fees are an obstacle to at least some transactions that would otherwise take place.

In recent years, it has become fashionable to argue for self-regulation by the market participants, on the grounds that statutory frameworks are expensive and cumbersome. Participants are better placed to identify bad behaviour, and to apply their own sanctions – e.g., refusal to deal with the offender. However, there are also dangers in such a system, as evidenced by the Guinness case. The fraud for which the defendants were convicted involved secret share support operations during the bid for Distillers. The grounds for appeal currently being addressed are apparently that the Serious Fraud Office failed to reveal to the defence that a City committee had looked at other contemporaneous cases of share support, and had concluded that no wrong had been done. The danger here is obvious: the opinions of market participants on what is, or is not, allowed are in conflict with the commonsense view that support schemes are deceptive of ordinary shareholders who will have no knowledge of what is going on. In other words, self-regulatory organisations may enforce only those rules which seem expedient to the market makers, overlooking the interests of outsiders.

Even were these regulatory frameworks, when added to the incentives for good behaviour that markets themselves generate, completely competent to ensure that economic actors told the truth and kept their promises, there remains the ironic comment of Joan Robinson: 'Honesty is much cheaper' (1962: 5). In utopian fashion, we could imagine an economy where traders told the truth about their products, and where contracts were always fulfilled to the best of the ability of the participants. Consumers would feel more secure, business would be able to focus on production, marketing and inno-vation without continually having to concern itself with contracts with suppliers and customers. Much of the accounting and legal professions would disappear. Economic life would be a lot simpler, and much less fraught. A strong social ethic to encourage honesty and trustworthiness in the populace at large may not be the *sine qua non* of markets that Hirsch suggested, but it might generate a much *happier* economy than we could otherwise hope to achieve.

Do markets (sometimes) deplete morals?

The preceding discussion has presupposed existing markets, and the sole question was how we can avoid market breakdown or failure due to bad beha-viour. However, the argument may also have something to say to the circum-stances in which it is appropriate to use markets to allocate resources to the provision of goods and services. The issue is whether markets can sometimes erode good behaviour. Given the current obsession with introducing 'market disciplines' into public services such as education and health, the question is not without interest.

The focus is on services which exhibit one or both of the following characteristics. First, some services cannot be precisely defined or even evaluated by the recipient. The best example is the relationship between doctor and patient, where asymmetry of information means that the patient has to *trust* the doctor to diagnose carefully and to treat effectively. Second, other services are close in nature to public goods. For example, basic scientific research in universities may never make an identifiable 'marketable' contribution, as there may be a large number of intermediate steps between a particular discovery and its application. The laser was regarded for many years as a scientifically interesting discovery, but practically useless. Advances in pure mathematics seldom have an immediate practical application.

The key feature of services with these characteristics is that their provision depends, to some degree at least, on virtuous behaviour by the suppliers. While it is true, for example, that doctors may develop reputations, it is doubtful whether reputations are always well founded, given that patients are not well placed to evaluate either the diagnosis or the treatment. For the vast majority of doctors, it is vital that patients are able to trust them to provide a good service without enquiring into their reputations. Traditionally, the incentives and rewards for talented people to engage in research have been recognition by the scientific community, and while this has sometimes involved an element of promotion to more responsible positions, this is by no means certain or predictable. Most scientists are driven by a passion for their subject, and view with some distaste colleagues who consciously set out to build a reputation. Where funds are allocated for basic scientific research, there has to be at least a tacit belief that the scientists involved are genuinely motivated by a spirit of enquiry. Obviously a good track record will help a scientist to get funding, but that cannot be the whole story. (The requirement of virtuous behaviour in services with these two characteristics has been traditionally captured by the concept of vocation, the idea that what is required is the commitment of the person to the task of serving others or pursuing truth, which brings its own rewards in terms of personal satisfaction.)

The issue is one of how far these virtues will survive 'marketisation'. Is it the case that the introduction of markets will tend to erode them, requiring even stronger regulation of behaviour by either statutory or self-regulatory bodies to ensure virtuous behaviour? To answer this question, we can draw on the insights of Holmstrom and Milgrom (1991) on a related issue. They consider the case of providing incentives for an agent who has to perform two tasks, one of which has clearly definable and measurable outputs, the other not being susceptible to accurate observation and measurement. Attaching incentives to the measurable output will lead the agent to concentrate his effort on that, to the detriment of the non-measurable activity. Indeed, Holmstrom and Milgrom show that the incentive payment for the measurable output should be zero where the other activity cannot be measured at all. The analogy with our question is obvious. If we wish the supplier to provide qualities which cannot be accurately observed or measured, then it is a mistake to attach incentive payments to that part of their activities which can be measured. Yet that is precisely what marketisation does: it links returns to the number of units supplied, tending to undermine any predisposition to virtuous behaviour.[2]

The problem is particularly acute if marketisation also involves competition. By driving monopoly rents to zero, competition ensures that there is no scope whatsoever for a particular supplier to provide a superior quality of service. To do so, evidently at higher costs, is to risk elimination from the marketplace. There is no simple way of signalling to consumers that what is on offer is a higher quality for which they should be willing to pay more. Indeed this points to another possible adverse consequence of marketisation: when the patient, or client, or other recipient of services becomes a 'customer', he or she rightly adopts a different set of standards in evaluating the supplier. In markets, *caveat emptor* is the rule, and as shown above, the customer has good reason to be cautious about trusting the supplier, especially if the customer knows that the rewards to the supplier are based on the number of units supplied. Yet again, a predisposition to virtuous behaviour on the part of suppliers is undermined, since it will receive no recognition from the customer. It is hard for a supplier to sustain virtuous behaviour, at considerable personal cost, if he or she receives no encouragement.

These deleterious effects of markets can be countered to some extent by the mechanisms discussed above. Regulation by some statutory body, or self-regulation of the profession, may go some way towards alleviating the justified fears of the consumers of services. However, it should be recognised that if quality of service is not easily defined or measured, then regulation faces an impossible task. Monitoring of quality can only hope to pick up the most blatant failures to conform to a professional code of conduct. Nor can the consumer always hope to rely on the personal ethical commitments of the suppliers: even doctors, to take one example, are not saints, and if the incentives are stacked against maintaining high quality, it is unreasonable to expect their conduct to remain unaffected.

If these arguments are correct, they suggest that marketisation of services such as education and health is likely to involve deterioration in the quality of service. But is the outcome likely to be any worse than that of non-market allocation systems? We should note that non-market allocation systems face some daunting problems. To create space for virtuous behaviour, resources must not be directly related to any quantity index, but have to be allocated to teams or individuals on the basis of their promises to provide a high-quality service. In other words, these teams have to be trusted to be careful stewards of the resources. However, it is difficult to prevent two types of undesirable behaviour. The first is that the teams may be less than efficient in their use of resources, and dissipate them in expenditures that are unnecessary or ill-directed but bring personal benefits. The second is that the teams may spend a lot of resources on 'lobbying' activities within the resource allocating institution, particularly where the institution has a bureaucratic structure. It is a moot point whether suppliers are more likely to be diverted from virtuous behaviour by this type of rent-seeking than by the lure of profit in a market situation.

However, the non-market mechanism has some obvious advantages. First, it *does* leave space for virtuous behaviour. Second, it makes virtuous behaviour the *ostensible* criterion for resource allocation; even if systems can be exploited by the non-virtuous, there is a greater opportunity for reputation mechanisms to weed them out, since the allocations can be made by those who are in a position to evaluate performance over time (unlike individual customers). Third, the ethos is likely to positively attract the virtuous and to deter the non-virtuous, so that good behaviour is maintained as the professional norm.

There is, however, a danger in building up a non-market service based on virtuous behaviour. The authorities (government) providing the resources may decide to cut expenditure (to promote 'efficiency'), free-riding for a while on the accumulated stock of virtuous professionals in the service. If this is done too shamelessly, the incentives to good behaviour may fall to such a degree that either the potential supply of virtuous workers will dry up, or even that the currently virtuous professionals within the service will be seduced into rent-seeking behaviour to protect themselves. The situation is doubly bad if the authorities decide to cut resources *and* introduce markets at the same time: in such circumstances it is hard to believe that virtuous behaviour will have any future at all in the service. This may take some time, of course. The erosion of virtue will be slow and gradual, and the full effects may take a generation to be felt.

To conclude, our analysis suggests that there are some services, the quality of which cannot be easily observed and monitored by the recipients of the service, where the introduction of market resource allocation mechanisms can have deleterious effects on the quality of the service supplied. Incentives for good behaviour are undermined, and scope for good behaviour may be eliminated if the markets are competitive. In such cases, the enthusiasm of the authorities for marketization of services may turn out to be a (socially) costly mistake.

Conclusions

Do markets need a moral framework? Not, apparently, if the conditions are right. The key condition is that there are incentives to suppliers to establish reputations in order to ensure that their customers will repeat their purchases. But that presupposes that there is a continuing market, and that information is sufficiently widely available to consumers, to make reputation building an option. Where these conditions are not met, and that could be in a wide range of markets, then we have to rely on regulation (either statutory regulation or self-regulation by the industry) to prevent bad behaviour. But regulation can be costly, and sometimes ineffective. Perhaps a moral code is not such a bad idea after all: at the very least, honesty is cheaper.

Do markets destroy morals? Again, not, apparently, if the conditions are right. As noted in the previous paragraph, there are markets where the incentives for good behaviour will reinforce any market virtues that the suppliers may already exhibit. However, where the conditions are not right, where reputations cannot be relied upon, where monitoring is difficult, and where virtuous behaviour is integral to effective supply, then markets, especially competitive markets, are quite likely to drive out good behaviour. Non-market allocation mechanisms may do a better job, since they can preserve virtuous behaviour.

Notes

1 For a very subtle and rigorous account, see Kreps and Wilson (1982).
2 It might be objected that this argument is too strong. Many markets exist in which a range of qualities are supplied, and there is no overwhelming tendency for quantity to drive out quality. The difference with the services we are considering here is that the quality of suppliers is not obvious to the consumers of the services.

References

Akerlof, G. (1970) 'The market for "lemons": qualitative uncertainty and the market mechanism', *Quarterly Journal of Economics* 84: 488–500.

Arrow, K. (1975) 'Gift and exchanges', in E.S. Phelp (ed.) *Altruism, Morality and Economic Theory*. New York: Russell Sage Foundation.

Atherton, J. (1992) *Christianity and the Market*. London: SPCK.

Coats, A.W. (ed.) (1971) *The Classical Economists and Economic Policy*. London: Methuen.

Dasgupta, P. (1988) 'Trust as a commodity', in D. Gambetta (ed.) *Trust: making and breaking cooperative relations*. Oxford: Blackwell.

Frank, R.H. (1988) *Passions within Reason*. New York: W.W. Norton.

Griffiths, B. (1984) *The Creation of Wealth*. London: Hodder and Stoughton.

Hirsch, F. (1977) *The Social Limits to Growth*. London: Routledge and Keegan Paul.

Holmstrom, B. and Milgrom, P. (1991) 'Multi-task principal-agent analyses: incentive contracts, asset ownership and job design', *Journal of Law, Economics and Organization*, 7 (special issue): 24–51.

Kreps, D. and Wilson, R. (1982) 'Reputation and imperfect information', *Journal of Economic Theory* 27: 253–79.

Robinson, J. (1962) *Economic Philosophy*. London: C.A. Watts.

17 Promoting integrity and virtue

The institutional dimension

Alan Hamlin

Introduction

Markets are often criticised for encouraging self-interested behaviour and thereby undermining virtue and personal integrity. How should such criticisms be interpreted and evaluated; and how should the underlying concern with the wider impact of institutional structures be addressed? This chapter is intended to sketch out a broad approach to these questions which operates at the general level of the economic analysis of institutions and which attempts to identify some of the ideas that contribute to an understanding of the issues involved. It may be the case that 'you can not legislate for integrity',[1] nevertheless I shall suggest that integrity may indeed be promoted or undermined by direct institutional means, but that the nature of the relationships between institutional design and virtue may not be as simple as they might seem.

Clearly much will depend on the particular ideas of virtue and integrity that are employed, and I shall offer specific interpretations of these ideas which attempt to capture important aspects of the underlying concepts while abstracting from the finer debates on the precise nature of virtue and integrity. Essentially I shall take virtue to be the disposition to act in the public interest even when such action conflicts with the agent's private interest; while I shall take integrity to be a property of the relationship between an agent's disposition to act and her higher order evaluation of that disposition. In short, integrity will involve the combination of a virtuous disposition and a higher order desire to be virtuous. The interpretations will be outlined in rather more detail below.

With particular ideas of virtue and integrity in play, I shall identify, in the third part of this chapter, a class of institutions that *economise on virtue* (a class which includes, but is not restricted to, the institution of the market) and distinguish between two variations on this theme. I shall also identify a class of feedback effects from institutions to dispositions which might be said to *promote* or *undermine integrity*. I shall then frame and address a range of questions which bear on the relationship between institutional design and motivational dispositions and, in particular, the question of whether institutions that economise on virtue must necessarily undermine either virtue or integrity. The last section will then offer some further discussion of the issues at stake.

The general line of argument I wish to suggest is one that accepts the idea of potential feedback effects from institutions to motivations and dispositions, but then attempts an essentially economic analysis of the further question of the detailed nature of these feedback effects arising from particular institutional arrangements. Although the analysis suggested here is clearly very preliminary in nature, it seems far from clear that there can be any general presumption to the effect that institutions that economise on virtue undermine either virtue or integrity. More generally, I hope to suggest that the arguments sketched out here hold out some hope for a broadly economic approach to questions of institutional design that recognises and accounts for the feedback from institutions to dispositions.

Virtue and integrity

As I have already noted, I take virtue to be dispositional – the virtuous agent is disposed towards the public interest in the sense that she is motivated directly by consideration of the public interest. More accurately, virtue might be understood as the dual attribute of a capacity to discern the public interest and a disposition to act as the public interest requires. Note that this idea of virtue is independent of any particular substantive theory of the public interest in that it merely requires the agent to be appropriately motivated relative to the relevant substantive concept of the good (or the right). In what follows I shall contrast the virtuous agent with the interested agent, who is motivated by consideration of her own interests. Of course, many other dispositions are possible, and even with respect to these two dispositions we should think of a continuum of possibilities between these two extremes, but the stark contrast between the virtuous agent and the interested agent will allow the argument to be sketched out in relatively simple terms.

If virtue is the disposition to act in the public interest, I take the value to society of virtue to be the increase in the value of social outcomes brought about by virtuous dispositions. Virtue, on this account, is not its own reward, but is socially valued only instrumentally as a means of serving the public interest. This view is adopted in part to focus on the possible trade-off between alternative institutional means of serving the public interest – some of which may rely upon virtue while others operate by economising on virtue in one of the senses to be identified below.

I must now be more specific about integrity and its relation to virtue. I want to focus on an aspect of integrity which seems of particular relevance in the present context – although I do not suppose that it exhausts the idea of integrity. The aspect of integrity that I wish to emphasise relates to Bernard Williams' use of integrity to denote the internal unity of the individual agent,[2] and is broadly consistent with the discussion presented by Gabriele

Taylor (1985) and by Mark Philp (Chapter 2, this volume). This contrasts with the use of 'integrity' to identify a particular virtue such as honesty or trustworthiness.[3]

More specifically, I take integrity to be a property of the relationship between the agent's first order disposition and her second order disposition. This suggestion clearly relates to the discussion of dispositional theories of value[4] where it is argued that values are those things which, under ideal circumstances, an agent desires to desire. Here I would amend this formula slightly to suggest that integrity is realised by an agent when that agent is characterised both by virtuous desires (first order) and by the desire to be virtuous (second order). Notice that this statement makes no reference to ideal circumstances. Integrity, on this account, is achieved whenever virtuous desires are sustained by the desire for virtue, whatever the external circumstances, and whether or not the desired states of the world are realised.

For an economist it is natural to think of this aspect of integrity as a type of long run stability condition. In the absence of this form of integrity, virtue might seem to be fragile or unstable. To the extent that first order motivations and dispositions are chosen, or otherwise adapt to second order desires, virtue will decline through time unless it is supported by integrity. It is this interpretation of integrity that provides a key to the economic analysis to follow, since it connects the notion of integrity to the idea of choice – a person of integrity would choose a virtuous disposition.

It should also be noted that I simply assume that a virtuous disposition is a necessary condition for the realisation of integrity, thereby ruling out the possibility of an interested agent of integrity. Of course, an interested agent may achieve states of internal consistency between first and second order dispositions analogous to integrity, but 'integrity' seems to require some moral component as well as simple consistency or integration. If we are to believe that promoting integrity is a worthwhile objective of social institutions (at least presumptively), it seems natural to believe that there is a necessary connection between integrity and virtue.

Economising on virtue and promoting integrity

Individual agents act and interact within social, economic and political institutional structures. Social outcomes can be thought of as the joint products of characteristics of the agents and characteristics of the institutional setting. For simplicity, suppose that institutions are valued only instrumentally; and that social outcomes and (possibly) the actions of agents are the only items of ultimate, intrinsic value. This leaves open the possibility that institutions matter (i.e., contribute – positively or negatively – to value) in each of two distinct ways. On the one hand, institutions may influence social outcomes by aggregating, structuring or otherwise mediating the fixed characteristics of a group of individuals. This is simply to say that varying the institutional structure may be expected to produce variation in the social outcome *ceteris paribus*.

We may call this the direct role of institutions. On the other hand, institutions may matter because they influence the characteristics of agents. This is to suggest that agent characteristics are endogenously determined (at least in part) by the institutional setting. We may call this the feedback role of institutions.

With respect to the direct role of institutions, we may identify two broad strategies for the design of institutions which add value – I shall say that institutions may either *economise on virtue* or not. With respect to the feedback role of institutions, I distinguish between institutional structures that *promote integrity* and those that *undermine integrity*. The role of the next few paragraphs is to offer some clarification and discussion of these ideas.

How, then, might an institution economise on virtue? Here I want to distinguish between two major possibilities.[5] The first possibility is that an institution attempts to economise on virtue when it attempts to secure the public good without relying on virtuous motivations on the part of the individuals who act under that institutional structure. This idea is perhaps most familiar under the description of *invisible hand mechanisms,* where the defining characteristic of such a mechanism involves the idea that the outcome emerges from the institutionally mediated activity of individuals who are not directly motivated by consideration of the emergent outcome. The market – at least in its pure competitive form – is often defended on the grounds that it economises on virtue in this sense. But the market is far from being the only institution that is defended in this way. It is clear, for example, that many aspects of the US constitution were designed explicitly to operate so as to economise on virtue in this sense or, in Hamilton's words, 'to make their interest coincide with their duty' (Krannick 1987). And it is equally clear that many aspects of our familiar social and political institutions can be understood in terms of attempting to channel interested behaviour towards socially acceptable outcomes. A general point here is that 'invisible hand' mechanisms operate via the medium of direct incentive structures – systems of rewards and sanctions which change the relative prices of various actions so as to encourage some actions and discourage others.

The second possibility that I want to consider here relies on a rather different interpretation of 'economising'. If the sense of 'economising' underlying the invisible hand idea is the simple one of reducing the extent of reliance on a particular scarce resource (virtuous agents), the second sense of 'economising' depends upon the equally simple idea of allocating scarce resources to their most valued uses. In this context we might think of attempting to ensure that virtuous agents fill those social roles where virtue is most important in terms of making the greatest contribution to social value, by the design of appropriate institutional procedures. The general idea here is not that of an invisible hand, but rather one of a selection or screening device.

It should be emphasised that these two sense of 'economising', and their institutional counterparts in invisible hand mechanisms and screening devices, are complementary. Taken together they provide the basis for an account of the economic approach to the question of institutional design. All too often the economic approach is cariacatured as consisting only of the idea of direct, private incentive mechanisms and invisible hand arguments; as if the economic approach was concerned solely with reducing the extent of reliance on a scarce resource and not at all with the most efficient allocation of those scarce resources.

To see this complementarity in a more practical light, suppose initially that there are just two spheres of social life, and that virtue is differentially productive across these two spheres, so that (at the margin) a virtuous individual in sphere 2 would add more to social value than a virtuous individual in sphere 1. Under these conditions it is easy to see that a screening device that tends to allocate virtuous individuals in sphere 2 will be socially valuable. It will tend to reduce the value of the outcome in sphere 1, but increase the value of the outcome in sphere 2 by a greater amount so that social value overall is increased. And this would be so even if the screening device were imperfect, so that it simply over-represented the virtuous in the second sphere relative to their proportions in the population at large. This seems to be a relatively straightforward application of the idea of comparative advantage in the context of the social division of labour. Now let us suppose, since it is surely true, that some aspects of social life are more easily and advantageously organised via invisible hand mechanisms than others. Assume again that there are just two spheres of social life, but that sphere 1 is such that an invisible hand mechanism operates tolerably well to generate acceptable social outcomes without relying in any way on virtuous agency. In sphere 2 there is no such tolerable invisible hand mechanism available, so that the achievement of acceptable outcomes depends crucially upon virtuous agency. In this case an institutional screening device which allocates virtuous agents to roles in the second sphere, working in tandem with the invisible hand mechanism in the first sphere, might be expected to improve outcomes overall by directly improving the outcomes in the second sphere without threatening the value of outcomes in the first sector. In this way the social effectiveness of institutions which attempt to screen or select virtuous individuals into the relatively virtue-intensive spheres of social life will be enhanced if invisible hand mechanisms are available elsewhere.[6]

The alternative to the strategy of economising on virtue is to rely on virtue.[7] This strategy sees the role of institutions as being concerned with the removal of problems which might prevent virtuous motivations from resulting in 'good' outcomes. Such problems might include the relatively standard range of game theoretic difficulties which can stand between individual motivations and social outcomes. Whatever the details, the strategy of relying on virtue is concerned with identifying such problems and finding institutional solutions so that the connection between virtuous motivation and 'good' outcomes is as tight and as direct as possible.

We can now turn to the discussion of the feedback role of institutions in promoting or undermining integrity. An institutional structure promotes integrity, on our reading of integrity, to the extent that it provides external circumstances conducive to a (second order) desire for virtue. That is, integrity is promoted to the extent that the institutional circumstances are such that a virtuous disposition (first order) is more likely to be chosen. This then re-connects the discussion of virtue and integrity to the analysis of choice.

Under what circumstances might we expect virtue to be chosen so that integrity is promoted? The answer to this question hinges on how we model choice at this level. If the choice is between a virtuous and an interested disposition, what is the relevant criterion of choice? This is a big question, and I shall not attempt to answer it fully here, but it seems reasonable to suggest that the relevant criterion must be sensitive to both private and public interests. We might think of the criterion, loosely, as an index of the *overall* value, to the individual, of a life-plan; and this should certainly include both private and public interests.

With a criterion of this general type in mind, the agent faces a potential choice between interested and virtuous dispositions, given a particular institutional environment which the agent may be presumed to expect to remain in place indefinitely. We are then concerned with the question of how a change in this institutional environment might be expected to impact on an agent's choice of disposition. To the extent that some institutional reform tends to shift the balance in favour of the choice of a virtuous disposition, we might say that the reform promotes integrity, while an institutional reform of the opposite type might be said to undermine integrity. Of course, we might also use these terms to indicate the overall impact of a particular institutional setting, rather than the direction of the impact of any institutional reform. In this case an institutional environment will support integrity to the extent that virtuous dispositions would be chosen under that environment.

The institutional dimension

These formulations of the ideas of economising on virtue, and of promoting integrity, suggest a variety of questions. Perhaps the most striking question – and the one which bears most directly on our introductory concern with the possibility of markets undermining virtue and personal integrity – is that of whether institutions designed to economise on virtue must necessarily undermine integrity. The first point to make is that, in the present context, this question can be interpreted as asking whether the institutional strategy of economising on virtue will raise or lower the 'return' to a virtuous disposition relative to the 'return' to an interested disposition, where the 'returns' are measured in terms of the relevant overall criterion of value. If the return to a virtuous disposition is increased, such dispositions will be more likely to be chosen and so integrity will be promoted and virtue protected; equally, if the return is reduced, integrity will be undermined and virtue eroded.

Once this basic question is seen in this way, it seems clear that there can be no general presumption that the strategy of economising on virtue will undermine virtue. The strategy of economising on virtue may increase the return to a virtuous disposition in several ways. First, and obviously, it can do so by improving social outcomes and so increasing one element of overall value. This point is emphasised by realising that, in the absence of any institutional feedback effects, the strategy of economising on virtue would certainly be of social value, since it would both utilise whatever virtue is available to the greatest social benefit, and substitute for virtue where it is not available. These effects remain when feedback effects are introduced, even though they are no longer the only effects.

A second, and slightly more subtle, way in which the strategy of economising on virtue may increase the return to a virtuous disposition is by means of an indirect incentive effect operating as the result of an institutional screening device. To see how this might work, return to the simple example of a world with just two spheres of activity, one of which operates under an invisible hand institution while a screening mechanism ensures that virtuous individuals are disproportionately represented in the second sphere. Think now of the impact of increasing the *private* benefits to individuals in the second, virtuous sphere. A first thought might be that such a move would attract interested individuals into that sphere and so reduce the value of outcomes but, *ex-hypothesi*, a screening device over-represents the virtuous in this sphere, so this thought must be abandoned. Nevertheless, the increase in private benefits will have an incentive effect at the level of dispositional choice. It will increase the return (measured in terms of overall value) to entering the second sphere and so provide an incentive for individuals to adopt that disposition which improves the probability of entering that sphere. In this way the institutional mechanism that operates as a screening device at the level of everyday (first order) choice, acts as an indirect incentive mechanism at the level of (second order) dispositional choice.

So it is possible for the strategy of economising on virtue to increase both the private and the social return to a social disposition, and we may, therefore, conclude that economising on virtue can promote integrity. But, of course, it need not. It is equally plausible to describe circumstances in which integrity may be undermined. The point is not that economising on virtue will necessarily promote virtue, but rather that it will not necessarily undermine virtue. It all depends on the details. Introducing a market-like mechanism in one sector of a society – health, say – may either promote or undermine integrity and, therefore, virtue itself depending on the precise details of the institutional arrangements, the private and social benefits on offer in that sector and elsewhere in the society, the interactions with other sectors, the pre-existing balance between virtuous and interested dispositions in the population, and so on. No simple claim that marketisation, or economising on virtue more generally, leads to motivational impoverishment can be sustained, any more than the simple counter-claim that such strategies provide universal support for virtue and integrity can be sustained. The real point that I wish to emphasise here is simply that the style of analysis that I have outlined, and described as an essentially economic approach to the questions of institutional design, seems to provide an appropriate basis for study of the more detailed questions by identifying the considerations on which answers to those questions must turn.

A further question is prompted by this line of thought: is promoting integrity necessarily a good thing? Again the answer is not as obvious as it might seem, If we continue to assume that the only items of ultimate, intrinsic value are the actions of agents and the social outcomes that are produced, it is by no means clear that the promotion of integrity is necessarily the best available strategy. It is at least possible that an institutional structure might induce 'good' behaviour and social outcomes while undermining integrity and virtue, and that any attempt to promote integrity may lead to 'worse' outcomes. Again, it will all depend on the details, but there are two rather distinct lines of argument that suggest that the promotion of integrity may not always be desirable. First, even if an institutional structure could reliably induce a completely virtuous population, there might still be a gap between virtuous motivations and good actions/outcomes. Furthermore, the institutional structures required to bridge this gap may not be consistent with the promotion of integrity. Second, it is unlikely that any institutional structure could induce a completely virtuous population, so that the real task is to identify the optimal balance of motivations in the population. The important question is not whether a completely virtuous society would generate better behaviour and outcomes than a completely interested society, but whether an increase in virtue and integrity *at the margin* will produce a social improvement. Now, assume, for the sake of argument, that a particular social reform which aims to economise on virtue will, in the circumstance of a particular society, undermine integrity and so reduce the extent of virtue at the margin. It is still possible that this same reform could improve social outcomes. So that, even if economising on virtue does tend to undermine integrity and virtue at the margin, it may still be the best institutional strategy available. Of course, as I have already argued, it may be the case that economising on virtue and promoting integrity can work together toward the improvement of social outcomes, but if they do pull in opposite directions the choice between them must be made by reference to the appropriate criterion of overall value.

Discussion

The arguments outlined here are sketchy at best and need much further work. In this final section I offer one or two, still more inchoate, comments which may contribute to the further development, or deeper understanding, of the argument.

First, it is important to note that while my account of the two alternative forms of the idea of economising on virtue – and of the institutional instantiations of that idea – stresses the complementarity of these ideas and institutions, this should not be taken as suggesting that they can always be invoked together. A simple example may clarify. Imagine the task of designing an institutional structure for a specific sector – the health sector, for concreteness – and focus on the possibility of a design that economises on virtue. Taken in my first sense this might suggest the adoption of an invisible hand mechanism – perhaps a market-like mechanism – to provide essentially interested incentives to doctors, nurses and other decision-makers in the sector. In my second sense, however, the idea of economising on virtue might suggest the use of a screening mechanism in the selection and training of doctors, nurses and other decision-makers intended to select for more virtuous and less interested individuals. The details need not concern us here, since I do not intend to argue for one strategy over the other (or indeed for the necessary superiority of either of these strategies over some third alternative); my point is simply that it makes little sense to attempt both strategies at once. If the screening mechanism works to over-represent the virtuous, you need an internal structure that allows those virtuous individuals to act as virtue dictates, rather than binding them with a structure intended to provide incentives to the interested. In this sense, then, the two forms of economising on virtue may interact perversely, but this is because they are employed inappropriately rather than because of some deeper problem with the underlying argument. The pattern of complementarity between the two types of institutional arrangement is a pattern that operates *between* sectors and not within a single sector.

My second comment returns to the distinction between integrity as I have interpreted it and the particular virtue of trustworthiness. The relationship between integrity and trust is important, not least because there is a considerable literature devoted to the analysis of trust in the essentially game-theoretic literature which might be brought to bear on the analysis of integrity.[8] I cannot provide anything close to a full account of the relationship between trust and integrity, but one distinction may be helpful – a distinction between what I shall term time-inconsistency trust and type-uncertainty trust.

The question of time-inconsistency trust arises in situations in which an agent may promise, agree or contract to perform action A at future time T, but may, when time T comes, face incentives to default or renege. A trustworthy agent, in this context, is a reliable promise-keeper. Note that this aspect of trust is independent of the nature of the agent's motivation. In particular, both interested and virtuous agents may face the time-inconsistency problem, and so trust of this type will be an issue for both. There is nothing in the least contradictory in the possibility of a virtuously motivated but untrustworthy agent – one who would default on past promises whenever this action is in the public interest. Institutional mechanisms that support time-inconsistency trustworthiness may be required even in the most virtuous communities.

Type-uncertainty trust differs from time-inconsistency trust in one important respect; the key doubt is still whether an agent can be trusted to perform appropriately, but performance is now determined by the dispositional type of the agent, rather than by the changing pattern of incentives over time. In a world containing both virtuous and interested agents and lacking any reliable means to distinguish between the two *ex ante*, it will often be in the interest of those concerned to masquerade as virtuous, and so the question of whether to trust in the proclaimed virtue of others will be an important issue. Here, then, type-uncertainty trust is directly related to dispositions, and the idea of a screening mechanism which selects (perhaps imperfectly) for the virtuous is clearly one way of supporting trustworthiness. The link from this aspect of trustworthiness to integrity, as I have interpreted it, is, then, via the discussion of the higher order choice of dispositional type, recognising the potential feedback effects of institutional arrangements.

At the level of the direct effects of institutions, the strategy of economising on virtue attempts to structure institutions in accordance with two basic ideas – that private interests should be channelled to public service (the invisible hand mechanism) and that the relatively virtuous should be allocated to those spheres of activity where virtue is most valuable (the screening mechanism). At the level of feedback effects of institutions, that strategy of promoting integrity attempts to structure institutions so as to encourage the choice of virtuous motivations. The relationship between these two strategies is complex.

If there were no feedback effects of institutions, the strategy of economising on virtue would be clearly appropriate – since it both utilises whatever virtue is available and attempts to substitute for virtue where it is not available. Once the feedback effect is admitted, matters become considerably more complicated. I have suggested that there can be no general presumption that economising on virtue will always undermine integrity and virtue, but it is also clear that it will in at least some cases. In those cases the choice of institutional structure is both the more important and the more difficult. The suggestion here is simply that by connecting integrity to the idea of choice – specifically the choice of dispositions under particular institutional arrangements – we can see some reason to hope that a generally economic approach to the question of institutional design may be fruitful.

Acknowledgements

An earlier version of this chapter benefited from discussion at the Balliol Colloquium from which this volume originates, and I am happy to acknowledge the helpful comments made by participants. Continuing discussions with Geoff Brennan are also gratefully acknowledged. The research reported here was supported in part by ESRC Research Grant No. R000233782.

Notes

1 Betty Boothroyd, Speaker of the House of Commons, in response to a statement of apology to the House by Sir Jerry Wiggin MP, 22nd May 1995.
2 Williams (1973); for a recent discussion, see Hollis (1995) and Williams (1995).
3 The Nolan Committee identifies integrity as one of the seven principles that should govern public life and defines the content of the notion of integrity as – 'holders of public office should not place themselves under any financial or other obligation to outside individuals or organisations that might influence them in the performance of their official duties.' This might seem to be one aspect of the notion of virtue, as that term is used here, rather than integrity. On trust, see the discussion on pp. 276–8 below.
4 See, for example, Lewis (1989) drawing on Frankfurt (1971) and others.
5 There are others; see Brennan and Hamlin (1995).
6 Further details of this argument can be found in Brennan and Hamlin (1995).
7 Of course, as I have just noted, the reliance on virtue in *some* domains is a part of the strategy of economising on virtue in the second sense outlined above.
8 Dasgupta (1988) provides an overview which is reinforced by the discussion in Gambetta (1988).

References

Brennan, G. and Hamlin, A. (1995) 'Economizing on Virtue', *Constitutional Political Economy*, 6: 1.
Dasgupta, P. (1988) 'Trust as a Commodity', in D. Gambetta (ed.), *Trust: Making and Breaking Cooperative Relations*. Oxford: Blackwell.
Frankfurt, H. (1971) 'Freedom of the Will and the Concept of a Person', *Journal of Philosophy* 68: 5–20.
Gambetta, D. (1988) 'Can we Trust Trust?', in D. Gambetta (ed.), *Trust: Making and Breaking Cooperative Relations*. Oxford: Blackwell.
Hollis, M. (1995) 'The Shape of a Life', in J. Altham and R. Harrison (eds), *World, Mind and Ethics*. Cambridge: Cambridge University Press.
Krannick, I. (ed.) (1987) *The Federalist Papers*. Harmondsworth: Penguin.
Lewis, D. (1989) 'Dispositional Theories of Value', *Proceedings of the Aristotelian Society*, Supplementary Volume 63: 113–37.
Taylor, G. (1985) *Pride, Shame and Guilt: Emotions of Self-Assessment*. Oxford: Clarendon Press.
Williams, B.A.O. (1973) 'A Critique of Utilitarianism', in J.J.C. Smart and B.A.O. Williams, *Utilitarianism For and Against*. Cambridge: Cambridge University Press.
Williams, B.A.O. (1995) 'Replies', in J. Altham and R. Harrison (eds), *World, Mind and Ethics*. Cambridge: Cambridge University Press.

18 Integrity in business

A real or illusory decline?

Robert Brown

Introduction

Most people believe in their own integrity yet think it rare in others. To speak of someone as a man of 'integrity' is to set him somehow apart from others. What is the meaning of this apparent inconsistency? Do most people delude themselves with their belief in their own integrity, or is it in fact a quality that is widely found? Even if most people are, broadly speaking, truthful and honest, the term 'integrity' is usually understood to mean more than just this.

How does one decide whether someone possesses integrity or not, and how elastic is such an assessment likely to be? Is integrity an absolute quality or is it relative to situation and context? Is it not so much one quality as a composite of qualities, with shortcomings in one area capable of being offset by virtues in others? If so, within what limits can the mix of qualities vary in different circumstances? Surely integrity implies dependability and consistency? Can someone only be held to be a person of integrity if there is a general feeling amongst those who know them that they have the quality? Is it a quality which can only be possessed by those who pass the test of the opinion of others?

In thinking about these questions, a particular challenge for me lies in the fact that two men for whose integrity I and many others have the highest regard have, quite separately, stood trial at the Old Bailey – one on tax fraud charges in the mid-1970s, and the other on charges of misrepresentation in relation to a securities issue in the late 1980s. The first was acquitted and the second had his conviction overturned on appeal. How do men of integrity come to be standing in the dock at the Old Bailey?

Clearly integrity is a complicated matter, and in the comments which follow I do not try to offer any general theory. I begin by reflecting on the different roles of the company as such, and of those who work in it, in bringing integrity to their joint proceedings. I then take as my main theme the seemingly general feeling that standards of integrity in the business world are falling, but suggest that this is basically a reaction to the growing complexity and transparency in the world. I illustrate this by drawing out the way in which structural change in business is bound to create doubt about the integrity of companies and those who manage them, whether or not this is justified by the facts.

In developing this line of argument, I am led to wonder whether a man of integrity is not simply one who, most of the time, can be counted on to do the right thing as he sees it, even though it may involve cost to himself. This may not sound very noble, but it would seem to be quite a good working definition. I want to find it possible to believe in the integrity of others and therefore need to apply a test which at least some can meet. I want a definition that recognises that most issues are capable of being seen in shades of grey rather than as black or white; what constitutes the 'right thing' is, after all, often far from clear. Finally, we have to recognise that people can make mistakes. And, surely, lost integrity ought, up to a point at least, to be capable of being retrieved?

The role of the individual and that of the company

Integrity is a quality which can be possessed both by individuals and by companies. A man of integrity, working for a company whose integrity as such is in doubt, may seek to bring integrity to its operations wherever it is in his power to do so, and only resign if a point is reached at which his own personal integrity is compromised. A company with integrity might employ a man lacking in personal integrity, but oblige him to work within a framework which guaranteed the integrity of his activities on the company's behalf. In terms of my definition, the role of the company is to define the 'right thing' for its agents to do and to reinforce their willingness to accept the various costs that they may incur as a result.

Furthermore, a man of integrity may still need the support of the company's institutional framework, if he is to preserve both his own and the company's integrity at all times. The individual lacks the collective wisdom of a company whose procedures may well have been established over a lengthy period of time and honed in a variety of different environments. Procedure based on collective wisdom will generally ensure integrity more effectively than individual judgement in the heat of the moment. Individuals must operate within boundaries laid down by the company which reflect its collective assessment not just of their commercial judgement and effectiveness, but of their ethical and moral judgement too.

This is, of course, a challenge which companies may fail to meet. Companies of integrity may fall short in the design and implementation of procedures to guarantee the integrity of their operations, especially when they are struggling to keep abreast of rapid changes in their marketplace. Weak procedures and management controls can permit individuals, who simply find themselves out of their depth, to generate all sorts of problems. These are particularly visible in financial markets, where their incidence is growing.

In my time in the City, Lloyds Bank has lost heavily through unauthorised money dealings in its small Chiasso branch in Switzerland, Rowntree has lost heavily through unauthorised dealings in the forward cocoa market, Allied Lyons has lost heavily through unauthorised forward currency dealings, Barings has been brought down by unauthorised dealing in Japanese stock-market index futures and Hammersmith and Fulham Council has lost heavily through unauthorised money market derivative dealings. These are only a few well-known examples; there have been plenty of others.

The increasing frequency of events of this nature may seem to imply an erosion of integrity. In fact the problem is not usually one of dishonest intent, but simply of human failing in a moment of crisis, which then compounds itself in an environment of weak management controls. Like a losing gambler, the trader doubles up in the hope of recovering a loss rather than admit to himself that his judgement has been proved wrong. The management fails to spot what is happening quickly enough and in no time the position is spiralling out of control. No theft has taken place. No-one in the company profits from it. No customer has suffered. No-one wanted it to happen.

To the outsider this looks like a breakdown of integrity, but in fact it is simply an operational risk of the business. It happens with increasing frequency, because there are today more markets available for trading than ever before, because these markets are more volatile, because more businesses are engaged in proprietary trading with their own capital and because it is a continual struggle to refine management controls at the same pace as the business is changing. The more markets and the more players there are, the more frequently this type of loss will arise. None of this demonstrates that there has necessarily been a decline in standards of integrity. 'There but for the grace of God go I', says everyone else in the business. The episode may suggest that the business had been too risky, but that is a matter of commercial judgement rather than one of integrity.

Organisations may, of course, themselves be flawed and a flawed organisation can let an employee down just as badly. This is one way in which men of integrity can come to find themselves standing in the dock at the Old Bailey.

A psychologist may put someone in a room with 20 others and ask them a simple question about something which they have all just observed. If the other 20 people have all been briefed to give the same, plainly wrong answer, the odd man out will eventually start to waver. After the exercise has been repeated often enough, he may well start to give the same answer as everybody else, even though it is plainly wrong.

Companies sometimes behave a little like this. After a while, that which at first seems odd comes to seem normal, and eventually that which is in fact wrong may seem to be right, simply because it has passed the test of time. A collective suspension of disbelief occurs. The risk of this happening is greatest where one man dominates an organisation, operating without the normal framework of checks and balances. He will surround himself with pliant people, paid well over the odds, and informed of matters only on a 'need-to-know' basis, whose integrity he progressively compromises until they are no longer capable of standing up for the integrity of the organisation. The organisation ends up by losing its independent moral character, which has become indivisible from that of its dominating figure. Companies at risk in this way can often be identified, but it may take years for the flaws to emerge. In the meantime the sheer drive of the dominant individual may well create an illusion of considerable success, while the laws of libel and slander provide ample shelter.

This may sound like the Robert Maxwell story in a nutshell, but it has happened quite often before on one scale or another. It is a common feature of many companies which have been the subject of DTI inspectors' reports over the years. It says nothing about whether standards of integrity in business today are in decline. Indeed standards of corporate governance are probably higher today than ever before as accountability has grown. However, it does show how a company may not necessarily possess integrity just because the majority of its employees are people of integrity. Those at the top have considerable power to corrupt a company without those beneath them realising quite what is happening.

The key forces at work in the business world

There are certain over-riding forces which affect all businesses and their employees around the world today. The first of these forces is that of globalisation. Falling trade barriers and improved communications have combined with commercial pressures to bring about a remarkable growth in multinational business. The Americans led the way in the postwar years, but UK, Continental European and Japanese companies have followed and we are now starting to see the first multi-national companies with headquarters in the developing economies of South East Asia.

The second force at work is technology. Everyone recognises the impact of technology, in particular of information technology, but many are inclined to see it as only one amongst a number of other equally important factors to be managed in any enterprise. This is a complete misjudgement. Many companies are now defined by their technology. Technology long ago ceased to be simply a means of automating existing business processes. Rather, it has moved centre stage in shaping the way businesses work and in opening up opportunities for competitive advantage.

The electronic point of sale system in a shop is, in one sense, simply a way of automating the process of paying for goods. However, it also makes new information available to management about the value and product mix of the average spend, and becomes a tool for managing the stock to best advantage. Once in place, it is a small step to start offering card payment facilities, and thus to gain access to the names and addresses of the customers. Individual buying patterns can then be analysed and offers to customers structured to attract their business. In no time the company has been re-defined by its technology.

The third factor at work is the changing regulatory environment. On the one hand, deregulation at the top has been the main trend in recent years, as belief in central economic planning has receded and the emphasis has shifted to fostering competition on level playing fields; lower down the scale, on the other hand, there has been a steady increase in the regulation of day to day business operations in such areas as health and safety at work, employment protection, employee rights, and service and product specifications. In military parlance, a company is freer today to pursue the strategy of its choice, while its tactics are subject to much more regulation. What effect do these forces have on the perceived integrity of a business and those who manage it?

Globalisation

Globalisation poses a stark choice for many companies. They must either become big enough to compete in world markets or they must be content to remain in a niche. By and large, the middle ground is an uncomfortable and transitory place to be.

The emergence of giant international companies, some with sales larger than the GDP of many countries, raises a great many issues which we need not dwell on here. However, one consequence is the export of jobs from high wage and high social cost economies to economies where such costs are lower. We used to have a television manufacturing industry in the UK. When televisions ceased to be a high technology product and became commodities, our markets were captured by imports from Japan – jobs were lost in the UK and gained in Japan. Subsequently, Japan lost many of those jobs to places like Korea and Hong Kong, where costs were lower still. Eventually some of the lost jobs have re-appeared in the UK as Japanese multi-nationals have chosen Britain as the site for their European television manufacturing plants. The relatively low labour and social security costs in Britain compared to the rest of Europe have meant that it has become cost effective to manufacture for the European market there rather than export to Europe from the Far East.

At every stage of this cycle doubts will have been cast on the integrity of the companies concerned and their managements. There will have been much complaint about cutting and running, short-termism, irresponsible attitudes to local communities and so on. However, at all points along the way televisions have become cheaper, better products available to more people; and this, of course, has contributed to the general quality of life.

The private sector is often the agent of such sweeping changes, changes which may work towards the common good, but which inevitably damage individual lives on the way. The observer may well doubt the integrity of the process. The individual manager handling such a change may do so in a way which preserves his own integrity in the eyes of those immediately around him; but they then often respond by transferring their doubts about the integrity of the process to that of the corporate entity itself. Does any of this mean that there is less integrity in the private sector? Is it not simply a bigger, more rapid and more visible process of change than those we have known in the past?

For example, I talked recently to a young manager who had been sent by a middle-ranking food company to turn round a subsidiary that was producing a specialist food ingredient for which there was only a relatively small and shrinking market, but one still of a size where, at the end of the process of returning the company to profit, it employed over 3,000 people. It had been a painful process, because the company was an important local employer; but the reduction in the work-force had been handled sensitively, a wages freeze accepted stoically and a good deal of pride taken in the return to corporate health. The managing director had called for goodwill, promising fewer but safer jobs and a profit-related element to pay once the company was back in the black. This was the deal; they were all in it together and they had succeeded.

At that point, a major competitor, which was the UK arm of a multi-national, appeared on the scene and approached the parent company with an offer for the subsidiary in question, which was felt to be too good to refuse. However, the purpose of the offer was to close the manufacturing plant, to reduce the capacity in the market place and to transfer production to the bidding company's own plant elsewhere.

This was a perfectly proper commercial response to a shrinking market – if this sort of thing was not permitted, there would still be companies making gas lights for the streets, which no one would buy. However, this young managing director had to explain to his work-force that he had not been able to deliver his side of the bargain which he had struck. What does this imply about his own integrity, about the integrity of the original owners of the plant and that of those who acquired it solely in order to close it down? Nothing. Everything that had been done was legitimate and, in the final analysis, necessary. The process had an inexorable logic to it – even a certain form of integrity. We may well ask, however, what was the effect on the perceived integrity of all concerned.

There is a second way in which globalisation may at first sight seem to work against (perceived) integrity, namely, the way in which – up to a point – it undermines the power of government.

Most citizens would prefer to be able to believe their governments to be fair and even-handed in their dealings. They want to believe that they will act as the custodians (as they present themselves to be) of the common national good. Beyond a certain point this is not, of course, realistic and never has been; but it matters that the comfort be there. However, the illusion only works in proportion to the government's perceived power to control events in the land.

Globalisation and the associated emergence of multi-national companies undermines the power of individual governments and exposes the illusion. The bigger the company and the smaller the country (and the bigger the difference in cultures between the company and the country concerned) the more the illusion is shattered. The unease some may feel about the role of American or Japanese multi-nationals in the UK is not at all the same as that which may be felt, for example, in economically weak but resource-rich countries playing host to multi-national mining or oil companies. Not only will the commercial decisions of these companies, such as their capital spending plans, have a very major effect indeed on the national economy and living standards; their corporate thought processes may, moreover, be quite alien to those of the local culture.

Multi-national companies must, of course, obey the law, but beyond that their objective is profit. They may choose to plough money back into the local community, but they are not entitled to do so out of straightforward benevolence. The money belongs to the shareholders – not to the company's board and certainly not to the local management. Such spending is part of the cost of operating in a developing economy – part of the price of the entry ticket. It maintains goodwill and so justifies itself. However, no-one doubts that the underlying objective of the company's operations is profit, so whenever it makes difficult decisions about priorities with important local implications there are bound to be doubts about the integrity of the process. The decisions are being made by alien entities with limited local accountability and are being driven by the profit motive.

Even the UK has experienced something a little like this in recent times. Sterling's withdrawal from the European Exchange Rate Mechanism was a defeat for government policy in an area fundamental to its whole thinking. Relative economic performance may have left the pound over-valued and vulnerable, but the UK and its European partners were prepared to expend reserves defending Sterling in order to buy time for economic policy convergence to provide fundamental support for the exchange rate. In practice they could not resist the global capital flows which were undermining the pound. Speculative pressures built up until the authorities gave up. In a global market-place only the markets themselves are powerful enough to determine exchange rates.

The whole episode provided ample scope for doubting integrity all round. Why did our European partners not do more to help? Were the Prime Minister, Chancellor and a whole host of other ministers being dishonest when they said they would not contemplate leaving the European Exchange Rate Mechanism? Were the speculators – in particular the hedge funds – unprincipled villains? Are the financial centres of the world full of unscrupulous wheeler-dealers? It was altogether a bad day for perceived integrity!

However, in practice everyone was simply the agent of an unstoppable process brought about by globalisation. Nothing illegal or dishonest occurred. Indeed the process had an integrity of its own. The pound was over-valued and needed to fall, the British Government and their European partners were bound to strike their poses, currency speculators were bound to sell Sterling, because it is their job to seek out opportunities for profit. The pound was bound to fall because currency speculators collectively have deeper pockets than do central banks. Looked at the other way round, where is the integrity in ending exchange controls, encouraging free markets and then seeking to defend a given exchange rate with limited resources?

Technology

As with globalisation, technology is both a destroyer and a creator of jobs. Most people equate technology with automation which means the replacement of people by machines. This is, of course, to neglect the jobs created in the technology sector itself – the making, marketing and distribution of computers, the programming of software, the networking of computers, the development of new businesses only made possible by computers and so on. However, to those on the wrong side of the equation, the substitution of machines for people will often seem to lack integrity.

The fundamental importance of technology in business has other side-effects too. I was a stockbroker for many years, and that is a business which has been completely transformed by advances in technology. Where once stockmarket dealings were conducted face-to-face on the floor of the Stock Exchange, the trade is now conducted on the telephone with the different market-makers and brokers all round the City being linked to each other electronically. The floor of the Stock Exchange has been replaced by a computer network. The business of trading in securities is now determined by the available technology.

On the whole these changes are to be welcomed and the Stock Exchange is now a more liquid and transparent market with lower execution costs than in the past. In that sense the quality of the market has improved. However, one drawback is that it is easier for a rogue trader to operate in the new environment. A man with a grudge against his employer is much better placed to do him damage by conducting malicious trades or by corrupting the computer network.

This is why people made redundant in securities trading firms are often bundled off the premises within minutes with their possessions in a bin-liner and a security man at their elbow. When a great many people are to be made redundant at the same time, they may well learn of the news only when their names are read out over the firm's loudspeaker system. If the redundancy programme is not carried out with great speed, security will be at risk.

This type of execution of a redundancy programme – which would cause outrage almost anywhere else – is an unfortunate necessity from time-to-time in the City and certainly does not look good! It does not look like the behaviour of managers and companies of integrity; it is nonetheless necessary.

The company's shareholders, its remaining employees and its customers and counter-parties all need protection and there is an integrity in the weighing of these interests, when it might be easier on occasion to neglect them. However, in practice, the effect on perceived integrity is no doubt unfortunate.

Regulation and de-regulation

I turn finally to the question of regulation; what does it say about integrity that business should need any kind of regulation at all? What is the meaning of de-regulation at the strategic, but increased regulation at the tactical level?

By and large, de-regulation at the strategic level reflects the conviction that the more competition, the better. With de-regulation it is easier for companies to enter each other's markets. Why, then, cannot competition be counted upon to look after health and safety issues, product safety issues and so on. Are companies and their managements so lacking in integrity that they have to be made to take an interest in the health and safety of their work-forces or the damage that their products may cause?

One consequence of deregulation is the way in which certain professions and quasi-professions have been turned into businesses. This poses some particularly interesting questions about integrity; and this is my last example.

In Pharmaceutical Society of Great Britain v Dixon (1968), in a Lords Judgement, Lord Upjohn stated:

> A profession is a vocation of the highest standing; it calls on the members to serve the public by offering to them highly technical and always confidential advice and services which require a different standard of conduct from the tradesman . . . those seeking the advice of a professional man are entitled to expect of him the highest standards of ethical conduct. This means that the professional man must submit to some restraints of trades such, to take an elementary example, as a prohibition against advertising and a refusal by under-cutting or otherwise to snatch work from another practitioner. Such restraints are necessary to establish, sustain and promote the profession and particularly its ethical standards. The restraints on professional men are justifiable in law for they are necessary not only in the interests of the profession but also in the interests of the public, who trust to the particularly high standing and integrity of a profession to serve it well.

Let us take the optician as an example. Before de-regulation, the optician was a white-coated specialist with whom one made an appointment through a receptionist some time in advance, whose time and attention one felt privileged to have and who then prescribed lenses coming in a choice of no more than the handful of frames available through the National Health Service or of a rather wider range of frames at a higher price on a private basis. Today, following de-regulation, a wide range of standard prescription spectacles are available off-the-shelf in a wide range of retail outlets and at extremely modest prices. One does not need professional guidance – one simply chooses the frame and looks at the sight test on the stand to see if the particular strength of the spectacles suits one's needs.

The fact is that the large majority of people who need spectacles, have a simple problem with the focusing of their eyesight, which various grades of standard prescription can rectify. What does this say about the integrity of opticians? Were they simply hiding behind a cosy cartel and practising a lucrative line in bogus science? Of course not. The opticians' defence is that the layman does not know the extent of his condition – the spectacles bought over the counter in the high street may seem to improve his eyesight, while leaving another, related condition to deteriorate. Regular, professional eye-tests will give early warning signs of other problems which may be developing and, of course, provide an insight into general health too. What does this say about the integrity of the high street retailer? Is he disregarding the complexity of optical health in order to steal the profession's bread and butter by undercutting it on price, or is he simply enabling the customer to shop around, buying the optical health check in one place and the simple spectacle requirement in another?

Once again, there are no black and white issues here; the 'right thing' is far from being clear. However, there is plenty of scope to doubt the integrity of all concerned.

Conclusion

I have here offered a small number of examples intended to illustrate the fact that the more our lives are complicated by globalisation, technology and changes in the regulatory environment, the more scope there is to doubt both the integrity of individuals and that of the companies within which they operate. Furthermore, given the growth in communications and a greater public demand that the workings of institutions be opened up to closer scrutiny, these trends are developing in an environment of much greater transparency than used to be the case.

I have sought to argue that integrity is not necessarily in decline, but rather that it calls for re-assessment in the light of the complexities and ambiguities of the real world. I doubt whether it is possible to establish a set of universal, constant benchmarks which can be used to determine whether someone possesses integrity except in a superficial way. Therefore, I return to my original thought, namely, that a man of integrity is simply 'a man who most of the time can be counted on to do the right thing as he sees it, even though it may involve cost to himself'. The role of the company or institution that he serves is to help him to do this when acting as its agent, whilst at the same time providing for the protection of its own integrity should he fail. I suggest that most of us would be very happy with such an epitaph!

19 Morality and the market

Integrity, responsibility and loyalty

Anthony Clunies Ross

The problem of morality and the market

My purpose here is to discuss the apparent conflict between the norms of personal behaviour that are commonly accepted in our culture as admirable or proper, and the ideology of the competitive market.

It has become common, during and since the Thatcher ascendancy, for critics of that régime to argue that it was not only amoral but positively immoral. Briefly, the market ideology which government policy of that period supported is thought to be one encouraging the unqualified pursuit of individual material self-interest. Moral behaviour, such critics assert, requires consideration for others and a readiness to subordinate one's own interest to the common good.

A further feature of this line of attack is that 'business' is presented as necessarily immoral. Business, we are told, involves competition, lack of scruples and ruthlessness rather than cooperation and mutual concern; there is often talk of profit as of something intrinsically wicked, obtained through exploitation. And yet all our major political parties believe, with whatever reservations, in the market; and a large part of the population could be said to be engaged in profit-oriented business in one form or another. Even those of us who work in the public sector, or are no more than stubbornly uncooperative employees in private enterprise, benefit materially in a number of ways from the existence of competitive business. We may not all perhaps hold equities but, if not, we are still very likely to hold deposits and insurance policies with institutions that do. Quite apart from that, our whole standard of life depends to a large extent on the present existence and past achievements of competitive industry and commerce. If business and competition and the market are immoral, then most of us are living on immoral earnings.

There is, thus, an awkward feeling that we are claimed by two contrary codes: that what we *need to do* if we would stay in business, what some of us *must do* if the economy is to keep turning, is inconsistent with what (in some sense) we think we *ought to do*. This inconsistency is potentially debilitating: bad for business or bad for morals or both. My impression is that a sense of conflict between business values and correct personal behaviour is not present, or is much more muted, in Japan; and that this is a source of strength. At the other extreme, Russia today suffers because the lines between business enterprise and criminality are not clear enough in people's minds. It would seem desirable, if we can conscientiously do so, to reach an understanding of personal and business values in which the two are not at odds.

Responses

The super liberal competitive ethic as response

The response to this criticism by supporters of the Thatcher régime involved resort to an ethic of a super-competitive-liberal kind, and a defence of the policy stance of the period as following from that ethic. Every economic agent *should* – it is argued – act 'independently', in the sense of giving no favour to any other agent. Policy should actually support, rather than discourage, such behaviour. Workers should have no solidarity with other workers in the same establishment; producers in the same industry should not coordinate policy with each other; employers should treat their employees like cattle, paying them as little as feasible except insofar as more pay would justify its cost in greater productivity; firms should be unbound by personal considerations or past habits in choosing their suppliers; they should be prepared to compete with rival firms to the death. It is right and socially desirable, according to this ethic, that they should act with as much freedom as the law allows to maximise their own utility, having no consideration within their utility function for the good or preferences of the other agents with whom they deal.

If checks to such behaviour have to be introduced for social reasons, that task is, in this view, the responsibility of government. People may properly take political action to have those checks legally imposed, but they have no obligation to act as if the checks already existed when they do not. Indeed, it is sometimes alleged or implied that, if people act against their individual material interests, the system as a result works worse for all. This is a highly individualistic code, implying that a person need recognise no responsibilities or obligations to those she or he encounters in commercial life except as the law provides.

Maybe few economic agents, if any, behave all the time exactly as if they held this view of how we ought to live. But the awareness that this ethic is often voiced, or at least implicitly held, gives a pretext for people to act in narrowly self-seeking ways of which otherwise they might be ashamed. To some extent too, law and policy inhibit combinations. Monopoly and restrictive-practices legislation tends to discourage firms from cooperating with others in the same industry or from showing any preference to particular customers or suppliers. Labour-market policy under the Thatcher government was one of generally discouraging associations among employees. The British

National Health Service reforms have been designed to break the ties of responsibility of Health Boards for their hospitals. Performance-related pay could be said to promote rivalry among workmates, even in nursing teams. Widespread sacking of workers has been held to be a symptom of good management: that virtuous process called 'slimming-down' or 'shaking-out' or 'downsizing'. Contested take-overs, leading to the dropping of management teams and often vast changes in the firm taken over, are seen as *prima facie* good because they can be expected to increase commercial efficiency; and the shareholders, who often have no personal connection at all with those who work in or run the company, are the only parties whose wishes should be consulted in the matter. Individuals, institutions, will better serve the common weal by acting altogether without sentimental attachments.

The Japanese ethic as response

By contrast, the Japanese ethic has a very different conception of business. This ethic prescribes that there should be a culture of personal commitment to one another among those who work together and have habitual dealings with each other. A number of management writers (see for example Peters and Waterman 1982) have argued over the last 15 years that this ethic has been adopted by the most successful Anglo-Saxon companies.

This ethic can be partly understood by looking at the large Japanese manufacturing firm. In such a firm, workers are expected to make a lifetime commitment to the firm and the firm to the workers. Those who work in the firm constitute the main stakeholders; the shareholders are outsiders who have provided capital; any attempts at contested take-overs are thus disreputable. Dore (1987) describes this as the 'community model' of a firm, in contrast to the Anglo-Saxon 'company-law model'.[1]

There are also in Japan well-known and accepted vertical commitments between firms – banks with those they finance and large firms with their smaller suppliers. Partners in joint ventures, and indeed any parties who have entered into commercial agreements, are expected to show loyalty and consideration to each other regardless of precise contractual obligations. Indeed, if we read the literature on commercial negotiations with Japanese firms, we are told that understandings based on personal trust are preferred to legally binding commitments.

These arrangements have their pros and cons; but clearly much of Japanese practice, conforming more or less to the stereotype, can be very successful in a sheer commercial sense. My impression is also that, although respected firms in the same industry compete vigorously against each other, they do not as a rule try to put each other out of business; so that such recently alleged or suspected attempts in Britain as that by a well-known press proprietor to bankrupt rival newspapers by pricing at a loss, or by a large international airline to drive out a smaller one by pursuing the other firm's customers individually and offering them special deals, would not have happened, or would at least have been generally condemned by the respectable mainstream.

It thus appears possible to have a very successful commercial system in which people consciously and explicitly work on a completely different ethic from the highly individualistic super-competitive-liberal one. And indeed it is quite credible that, even in the strict commercial sense, an enterprise in which all the workers feel a strong commitment to each other and identify with the purposes of the institution tends to be much more effective than one in which they see each other as rivals, or at best impersonally, so that each has to be given material carrots and sticks to induce her or him to do what is necessary.

Steps towards a resolution

It seems that there may be elements of truth in both of these responses. Competition between economic units, and commitment within them are both important. An attempt at an integration of these requirements first suggests that it may be critically important to analyse what the competing units are and how far the competition between them is carried. Second, it suggests a need to carefully discuss which elements contrary to the individualistic ethic are required in order to obtain forms of cooperation and commitment which promote economic efficiency – and I will identify responsibility, loyalty and creativity. Third, as I shall argue in the next section, it suggests that these elements contribute to human welfare in ways not covered by the utilitarian concept of economic efficiency.

Getting the boundaries, and extent of competition right

Firms quite properly compete against one another, but the above brief discussion suggests that it is likely to make both for the commercial efficiency of the firms concerned and also for social efficiency in the simplest utilitarian sense, if the individuals within them cooperate and are committed to each other. However, this does not tell us at exactly what level of organisation cooperation should end and competition begin. We could move towards what Norman Macrae has called the 'intrapreneurial' firm: one that contracts out as much as possible to competing tenderers, so that the realm of cooperation tends to be limited and commitment reigns mainly in small units (Macrae 1982). Alternatively, the large institution may remain organisationally as one in terms of allegiance, with a potential for mutual commitment running from top to bottom, but competing with other organisations.

Moreover, 'competition', in the sense in which the term is used in economists' discourse, covers a range of phenomena rather different from those included in the everyday usage of the word. Under competition in the economists' sense, the parties need not be consciously playing against each other. It is precisely those industries that are said to approach 'perfect competition' –

farming, for example – where the agents have no sense of a need to do down their counterparts. Neighbouring farmers see themselves as playing against the elements, against the government perhaps, but not against each other. A farmer normally gains nothing of which he is aware by his neighbour's ruin. It is only in 'imperfect competition', where the agents are large in relation to the market or to their differentiated niches within it, that competition becomes anything like warfare, or even like a football match or a game-show. Competition in the desirable sense does not necessarily entail rivalry.

Where conscious rivalry exists, it is important what the conventional limits to competition among the relevant entities are. If competing firms succeed in taking each other over or putting each other out of business, that is the end of competition. And there is after all a by-no-means-alien, indeed rather British, idea of sportsmanship that appears to be capable of application: that you competed vigorously but within strict rules, 'hated the foe with a playing at hate', as one famous school song puts it. You don't aim to kill the members of the opposing team, or the referee. Practices that would spoil the game are banned, whether by the letter of the law or by unwritten convention.

To vary the sporting analogy, the social function of commercial competition is not to let a small number of tycoons emerge like Olympic champions by vanquishing all opposition, but to keep lively incentives for the satisfaction of human needs, and that may require structuring the rules in such a way as to ensure that a significant number of players continue to be in the game.

Furthermore, for some types of entity, only a very limited degree of competition among individual autonomous units is efficient. The idea that schools and universities and hospitals should be publicly scrutinised, whether by their customers or by a quango, and hence have at least a symbolic incentive to outdo one another in performance and service, is probably healthy.[2] Universities with a good reputation attract good students and staff; and competing on that ground does no harm at all. But at the same time we need to realise that there are certain matters on which we need to cooperate freely without worrying about the effect on the relative scores. Between hospitals too it may be all very well to have competition over which has the most favourable rating among patients, but Chapter 4 in this volume draws attention to the wasteful and damaging results when they treat each other like rival software agencies, hoarding commercial secrets, or like rival used-car merchants, concealing the deficiencies of what they are purveying.

Competition among parallel service organisations such as these is fine as long as it is not carried to the point at which it blocks the inter-organisational cooperation that health and education, for example, often require. Indeed many productive enterprises, in the private, as well as in the public, sector, practise informal cooperation precisely where the super-competitive-liberal model supposes that they should be keeping each other at arm's length. It is common enough, after all, for neighbouring farmers to cooperate. Even among manufacturers and traders, and by no means only in East Asia, the phenomenon of symbiosis as a substitute for vertical integration has come to be recognised by industrial economists: firms that have dealings with one another develop understandings under which they will consult each other's interests (for a résumé see Schanze 1993). The conventional economists' view of competition treats this as a restrictive practice, but it could be said to achieve informally what vertical integration achieves by formal and legal means. Like vertical integration, it does not necessarily involve a conspiracy against the public.

Responsibility and loyalty

I will now discuss the extent to which elements contrary to the super-competitive individualist ethic are necessary in order for economic efficiency to be achieved. It is widely recognised that trust, and consequently trust-worthiness, are necessary for efficiency. Without trust the costs of trading become unduly high. This is explored by Donald Hay in Chapter 16 of this volume. Even extreme supporters of individualistic competition may have no objection to advocating behaviour that makes for trustworthiness in this sense.

There is a further element, which we can call responsibility, that is also necessary. The term 'responsibility' is a tricky one, with several closely related, but not identical, meanings. The meaning of the term employed here is what might be called a sense of responsibility or an expressed responsibility. If I act as if another person's welfare is an element in my own utility, then I may be said to act with responsibility toward that person.

Responsibilities may be expressed to a particular person, or to a class of people, or perhaps even to humankind as a whole. The wider the class, inevitably the more limited the responsibility expressed can be. Where substantial responsibilities are expressed consistently to a particular person or group or class of people, that behaviour can be characterised as loyalty.

Loyalty is commonly regarded as a virtue. It is a somewhat different species of virtue from honesty, truthfulness, impartiality and fair-mindedness, which between them might be held (on one understanding of the term) to constitute moral integrity. This latter virtue (or these virtues) could be regarded as having a universal character. Loyalty, by contrast, is by its nature particular.

When we talk of the value of trustworthiness in commercial life, we are normally considering those universal virtues. A trustworthy customer or supplier is one who will pay debts, keep promises, describe products truthfully and interpret contracts fairly. No specially favourable disposition to the other party is implied.

I submit that, beyond trustworthiness in this sense, considerable mutual responsibility, indeed a measure of loyalty, is required if commercial and industrial life is to work at its best.

An influential strand of Atlantic management thought and description of the past 15 years (such as Peters and Waterman 1982; Stewart 1990;

Semler 1993; Waterman 1994) seems indeed to be saying that certain types of mutual responsibility and loyalty may be almost necessary conditions of the consistent commercial success of enterprises. These are responsibilities to all members of their workforces, to their customers (where customers are sufficiently close and limited in number for such responsibility to be relevant), and even perhaps a commitment to certain national or human objectives.

'Today's top enterprise does the best for its shareholders by treating them as only one of three constituent groups essential to their success. The other two are quite clearly their people and their customers' (Waterman 1994: 25). Waterman assembles a sheaf of case-studies as evidence for this proposition, including some from among the biggest and oldest US companies.

'The successful companies will be the ones that put quality of life first', writes Ricardo Semler in winding up the extraordinary tale of his own family firm in Sao Paolo. 'Do this and the rest – quality of product, productivity of workers, profits for all – will follow' (1993: 232). The story, incidentally, includes a defiance of official corruption that requires an extremely long-term perspective if it is to be regarded as self-interested.

'The transformational leader', says Valerie Stewart, 'is clear about his or her values. . . . Somewhere in that value-system, you'll find a deep and abiding respect for other people, and a need to create a better world.' (Stewart 1990: 125)

These writers, to translate them soberly, are not saying that mutual responsibility among fellow-workers, and responsibilility for customers, and even the wider social responsibility that is sometimes invoked, are sufficient for commercial success, rather that they provide a fertile field for some of its ingredients. This is morally and prudentially the negation of the conventional wisdom expressed as 'business is business', 'at the end of the day nothing matters but the bottom line', 'my sole duty is to the shareholders': that was discussed at the beginning of this chapter. Japanese examples have understandably been used to support the idea that mutual responsibility among those working for a firm, and between a firm and its suppliers or its customers, are potentially positive factors for commercial success and indeed for the economic efficiency of an industrial sector. And it is the more admirable features of Japanese life, as they seem to outsiders, that would appear to be the crucial inputs: not the conformity, secrecy, racism and political corruption, but consideration, courtesy, cooperativeness, trust and loyalty.

If this is so, why is it so? Why should commercial success and economic efficiency depend, to any degree, on responsibility within each firm or productive organisation, and why on responsibility between them? I shall attempt some explanations to fit the descriptive material. The former question is the easier.

The importance to economic efficiency of high levels of mutual responsibility within individual firms can be explained with reference to the ideas of *X-efficiency* and *adaptability*.

First, the physical efficiency with which a group of people work depends in large part on their enthusiasm, care and general assiduity. This is likely to be enhanced if they see themselves as a team working in their common interest. They may need to satisfy 'outside' (non-employee) shareholders, but, if so, that may be seen simply as one of the constraints under which they operate rather than a primary and overriding objective. A considerable element of workershareholding or a transparent system of bonuses or profit-sharing will of course make it easier for this view of the enterprise to prevail; these in themselves require, perhaps, no more than trust to make them work. But for a selfless commitment to the purposes of the corporate being, a culture of mutual concern, coupled with demanding aspirations, will also be necessary. Dore (1987) explained the relative success of Japanese manufacturing (in spite of what might seem to Anglo-Saxons as wasteful use of labour) by supposing that the gains in X-efficiency (the addendum due to care, diligence and enthusiasm) outweighed any negative effects. Workers were not only ready to observe rigorous standards but were also forthcoming with ideas for improvement. Reports on the Nissan subsidiary in Sunderland, and other Japanese-owned plants in Britain, tell a similar story.

But maybe X-efficiency gains are not the whole story. There is, second, *adaptability*: the readiness of people, including of course those at the top of the organisation, to take cuts in pay on occasion so that the enterprise may survive, to change the way they work, to re-train, to take on each other's jobs where that is necessary. Confident that they will not be simply exploited, that their interests will not be ignored, that the burdens will be shared, seeing themselves as part of a team with a common purpose, employees are ready to act more like small, family-style entrepreneurs in being prepared to do whatever is required to keep the vessel afloat. So the advantages of large and small firms are combined.

Such ready adaptability of rewards, tasks, organisation and skills within firms may be, more and more, a precondition of acceptable levels of employment and prosperity in high-wage, old-industrial countries as they face the shocks of increasing global competition. The business-is-business ideology commonly goes with the view that there is a fight to the death with our overseas competitors: it is us or them. The principle of comparative advantage, by contrast, together with comforting identities such as that world exports equal world imports, reassure us that the explosive rise of industry in hitherto poor countries is to be seen as an opportunity rather than a threat. Yet considerable agility, both in what is offered and in its price, is needed if the opportunities are to be taken and our resources are to remain fully employed. The ideal may be to combine the resources of knowledge and imagination available to a Toyota or an ICI with the nimbleness of a Punjabi all-hours corner shop.

The adaptability of firms affects not just their own particular levels of productivity and profitability but also the efficiency of the whole system, insofar as it provides a mechanism for keeping people fully and productively occupied.

Creativity

A sense of mutual responsibility within firms, bolstered by mutual trust, is not a sufficient condition or panacea. Organisation, the character of leadership, and other elements of management practice are also critical. If there is another factor that stands out in many case-studies of innovative and successful management, it is the way in which the creative powers of individuals are elicited and harnessed to the purposes of the organisation. Consultation of ordinary workers, pressing them for ideas on improvement, organising so that groups of a human size are largely autonomous, dispersing authority, encouraging experiment, relying as far as possible on a common purpose rather than orders and rules: these in various forms and combinations are the stock-in-trade of a number of striking studies, both Japanese and Atlantic.

There is no named virtue that relates to the encouragement of creativity, as integrity (in at least one of its senses) relates to trust, and loyalty to responsibility. But allowing and nurturing the creative activity of others is one of the greatest boons that can be granted to them.

Restraints on competition (again)

Between firms and organisations too, mutual responsibility, and not merely trust, may have a positive bearing on economic efficiency. Generous customer-care, increasingly recognised as commercially prudent in the activities in which it is relevant, is also likely to be efficient in a social sense. The supplier is likely to be able to deal with hitches at a lower cost than the customer. One of the firms studied by Peters and Waterman (1982) instructed its salesmen to act as if they were on their customers' payrolls. Moreover, a firm that is a large customer, may, by loyalty to its smaller suppliers, provide them with a reliable market that reduces the risks of their investments, while at the same time giving itself leverage for enhancement of their performance. Risk discourages productive innovation; and the death of firms is *prima facie* a more wasteful way than their improvement in performance for increasing the productive efficiency of the system.

It was also suggested above that a certain restraint towards competitors may be functional for the economy, at least to the extent that firms should not take action, the sole purpose of which is to reduce the number of competitors. Where the 'competitors' are hospitals, schools or universities, a greater departure from the canons of the super-competitive model is needed. There are considerable social economies arising from the existence of what might be called commonwealths of healing, learning and scholarship, where information is fully shared, and the social objectives are explicitly accepted by the players as having to override their own competitive advantage.

This is not to question the importance of competition in due measure and in its proper place and in a framework that internalises social externalities. The necessity of surviving in a competitive market and of satisfying the outside shareholders is a vital discipline in many activities, directing attention to the delivery of what is needed by the public. Even among hospitals, schools and universities, competition in esteem is salutary, and the esteem needs to be in large part that of the customers.

Mutual trust, mutual responsibility and creativity: public goods of a special order

Discussion of economic (social) efficiency has been conducted here so far on the usual assumptions made by economists: that what is to be maximised is 'welfare' ('material welfare') and that the criterion of a person's welfare is her revealed preferences. Yet most of us probably do not believe that people's welfare is in fact entirely defined by what they spontaneously choose. If that were the case, we should not seek to prevent people from becoming drug addicts unless their addiction would impose burdens on others. We should not introduce children to literature, even to literacy, unless it was what they spontaneously chose or their doing so was entirely justified by benefits external to themselves. All directive education (except in so far as it is designed to make the pupils more useful to others) supposes that there are certain abilities, items of knowledge, experiences, for which the pupils would be themselves the better but which they might not acquire spontaneously. Implicitly, I believe, those parents and educators whom we should regard as wise and benevolent aim to give their charges the experience of mutual trust, mutual responsibility, and creative activity, in the hope, even the confidence, that, once enjoyed, these experiences will be valued.

Mutual trust, mutual responsibility and creativity, are in fact valued by those who have enjoyed them; but we do not naturally seek them by unerring impulse, as we do with food, water or shelter. We often need to be led into experiencing them, or indeed to experience them by accident, before we realise that they minister to our needs.

Economists use the term 'public goods' for benefits such as law-and-order or urban street-lighting. The characteristic signified by this term is that the provision of these goods for one person entails their provision for others as well, and that one person's use or enjoyment of them does not diminish that of anyone else.

Mutual trust, mutual responsibility and creativity, may be described as public goods in this sense. The element of mutuality in shared trust or shared responsibility means that enjoyment by one party entails also enjoyment by another. But, beyond that, their mutual trust and responsibility provide the seedbed for the productivity whereby third parties can be better served. Creativity on the part of one person may clearly also entail free benefits for others. What I am suggesting, then, is that all three, if correctly channelled, can be important contributors to general economic efficiency, that is, to potential material welfare on the conventional utilitarian understanding of the term.

But we can say more than that. Whereas street-lighting and policing have resource-costs, by contrast, mutual trust, mutual responsibility and creativity are in the most obvious sense free goods, while at the same time they are valuable not only for those who engage in them, but also potentially for the whole productive process and hence for others. We might call them super-public-goods. We can see them as at once public goods, free goods, and free productive resources.

This perhaps explains the apparently astonishing reports of achievement on the part of some of those enterprises that have contrived to tap into these wellsprings. Their use provides its own reward. Systems of management based upon them are self-reinforcing.

The difficulty of course is to break into the virtuous circle. But it is a difficulty of practical management, not a moral dilemma.

Conclusion

'Competition' has an important role in the organisation of modern societies, but not all that is competition in the relevant sense entails rivalry. Moreover, rivalry within working organisations has to be strictly limited so as not to impair vital cooperation and teamwork. Rivalry between firms or service organisations also requires conventional, as well as legal, limits – rules of the game – which vary according to the social function of the organisation, if it is to be beneficent.

An economy in which the disciplines of competition are operative does not need to be one of extreme individualism. Indeed, for a successfully functioning economy, we must qualify the individualist ethic by precepts and incentives and institutions which encourage the exercise not only of trustworthiness but also of responsibility and creativity. A society guided by unrelieved super-competitive individualism in its productive sectors will thus be one in which there are inefficient outcomes – in which important sources of material benefit are forgone.

Correspondingly, some of the norms of personal behaviour that are commonly accepted as morally admirable provide the foundation for elements vital to full economic efficiency, as well as for benefits that transcend the framework in which economic efficiency is usually defined. Because, once experienced, mutual trust, mutual responsibility, and individual and group creation, tend to be valued and indeed to be their own rewards, there is a self-reinforcing mechanism for any institutional or social achievement that depends on the exercise of these characteristics.

Notes

1 To focus on such firms inevitably involves something of a stereotype, especially as such firms never represented the whole of the economy; also, reality has probably started, in the 1990s, to diverge somewhat further from the stereotype. Nevertheless it is helpful.
2 We support this idea, even though we all agree, unless we happen to come out on top, that the criteria, whatever they are, are flawed.

References

Dore, R.P. (1987) *Taking Japan Seriously*. London: Athlone Press.

Macrae, N. (1982) 'Intrepreneurial now', *Economist*, 17 April: 47–52.

Peters, T. and Waterman, R. (1982) *In Search of Excellence*. New York: Harper & Row.

Schanze, E. (1993) 'Symbiotic arrangements', *Journal of Institutional and Theoretical Economics* 149(4): 691–97.

Semler, R. (1993) *Maverick*. London: Century.

Stewart, V. (1990) *The David Solution*. Aldershot: Gower.

Waterman, R. (1994) *Frontiers of Excellence*. London: Nicholas Brealey.

Section II
Integrity and the public service

20 Integrity and public accountability

Peter Kemp

I come to this subject from a mainly practical point of view, as someone who has spent some 25 years of his life in the Civil Service, ending with senior positions in the Treasury and Cabinet Office. Questions of integrity and public accountability, and how they affect the ongoing work of government and public administration and *vice versa*, can be among the most difficult questions which the process of government throws up.

The conclusion that I come to in this chapter is that there need be no conflict between the distinct demands of integrity, public accountability and good government, but that to ensure that in practice these come together can give difficulty both to the individuals and to the institutions involved.

What are we talking about?

There has been much discussion about 'integrity' and this is not the easiest of subjects. Still, I propose to add my tuppence worth. I start by way of two quotations. The first is from W.H. Auden:

> You need not see what someone is doing
> to know if it is his vocation,
> you have only to watch his eyes:
> a cook mixing a sauce, a surgeon
> making a primary incision,
> a clerk completing a bill of lading,
> wear the same rapt expression,
> forgetting themselves in a function.
> How beautiful it is,
> that eye-on-the-object look. . . .
> ('Sext', from *Horae Canonicae* (1954) 1979)

The second comes from Psalm 15:

> 'Lord, who shall dwell in thy tabernacle: or who shall rest upon thy holy hill?

Even he that leadeth an uncorrupt life: and doeth the thing which is
   right, and speaketh the truth from his heart.
He that hath used no deceit in his tongue, nor done evil to his neighbour.
He that setteth not by himself, but is lowly in his own eyes; and maketh
   much of them that fear the Lord.
He that sweareth unto his neighbour and disappointeth him not: though
   it were to his own hindrance.
He that hath not given his money upon usury: nor taken reward against
   the innocent.
Who so doeth these things: shall never fail.'

The first quotation seems to me to capture the personal internal integrity of
someone owing his loyalty to his job and to himself, while the second captures
that of someone owing his loyalty to other people. Both are marvellous pieces
of language, but they are more than that; they encapsulate a real and solid
view of what the author saw as right. And so, still, do many others also see
it as right; but it is not always fashionable to say so just now.

I think that this is rather a pity. In too many contemporary discussions of
integrity we hear little about God or religion or the ancient traditions.
Indeed, in the typescript of one of the papers circulated before the Balliol colloquium the word 'religious' had been crossed out and 'ideological' put in its
place. There is an interesting separate question as to why we are so nervous
about this dimension; and it is a practical point too, because it leads us
into looking for solutions for things for which it may be that there are no
solutions to be found. And from the point of view of government and the
State it is even more practical; because these have to pick up the bits left
behind when religion becomes unfashionable – to pick them up both physically, in the sense of providing for a good deal of material welfare and the like,
and spiritually, in the sense of the overriding eventual fall-back position.

Today we find ourselves confronted with a 'culture of blame'. Perhaps I
write as an older person, but there was a time when it was accepted that certain things just happened; you could not really blame anybody tangible, so
you blamed Nature, or God, or circumstances or whatever. Now we have
moved into a situation where every accident has to have a cause; we are turning on its head the old adage, so that success is now an orphan, while failure
has a thousand fathers. Hence the habit, encouraged by greedy lawyers, of
chasing the parentage of failure: a sort of super universal Child Support
Agency. And while this afflicts both the public and private sectors, it is
most noticeable in the public sector and in the public services.

Public accountability

I am going to limit myself to public services as commonly understood. Note
that I am not going to talk about the public *sector*; there is an increasing, and
in my view welcome, blurring of the distinction between the public and the

private sectors when it comes to the delivery of services. What matters here is the position and condition of the recipient of the services. Under these circumstances the question of what constitutes the public services as such can be endlessly debated; considerations of elements of choice or its absence, optionality or absolute need, payment or non-payment at the point of service and so on all enter into the debate. Today we might like to restrict ourselves to a determination by choice, or lack of it, in the use of the service, which is the point of view of the citizen; and to couple this with the need to deliver the service, which is the point of view of the State. Not everything that a citizen needs has to be delivered by the State – there may be other providers. Not everything that the State has to provide is required by every citizen; for example, we are not (yet) all retirement pensioners.

But this gives us a position to go at, and we see the first problem. For if the State is seen as provider of services for those particular people, when not every one of us needs the services, how is the State's responsibility to those people to be reconciled with its responsibility to the rest of us, who at the lowest level have to pay the taxes necessary to provide these services, and more generally and in differing ways may be inconvenienced by the State's action in its first role? Humps down a quiet road may be good for the children who want to play there, but they may be seriously unhelpful to an ambulance trying to get an elderly resident of that street to hospital in time. Better conditions for social security claimants may be highly desirable, but are going to add to, or at least prevent any reduction in, the taxes paid by the rest of the public.

Accountability and integrity

I have just said something about what we might mean by integrity. And I have described the area that I want to look at. But what, then, *do* we mean by 'integrity' and how does it sit with 'accountability'? Are they the same thing, or are they mutually reinforcing concepts – or, indeed, concepts that are opposed? At this stage I do not wish to generalise. As I have said, the conclusion that I shall come to at the end is that there need be no conflict between the distinct demands of integrity, public accountability and good government; but that is not always – some might say ever – going to be easy to achieve. If one *had* to seek to generalise, one might, for instance, regard accountability as literally an accountability to other people – usually the 'customer', or the superior up the line at various stages in the chain, or indeed to one's juniors, or the environment in which one works. Conversely, one might define integrity as something internal to oneself – a sort of inwardly directed accountability, in contrast to the outwardly directed accountability more usually covered by that term. Such an approach certainly works in the sense that one can see the confusions that may come up, and the cases where accountability and integrity are not the same and efforts have to be made to reconcile them.

How we got here

It is worth looking at how we got here. I have written a little book about this (Kemp 1993) or at least a book that touches on this so far as the central Civil Service goes. We see a combination of factors which have led to a public sector (note that I do use the word here) of the size that it is today – taking up 40 per cent or more of Gross Domestic Product. We see an increasing expectation on the part of people for better public services, spurred on, of course, by governments who on the whole have never lost a vote by promising this sort of thing. We have seen the failure of the historical capacity of the private sector – in which one would include the Church – to meet these expectations. We see a touching faith in the capacities of economies to grow and to deliver better standards of living to everybody. And we see an arrogance on the part of governments, or perhaps I should say on the part of some of the creatures employed by governments, that only they know how best to do these things.

The result is the growth that we have seen: growth of expectations; growth in resources devoted to trying to meet these expectations, though often without the underlying economic growth honestly to meet them; and the development of the 'nanny knows best' approach, which creates individuals and institutions who take advantage, in one way or another, of the first two factors.

We also see the growth of the 'expectation gap', both in terms of actual delivery and performance, and in terms of integrity. So far as performance and performance expectation are concerned, engineering is clearly possible. A sensible private sector company, for instance, can engineer things so that on a scale of 1 to 10, expectation may be at 5, while performance is at 6, thus creating satisfied customers. Public services do not have that luxury; expectation is always up towards the 8 or 9 mark. But since public services are on the whole no better and no worse delivered than Marks & Spencer's service, performance is still around 6. So there is a gap. The gap is even greater with integrity; even with those private concerns that are seen as the best in these terms – again your Marks & Spencer, your Sainsbury, perhaps some of your banks – you are not *totally* sure how far you can trust them, nor are you altogether surprised if things go wrong. But try telling that to people who have to deal with your Social Security Office, your Passport Office or your Coastguard, and you find that here there are very high expectations indeed. There can be no engineering here, and the public provider has to seek to match what is expected of it in terms of integrity.

Some examples

Enough of generalising; let us come to government and indeed public administration as a *practical* subject. It is indeed extremely difficult. Let us take a recent example: the events covered by the Scott Inquiry looking at the arms for Iraq affair. We have now had the Report itself and the debate in the House of Commons, which the then Government won. Arguments rumbled on about the form of the inquiry and events surrounding its publication, and about whether or not particular ministers should or should not have resigned; and whether or not individual civil servants should be disciplined, something which, no matter how technically justified, could be difficult with ministers staying in place. Yet in a way all these matters, exciting though they are, are not what the Scott events were really all about.

What they were about were various conflicts. Patently there were conflicts between two government policies; on the one hand there was the industrial view, in bureaucratic terms sponsored by the Department of Trade and Industry, that all exports were desirable because they created or retained jobs in the United Kingdom, while on the other hand there was the foreign policy point of view, sponsored by the Foreign and Commonwealth Office, which had its own ideas about the extent, if any, to which help and support should be given at that particular point in time to Iraq. And then there was the Ministry of Defence, torn between hoping to support British armaments, which indirectly helped their product, on the one hand, and on the other hand, the wish not to supply a potential enemy with weapons which might at some time be used against us. A second conflict was that between a generalised wish not to mislead Parliament or the public and a specific feeling in this case that the fact that the stated guidelines pertaining to arms sales had been modified should not be revealed in public. And a third series of conflicts, which must have come up, was one among the individual protagonists involved on either side in these first two debates, between the 'line' that they were taking in terms of their professional activity and of support for their side, and a different line, which, just possibly, some might have preferred to take from the point of view of their personal integrity.

Public debate has, so far, been largely about the second of these conflicts – namely, whether or not Parliament should have been told of the change – and not much about the first or the third. It is interesting, indeed, that the first has not been much debated, since after all that ought to have been the heart of the whole matter: the substantive government action that was taken, and whether selling those arms to Iraq was or was not in the British national interest. It could be argued, and I would so argue, that the second issue – whether or not Parliament should have been told about the change in the guidelines, and the third issue – the personal conflict with the integrity of some of the individuals concerned – are, from the point of view of good government of the State, secondary consequential issues. This is not to say that they are not important, but simply that when dealing with government administration as a practical subject, we ought to start from the substance of the matter.

We can all come to our own conclusions. My own conclusion on the first conflict is that we do not know enough, still, to judge whether the right outcome was arrived at; on the second conflict it is that, if ministers genuinely thought that the interests of Britain would suffer if Parliament were told of the change, then they were right not to do so, (though no-one can deny that, even if this decision had been taken and was accepted, the actual handling of the various communications to Parliament and MPs over the years was less than competent); and on the third conflict it seems that the vast majority of ministers and civil servants involved, whatever their personal view, could in fact square their own integrity, and did so – (though again this is not to say that some of the handling of some of the events does not seem to have been very clever). The question we ask is whether, as citizens, we are content with this sort of analysis and apparently comfortable conclusion, and, if not, what we would have done personally, if we had been involved – bearing in mind the 'can-do' spirit of the age, and what changes of machinery, if any, we would like to see to prevent, or at least help the protagonist with, such episodes in the future.

Another example of this sort of 'set-piece' issue is to be found in the recent programme of change in the public service, most particularly in the Civil Service. We have achieved a great deal and there is no doubt that in most areas services are being delivered better, and better value for money is being delivered for whoever pays for them. But issues now arise – most notably in the excitement over the prison service – about questions of Parliamentary accountability and who does what. Here the critics, some of them using a rather wide sort of scatter shot gun, imply that the admittedly difficult and not always solved problems of accountability which have been emerging, do verge on questions of integrity for the individual and, indeed, for the system itself, in the sense that I have just described – a respecting of internal truths. I doubt if this is so, but it is an example of where issues variously described as involving matters of accountability and integrity are up for critique, and are frequently confused – though they have necessarily to be seen against the overall background of what a government, pursuing its own actions or reactions in the light of what it was democratically elected to do and of what it judges to be correct, has to face.

There are, then, major policy issues which arguably present themselves as set pieces. But let us look also at day-to-day work. People are faced with events as they occur, and, to paraphrase Harold MacMillan, events are the most difficult and dangerous things that are going to come up. Faced with the on-rush of events, ministers and civil servants are often confronted with dilemmas which, to be fair or, as you might say, unfair to them, they perhaps do not always recognise. Tensions arise between long-term and short-term policies, between loyalties to personal beliefs and loyalties to the State, between the interests of this set of people and the interests of that other set, between the need to make a decision now and the desirability of thinking things over.

Among the 'stake-holders' there are many whose claims have to be reconciled. These include the State, whatever exactly one may mean by that, the government of the day, its policies and its wish to be re-elected; the immediate 'user' whoever he, she or it may be; the future as contrasted with the present (are we laying in trouble or benefit for the year 2030?); and, indeed, in an increasing number of cases, other countries and other overseas interests, who have to do business with us, as we with them. The notion of a 'stake-holder society' may well be successful, but it has to stay out of detail if it is to stay out of trouble.

While government has always been a difficult task and the ethical and accountability issues always troublesome, these have arguably become even more difficult in recent years. The problems of 'rationing' and the prioritisation of resources, which give rise to so many of the issues, are much sharper now than they were in the 1950s and 1960s. There is the increased consciousness of people *qua* citizens of their rights and wrongs. Their entitlements and expectations (exemplified by the Citizens' Charter), though in themselves right and proper, also give rise to more issues for government than used to be the case. And there is the phenomenon of the increasing and, seen from the point of view of the citizen, welcome tendency of the courts to examine governmental actions and decisions. Issues of integrity seem to me to arise at quite simple levels with the introduction of these 'outside' forces. Consider, for instance, what their existence does for decision-makers in leading them to make other and, from some points of view perhaps, better decisions than they would otherwise have made: and the impacting of different forces on the integrity of decision-makers, even though they may have taken their original decisions in a way that was consistent with their own integrity.

A case-study

At this point I should like to lay out a case-study. It concerns the delivery of a particular social security benefit. Amongst other things it illustrates the problems of distinguishing accountability and integrity in the delivery of a public service.

The Social Security Benefits Agency costs about £2–3 billion per annum (and that is only the administrative cost – the full annual cost of the programme is around £90 billion). There are, I believe, about 14 million benefits paid every week to people who are, by definition, the worst off and the least able to manage in our society. And there are about 70,000 or so people employed by the agency. Together with certain aspects of local authority work, they underpin society; they prevent riots in the streets; in a sense they *are* society.

So here we have, in a very clear form, a simple conflict in public policy between, on the one hand, the social needs and expectations of those who rely wholly, or in part, on the social security system and, on the other hand, the legitimate expectations of those who fund that system. Let us look at what happens at various levels.

In the first place, at *level one*, the State may, for one reason or another, perceive a need for some kind of change, which may well involve finding further funds. If it is sufficiently important, the minister in charge will take it to the Treasury. Let us assume that he or she gets approval there. Then he or she may have to take it to the Cabinet. At this point we have the dilemma, together with the questions of integrity that it entails, which faces the minister in his or her arguments, as he or she tries to balance the need to relieve the newly perceived disability or discomfort experienced by some section of the population against that of improving the lot of existing claimants, or, again, against those of imposing taxation on the rest of us, or of reducing our general borrowing, (an objective which should not be scorned, for it is one which, if achieved, will eventually benefit us all). This is a genuine dilemma, which is what government is there to sort out.

Next we have *level two*, which is where the Benefits Agency comes in. Assuming that ministers have decided that such and such an improvement is to be made and that funds are to be made available, the agency itself then has to start setting the targets in detail. There we have the dilemmas of having to set one target against another and of having to rate one area as less important than another. Again, we must not underrate the difficulties or the importance of setting targets and objectives. It is not an easy art, but it is a necessary one; and well set and thought through targets – particularly those of a non-financial and qualitative kind – bring benefit by their very existence to both claimants, staff and tax-payer.

Level three is that of what happens at the local office. The decisions taken at level two have been translated into broad instructions, but at the local level we still have flexibility and alternatives, which local managers have to decide, interpret and choose between. They may believe in their received instructions or they may not. But they have a job to do, here as elsewhere. If their personal integrity – as illustrated by the piece from Auden above – comes up against their collective accountability – as illustrated by the piece from the Psalms, then there is a problem.

Level four is that at which the individual man or woman on the desk has to do the work. In this day and age a good deal of discretion and flexibility is, in my view correctly, given to such people. This is necessary because, particularly in the social security world, people's circumstances are all different. But this does mean that the man or the woman on the desk has to make up his or her mind in many very difficult circumstances, and often very quickly, against the background of some broad guidance which may not, indeed can not, cover every eventuality that may arise, and the guidance may not always fit what the desk officer thinks is right. But he or she must go along with it; their duty must be to their employer – and through their employer to the benefit claimants – and not to themselves. The alternatives are to get a transfer to another job or, at the extreme, to resign. This has not been unknown.

Finally we have *level five*, often overlooked and particularly by the '*bien-pensants*', which is that of the claimants themselves. They too have a duty of integrity: not to tell lies, to turn up at the times when appointments are made for them, to report changes of circumstance, to treat the man or the woman who is trying to help them with courtesy and diligence. One of the most trying issues about integrity in the public service is the way in which many people think of it as a one-way affair. The State must have its integrity; but individuals tend to cop out. It should not be like that.

The democratic dimension: the public

One thing that comes out of this very simple example, particularly at the last level that I have identified, is the importance of the question of whether, in a democracy, people generally feel that they all have a duty to help the State and its agents when they wrestle with questions of integrity. For in the general area of planning and providing public services it seems to me that the individual out there must accept his or her share of responsibility. Of course, there is a wide variety of circumstance; if a doctor is face-to-face with a particular patient, then, while the two may owe to each other (amongst other things) duties of integrity, the rest of us are not directly involved in what goes on between them. But in general it seems to be important that people do not use democracy, or seek to fulfil their electoral duties simply by voting in general and local elections every so often, as their sole contribution towards solving all the subsequent problems that the State and its agents may have – in short, as a simple way of passing the buck.

This issue comes up in many ways. There is the obvious way that I have just discussed, where people expect standards from the providers of public services, which sometimes they are not prepared to observe themselves, whether in their private lives or as partners in the public service provision. And then there is the more basic point, which concerns the whole question of 'getting the eats on the table'. Does integrity have a cost and, if so, does it mean different things as between societies which are rich and profitable and societies which are poor and struggling?

In either case there are the questions of personal versus communal integrity, and of the extent to which an individual can, or is entitled to, unload his or her integrity problems on to another. This is a particular problem for the State. For when people vote, they are not always totally honest. Certainly, they say that they would be prepared to pay more income tax, let us say, if the health service or the social security system, or whatever it may be, was improved. (Let us leave aside for the moment the perceived fact that people who are prepared to say this in answer to opinion polls, when it does not matter, frequently do not sign up to it at elections.) But is it just the provision of services that they are trying to buy with their money? Or are they also trying to buy out of the responsibility, the integrity and all the other problems of the delivery of the public services? Are they in fact doing what they perceive recent governments to have been doing – 'contracting out', but in this case contracting out of their consciences? Are they seeking to buy out of the problems of integrity at their level by exporting them, at a price which they can afford, to those who have to operate at different levels?

The administrative dimension: the players as a group

So what about the people who have to decide and who have to deliver the services? What happens when individual consciences and beliefs as to what is right and wrong come up against the wider demands of the State and, in the jargon, of *realpolitik*? Are there times when it is defensible and necessary to tell lies? Wartime conditions clearly constitute one of these times, when winning the war and saving the lives of people on your own side has to be an overriding requirement. But there has been much debate about an event of many years ago now when Mr Callaghan (as he then was) gave what some saw as having been an incomplete reply in relation to plans concerning devaluation, (which had in fact been already settled), when in his judgement the fuller answer would have done damage to the State. More recently we have had accusations that the government of the day was less than fully open in its replies about the discussions which had been taking place with the Republican elements in Northern Ireland, even though it subsequently became evident that the upshot of this was a cessation of the violence, murders and deaths that has been taking place for so many years in that Province. Was this right or wrong? Should the ministers and the officials concerned have maintained their own personal integrity by telling the truth, if that was going to mean yet more atrocious murders? At least part of the answer comes from considering where people stand at the point where they have to decide; as I said earlier, the benefit of hindsight and the courage of the non-combatant are cosy comforters – but only after the event.

The problematic question is whether there is any inconsistency, whether what a person believes is right in himself can then be wrong when delivered publicly; or, indeed, *vice versa*. Perhaps we reach a situation where 'high', or public, integrity has to subsume personal integrity; in many walks of life people are put in charge of potential temptation, if that is the right way of putting it, and are trusted nevertheless. Perhaps the only way of dealing with the inconsistency is to ensure that within the system people are fully aware of what they are doing, and of what they themselves think is right and wrong.

From the point of view of the on-going management of the State what is needed is a perceived high standard of behaviour. People need to trust and to be able to trust the machine, whether or not it has got internal flaws, and (dare I say it?) whether or not the personal or internal integrity of the State's agents is strained. Whatever T.S. Eliot may have said, I would argue that in public affairs the right decision wrongly taken is better than the wrong decision rightly taken. The perceived presence and performance of accepted, and hopefully better than accepted, standards of behaviour are what matters.

The individual dimension – the player as a person

But where does that leave the individual? On my argument the agents of the State should not be allowed for the sake of their personal integrity to disbenefit the rest of us by letting the State take less than the optimal overall course. But does this mean that people have to subject their standards to this wider belief? I think not. This is because I think that one can trust the State to function with integrity only if its agents have themselves a high standard of internal behaviour. Indeed, you can only entrust such power to such people, in the same way as you can only entrust the key of the wine cellar to people who know of the dangers of alcohol and are temperate in its use. The individuals whom I have come across in 25 years or more of Civil Service life have been of this high standard, whether ministers, officials or advisers. They have been people of high personal integrity, who knew that they were working in a very difficult field, and who, if they had to depart from what might be required by their own high standards, knew what their duty was: to go along with it, while believing in it, or to resign.

Let us not pretend that this is easy. The appearance and delivery of high standards, standards in which citizens can believe and on which they can rely and which give good government, do not always sit easily or in a simple way with what individual persons themselves might wish or believe. But it can be made to do so. We pride ourselves in Britain on the apolitical nature of our public services, and we spend a lot of time seeking to ensure it; and that is what, generally speaking, is actually delivered to us. But it is often overlooked that this is achieved only at the cost of many personal dilemmas and sacrifices made all the way down the line. On the whole, my belief, based on experience, is that individuals do manage to make this reconciliation, though it is not always easy.

There is commonly much talk about why people join the public service. Why should men and women who might earn a great deal more money, and perhaps in some senses have more power, go into the Civil Service, into teaching or into health, when they could go into industry or the City? There is reality in the belief in 'public service' as a vocation and a willingness on the part of many people to give up the monetary and other rewards of the private sector in return for helping to deliver better public services. But one of the issues very seldom discussed is the way in which such a decision may lead, sooner or later in the individual's career, to some kind of conflict of conscience, when what he or she might personally believe, the way in which he or she might personally wish to behave, comes into conflict with the wider need of the public service, which he or she has chosen to join and support. At that point a certain kind of moral sacrifice may be required.

Compare the 'private' side

A point before I close. This chapter has been about the public services, whether or not they are delivered by 'the public sector'. But much of what I say applies to 'private service', however that may be defined. There is no doubt that public service and private service are often different, and can come under different rules. But it would be quite wrong to think that the rules applicable to private service are less responsive to considerations of proper integrity and ethics, or that they are any easier to apply. How they might differ from those applicable to the public services could be and has been the subject of a great deal of discussion, and is a topic beyond the scope of this chapter. For present purposes, all I would say is that the public services have no monopoly on the sort of issues and problems that I have tried to describe here.

A general conclusion

To sum up, my own personal belief is that in the management of the State and in the delivery of public service the needs of the State must, when it comes to the crunch, be put ahead of those of the individual. But I do not believe that such a conflict often arises. This is because the totality of the personal integrities of the agents of the State feed back into what is the State's overall integrity, and the two mutually support each other. We are dealing with a very large number of different people and a very large number of different decisions. There will always be accidents and exceptions. But my belief is that the overall integrity of the State and of good government relies on and derives from the individual integrity of all its agents, whether these be ministers, civil servants or any other; and, *vice versa*, the individual's personal integrity draws strength from the fact of acting as an agent for the collective integrity. This may sound like an attempt to have it both ways and to see the world through over-optimistic spectacles. But then I am an optimist.

References

Auden, W.H. (1954) 'Sext', *Horae Canonicae*, in *Selected Poems* (1979) ed. Edward Mendelson. London: Faber & Faber.

Kemp, Sir Peter (1993) *Beyond Next Steps: A Civil Service for the 21st Century*. London: Social Marker Foundation.

21 Moral integrity in the public service

René Sève

It is not uncommon to compare the principles governing public with those governing private morality with a view, among other things, to seeing whether public morality, which would seem to call for a level of dedication appropriate to the generality of the interests with which it is concerned, does not in reality present certain risks for the moral integrity of the individual, who may be more carried away by the importance of the role that he finds himself occupying rather than raised to a higher level of moral responsibiity. Such, at any rate, would seem to be the point of view underlying certain aspects of Thomas Nagel's excellent article 'Ruthlessless in public life'.[1] This approach would seem to be mainly justified in those extreme cases where the importance of the public role in question and the pressing nature of some exceptional danger or need combine in such a way that the superior interests of the nation may be at stake. But in more ordinary cases, such as those in which a civil servant, whatever his rank may be, has to manage some fiscal system, to establish a standard of excise duties for a particular range of products, to organise some minor road equipment programme, to authorise the availability for general use of a new drug, etc., the problems of public morality are certainly more similar to those to be found in other forms of professional life, at all events to those implied by the fact of belonging to some organisation.

The fact of an individual's belonging to an organisation would seem, indeed, to involve a divide between his or her immediate interests, on the one hand, be they self-regarding or, on the contrary, linked to some higher moral concerns, and, on the other hand, the wider or narrower interests of the institution. To take a (by now) classic example, the sentry must leave his post neither to flirt with a passer-by nor to separate two of his comrades who are fighting with each other.[2] If it is easy to understand that the acceptance of a given role within an organisation will impose certain limits on the outlook of whoever occupies it, in regard both to ends and to means, one might suppose it to be a peculiarity of an administrative or a political role, at any rate in theory, that it should work in favour of a general interest which would allow the individual's horizon to extend further than his or her merely private interests. Such a point of view was expressed by Lord

William Beveridge. 'To-day as tomorrow, the civil servant, when he joins the Civil Service, will take the triple vow of poverty, anonymity and obedience' (1922: 231; quoted in Kerauden 1994: 132). By way of contrast, the employee of a business might be justified in allowing his duties as a citizen to weigh against the interests of his employer in order, for example, to protect society from damage to the environment, or quite simply from a form of unfair competition that might lead to excessive prices for the consumer or to a position of unfairly restricted competition for competitors.[3]

Nevertheless, the description that I have just outlined of the public role as compared with a private role within some economic organisation, calls for some qualification. The first thing to note is that this account of the public servant whose role it is to realise the general interest, and who has therefore simply to preserve himself from contamination by private interests, not least his own, is imprecise and inexact, even if it largely inspires the penal law and that governing public administration. Here it is necessary to take the most serious account of the division of labour within the State and its systems of administration. To take just the case of France, the powers of the State are organised through a series of ministerial departments, sub-divided under certain main heads, services, sub-heads and offices of central administrations, which themselves constitute no more than the visible aspect of a whole host of ground-level civil servants, with their own organisational structures, of associations dependent on the State, and of public enterprises; and all this for the State public service alone. To this one must add those administarations which are responsible to local government of one form or another, whether of the regions, the departments, of groups of communes or of municipalities, not to mention inter-regional and even cross-frontier institutions etc. Without going into the detail of this quasi-monadology,[4] one has to take account of the fact that in reality the 'fonctionnaire'[5] moves in a universe that is at least three-dimensional, consisting (according to convention) 'at the bottom level' of his private interests, 'at the top' of the general interest and in between the interests of his national or local administration, as well as of his particular branch or office. Implicit in this organisation, as in any other, is the underlying assumption that in appointing individuals to specific tasks, they will be in a better position to promote the general interest, at the cost, if necessary, of certain conflicts or of a sometimes absurd competition between the different sub-organisations separated out in this way. One might supppose that this situation of a highly particularised role is essentially characteristic of the position of civil servants on the bottom rungs of the hierarchy, the obscure representatives of the whole executive army. But a somewhat more careful description of the ways in which the higher spheres of the State operate shows that that even at that level the capacity for integrating the general interest is not necessarily as marked as one might believe.[6]

Inevitably, this way of looking at the matter leaves a certain number of questions unanswered, among them the following:

If one holds that the interest attaching to the role lies indeed in making its proper contribution to the general interest, one may well doubt whether this general interest really represents an absolute ideal. Or to put it another way, is the 'general interest' really in the general interest? For example, even if something is in the national interest, is this truly the interest of humanity in general or, at the very least, of a group of nations of which one's own country is just one? Assuming that the answer to this first question is positive, is that general interest which is held to justify the behaviour of the 'fonctionnaire' within the framework of his role, the interest of the country or in fact rather that of the State, which, *qua* organisation, necessarily has its own special interests, those of preserving its own power, of avoiding conflicts with its own agents and of making civil society in general pay the costs of its own working? If it is said that the interest of the country and that of the State coincide, is the 'fonctionnaire' to regard himself as the servant of the State or of the government of the day?

If we turn now from questions concerning the general interest and its different interpretations to the relation between this interest and the morality of the 'fonctionnaire's' role which is to guide the him in his daily work, one may well ask oneself whether this role-morality should not be re-examined in the name, precisely, of the general interest, even if that might mean disobeying immediate disciplinary rules in the broadest sense of the term, that is to say those not only of the discipline to which the 'fonctionnaire' is submitted within the vast overall organisation of the State, but equally those which a minister is expected to observe in relation to the government as a whole.

Again, must the lower limit, that of private interest, be seen as similarly unbreachable? Must particular interest always be subordinated to that of the role or the function and, beyond that, to the general interest? Can one really condemn the official who, at the beginning of a new school year, writes a recommendation urging the admission of a child – a relation, the child of a friend or that of a relation? Or the hospital doctor who similarly intervenes in order to obtain treatment for someone by a team in whom he has confidence? Or the 'fonctionnnaire' in love, who flirts not only with his beloved, but also with absenteeism or with bogus certificates of unfitness for work? The law condemns the policeman who loves the prostitute, but might not certain forms of moral judgement rather absolve him?

At the end of the day, are the general interest, the interest of the particular function and private interest truly what they represent themselves as being? When the 'fonctionnaire' sacrifices his family for his work in the name of the general interest, is not this general interest really simply the interests of his own career, or at a slightly higher level, that of his administration, whose interest no longer strikes him as sectional in relation to those that are more general. Is particular interest always as particular as all that? The celebrated writers, Paul Claudel and Saint-John Perse may have been supported in part by the tax-payer's money, but in the end has not what they were thus enabled to produce brought benefits in return, if not to the whole of the population that contributed to their support, at least to an élite capable of appreciating their work?

Finally, and following the same train of thought, who is in a position to know what *is* the general interest, the interest of the particular function or even his or her own interest, and *a fortiori* how is one to determine in any particular case the proper order of priorities as between these three dimensions? In other words, as is said by certain branches of the State, 'where is one to place the cursors?'

In an attempt to provide some elements of response to these different questions, and still within the context of the French administration, I propose to look in closer detail at the rules, presently in force, which are presumed to establish reasonably clear distinctions between the spheres of interest which I have just described, and second, at the customary practices which may intervene to bend, but also to enrich, the juridical norms.

I aim at providing an account of positive law, which will be neither exhaustive nor precise, but which will provide certain broad indications, indications which indeed are classical enough. Before embarking on the more detailed examination of this theme, I must make it clear that the juridical rules which govern the organisation of the public service and the duties of its 'fonctionnaires', have it as their essential concern (to use the terms of the model previously set aside as being much too simple) to protect both the State itself and even those to whom the rules are to apply from the temptations which private interest might bring to bear. To this first general observation, one must add a second, which leads one to consider the rules governing the organisation of the public service in France as relatively liberal. The 'fonctionnaire' is able to pursue either his private interest or his own vision of the general interest, that is to say perhaps, another form of private interest, under relatively flexible conditions.[7]

Restrictions on the pursuit of private interest in the strict sense of the term

The rules in force

Even if the possible conflict between the demands of moral integrity and those of the 'fonctionnaire's' social role does not in general arise as a result of his pursuit of his own private interests, but rather from a concern, going beyond the obligations of his given role, for the more general interest, the State nevertheless does set certain limits to the pursuit of their private interests by salaried public servants, on pain of penal and/or disciplinary sanctions. The first area of concern is naturally that of corruption and of improper interference, a concern on which I shall not dwell here. Second, the duties of a 'fonctionnaire' are incompatible with any regular pursuit of any outside gainful activity, even one completely distinct from his normal occupation and thus incapable of giving rise to any direct conflict of interest with it. In other words, the question here is not so much one of corruption as of not engaging in a job parallel to one's employment as a 'fonctionnaire', that is to say it is that of the holding of a plurality of paid posts.

In principle, then, the 'fonctionnaire' may not occupy several different posts, especially not more than one public post. This rule naturally makes for the avoidance of any confusion of roles within the framework of the division of labour to which I referred above, and commits the State to making sure that its employees are properly paid. One can understand the reasons for this; on the one hand, it is perhaps difficult to expect a genuine disjunction between public and private activities, and so one finds oneself back with the first case, while, on the other hand, the 'fonctionnaire' may be tempted to give priority to that among his activities which pays him most. Nevertheless, with appropriate hierarchical authorisation, the 'fonctionnaire' may, even within the scope of the public service, pursue certain ancillary activities, in particular that of teaching. But it is also possible for him to develop a genuine private activity, which is profitable to him, whether by way of producing works of the mind, (an activity which may lead him to express views distinct from those of his administration – see below) or by way of developing consultative activities, something which is particularly appreciated in the case of members of certain teaching bodies (where it is possible to add the profession of barrister ('avocat'), arbitrator or consultant to that of Professor of Law or, at a somewhat lower level, that of physical education instructor or proprietor of a gymnasium to that of masseur-physiotherapist).[8] Of course, certain general conditions are attached to these various exceptions to the rule – as noted above concerning appropriate hierarchical authorisation; or there may be particular conditions attaching to the peculiar nature of the consultancy or the teaching in question, (a taxation official is not allowed to advise the very businesses of whose taxes he is the inspector). At the same time, a ceiling is placed on the permitted level of remuneration; where private activity is concerned, this must not go beyond 100 per cent of the 'fonctionnaire's' basic salary, not counting bonuses (cf. the decree of 11 July 1955).

These constraints apply equally to such professional activities as may be carried on by those 'fonctionnaires' who are no longer on the staff or who are on temporary leave of absence; in their cases the State is concerned to prevent its agents or former agents from carrying on any activity that might prove detrimental to that branch of the administration to which they belong or had belonged. In this area, the principal measure in force is one which disallows 'fonctionnaires' from undertaking any professional activity within private companies that their previous official duties might have led them to supervise, inspect or negotiate contracts with (cf. the decree of 17 January 1991; Article 432–33 of the Penal Code). It is to be noted that these restrictions on the well-known passage from service of the State to posts with private companies do not apply to public enterprises, something which might well be a matter for discussion.

One may note, finally, that these measures aim at preserving a certain equilibrium between two posible meanings of the word 'integrity': one has to preserve the integrity of the 'fonctionnaire', by avoiding any illegitimate contamination by private interests; but, conversely, one has also to preserve the integrity of the human being, and in particular the development of his competences and his 'excellences', including those which have nothing to do with the performance of his role in the public service as such.[9]

Customary practices

The provisions of the law have naturally to be linked to what actually happens in practice; and the two do not always exactly correspond. Here it would seem that the state sins by lack of follow-up and of verification, something which, it is true, is very difficult to effect at the level of civil society and *a forteriori* at the level of the 'fonctionnaires' themselves, given that between themselves they can always look for the sort of mutual understanding that limits the effective capacity of the State to impose sanctions on them. As one of the overall Heads of Central Administration put it recently, 'If one wishes to exert any real check on the administration, one will have to call in inspectors external to it and not simply rely on an established Inspectorate, above all one fully integrated within a Ministry.' As in any other organisation, self-denunciation has its limits.

In the cases with which we are concerned, there are two points which deserve particular emphasis. So far as the amassing of more than one source of income is concerned, it is not obvious that the State makes all the necessary efforts to check, in particular through its fiscal services, whether the rules governing the overall ceiling are respected. It is the same story so far as the salaries of those 'fonctionnaires' who are seconded to public companies or other public bodies are concerned, salaries which, in theory, may not exceed the same 'fonctionnaire's' salary by more than a certain percentage. Finally, there are certain well-known instances, or instances which deserve to be well-known, which show that the limits set to the passage from public service to private company are far from being always respected, especially in the case of high Civil Servants, such as, for example, those whose work will have brought them into close and regular contact with ministers. We have here an interesting case of self-censorship within the French body politic; in the private sector, by way of contrast, one would expect a company in competition with one benefitting from the illegal arrival on its Board of a former 'fonctionnaire' would raise questions about it before the courts or otherwise move to alert public opinion.

Nevertheless such phenomena remain marginal; so too, moreover, do cases of corruption at least so far as the agents of the State are concerned (as compared with elected representatives or with the agents of local or regional bodies directly responsible to them).The first reason for this is probably that 'fonctionnaires' have, in general, little real opportunity to sin, at least so far as the majority of them are concerned. The second reason, which goes some way to explain the first, is that it does not enter their minds, in the first place because of their sense of duty, and second, perhaps equally, because they lack the necessary imagination. One can understand why the State, quite apart from any spontaneous feelings of indulgence that 'fonctionnaires' may have towards each other, renounces any idea of public sanctions for dubious practices, whether through penal measures or such severe disciplinary measures as suspension, demotion, compulsory retirement or dismissal, at any rate so long as these practices remain below a certain degree of gravity. One has the impression that the fact of malpractice becoming known, an inevitable consequence of its being punished, is judged to be more damaging in the long run than the impunity of the offender, especially given that between the one extreme and the other there exist such means of warning and other pressures as are sufficient to avoid too many excesses. It would be interesting to examine whether the cultural practice, so to speak, which consists in shutting one's eyes or at least in discreetly half-shutting them to lapses from integrity committed by 'fonctionnaires' is peculiarly characteristic of certain nations (the Latins) or whether in the end, as seems likely enough, it is peculiar to any corporation or organisation of this type, which takes the overall view that *de minimis non curat praetor* (roughly, 'the highest magistrates do not concern themselves with minor cases'), a view of which it is hard altogether to disapprove.[10] In short, regulation by established custom seems preferable to one by formal juridicial apparatus. One may also note in this connection that the State does not show itself to be over-zealous in making its 'fonctionnaires' aware of the possible authorisations of multiple activities from which they might benefit.

Restrictions on the pursuit of the general interest outside one's employment

The rules in force

The basic condition making posible the pursuit of the general interest outside the performance of one's role would seem to be that one should possess the necessary freedom of thought or of opinion.[11] In France this freedom is of considerable extent, since, despite certain attempts to restrict it made during the Fourth Republic, any degree of incompatibility between belonging to the public service and adherence to a political party or to other movements of thought is ruled out; in the same way, only relatively limited use is made of the oath which the 'fonctionnaire' may be called upon to swear to certain quite general moral principles.

One concrete manifestation of these arrangements is to be found in what is proclaimed to be the complete irrelevance of a 'fonctionnaire's' opinions so far as his recruitment or his career propects are concerned. This principle is even enshrined in the constitution, as it is expressed in paragraph 5 of the Preamble to the Constitution of 1946, and applies equally to civil servants and to members of the Armed Services. This implies that the administrative files needed for the management of the careers of 'fonctionnaires' bear mention neither of their political, religious or Trade Union opinions nor of their activities in any of these domains. One may nevertheless note with René Chapuis (1994, 2: 219, §252) that the impact of this principle has been somewhat attenuated by the judgement of the Council of State according to which, notwithstanding the irregularity constituted by any mention of personal opinions on the files, it is only if knowledge of his opinions has actually influenced a posting or a sanction imposed on a 'fonctionnaire' that such a measure is to be deemed irregular; while a more liberal interpretation ought to lead to the position that, even if there is no causal link, any measure affecting him should be deemed to be null and void, if any comments of a political or religious nature are to be found in his dossier.

The principle of freedom of opinion has nevertheless two limits, limits which are natural enough and which concern, on the one hand, agents nominated at the discretion of the Government and, on the other, the sub-prefects, who represent the State in the departments and in the regions, and who are, as it were, the instruments, possibly the armed instruments, of its intervention.

The first category is perhaps the more interesting one. It covers those high officials who occupy the highest roles of the State, the list of which is at present determined by the decree of 24th July 1985, and in which are to be found mainly the General Secretaries of different Ministries and Directors-General and Directors of different branches of the central administration, Heads of diplomatic missions with the rank of Ambassador and Rectors, Prefects and Directors of a certain number of public administrative establishments.[12] The fundamental point here is that this category also constitutes an exception to the principle that recruitment to the public service should be by open competition and that it is open to 'fonctionnaires' already in service to take advantage of it; if they do so, however, they do not, of course, acquire tenure of their new posts, and in certain (in practice more exceptional) cases they may come to stand outside the public service as such.[13] Finally one should make it clear, from a sociological point of view, that the number of posts affected by these particular rules is less than one thousand.

So far as freedom of expression is concerned, that is to say the public presentation of the above-mentioned opinions, the French system remains faithful to its principles, which, when compared with the arrangements prevailing in certain other states, are strikingly liberal. In carrying out his actual functions, the 'fonctionnaire' must, of course, observe the strictest possible neutrality, both in the expression of his opinions and in the performance of such acts as might result from them.[14] As for teachers (or, more generally, for those who have an intellectual role within the State employ) if, on the one hand, they must not, for example, mark certain students more generously in the light of the convergence of their respective beliefs, they enjoy, on the other hand, the widest possible degree of liberty, even in carrying out the functions of their role, this being considered necessary to its proper performance.[15]

Outside his professional activities, properly speaking, the 'fonctionnaire' enjoys complete freedom of expression provided that he respects certain limits.[16] Here too, the general principle is relatively liberal. So far as religion is concerned, he is free to participate in any form of observance or in any proselytising activity. As for political expression, the agents of the State are free to take part in demonstrations, to play an active role within a political party or to put themselves forward as candidates in elections.[17]

One general limitation on this freedom of expression, apart from certain special conditions applying to magistrates and members of the Armed Forces (see Chapuis 1994, 2: 225 §259), concerns the well-known obligation of discretion, which applies to every expression of opinion, even when it takes place in the context of a candidature for public employment, though in that case to a modified degree. In the texts in which it is formulated this obligation is defined in an almost tautological manner; jurisprudential interpretation has, therefore, tended to the view that it is to be seen as carrying greater weight in relation to several parameters, of which the most important are the fonctionnaire's rank, the topic on which views are to be expressed and the context of their expression.

This jurisprudential consideration allows us to hold over to the following section, devoted to actual practice, certain reflections on the extent of this obligation of discretion, as well as on the previously mentioned rights and obligations.

Customary practice

As in the case of restrictions on activities devoted to the pursuit of private interest, the rules, in the last resort protective both of the 'fonctionnaire's' freedom and of his moral integrity, may perhaps suffer in their application from the complexities involved in their interpretation and in checking on their observance.

So far as freedom of opinion is concerned, it is certain, for example, that the subsequent careers within the military institutions of the small number of communist officers who, at the moment of the Liberation and thanks to the integration into the Regular Army of the irregular forces belonging to the Resistance, were appointed to positions in the military hierarchy, sometimes of considerable importance, were not marked by any great brilliance; but this is understandable, when one remembers that the military were at that time faced with wars of independence, which the Communist Party was clearly engaged in campaigning against. More generally, once his or her opinions are known, either because they are revealed naively, as it were, or because they may be inferred from membership of a Trade Union, from the fact of being a candidate at an election or from that of being appointed to a post reserved for certain categories of persons, how can one ever be sure that this knowledge has had no influence on the career of the 'fonctionnaire' concerned? The same is true for any anti-discriminatory measure whatsoever: it will always be possible to get round it, because one will always be able to find some other reason to justify a decision tinged in reality with political, religious or racial prejudice.[18]

This type of rule must, then, be checked against what actually happens in practice. This, in fact, turns out to be not as contrary to the spirit of the legal directives as it might have been. In reality, everything depends on the prevailing general political situation; one of sharp divisions, of society in a state of semi-revolution or, on the contrary, of an overall consensus on certain major aspects of the role of the State, in the diplomatic or economic sphere, for example – all these factors have their impact, in one way or another, on the neutrality (or non-neutrality) of nominations and careers. It is to be noted that if, in recent times, certain traditionally political posts, such as those depending on the Ministry of the Interior, or on certain judiciary functions, have not always been filled on the basis of competence alone, other posts, on the contrary, in particular those associated with Ministries that are more involved with the economy, (the Ministry of Finance, the Ministry of Industry or even the Ministry of Labour) have provided their holders with a surprising degree of permanence, lasting through three distinct parliamentary majorities and and five different Prime Ministers. And what is true of the most visible of the posts to be filled at the discretion of the Government, is equally true of those of lower rank. In reality, and the overall political situation apart, the State, like any other organisation, has to manage its human resources intelligently, resources which are not limitless (and which, in the case of the most competent 'fonctionnaires', may also be covetted by the private sector), and has for all these reasons to insure for its servants the prospects of a reasonable career. What all this comes down to is that the management by rule and by custom of the public service ends up by favouring something which is doubtless not contradictory to the desired end, namely, a spirit of public service or, to put it in less favourable terms, a common way of thinking or a conformism, which, despite certain differences of opinion, allows each individual to reconcile his or her own interests with those of the State and the requirements of the hierarchy.

From the standpoint of principle, this practice of political appointments, whether explicit or underhand, may shock, but its widespread character, even over and above the French case, which presents perhaps only a relatively limited illustration of the phenomenon, should prompt one to weigh its advantages. To put the point in Thomist terms, to take account of special personal considerations is not necessarily vicious. It seems natural enough that a monetarist Minister of Finance should seek not to lumber himself with Keynesian 'fonctionnaires' and, therefore, to replace them. The notion of competence, above all in a post close to the sources of political power, must somehow take on board the relevant subjective and political parameters; (a minister must appreciate the human qualities of those who work with him). It is not in a Minister's interest to give such weight just to these considerations as to surround himself with 'fonctionnaires' who, though devoted, are professionally somewhat limited. In the same spirit, but conversely, one may note that certain 'fonctionnaires', who may often have taken a very close part in governmental action, have seen their careers suffer in consequence after a change of majority. But in general, by way of contrast with the private sector no doubt, suffering of this sort is not so great as to call for any serious moral condemnation. In reality, procedures which might make it possible to avoid this kind of injustice or this kind of inefficiency in the use of resources for political motives, whether that of under-utilisation or of unjustified advance in a career, would involve such ponderous counter-measures or counter-devices as to make all too likely the appearance of other abuses, in particular those of the formation of internal lobbies or pressure groups, which, on the pretext of defending the neutrality of the administration, would be engaged in defending their own power. Here again, the public service faces a problem which arises more generally in the management of institutions. One has to ensure a balance between the normal conditions of recruitment and predictable promotion on the one hand, and on the other hand, the use that may be made either of the accelerator or the brake, decisions to do either of which are bound to depend on closely arguable considerations.

Finally, mention should be made of the obligation of discretion. Interpretation of the law is more restrictive in this domain than the texts might lead one to suppose. For example, a Director of the Centre National de Recherche Scientifique has been dismissed for having given his approval to a petition drawn up in terms which, though very strong, did not seem particularly excessive.[19] In fact, what has to be compared is an interpretation of the law that is relatively strict (partly because of a reluctance to undermine the administrative sanctions) and the relatively small number of cases in which the administration actually punishes its subordinates. Other methods of pressure and other systems of self-censorship exist, which together reduce the need for recourse to heavy sanctions, which in their turn are to be explained in the light of the gravity of the case as such as much as by reference to other parameters, be they psychological, political or a matter of relationships.[20]

Again, these essential parameters have to do not so much with the nature of the public service as such as with the running of any organisation. The margins of manoeuvre available to the various parties concerned are to be explained in terms of a complex balance of forces, whereby the subordinate is not always bound hand and foot in relation to his hierarchy, on which he is able to bring to bear various forms of direct or indirect pressure. It is not so much to the sociology of administration as to the sociology of business that one may look to find the greater number of empirical studies of the networks, countervailing powers, and underlying or interlocking hierarchies, the nature of which, over and above the rules, explain, in part at least, the actual behaviour of the individuals and groups involved (cf. Moullet 1992).

The pursuit of the general interest within the framework of the post

The rules

Independently of the above-mentioned problems relating to private activities, the law of 13 July 1983 sets down, in its articles 26 and 28, the two principle obligations to be respected by the 'fonctionnaire': that of respect for professional confidentiality and that of carrying out the tasks which are entrusted to him or to her.

So far as professional confidentiality is concerned, the meaning of the rule is clear enough. 'Fonctionnaires' have a duty not to disclose facts relating to particular individuals, whether they be 'moral' or physical persons: the financial situation of a company for which the 'fonctionnaire' is reponsible for drawing up a dossier of aid or recovery, the state of health of someone who is ill, a tax-payer's declaration of income.[21] On top of this, there is a more general obligation concerning the organisation and ends pursued by the administration itself, which must not be disclosed to third parties without the authorisation of someone of superior rank in the hierarchy. For example, before taking part in a public conference 'fonctionnaires' have to obtain the authorisation of their superiors, whose business it is to check whether the facts that may be disclosed will not damage the good running of the administration, but will, on the contrary, serve to make it if not better appreciated, at least better understood.

The obligation of obedience for its part lies under a double limitation, set out in the same article 28 of the law of 13 July 1983. The 'fonctionnaire' 'must act in accordance with the instructions given to him by his hierarchical superior, except when the given order is manifestly illegal and liable seriously to damage the public interest'. Jurisprudential interpretations, established even before the promulgation of the law which takes its cue from them, indicate that these two conditions are cumulative and that, if both are satisfied, the 'fonctionnaire' actually has a duty of disobedience to the order which is addressed to him.[22] The cumulative character of these conditions means that when one of them, and in particular the second, does not hold, the 'fonctionnaire' finds himself back in the ordinary situation of having a duty of obedience, even if his superior remains, of course, liable to penal or disciplinary sanctions. For example, his subordinates must obey an officer who makes an improper use of the right to requisition, even though they perceive the illegality of the act, if it is nevertheless not of a nature to cause sufficient damage to the public interest; in such a case the officer in question is liable to sanctions which concern him alone.[23] If both conditions do hold, and the 'fonctionnaire' carries out the illegal order, then he too becomes liable to sanctions, the fact of his having received an order not being sufficient to exonerate him from all fault. Finally, it must be made clear that, apart from the case where those in authority, when faced with a refusal to obey, recognise the improper nature of their order and withdraw it, the practical effect of these arrangements, in a case where sanctions are imposed on the reluctant subordinate, is for these to be annulled by judicial procedure, if this is requested by the subordinate concerned, and if indeed he is not exposed to such pressures as might prevent him from proceeding in this way. Obviously, the commonest case is one where doubt subsists as to the irregularity of the act or its consequences: this is why, when they are called upon to carry out unusual orders, 'fonctionnaires' ask for written confirmation of them (sometimes a simple matter of having a document initialled), so that they cannot subsequently be accused of having acted on their own initiative.

Customary practices

The recall of these regulations, which make use, as do others which we have looked at previously, of blurred and not very well defined concepts, leaves it to be understood that behind the rules lie a set of practices that are much more complex. The main one brings into play a set of subtle divergences between the procedures which are set down in writing, and are for that very reason open to proof, and indications given by word-of-mouth. So far as the obligations of discretion and of confidentiality are concerned, a distinction has to be made between the severe restraints that are placed on the transmission of documents (even if today's practice has become very lax in this respect, in particular among the magistracy), and the tacit acceptance of the discreet provision of information.[24] A 'fonctionnaire', who, out of consideration for the general interest, as one should hope, has the feeling that an administrative or governmental decision is going in a direction that he judges to be undesirable, retains a certain margin of discretion to alert the parties concerned, who, provided that they respect the confidentiality of the sources on which they are relying, may go into action to try and influence the probable outcome of the decision. Interministerial practice provides endless examples of this type of intrigue. In order to offset the weight of an influential minister, the representative of a branch of the administration that sees the balance of decision about to swing against it, may discreetly warn the interest groups concerned, for example certain businesses or professional bodies, of the decisions in preparation, so that they may more-or-less publicly make known their opposition, for instance by referring the matter to the Prime Minister. Within one and the same administration, the branch responsible for looking after certain interests, faced with the indifference of their hierarchy, of their Director General or of the Minister, may have recourse to the same procedure with a view to influencing them.

This extremely widespread type of custom may act as a screen for more subtle forms of disinformation. The rumour may be spread that a given individual is likely to be appointed to a particular post of reponsibility in order, precisely, not to render his appointment more likely than it already is (which would be the simple case), but to conceal a choice that has already been made in favour of someone else and to take the sting out of any accusation of partiality that this decision may give rise to when it becomes known. In other words, and as in every organisation, a given sub-group may seek to bring external pressures to bear in order to reinforce its own position within the system.

On the level of principle, the moral conscience is torn. One may disapprove of the leak organised by the Minister himself in opposition to one of his colleagues, as in the case of the Westland affair, for example. Conversely, one may be inclined to approve the courageous gesture of a Ponting in making known to a Member of Parliament some disasterous failure of the British Navy. (Clive Ponting was a British civil servant who made public certain officially confidential information on the grounds of public interest, claiming that it was a matter of conscience to do so. He was subsequently prosecuted by the Government.) In this second case, is it really so easy to condemn the administration for prosecuting its agent, guilty, in the name of his own personal assessment of where his moral duty lay, of having infringed the professional ethic of his service; for if it failed to prosecute him, it might give encouragement to others to act in similar ways in the future, with, no doubt, still less moral justification than in the particular case in question. We find ourselves here, as always when faced with questions of casuistry, in a situation where one can see how each moral position (through all the varieties of absolutism to the different consequentialisms) may *within its own terms of reference* find justification for one or another of the alternative courses of action to which we have just referred. In fact, very often the concrete solutions may be found to lie in the different gradations of sanctions that are available. In the short term Sir Leon Brittan, while escaping the penal sanction, was unable to avoid the political one. The same was true for Ponting, though he was subject to the administrative sanction. As for any moral sanction or approbation, judgements may have evolved with the lapse of time and sheer forgetting.

From a more general point of view, this practice of 'leaks' in advance of governmental or administrative decisions renders the duty of obedience less stringent than it might seem simply on the basis of the texts. *In fine*, indeed, the tactics of influence, if they do not produce a consensus over public decisions, at least mitigate conflicts to the point at which the consciences of those who have to carry out orders are not subject to too violent a shock, However, in addition to these considerations, there are others, likewise common to all organisations, which bring us back to the inherent unclarity, if not of duty, then at any rate of obedience itself. Moreover, in the kinds of cases with which we are concerned, any on-going attempt to impose on subordinates, whose security of tenure is effectively guaranteed, decisions of which they disapprove and/or which they have difficulty in understanding, risks resulting in a reduced efficiency in the functioning of one's own administration and hence in an imperfect carrying out of the decisions in question. Thus, it is to be noted that a Minister will rarely take a decision, even one which is perfectly legal and appears to be in no way contrary to the public interest, if it meets with the disapproval of his own administration. There are different ways of looking at this type of reality. During those periods when society is politically deeply divided, one will tend to welcome this relative strength of the administration in being able to maintain its own neutrality *vis-à-vis* initiatives which are over-political (the 'one' who, one supposes, will welcome this neutrality is, of course, the 'moral one' and not that of the supporters either of the party of the majority or of the opposition). Conversely, however, during periods such as the present, when the economic parameters tend to become dominant and lead people to look on the State less from the political angle as the guarantor of fundamental rights and duties than from the practical angle of a cost/benefit relationship, then this 'compactness' of the administration is more readily seen as a form of inertia, and there is a tendency to deplore the way in which the political powers-that-be find their way blocked by administrative citadels, the refuge of different corporations and of a diversity of vested interests.

The above observations, based upon the positive law and supplemented by certain sociological considerations, do not provide answers to all the questions raised at the beginning. The impression that one derives from these brief accounts is that the State regulates itself in such a way as to avoid the crises which might set different branches of its administration against each other or create divisions internal to them. But it is clear that from an outside and more moral point of view, this self-regulation means that individual members of the administration come to make use of certain principles of reasoning, which, without anyone noticing what is happening, progressively lead the 'fonctionnaire' to renounce a certain freedom of judgement. In fact, for the 'fonctionnaire' – and more particularly, if we are to focus our attention on the case which would seem to call for an even greater sense of personal responsibility, for the senior 'fonctionnaire' – the hypothesis of a conflict between the duties attaching to his role, on the one hand, and the general duties of citizenship or of human beings as such, on the other hand, seems very remote, given that in a democratic society in time of peace, the legal framework offers sufficient guarantees for the protection, both within and without the national frontiers, of the basic interests of humanity, (apart from such exceptions as, for example, the affair of the Greenpeace boat, the *Rainbow Warrior*) which was blown up by French security services in a New Zealand harbour.[25]

It remains the case that administrative practice, and in particular the administrative division of labour, prevents individuals from having an overall view of all relevant factors or, if they do have access to such a view by virtue of their position in the hierarchy, to possess it in sufficient precision of detail, or to find themslves in situations such that they are able to bring to bear on the data a critical and well thought out judgement, when only too often they are under the pressure of the real or imagined urgency of the need to come to a decision. This situation reinforces principles of judgement, which, to put the matter very neutrally, one might take to be conformist. In particular, administrative practice supports the idea, which, it has to be said, is not altogether false, that the decisions to be taken are complex and that even if one feels a certain degree of disapproval towards them, this is perhaps tied to a lack of sufficient information: for example, the maintenance of important links with states that fail in their respect for the principles of democracy may be explained by reasons of which not everyone is aware. Moreover, even in the situation where he has direct responsibility for a dossier, the 'fonctionnaire' knows that the two alternatives between which he has to decide (to put it very simply) are set apart from each other by different prudential considerations, without there being any purely rational procedure on the basis of which he might come down in favour of either the one or the other in perfect certitude of having made the best choice. Thus, so long as certain fundamental principles are not explicitly violated, any decision taken within the framework of the rules may be deemed to be a good one and hence becomes acceptable.[26] Awareness of the complexity of the decision and of the lack of complete information render any judgement as to how far the decision may depart from principles of an overriding general interest much more uncertain.

But to this there are other types of argument to be added. One may indeed take the view that even a decision which may appear to be morally debatable may be found acceptable by reference to a sort of collective sin. One sees this very clearly in the international field. Practices which are suspect, but whose harmful consequences have not been absolutely proved, are continued because others do likewise: one will lose such and such a market if one is not ready to shut one's eyes to the corruption involved. In internal affairs, one aims a few blows below the belt in order to stave off those of one's adversaries.

This conception rests, it would seem, on the idea that competition and victory have a certain moral significance. In the competition between different companies, to which the State is by no means indifferent, above all in the international field, or in the competition between different branches of the administration as they seek to obtain decisions that come down in their favour, one takes the view that the best product, or the best set of arguments, if they are really to be the best, must come from people whose professionalism is not simply limited to the development of the product or to the construction of the arguments, but extends to the elaboration of the means, possibly tortuous, by which they justify the value of their product or their position. Thus, in a well-known formulation, Dean Ripert expressed the view that 'The law does not protect imbeciles'; along similar lines, one might say that it is not the point of morality to encourage the naive.

Provided, however, that competition at least stops at the point where fundamental legal or moral principles are brought into question: to bribe an intermediary, coming from a country where baksheesh is a current practice, is not the same thing as to sabotage the plane in which the delegation from the rival company is travelling. To attract a company to invest in one's own electoral constituency is not the same thing as to force it to shut down its factory in the constituency of one's political opponent. To award a public contract to a company which happens to have the audio-visual facilities by which to provide publicity for politicians is not altogether harmful, if the company's technical bid is as satisfactory as that of any other.[27]

In conclusion, and especially for those who do not believe in the virtues of competition, the administrative world may seem, in many cases, to be poorly equipped to respect the principles of moral integrity, that is, those rules which appear normal in relations between human beings. In the administrative world, as in that of business, one uses tactics for the manipulation of others, one keeps one's script hidden, one gives to be understood pieces of information that one knows to be false, one holds up the transmission of certain data in order to throw off balance whoever one is dealing with, one makes demands that one knows to be unacceptable in order to make sure of obtaining that which is essential – even if, in the domain of the public service, such practices appear to be relatively amateurish (due to a lack of training) when set against the advice presented in textbooks aimed at the directors or managers of private enterprise, they seem nevertheless to stand in a certain contrast with the abstract ethic as presented, for example, in the quotation from Lord Beveridge, with which we began.

But this type of disapproval may be reproached for directing its criticism not so much to certain administrative practices as to the acceptance by the individual of a certain social role which, inevitably, is going to limit his point of view. The alternative to such ways of going on would be not so much to look for mechanisms by which to correct them (for these already exist) as to give up all idea of a genuine commitment, a choice which, of course, is only likely to appeal to academics or philosophers, whose very existence nevertheless relies on the readiness of others to get their hands dirty. Conversely, however, the rejection of the purely abstract moral point of view must not be allowed to result in a sort of sociological pragmatism, which would consist in presenting as commonplace all the ways in which things actually work and thus to encourage downward spirals of a dangerous moral indifference. Faced with the difficulty of determining which is the best course of action, of gaining access to the right information, and with the limited nature of our rationality and the notably chancy character of collective decisions, with the slight impact of individual actions on what happens overall, one looks for a decisive point of view and ends up, of course, by sticking, and even then with difficulty, to that of one's own personal interest.

Notes

1 First published in *Philosophy and Public Affairs* II, 4 (Summer 1973) and reprinted in Nagel 1979.

2 In this example, the general interest would indeed consist in the sentry remaining at his post in order to avoid giving a bad example, which, in other circumstances, could have dramatic consequences, even if, in this particular case, he might prevent his two comrades from damaging each other at no risk at all to the garrison.

3 It is to be noted, however, that in the French context, so far as one can tell at least from those cases which have achieved a certain degree of notoriety, it is comparatively rare to come across instances of the employees or directors of companies bringing the law into play and denouncing the practices of their employer or their parent company. It was only after having been dismissed, for example, that the employees of Alcatel disclosed its practice of overcharging France Telecom. It is also true that a company which, naturally, may make use of techniques of moral desensitisation in relation to its own members, is at the same time aware of the limits of such techniques, and, at any rate in certain sectors, probably only in exceptional cases acts on the outer margins of legality, or in conflict with it.

4 For further details, see Dupuy and Thonig 1983.

5 The term 'fonctionnaire' is properly applicable to anyone who is a paid employee of the State in France – teachers employed in state schools are, for example, 'fonctionnaires'. The term thus covers a much wider range than the English 'civil servant'. It has seemed best, therefore, to leave it untranslated [translator's note].

6 For one celebrated example, see the well-known work by G. Allison (1971).

7 Historically speaking, there is a certain paradox to be found in the fact that the origin of this statute, allowing the 'fonctionnaire' to pursue his political activities outside his professional functions is to be found, no doubt, in the strength after the Liberation both of the Communist Party and of its effective Trade Union extension, the CGT, something which has clearly protected French society from a good number of attempted witch hunts.

8 For these questions, cf. the statutory order of 29 October 1936, an order which is still in force, and in particular article 3, which sets out the principal dispensations. It would be interesting to discover what influence teachers of Law and lawyers had in the drawing up of this order, and *a fortiori* that exercised by those teaching lawyers who happened to be exercising parliamentary functions at the time, something which, as one knows, was particularly common among members of these professions.

9 From a more utilitarian point of view, it is equally important to be able to retain a sufficient number of 'fonctionnaires' in the service of the State, by authorising them to undertake gainful outside employment and in this way allowing them to obtain a complementary source of income.

10 It is to be noted that in the inquiry which followed the Westland affair, the report drawn up by the Head of the British Civil Service (Sir Robert Armstrong) was criticised by members of Parliament for having exonerated the civil servants concerned from all responsibility for the leak, for which Leon Brittan alone was held to be responsible.

11 For the freedoms guaranteed to 'fonctionnaires', cf. the law of 13 July 1983: article 6, freedom of opinion; article 7, candidature at elections; article 8, Trade Union rights.

12 It is to be noted that, legally speaking, this list is not considered to be exclusive, and that it may be extended, depending on the nature of the posts falling under the appropriate constitutional jurisdiction (cf. Council of State, 13 March 1953, Teissier, *Recueil* 133).

13 This practice is, however, not at all widespread in France, particularly when one compares this country to the United States or even to Great Britain.

14 For example, the 'fonctionnaire' must not promote a co-religionist of lesser worth over a competitor, who might be completely indifferent to his faith.

15 Hence the occasional rare objections by academics to the sanctions, sometimes in fact relatively light, imposed on those who defend revisionism or who deny the existence of the gas chambers, not because the objectors share these opinions, but because they see in their expression the price to be paid for the general freedom from which all benefit.

16 I do not here include the exercise of Trade Union freedoms or the right to strike, even if this does raise the problem of integrity.

17 This includes members of the Armed Services, who are authorised by the law of 13 July 1972 to present themselves as candidates for any publicly elective post.

18 For example, one may refuse to let an apartment to a tenant of a given race on the pretext that his credit is not good enough.

19 cf. the above-mentioned judgement Teissier. Other examples are to be found in Chapuis (1994, 2: 223, §257).

20 But this argument can turn out to be double-edged, in as much as the sanction is open to criticism on the grounds of having been imposed not so much for a failure to respect the obligation of discretion as for political reasons (something which, within certain branches of the Administration, ensures a reaction on the part of the Trade Unions).

21 This obligation of secrecy does not apply to the individuals who are protected by it and who, on the contrary, have a right to have the contents of their administrative records freely communicated to them. Thus, the mark recorded on a piece of written note-paper has the status of an administrative act, of which the possible victim is to be informed on demand.

22 For a relative exception concerning members of the police, cf. the deontological code of the national police force, article 7. This lays it down that in such situations the police 'fonctionnaire' must report his reservations to a higher authority; if this authority confirms the order, the 'fonctionnaire' is obliged to act in accordance with it.

23 For this example, cf. the Code of Military Justice, article 463.

24 That is to say, information provided by word-of-mouth, 'off the record', as it is said.

25 cf. Keraudren (1994: 242):

> Contrary to the democratic legend of their professional body, 'fonctionnaires' have been described as individuals in pursuit of their own personal or corporative interests without regard for considerations of democracy. Either because they set out deliberately to put obstacles in the path of elected governments: the evidence of former ministers such as Tony Benn, Anthony

Crosland, and Barbara Castle as to the obstructions and delaying tactics employed by civil servants in order to sabotage the policies pursued by those in government has received very wide publicity. Or because they cynically ignore the legitimate requests of ordinary citizens: journalists in particular have made it their business to underline the excesses of the bureaucratic machine when it operates counter to the interests of the citizens, whom it is supposed to serve. Or again because 'fonctionnaires' form part of a social élite that is wholly removed from the reality of modern society.

26 The work of Allison (1971) shows that the process of decision in the affair of the Cuba missiles resulted in part from the balance reached between the positions of the different parties within the American administration, who, if they were not altogether sure of what should be done, at least had a clear idea, which they were committed to defend, of what it was absolutely imperative not to do.

27 For a minister, to appear on television is not only to provide himself with personal publicity, but is equally an opportunity to present the activities of his ministry in a favourable light and, more generally, the values and interests which it is concerned to promote, which, in most cases, are quite legitimate.

References

Allison, G. (1971) *Essence of Decision: Explaining the Cuba missile crisis*. Boston: Little Brown.

Beveridge, Lord William (1922) *In the Development of the Civil Service*. Westminster: HMSO.

Chapuis, René (1994) *Droit administratif général* (General administrative law). Paris.

Dupuy, François and Thonig, Jean-Claude (1983) *Sociologie de l'administration française*. Paris: Armand Colin.

Kerauden, Phillipe (1994) *Les modernisationes de l'Etat et le thatcherisme*. Brussels: Bruylant.

Moullet, Michel (1992) *Le Management Clandestin*. Paris Interéditions.

Nagel, Thomas (1979) *Moral Questions*. Cambridge: Cambridge University Press.

22 Responses to each other

Peter Kemp and René Sève

Peter Kemp: response to René Sève

Since writing my own chaper, I have had the opportunity to read that by René Sève. This is a first class chapter, and, as a former Civil Servant, I recognise and agree with much of what he says. Broadly, I think that the conclusions of his chapter and those of my own are much the same, namely that in the field of State service and public administration the State is larger than the individual and that, if any conflict of whatever kind arises between the State and the individual public servant, it is the individual who must give ground.

However, it is worth noting what seems to me to be something of a difference in emphasis between us as to the way in which this result comes about. It seems fair to say that, in reaching his conclusions, René Sève bases himself more on a rather legalistic view, or at least on a view more bound by law, in its approach to the delivery of public service, while I base myself more on the less rule-bound and codified, and more unwritten, approach that I think I see in the United Kingdom. For instance, in his paper René Sève cites a number of formal rules and acts; we have no Civil Service Act or anything similar here, and only recently have we had the notion of formal contracts for Civil Servants and a (non-legally based) code of conduct.

However, it may be possible to exaggerate the differences. René Sève suggests that in France the formal rules tend to be known only to a few specialists, and that the 'unwritten' code is strong; while in this country the general law and specific Civil Service 'law – e.g., disciplinary proceedings – do have a place alongside the non-codified rules. (And René Sève has suggested to me that the nature of many public administration decisions makes possible gradations which help the individual to live with the decision, whatever the regulatory ideal; this is an interesting concept, about which I am not sure. While decisions are never black or white, I do not think that in this country at any rate gradations are often, if ever, consciously adapted to the decision maker's personal integrity.)

René Sève and I agree broadly, then, in our conclusions, and any difference of emphasis in the different routes by which this is achieved is probably to be put down to much wider and longer standing differences in French and

British styles and cultures than to differences specifically related to public administration. The point is nevertheless an interesting one, and worth bearing in mind when examining examples of areas in which French and British Civil Servants work alongside each other.

Response to Peter Kemp

It is true that French law (public or private) rests more on formal regulation than does the British legal tradition. However, this does not imply that English law does not include rules clarifying the notion of integrity of the civil servant. In particular the trials in which civil servants are prosecuted (like that of Ponting, to which I referred in my paper) may be an opportunity to formulate or indicate general principles or rules. Moreover, in France the formal rules organising the public service are only very dimly known (except by specialists and trade unionists) and they are immersed in day-to-day practice and custom, which constitute the real regulation. In short, I believe that the discrepancies between our two countries should not be over-estimated, even if in theory our visions of law, and even maybe of education, differ.

On the matter of substance, namely, your thesis that 'there need be no conflict between the distinct demands of integrity, public accountability and good government, but to ensure that in practice these come together can give difficulty to the individuals and the institutions involved', you kindly note that we agree. I think that this right, but I should like to stress that this lack of conflict must be seen as a *regulative ideal* to which reality never totally conforms. In practice, governments and public servants nearly always succeed in finding a middle ground between the general interest (itself quite hard to define) and their particular interests (their own interest as individuals or the interest of the group to which they belong). This remains a possibility because the substance of their decisions allows for gradations and compromises; and it is legitimate because here the general interest is the outcome of 'conflicting' particular interests. In any case, I do not think that this formulation really contradicts your reasoning.

BELFAST PUBLIC LIBRARIES

Index of names

Sci186

£60.00

51AIN